Office 2010 Workflow:

Developing Collaborative Solutions

MARK J. COLLINS

Apress®

Office 2010 Workflow: Developing Collaborative Solutions

ISBN-13 (pbk): 978-1-4302-2904-9

ISBN-13 (electronic): 978-1-4302-2905-6

Printed and bound in the United States of America 9 8 7 6 5 4 3 2 1

President and Publisher: Paul Manning
Lead Editor: Jonathan Hassell
Technical Reviewers: Robert Garrett and Michael Mayberry
Editorial Board: Clay Andres, Steve Anglin, Mark Beckner, Ewan Buckingham, Gary Cornell, Jonathan Gennick, Jonathan Hassell, Michelle Lowman, Matthew Moodie, Duncan Parkes, Jeffrey Pepper, Frank Pohlmann, Douglas Pundick, Ben Renow-Clarke, Dominic Shakeshaft, Matt Wade, Tom Welsh
Coordinating Editor: Anne Collett
Copy Editor: Kim Wimpsett
Compositor: Kimberly Burton
Indexer: Potomac Indexing, LLC
Artist: April Milne
Cover Designer: Anna Ishchenko

Distributed to the book trade worldwide by Springer Science+Business Media, LLC., 233 Spring Street, 6th Floor, New York, NY 10013. Phone 1-800-SPRINGER, fax (201) 348-4505, e-mail orders-ny@springer-sbm.com, or visit www.springeronline.com.

For information on translations, please e-mail rights@apress.com, or visit www.apress.com.

Apress and friends of ED books may be purchased in bulk for academic, corporate, or promotional use. eBook versions and licenses are also available for most titles. For more information, reference our Special Bulk Sales–eBook Licensing web page at www.apress.com/info/bulksales.

The source code for this book is available to readers at www.apress.com. You will need to answer questions pertaining to this book in order to successfully download the code.

To Donna, my beautiful wife and my best friend

Contents at a Glance

Contents

Preface

Henry Ford has been called the father of the automobile. Although he did not invent the car, he did devise a way to make them affordable. His novel idea: bring the work to the workers. Prior to this, cars were made one at a time, or each worker would move from car to car. The assembly line allowed workers, their tools, and their materials to stay in one place, and the cars were brought to the workers. This saved such an enormous amount of time that the cost of each vehicle was drastically reduced.

I had the opportunity to visit an automobile plant, and the precision of the assembly line was utterly amazing. One area that particularly impressed me was the place where the wheels were being mounted. There was a person on each side of the car, and each had two chutes (one for the front wheel and one for the rear wheel) where wheels and tires were staged. If you looked up the chute, you could see 15 or so wheels ready for the next cars. What was amazing was that each car had different wheels and tires. Some were steel wheels; others were chrome or alloy. However, as the car approached the mounting area, the correct wheel and tire was presented at each of the four chutes. At the top of each chute were four groups of workers preparing the wheels and mounting the appropriate tires. For this whole thing to work, each person had to do their part in the exact order needed to supply the assembly line.

An automobile assembly line is simply an enormous workflow. It is the precise arrangement of hundreds, perhaps thousands of activities. A workflow describes the steps of a process, which are modeled as activities. As the car works its way through the workflow, activities are performed on it.

Office Workflows

People are generally interested in the tasks that they are responsible for. Workflows should perform as much of the work for you as possible. Our focus is primarily on the activities that a workflow can't do—the ones that require a person to do something. These human activities are modeled as tasks. A *task* is a step in a workflow process that requires a person to do something such enter the specified data, approve a document, make a decision, and so on.

Imagine hundreds, even thousands, of workflows running simultaneously. As they work through their defined processes, they continually spawn new tasks. From a user perspective, the task list is the key to the whole process. From there, each person can see the work they have to do. They can plan their day's activities based on what is in their task list.

Workflows in Microsoft Office are particularly powerful because the workflow activities are so well integrated into the tools you already use such as Word, Outlook, and Excel. The task item can have links to the Office document, form, or web site that is needed to complete the task. And the task forms can be embedded in the Office documents.

Integrating External Data

The Office 2010 release provides some significant improvements for integrating the enterprise data into the office workflows. This feature is called Business Connectivity Services, and it gives you several ways to link external data.

For example, suppose you have a workflow process that generates a task to make a follow-up call to a customer after a large order is fulfilled. The customer's contact information, order details, and order history all reside in the enterprise system. This data can be provided in SharePoint as an external list and can be included with the task details. If the customer needed some help or wanted to submit some feedback, this could be entered on the task form and pushed into the enterprise system automatically.

The Office tools such as Outlook and Excel can now be used as front-end applications to your enterprise system, augmenting your existing applications.

Diverse Authoring Tools

One of things that most impresses me about this release of Office is the breath of tools that are provided. Workflows can be authored in any of the following:

- SharePoint, using out-of-the-box workflows

- Visio, to design the high-level process

- SharePoint Designer, creating declarative (no-code) workflows

- Visual Studio, creating workflows using the Workflow Foundation in .NET

In addition, they provide ways to move a workflow between tools. For example, you can start a workflow in Visio, import it into the SharePoint Designer for implementation, and then send it back to Visio for documentation. Declarative workflows can also be imported into Visual Studio for advanced, code-based implementations.

You can also create custom actions in Visual Studio, which can then be used in declarative workflows implemented by power users.

Summary

This book will demonstrate these features and show you how to implement them. After working through the projects presented in this book, you be able to employ this technology to create amazing office automation solutions.

About the Author

■ **Mark Collins** has been developing software for 30 years in a variety of industries and an enormous range of technologies. A common thread throughout his career has been a vision for the automation of existing processes. Fortunately, recent technological advances have provided significant improvements in the tools available for process automation. The Office 2010 release marks a pinnacle in this progress, and this book represents a giant step forward of this vision.

A second underlying theme has been the improvement of software development methodologies. The process and structure applied in development projects will determine the quality and productivity you can achieve. To that end, Mark has developed several CASE tools. His latest application suite is called Omega Tool (`http://www.TheCreativePeople.com`).

About the Technical Reviewers

■ **Robert Garrett** has worked with SharePoint since the early beta version of MOSS 2007 and has leveraged his talents for SharePoint architecture and design with Portal Solutions, a SharePoint consultant company in Rockville, Maryland. Rob has an extensive background in .NET technologies and has developed software for Microsoft frameworks since the early days of C++ and MFC. In pursuit of his career dreams, Rob left his birthplace in England for a journey to the United States on Thanksgiving Day 1999 and enjoyed his first American meal from a gas station.

■ **Michael Mayberry** currently helps lead a software team for a nonprofit organization to build .NET enterprise applications. He serves as a lead architect and focuses on adopting new technologies toward solid solutions. Michael's experience includes the development of web-based extranet solutions, along with data collection and analysis applications within the auto industry. Michael moved to build CRM and BI solutions for the nonprofit industry more than seven years ago.

Acknowledgments

First, I want to acknowledge that anything that I have ever done that is of any value or significance was accomplished through the blessings of my Lord and Savior, Jesus Christ. This book was well beyond my own ability, and it was nothing short of God's amazing grace that enabled me to complete it. He has once again proven that "I can do all things through His annointing" (Phil 4:13).

Next, I want to say a big "thank-you" to my beautiful wife, Donna. I can honestly say that I would not be who I am if it were not for what you have sown into my life. You are the embodiment of a Proverbs 31 wife. I am truly blessed to be able to share my life with you. Thank you for your loving support and for making life fun!

I am also very thankful for all the people at Apress who made this book possible and for all their hard work that turned it into the finished product you see now. Everyone at Apress has made writing this book a pleasure. Thank you!

Finally, I want to thank Anne Collett, Kim Wimpsett, Rob Garrett, and Michael Mayberry. Each of you contributed your time and talent to make this book a success. Thank you!

Introduction

The 2010 release of the Microsoft Office suite, including SharePoint 2010, provides a huge step forward in office automation. This book was designed to help you quickly master the key concepts so you can start building Office workflows. Using the techniques demonstrated in this book, you'll be able to take advantage of all the really cool features of Office 2010.

About This Book

After the first three introductory chapters, this book then presents a series of projects with step-by-step instructions so you can implement them yourself. As you work through these exercises, you will learn the concepts introduced in each chapter.

The projects cover a broad spectrum, from no-code workflows that might be implemented by a power user to Visual Studio solutions requiring a developer. The projects were intended to be followed in order because they tend to build upon concepts presented in previous chapters. However, you can skip around if you so choose. I will usually refer to previous chapters when earlier concepts are used. You can then go back and review if necessary.

What You Need to Use This Book

This book presents a series of projects that demonstrate features of Office 2010, SharePoint 2010, and Visual Studio 2010. It is expected that you will work through these exercises to gain hands-on experience with these applications. To do that, you'll need a 64-bit computer with lots of memory. And, of course, you will need to install all of these products. If you don't already have a license for these products, you should be able to use a trial license, which will give you enough time to complete the projects in this book. Chapter 2 provides instructions for setting up a development environment.

Alternatively, you can read the book without working through the projects. There are plenty of screenshots, so you will get a good sense of how the solutions work. This approach will provide an introduction to the available features so you can decide if and when you want to start using Office 2010. When you later decide to implement an Office/SharePoint 2010 solution, refer to this book for ideas and sample implementations.

Code Samples

You can download the Visual Studio 2010 solutions described in this book from `http://www.apress.com`. You will need to answer questions pertaining to this book in order to successfully download the code.

Feedback

For questions and comments, you can e-mail me at markc@thecreativepeople.com.

PART 1

■■■

Introduction

Implementing a Office workflow solution can be a bit daunting at first glance. Before I get into all the technical details, I think it would be useful to set the stage in order to establish a common perspective. In Chapter 1, I'll present the big picture to help you see how all the pieces fit together and describe the areas that I will focus on in this book. Chapter 2 will show you how to set up a development environment so as we start to build real solutions, you be able to deploy and test them. Chapter 3 provides a brief primer on SharePoint development for those who are new to SharePoint. It explains the basic concepts of columns, content types, and lists.

The remainder of this book will present sample projects that demonstrate how to build workflow solutions in Office 2010. I'll start with some fairly simple projects and gradually build more complex solutions. Along the way, I'll explain key concepts that will help you master this technology.

■ ■ ■

CHAPTER 1

Overview of Microsoft Office

In this book, I'll be discussing a lot of software products such Microsoft Office, SharePoint, Workflow Foundation, SQL Server, and Visual Studio. In this Chapter, I'll explain how these work together and how (and when) each of these is used.

End-User Perspective

But first, let's take a step back and view all this technology from the perspective of the people who will benefit the most—the end users.

Office Overview

The Microsoft Office suite of products allows you to author all types of *documents* including spreadsheets, diagrams, presentations, calendars, and so on. SharePoint then provides a repository for storing, sharing, and maintaining those documents. Through a flexible security model, SharePoint controls what each person can see and what they are allowed to change (and who is notified when a change is made).

   The concept of *lists* used in SharePoint is a slight departure from that model. Although these can be thought of as a list of documents, the things we generally keep lists of such as requests, tasks, and bugs can't really be called documents. *Discussions* are a special type of list that allows for items to be associated with other items in the list. So, a SharePoint site is a collection of Documents, Lists, and Discussions. Figure 1-1 shows the navigation window of the default SharePoint portal, which emphasizes this point.

Documents
Site Pages
Shared Documents

Lists
Calendar
Tasks

Discussions
Team Discussion

Figure 1-1. Default SharePoint navigation window

The documents are created through one of the familiar Office products such as Word. The items in a list, however, are usually created though a SharePoint form. Figure 1-2 shows the standard **Task** form that comes with SharePoint 2010 "out of the box."

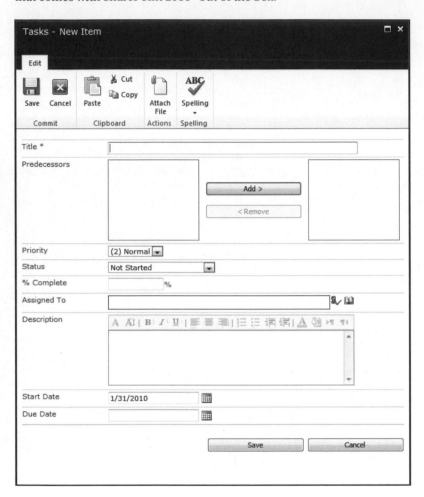

Figure 1-2. *The standard Task form*

This is all really cool and way better than a room full of filing cabinets. But this is still fairly static.

Workflows in SharePoint

This is where workflows come in. Workflows define the processes that are applied to each of these documents, lists, or discussions. For example, suppose you had a list of service requests. Someone would use a form to initiate a request, and someone else will, ideally, respond to that request. A workflow-driven list could add the following:

- Forward the request to a manager for approval

- Route the request to the correct person or group based on the nature of the request

- Escalate the request to a supervisor if not completed in a reasonable amount of time

- Request feedback from the initiator when the item is complete

As you'll see, workflows can make your lists come alive. Workflows can also be applied to documents. Suppose you need to produce a bid in response to a request for proposal (RFP). For a large contract, this job will require a number of people from several departments throughout the organization such as Marketing, Accounting, Legal, and Human Resources. A workflow can be used to require that the appropriate reviews and approvals are obtained while ensuring no one is "sitting on it."

Workflow Overview

There are three types of workflows that you will use:

- Workflows predefined by SharePoint Server (or SharePoint Foundation)

- Workflows created through the SharePoint Designer

- Workflows generated by Visual Studio

Figure 1-3 shows some of the predefined workflows.

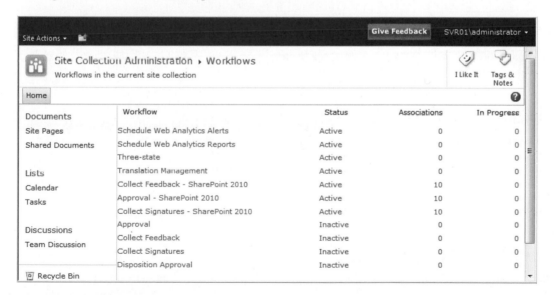

Figure 1-3. *A list of predefined workflows*

Once a workflow has been deployed to the SharePoint Server, you can associate the workflow with a list, document library, or content type. A special type of workflow called a *site* workflow is *not* associated with a list or other SharePoint object. It can run stand-alone and independent of these other objects. This is a useful feature since some workflows don't really fit as a list workflow.

A workflow can be configured to start automatically. For example, when an item is added to a list, a workflow that is associated with that list can be started as soon as the item is created. Alternatively, you can start a workflow manually through some end-user action on a SharePoint form or even from an Office application such as Outlook.

Code-less Workflows

The first two types of workflows are sometimes referred to as *code-less* (or no-code) workflows because they are created with GUI-type applications and require no "code." These workflows can be created by power users or IT staff. Code-less workflows are a convenient way of automated existing manually processes. They are basically limited to the types of things you would normally do with SharePoint objects such as creating tasks, updating calendars, sending e-mails, approving documents, and so on.

In Part 2, I'll provide several examples of ways to use no-code workflows. They are pretty easy to set up and provide a great deal of functionality. For many of your workflow requirements, these will fit the bill quite nicely.

Visual Studio Workflows

The third type of workflow uses the power of Visual Studio to create more advanced workflows. It relies on Microsoft's Workflow Foundation (WF) based on .NET version 3.5.

■ **Note** With .NET 4.0, Microsoft introduced a whole new approach to WF, a complete departure from previous implementations. Unfortunately, SharePoint 2010 does *not* use .NET 4.0, and all your SharePoint workflows must be built with version 3.5.

In Part 3, I will show you how to use Visual Studio to build custom workflows. This approach will require a developer to create the workflows. However, power users will still have the ability to associate and configure these workflows to suit their specific requirements.

Visual Studio workflows are virtually limitless in terms of what you can do with them. You can use the same SharePoint objects such as task lists and e-mails that you'll use with code-less workflows. In addition, you can also integrate custom applications and data into your workflow process. Also, you can implement your own custom workflow forms using familiar ASP.NET tools.

Business Connectivity Services

SharePoint is traditionally associated with office automation and typically deals with documents, calendars, tasks, and e-mails. Often, separate enterprise software handles the core business operations such as fulfilling orders, responding to customer service requests, and following up on sales leads. Most of the time, people have to work in two different worlds—one system to operate the business and a separate system for completing the paperwork.

SharePoint 2010 provides Business Connectivity Services (BCS) that enable you to access your enterprise data from within SharePoint. Essentially, BCS makes the external data available to you as a SharePoint list so you can access it just like any other SharePoint list.

In Part 4, I'll show you how to take advantage of these services to use (and update) your existing enterprise data from the SharePoint workflows that you'll build. This will allow you to use Office clients such as Outlook to participate in workflows that integrate with the enterprise systems, thus bringing these two worlds closer together.

Technology Overview

Now let's take a look at the different software products that you'll use to implement workflow. In the next chapter I'll cover this in more detail and show you how to install and configure the products, but for now, I'll present this at a high level. Since this book is about workflow, I can't begin to cover all the really neat features provided in the latest version of Office and SharePoint. I will show you how to build enterprise-class workflow solutions, but to get there, out of necessity, I'll will need to largely ignore many other useful nonrelated features.

Software Products

The products that you'll be using to create the workflow solutions in this book are described in the following list. I will cover these in more details is subsequent chapters.

- **SharePoint Foundation 2010**: SharePoint Foundation (SPF) provides the core services that are used by the SharePoint Server. This product is roughly equivalent to the Windows SharePoint Services (WSS) in SharePoint 2007. I say roughly equivalent because there have been some significant enhancements from the previous version. The services that we are particularly interested in include Workflow Services and Business Connectivity Services (BCS). The Business Data Catalog from SharePoint 2007 provided read-only access to external data sources. It has been replaced in 2010 with BCS, which provides both read and write capabilities.

- **SharePoint Server 2010**: The SharePoint Server (SPS) 2010 is the server component that provides the portal to all of your document, lists, and discussions. Previous versions were known as Microsoft Office SharePoint Server (MOSS). There is not a real clear line between what features are provided by SPF and which ones require SPS. It is possible to install SPF only (and not install SPS) and still use workflows, but some of the features will be limited. This book will assume that you are using SPS.

- **SharePoint Designer 2010**: The SharePoint Designer allows you to create a SharePoint site without writing any code. You can use it to create lists, pages, and views. More importantly for our purposes, the SharePoint Designer can be used to create code-less workflows. The 2010 release includes significant improvements in the workflow editor. You'll use this in Chapter 6, and in Chapter 7 I'll provide a more thorough explanation of its features. The 2010 release has also been redesigned to focus on the building blocks of a SharePoint solution such as columns and content types rather than just being a list editor.

- **SQL Server 2008 or 2005**: The SharePoint configuration data is stored in a SQL Server database. The database can reside on a separate server or as a local instance on the same server running SharePoint. Unless you provide your own SQL Server instance, a built-in database will be created when you install SharePoint Server. The built-in database uses SQL Express 2008.

- **Visual Studio 2010**: Visual Studio 2010 provides a development environment for building more complex workflow solutions. The 2010 version has some really nice enhancements from the 2008 release. For starters, in VS 2010 you can press F5 to automatically build, deploy, and debug your workflow. That alone should convince everyone to upgrade. You can also use VS 2010 to build ASP.NET forms instead of the forms created by the SharePoint Designer. VS 2010 has built-in templates for creating SharePoint-enabled solutions including workflows and forms. You can still use Visual Studio 2008 to create SharePoint workflows, but the examples in this book will use only 2010 because of its improvements.

- **Visio 2010**: Visio 2010 is part of the Office suite of application but is not part of the standard Office bundles. It must be purchased and installed separately. Visio is used in conjunction with the SharePoint Designer to construct code-less workflows. Visio provides the graphical visualization of workflows implemented by the SharePoint Designer.

- **InfoPath 2010**: InfoPath is also part of the Office suite of applications and is used to generate SharePoint forms. In Chapter 11, I'll show you how to use InfoPath 2010 to build custom task forms.

- **Office 2010 Applications**: Many of the Office applications such as Word, Excel, and Outlook are already workflow-enabled, which means that they can easily participate in a workflow. You can use either Office 2007 or Office 2010 applications and for the projects in this book. Either will work, although the text and figures are based on the 2010 versions. The 2010 release includes some useful integration with SharePoint. For example, the new Office Backstage UI provides a more seamless experience when editing documents in a SharePoint document library.

- **SharePoint Workspace**: SharePoint Workspace is the new name for the product previously known as Microsoft Groove. SharePoint Workspace allows you to make an offline copy of SharePoint lists and documents. This copy is synchronized with the server when you are connected to the network. This enables you to work offline in a relatively seamless fashion. This has been enhanced to also provide offline support for external content, which I'll demonstrate in Chapter 20.

Client-Server Topology

Figure 1-4 shows the primary components of a workflow-enabled SharePoint system.

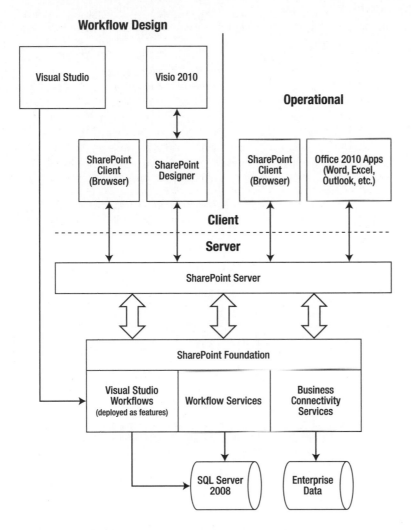

Figure 1-4. SharePoint system components

SharePoint Foundation and SharePoint Server, along with the database engine(s), are the server-side components. Pretty much everything else runs on the client. Because often in a development environment everything runs on a single machine, the distinction between client and server can be blurred. The important thing to note is that once you have set up the server, all you need on the client is a browser and whatever Office apps you want to use (Outlook, Word, and so on).

Summary

We hope you now have a sense of what workflow-enabled SharePoint solutions can do and the major components that are used. Don't worry if this seems a bit sketchy; for many, the concepts will become clearer as you work through the details. In the rest of the book, I'll show you, step-by-step, how to create various workflow implementations. In the next chapter, you'll set up your development environment for the projects you'll build in the remaining chapters.

CHAPTER 2

■ ■ ■

Setting Up a Development Environment

In this chapter I'll show you how to set up a development environment. As you probably noticed from the previous chapter, you need to install and configure several software products. The easiest approach is to put all of this on a single machine, and I'll explain how to do that. In addition, you will need to configure e-mail and set up multiple user accounts to simulate a production environment.

Single-Computer Installation

The SharePoint products require a 64-bit operating system and lots of memory; they require 4GB at a minimum, but 6GB or 8GB is recommended, especially if you're installing everything on a single machine. Your operating system choices are narrowed down to Windows Server 2008 or Windows Server 2008 R2. To make it easier for developers, Microsoft enabled the SharePoint products to also be installed on Vista or Windows 7 for development only. You will need a 64-bit version, however.

There are numerous ways to configure a development environment. In this chapter, I'll explain two of the more common scenarios. The easiest and preferred approach is to install on a server OS with a separate instance of SQL Server. The second is to install SharePoint on Windows 7 with an embedded instance of SQL Server Express. Installing SharePoint 2010 on a desktop OS requires some extra work.

I recommend a dual-core or quad-core processor and all the memory you can afford. You'll be running several memory-intensive applications including SharePoint Server, SQL Server, Visual Studio, and Office. For my development environment, I'm using Windows 7 Professional on a quad processor with 6GB of memory. This platform should work fine for the solutions you'll be building in this book.

Initial Setup

For these instructions, I'm assuming that you have a new install of the operating system with nothing loaded on your system yet. You might need to adjust these steps if you are using an existing system with some software already installed. Because of all the products you'll need, it would be best to start with a clean system to avoid any conflicts. For example, installing a 64-bit version of an application when there is an existing 32-bit version installed can cause problems.

■ **Caution** For Windows Server 2008 R2 and Windows 7, you will need to install hotfix KB976462, which adds the `AllowInsecureTransport` property. Without this, the SharePoint installation will fail because of an unrecognized config file entry. To download this file, go to `msdn.microsoft.com`, and enter **KB976462** into the search box. You can get more information from the MSDN site. If you are using Vista or Windows Server 2008, search for **KB971831**.

SQL Server

When installing SharePoint Server in stand-alone mode, it will install SQL Server 2008 Express for its internal databases. If you want to use a different instance of SQL Server (local or otherwise), you will need to use Active Directory and set up domain accounts to access SQL Server. When installing SharePoint, choose the Server Farm option, and you will be prompted for the SQL Server details.

Active Directory

For practical purposes, you will need to have Active Directory available. Technically, SharePoint will run without it, but it relies on it for some user information, such as e-mail addresses. So, you can add users to your site but won't be able to set up the e-mail address. Active Directory can run only on a server OS. You can install SharePoint on a desktop OS, but it will need to be on a network with access to an Active Directory domain controller.

■ **Note** When you install SharePoint Server (SPS), the SharePoint Foundation (SPF) is installed as well; you do not need to install both. Although some of the solutions in this book will work with only SPF (SPS not installed), many will not. This book assumes that you have installed SPS.

Installing SharePoint on a Server OS

Before installing SharePoint Server (SPS), you'll need to install the necessary prerequisites. If you're installing on a server OS (Windows Server 2008 or Windows Server 2008 R2), this is pretty easy. When you first launch the install program, it will provide options for preparing your system, as shown in Figure 2-1.

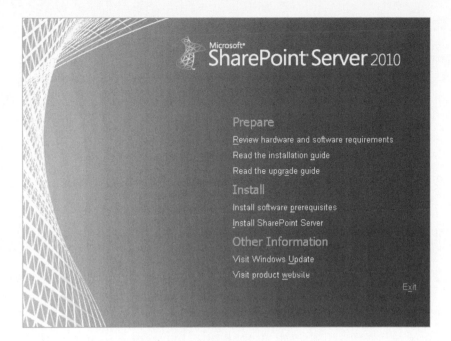

Figure 2-1. *The SharePoint Server installation program*

The first three links in the Prepare section are links to online documentation that you might want to read for tips on setting up a production environment.

Installing the Prerequisites

The first link in the Install section launches the Preparation Tool, which ensures all the necessary prerequisites have been installed. You'll need to run this first. After you click this link, you should see a window similar to the one shown in Figure 2-2.

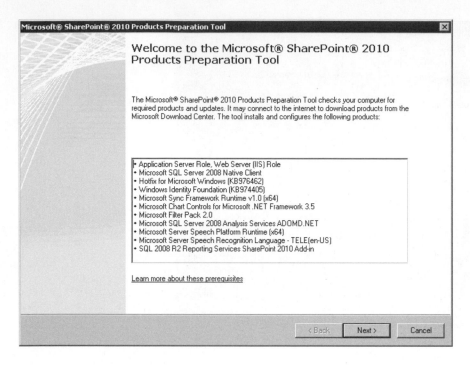

Figure 2-2. Installing prerequisites

Click the Next button, and all the missing prerequisites will be installed for you. When this finishes, another window will be displayed that explains the actions that were taken.

Installing SharePoint Server

After the prerequisites have been installed, the setup application will ask you for the product key, as shown in Figure 2-3.

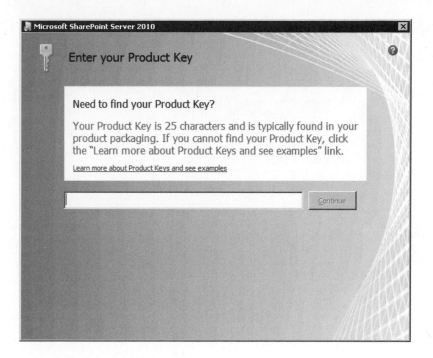

Figure 2-3. Entering your product key

SharePoint Foundation (SPF) and SharePoint Server (SPS) will then be installed without requiring any user action. After that's finished, you'll need to run the Configuration Wizard. Just select the box on the confirmation page shown in Figure 2-4, and the wizard will be started automatically.

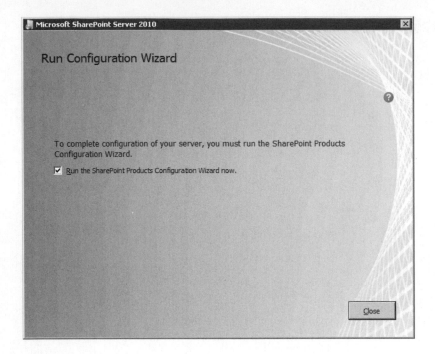

Figure 2-4. Finishing the installation and launching the Configuration Wizard

Running the SharePoint Products Configuration Wizard

The SharePoint Products Configuration Wizard will create the configuration database and set up the farm information. The initial page shown in Figure 2-5 summarizes the information that will be required.

Figure 2-5. Starting the SharePoint Products Configuration Wizard

To complete the configuration changes, some of the Windows services may need to be restarted, as explained in the dialog box shown in Figure 2-6.

Figure 2-6. Restarting services

The next page, shown in Figure 2-7, gives you the option of connecting to an existing farm or creating a new one. Since this is a new installation, you will need to create a new farm.

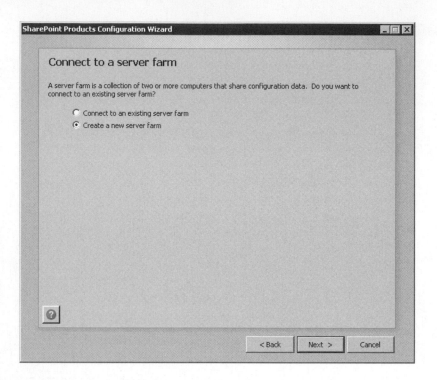

Figure 2-7. Creating a new server farm

The dialog box shown in Figure 2-8 allows you to specify where the configuration database should reside. The wizard will create the database; you will specify the name of the database and which server it should be on. By convention the database name should be `SharePoint_Config`. You'll also need to specify the logon and password to use when connecting to the database. This must be an Active Directory domain account with permission to create a database.

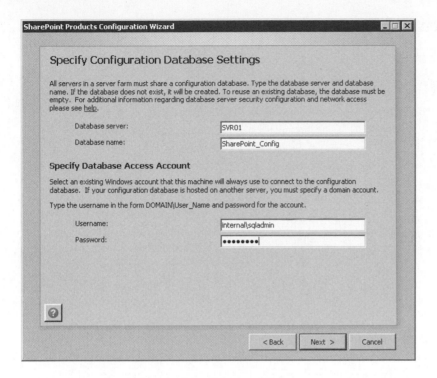

Figure 2-8. Specifying the database connection

You will also need to specify a password, called a *passphrase*, that will be used if you want to add more servers to this farm. For a development environment, this will probably not be used. However, in the dialog box shown in Figure 2-9, enter a passphrase, and write it down in case you need it later.

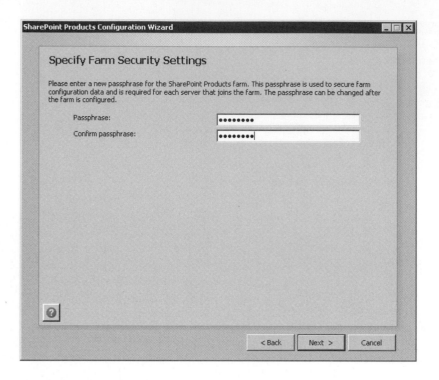

Figure 2-9. *Establishing a SharePoint farm passphrase*

The dialog box shown in Figure 2-10 allows you to configure the port that is used by the Central Administration application. This web app requires special permissions, and you'll use this page to configure how that authentication is done. NTLM will work fine.

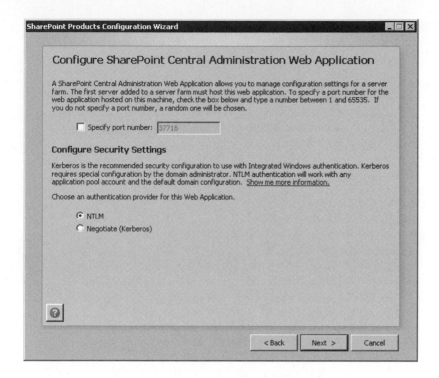

Figure 2-10. Configuring the Central Administration application

The last page, shown in Figure 2-11, summarizes the configuration options that were specified. The farm will be set up after you click the Next button.

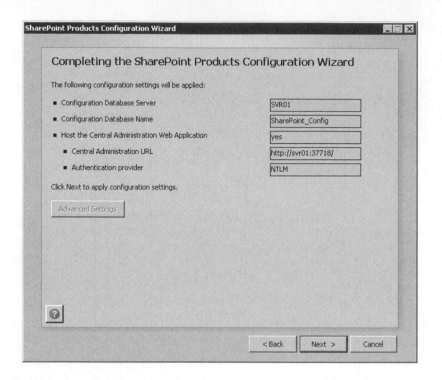

Figure 2-11. Configuration summary

Using the Central Administration Web Application

After the farm has been configured, the Central Administration web app will be started automatically. There are a few more settings that you'll need to set up. The first page, shown in Figure 2-12, gives you the option of configuring it manually or letting the application walk you through it. Click the Start the Wizard button.

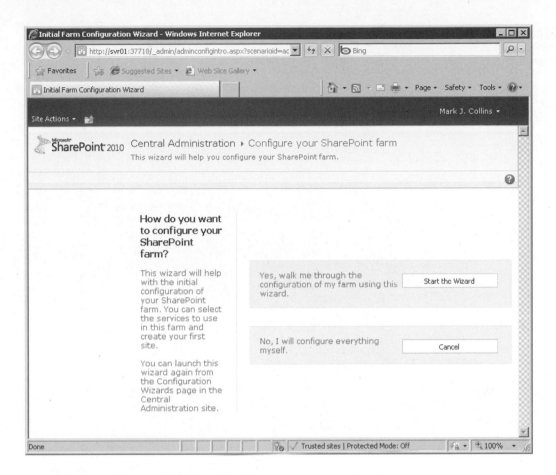

Figure 2-12. Configuring the SharePoint farm

You'll use the next page to configure the SharePoint services. Select a user account that the services will run as. This can be the same account used to connect to the database, as shown in Figure 2-13. You can also use this page to specify the services that should be available. You can use the default settings.

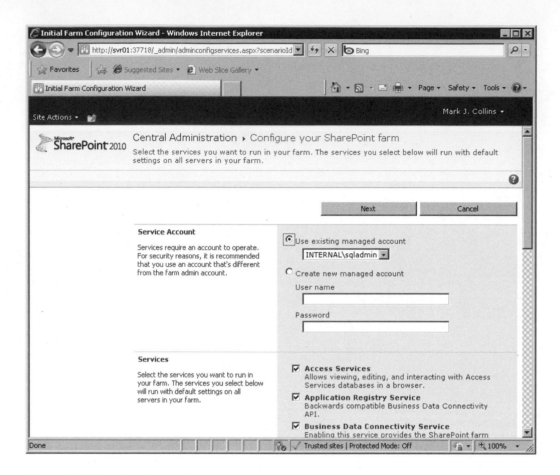

Figure 2-13. Configuring services

On the final page shown in Figure 2-14, you'll set up the home site. Enter a title and description, and specify the URL for this site. You can also choose the template to be used for this initial site.

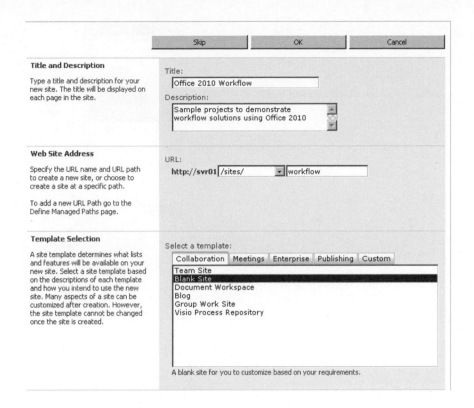

Figure 2-14. Creating the home site

The page shown in Figure 2-15 provides a summary of the farm's configuration.

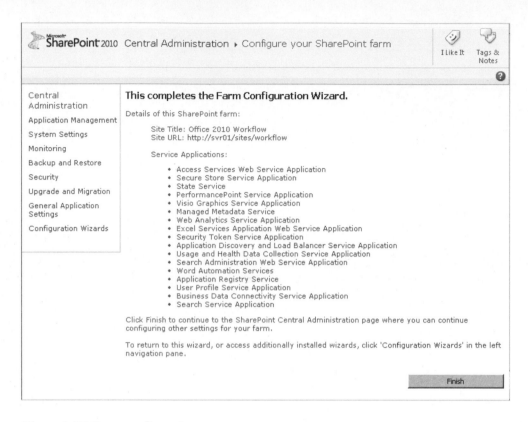

Figure 2-15. Farm configuration summary

Installing SharePoint on a Desktop

The setup application was designed for installing on a server OS. If you try to install on a desktop OS, you'll get the error shown in Figure 2-16.

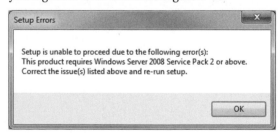

Figure 2-16. Unsupported OS error

To install on Windows 7, you'll need to customize this process by using the following instructions.

■ **Note** You can also install SharePoint on a 64-bit version of Windows Vista; however, it requires a few more steps. If you are using Vista, refer to the MSDN documentation for details.

You will need to modify a configuration file used by the setup program. To do that, you'll need to copy the installation media to a writable location. If you have the installation on a disk or disk image (ISO file), copy the entire contents to a folder on your hard disk. If you have the installation as a single self-extracting file such as `SharePoint.exe` or some other name (such as `en_sharepoint_server_2010_rtm_x64.exe`), then you'll need to extract this to a folder on your hard disk. To extract the files, run the following from a command prompt:

```
SharePoint.exe /extract:C:\SharePointInstall
```

Make sure to change `C:\SharePointInstall` to the actual location of the folder you created. Change `SharePoint.exe` to whatever your installation file is named. The contents of your installation folder should look like those shown in Figure 2-17.

Figure 2-17. Contents of the custom install folder

There is a `config.xml` file in the `Files\Setup` folder. Open this with a text editor such as Notepad, and add the following entry in the `Configuration` section:

```
<Setting Id="AllowWindowsClientInstall" Value="True"/>
```

The complete file should be similar to this:

```
<Configuration>
  <Package Id="sts">
    <Setting Id="LAUNCHEDFROMSETUPSTS" Value="Yes"/>
  </Package>

  <Package Id="spswfe">
    <Setting Id="SETUPCALLED" Value="1"/>
  </Package>

  <Logging Type="verbose" Path="%temp%" Template="SharePoint Server Setup(*).log"/>
  <!--<PIDKEY Value="Enter Product Key Here" />-->
  <Setting Id="SERVERROLE" Value="SINGLESERVER"/>
  <Setting Id="USINGUIINSTALLMODE" Value="1"/>
  <Setting Id="SETUPTYPE" Value="CLEAN_INSTALL"/>
  <Setting Id="SETUP_REBOOT" Value="Never"/>

  <!-- Add this line for Window 7 install -->
  <Setting Id="AllowWindowsClientInstall" Value="True"/>
</Configuration>
```

Installing the Prerequisites

Now you'll need to install each of the prerequisites manually by following these steps:

■ **Note** When installing some of these prerequisites, you may get an error indicating that a later version has already been installed. If that happens, you can cancel the install and skip this prerequisite. Also, at the time this was written, some of these products were still in a Beta release. The download link may change when the final release version is available.

---

1. *Microsoft FilterPack*: Run the `FilterPack.msi` install file, which is found in the `PrerequisiteInstallerFiles\FilterPack` subfolder in the installation folder that you created.

2. *Microsoft Sync Framework*: Download and run the synchronization framework (`Synchronization-v2.0-x64-ENU.msi`) using the following link: `http://www.microsoft.com/downloads/details.aspx?familyid=109DB36E-CDD0-4514-9FB5-B77D9CEA37F6`. Download the appropriate 64-bit version of the core Synchronization installation file. At the prompt, choose Run. You will also need to download and install the Provider Services and Database Providers products.

3. SQL Server Native Client: Download and run the SQL client software using the following link: http://go.microsoft.com/fwlink/?LinkId=123718. At the prompt, choose Run.

4. *Windows Identity Foundation*: Download the Windows Identity Foundation (previously known as Geneva Framework) using the following link: `http://www.microsoft.com/downloads/details.aspx?FamilyID=eb9c345f-e830-40b8-a5fe-ae7a864c4d76&displaylang=en`. Download the appropriate version for your OS.

5. *ADO.NET Data Services (1.5)*: Go to the Microsoft site using this link: `http://www.microsoft.com/downloads/details.aspx?FamilyID=a71060eb-454e-4475-81a6-e9552b1034fc`. From this page, select the download link for the Runtime Only version, and follow the instructions.

6. *Chart Controls*: Download and run the chart controls using the following link: `http://go.microsoft.com/fwlink/?LinkID=122517`. At the prompt, choose Run.

7. *SQL Server Analysis Services*: Download and run Analysis Services using the following link: `http://download.microsoft.com/download/A/D/0/AD021EF1-9CBC-4D11-AB51-6A65019D4706/SQLSERVER2008_ASADOMD10.msi`. At the prompt, choose Run.

8. *SQL Server Reporting Services (SSRS) add-in*: For SQL Server 2008, download the SharePoint add-in from this link: `http://www.microsoft.com/downloads/details.aspx?familyid=200FD7B5-DB7C-4B8C-A7DC-5EFEE6E19005&displaylang=en`. For SQL Server 2008 R2, use this link: `http://go.microsoft.com/fwlink/?LinkID=164654&clcid=0x409`. Then run the `rsSharePoint.msi` installation package.

■ **Caution** The installation described in step 8 will configure the reporting add-in for local mode. This means that it will function without an actual instance of SSRS. Most of the reporting functions will work, but you will not have the server-side benefits of SSRS such as subscriptions. If you are using an actual instance of SSRS (either on the local server or on another network server), there are additional steps needed to configure SSRS for use with SharePoint 2010. For more information, refer to the following MSDN article: http://technet.microsoft.com/en-us/library/ee662542(office.14).aspx.

Enabling Windows Features

A number of Windows features must be enabled for SharePoint to work correctly. The easiest way to do this is to run the script shown in Listing 2-1 from a command prompt.

Listing 2-1. Script for Enabling Windows Features

```
start /w pkgmgr /iu:IIS-WebServerRole
start /w pkgmgr /iu:IIS-WebServer
start /w pkgmgr /iu:IIS-CommonHttpFeatures
start /w pkgmgr /iu:IIS-StaticContent
start /w pkgmgr /iu:IIS-DefaultDocument
start /w pkgmgr /iu:IIS-DirectoryBrowsing
start /w pkgmgr /iu:IIS-HttpErrors
start /w pkgmgr /iu:IIS-ApplicationDevelopment
start /w pkgmgr /iu:IIS-ASP
start /w pkgmgr /iu:IIS-ASPNET
start /w pkgmgr /iu:IIS-NetFxExtensibility
start /w pkgmgr /iu:IIS-ISAPIExtensions
start /w pkgmgr /iu:IIS-ISAPIFilter
start /w pkgmgr /iu:IIS-HealthAndDiagnostics
start /w pkgmgr /iu:IIS-HttpLogging
start /w pkgmgr /iu:IIS-LoggingLibraries
start /w pkgmgr /iu:IIS-RequestMonitor
start /w pkgmgr /iu:IIS-HttpTracing
start /w pkgmgr /iu:IIS-CustomLogging
start /w pkgmgr /iu:IIS-Security
start /w pkgmgr /iu:IIS-BasicAuthentication
start /w pkgmgr /iu:IIS-WindowsAuthentication
start /w pkgmgr /iu:IIS-DigestAuthentication
start /w pkgmgr /iu:IIS-RequestFiltering
start /w pkgmgr /iu:IIS-Performance
start /w pkgmgr /iu:IIS-HttpCompressionStatic
start /w pkgmgr /iu:IIS-HttpCompressionDynamic
start /w pkgmgr /iu:IIS-WebServerManagementTools
start /w pkgmgr /iu:IIS-ManagementConsole
start /w pkgmgr /iu:IIS-IIS6ManagementCompatibility
start /w pkgmgr /iu:IIS-Metabase
```

```
start /w pkgmgr /iu:IIS-WMICompatibility
start /w pkgmgr /iu:WAS-WindowsActivationService
start /w pkgmgr /iu:WAS-ProcessModel
start /w pkgmgr /iu:WAS-NetFxEnvironment
start /w pkgmgr /iu:WAS-ConfigurationAPI
start /w pkgmgr /iu:WCF-HTTP-Activation
start /w pkgmgr /iu:WCF-NonHTTP-Activation
```

To verify that these features were enabled, you can select them from the Control Panel. From the Programs and Features group, select Turn Windows features on or off. Figure 2-18 shows a partial list of these features.

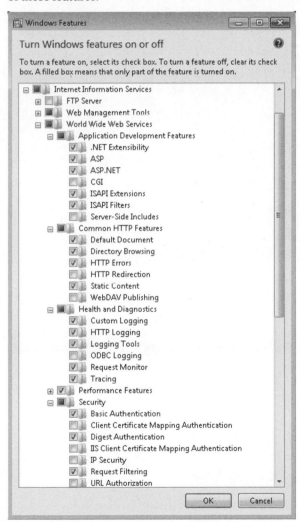

Figure 2-18. *Listing of Windows features*

Installing SharePoint Server

Now that you have all the prerequisites loaded, you can install SharePoint Server. To do that, run Setup.exe from the folder that you created for the extracted files. You will be prompted for your product key, as shown in Figure 2-19

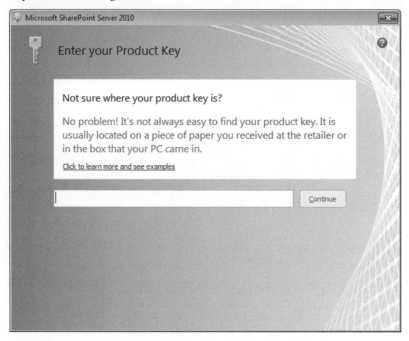

Figure 2-19. Entering your product key

The SharePoint Server has two installation options, as listed in Figure 2-20. You will probably want to use the Standalone option. The Server Farm option is used when the database is hosted on a different machine or there are multiple SharePoint servers in the farm. However, this option will require an Active Directory domain controller and domain user accounts.

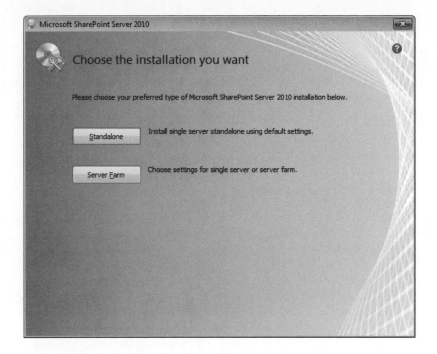

Figure 2-20. Selecting the installation type

When the installation has finished, the dialog box shown in Figure 2-21 will appear.

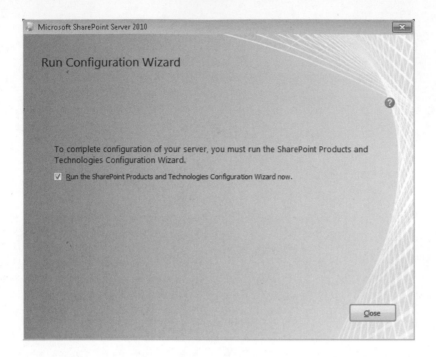

Figure 2-21. Starting the Products and Technologies configuration

Installing Hotfix KB970315

The install program is now prompting you to run the Products and Technologies Configuration Wizard. Before you run this, however, download and install the SQL Server hotfix KB970315. To get this hotfix, use the following link: http://support.microsoft.com/kb/970315. Click the link to request the hotfix (choose SQL_Server_2008_SP1_Cumulative_Update_2). You will be prompted for your e-mail address, and a link to the hotfix will be e-mailed to you. Download and run this hotfix. The Select Features dialog box, shown in Figure 2-22, will be displayed. The instances should already be selected; if not, click the Select All button. The patch level could be different from the one shown here.

■ **Note** If you are using SQL Server 2005, you'll need to install the cumulative update package 3 for SQL Server 2005 Service Pack 3 if you haven't already. You can download that update at http://support.microsoft.com/kb/967909.The following instructions are for the 2008 update.

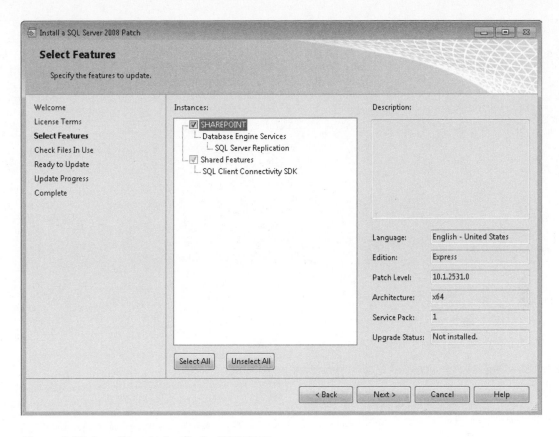

Figure 2-22. Installing the hotfix for KB970315

Running the Configuration Wizard

Once the hotfix has been installed, go back to the SharePoint Server dialog box. Leave the check box selected, and click the Close button. The Configuration Wizard will then start, as shown in Figure 2-23.

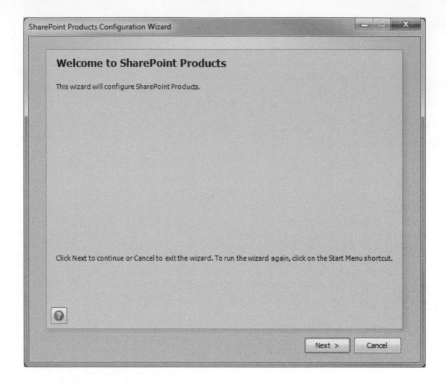

Figure 2-23. Starting the Configuration Wizard

If you are installing on Windows 7 or Vista, you will get a warning (shown in Figure 2-24) reminding you that running a SharePoint workstation is not supported for production environments. Just click OK. You might also get a warning that some services will need to be restarted.

Figure 2-24. Windows 7 not supported for production environments

When this has completed, you should see the message shown in Figure 2-25.

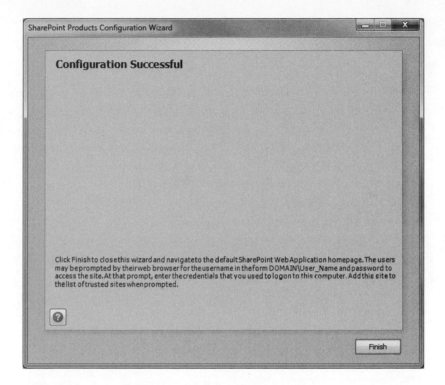

Figure 2-25. Configuration Wizard completion message

Initial Site Configuration

■ **Caution** When installing on a desktop, a home site is created for you. The steps in this section assume that a desktop OS (Windows 7 or Vista) is being used.

After you click the Finish button to close the Configuration Wizard, the SharePoint site will be launched. You will be prompted to select a template for your initial site, as shown in Figure 2-26. Select the Blank Site template.

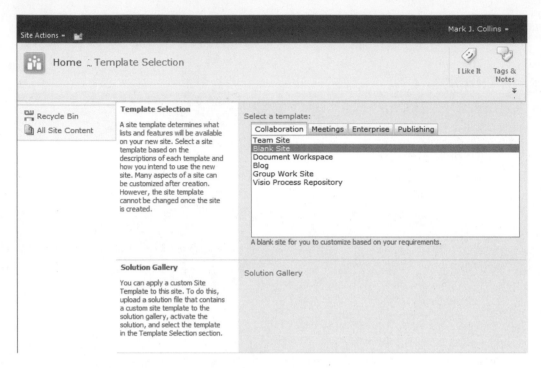

Figure 2-26. Selecting the Blank Site template for the initial site

Next, you will be prompted to set up the groups that will be allowed various access rights to your site (see Figure 2-27). You can use the default groups that were already created.

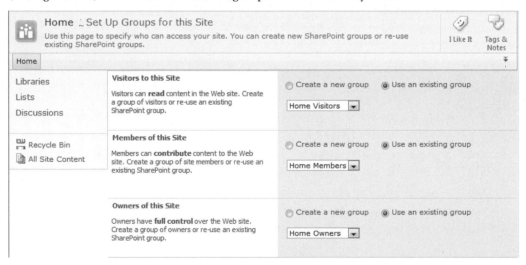

Figure 2-27. Selecting the user groups for your site

Congratulations! Your initial SharePoint site should be available. The URL for the home page will be `http://<YourComputerName>/default.aspx`.

Installing Other Applications

Some of the solutions in this book will require other applications to create more advanced workflows. For best results, install these applications on the same machine that you're running SharePoint on. The order that these are installed is not critical. You can install Visual Studio and the Office applications before installing SharePoint Server. If some of these are already installed, that's fine; you can just skip these steps.

Installing Visual Studio 2010

You will need Visual Studio 2010 for some of the advanced workflows that you'll be creating. Visual Studio can also be used to create the forms used by SharePoint. Install Visual Studio 2010 on the same machine that you installed SharePoint.

Office Client Applications

You will also need to install the Office 2010 client applications such as Outlook, Word, and so on. Although the server applications (SharePoint Foundation and SharePoint Server) must be 64-bit versions, the client applications can be either 32-bit or 64-bit. The one primary consideration here is that you cannot mix versions; they must be all 32-bit or all 64-bit. So, once you make a decision here, you are pretty much stuck with it. For example, I tried to install a 64-bit version of the SharePoint Designer and received the error shown in Figure 2-28. Apparently, one of the prerequisites had installed a 32-bit Office component.

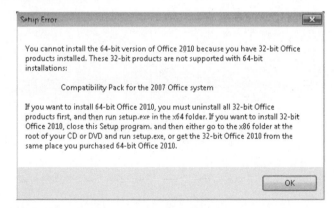

Figure 2-28. Office product incompatibility message

■ **Tip** The primary advantage of using the 64-bit versions is that they support larger files. Excel, for example, will support more than the ~65,000 rows that we've all become familiar with. This, however, is probably not a big concern for your development projects. The downside of using a 64-bit version is that any add-ins that you may want to use must also be 64-bit versions. You may run into a situation where something doesn't work because a 64-bit version is not yet available. The safe choice is to stay with the 32-bit version—for now anyway. That is not to say that using the 64-bit version will cause problems; it should not. If you have compelling reasons to use the 64-bit version, then you should install the 64-bit version.

SharePoint Designer 2010

Install the SharePoint Designer, which is a free product available from Microsoft. To download the 32-bit version, use this link:

```
http://www.microsoft.com/downloads/details.aspx?FamilyID=D88A1505-849B-4587-B854-
A7054EE28D66
```

For the 64-bit version, use this link:

```
http://www.microsoft.com/downloads/details.aspx?FamilyID=566d3f55-77a5-4298-bb9c-
f55f096b125d
```

Download and run the installation program. You should see the installation options shown in Figure 2-29.

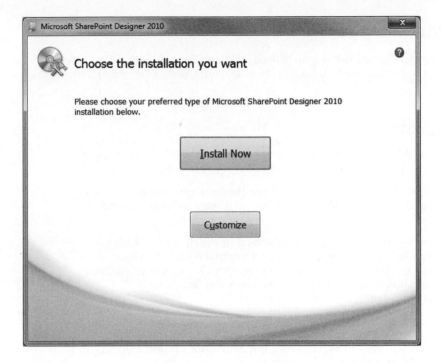

Figure 2-29. Installing the SharePoint Designer 2010

Click the Install Now button, which will install the SharePoint Designer 2010 with all the default options.

Installing Office 2010

Microsoft Office 2010 comes in five editions that contain various combinations of the Office products. The most important product for our purposes is Outlook, which comes in all editions except Home and Student. Any of the other editions should work fine. Here is a link that explains what is included in each edition:

`http://technet.microsoft.com/en-us/library/ee523662(office.14).aspx`

Installing Visio 2010

You will use Visio 2010 to design a workflow in Chapter 5, so install it now, if you have a copy of it. (It is normally purchased separately and not included with the standard Office bundles.)

Configuring E-mail

The workflows that you will be creating will use e-mail to send task notifications. SharePoint Server will need access to an SMTP server that it can use to send e-mails. Also, your Outlook client will need to be able to receive these e-mails.

Providing an E-mail System

Windows 7 does not provide an SMTP server, so you'll need to find another solution to support incoming and outgoing e-mails. I can offer three suggestions, starting with the easiest:

- *Exchange*: If you have access to an Exchange server, then you can simply point the SharePoint server and your Outlook client to it. You may want to create some test accounts to work with.

- *Open source mail server*: You can install one of several free mail servers, which work fairly well, especially if you're only using it for internal e-mails between Office applications. One that I have used and found pretty easy to set up is called hMailServer. You can find more information and download details at `http://www.hmailserver.com`.

- *Private mail server*: The last option requires setting up your own mail server. The details for doing this are beyond the scope of this book. I'll let you know that Windows Server 2008 provides an SMTP server, but it does not support POP. Windows Server 2003 does support POP, so you may want to use that.

Configuring SMTP

To configure SMTP in SharePoint Server, you'll use the SharePoint Central Administration application, which you should have in your Start menu. Select the System Settings group, and then under the E-Mail and Text Messages (SMS) heading, select the `Configure outgoing e-mail settings` link. Enter the appropriate information in the Mail Settings page shown in Figure 2-30.

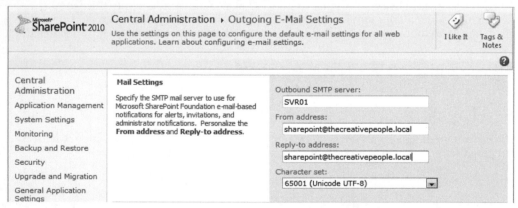

Figure 2-30. Entering the outgoing e-mail settings

Summary

Getting all the various products installed and configured may seem like a lot of work. But getting that done now will help with the remaining chapters. You'll be able to focus on the task of creating workflow solutions.

There are a lot of different scenarios, and I didn't cover all of them. Also, as we all know, these products can change over time and may require some adjustments to these procedures. If you're having any difficulties in getting these to install or work correctly, a lot of information is available online. Check out Microsoft's MSDN site (`http://msdn.microsoft.com`).

CHAPTER 3

SharePoint Primer

This chapter is intended for anyone who is fairly new to the SharePoint technology. I'll give you a brief description of the various types of objects that are used to implement a SharePoint solution. In a very loose sense, you can think of SharePoint as a database where the "tables" are the lists and the "rows" are the items you put in the lists. Because SharePoint also provides the visualization of this data, presentation aspects are considered at every level in the "database" design.

Columns

The basic building block is the *column*, which holds a single piece of information.

■ **Note** Columns are also referred to as *fields*. In the SharePoint object model, which you'll use in Chapter 9, you access columns through the SPField class. The SharePoint Designer calls them *columns*. So, you will see both terms *column* and *field* used interchangeably.

Each column definition must include the column type, which specifies both storage and presentation details. Figure 3-1 lists the available column types.

Column Types
Single Line of Text
Multi Lines of Text
Choice
Number
Currency
Date & Time
Yes/No (checkbox)
Hyperlink or Picture
Lookup (Information Already on This Site)
Person or Group
Calculated (calculation Based on Other Columns)

Figure 3-1. Column types

Text Columns

Notice that there are two text types: `Single Line of Text` and `Multi Lines of Text`. Although the storage requirements of these two are identical, the display details are not. A multiline text field will take up more space on the form (you can specify the default size) and has additional display options. Figure 3-2 shows the Column Editor for a `Multi Line of Text` column.

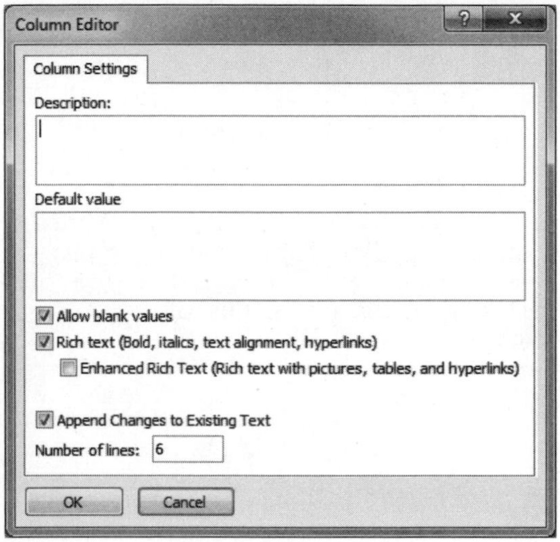

Figure 3-2. *Multiline text field settings*

One of the particularly interesting features of the multiline column is the append option. If you select the `Append Changes to Existing Text` check box, whatever text is entered in that field is appended to the existing contents. This is often used on a comments field. If the item is edited multiple times, the comments are appended at the end of the previous comment, giving you a running history of all the comments. A multiline column can also support rich-text formatting and even pictures.

Contrast this to the settings for a `Single Line Text` column, as shown in Figure 3-3.

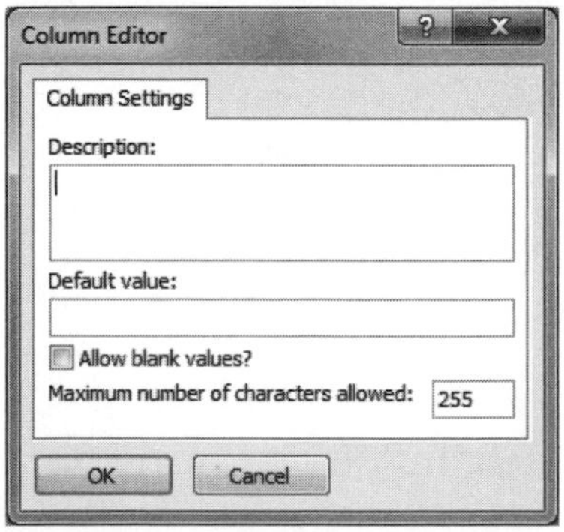

Figure 3-3. *Single-line text field settings*

Date & Time Columns

When defining a column, you can also specify a default value. For example, when creating a `Date & Time` column, you have an option to default to the current date/time or a fixed date, as shown in Figure 3-4.

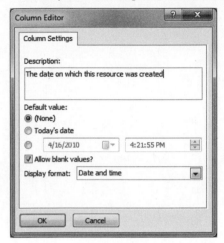

Figure 3-4. The `Date & Time` *column settings*

Notice also that you can choose to display the value as a date only or as both a date and a time.

Person or Group Columns

If you use a column type of `Person or Group`, the edit form will use a `PeoplePicker` control. You'll use this control a lot, and it's a very useful way to select users, ensuring only valid choices are allowed. The Column Editor shown in Figure 3-5 illustrates the settings you can use to configure how this control works.

47

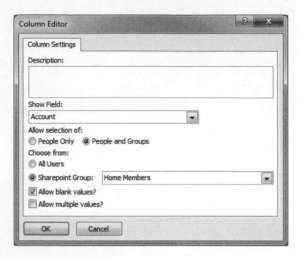

Figure 3-5. Column Editor for Person or Group

You will use these settings to determine what attribute of the user to display. By default this is the account or login name. However, you could display the name, e-mail address, phone number, or whatever is appropriate for your application. You can also control which users or groups are allowed and whether multiple people or groups can be selected.

Choice Columns

The Choice type is another interesting column type. You'll use this when you want to provide fixed values for the allowable options. Figure 3-6 shows the Column Editor for a Choice field.

Figure 3-6. Column Editor for a Choice field

When defining the column, you'll specify the available option in the Choices list. You can decide how the choices are presented. There are three options:

- Drop-down menu
- Radio button
- Check boxes

Lookup Columns

The Choice type should not be confused with the Lookup type. A Choice column has a fixed set of allowable values. Often, however, you'll want to restrict values to a dynamic list. The Lookup type allows you to do this by specifying another list as the source of the allowable values. For example, if you have an Order list and you want to select the customer for this order, you can create a list of customers and then use that list to look up customers on an Order list.

Figure 3-7 shows the Column Editor for the Lookup column type.

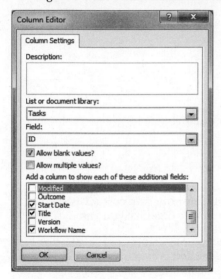

Figure 3-7. Column Editor for the Lookup column type

You must first choose the list to be used for the lookup. You'll then select the field that will be stored in the new column. This is typically an ID field or some other unique identifier. You can also select additional fields that will be displayed on the form.

Lookup columns are the mechanism that you'll use to ensure referential integrity. In database terms, this is equivalent to a foreign key relationship. By defining a Lookup column, you ensure that selected values are valid. This also improves the user interface. The user can search for the customer, using any of the additional fields that you specify.

Calculated Columns

A `Calculated` column allows you to define a column with a formula that includes the values of other columns. Figure 3-8 shows a sample.

Figure 3-8. A calculated column

In this example, the `Title` and `Request Status` columns are concatenated to form a new column.

Site Columns Collection

SharePoint provides a set of column definitions, referred to as a `Site Columns` collection. These are defined as independent pieces of information that you can assemble into your own custom lists. When creating a list, you can use any of these existing columns. Site columns are organized into groups. You can also define new site columns and new groups to help organize them.

When creating a list, you also have the option of creating a new column that is used only by that list. The difference is in how the column is created. In the first case, the column is created, added to the `Site Columns` collection, and then added to the list. In the second case, the column is created and added to the list. It requires an extra step to create reusable column definitions.

In SharePoint, the mantra is "Build once, use often." A column definition should be reused wherever appropriate. This means taking the extra step to define the column first and then adding it to the list. But it also means carefully considering the design of the column and how you expect it to be used. Keep in mind that if you change an existing site column, everywhere it is used it will change. That can be a good thing if used properly. Give your columns meaningful names and a description that explains the intended use. When choosing an existing column, don't just look for one with the correct column type. Make sure the description matches what you're planning to use it for.

Content Types

Content types define a reusable collection of properties and are used throughout SharePoint. One use of content types is to define the items (rows) that are contained in a list or document library. A content type specifies a collection of columns. For example, Figure 3-9 shows the columns included in the Task content type.

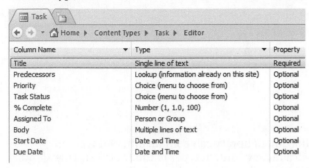

Figure 3-9. The columns included in the Task content type

Columns can be specified as either Required, Optional, or Hidden, which controls how the field is displayed in the form. For each content type, you can specify a custom form to be used. In Chapter 11, you'll use InfoPath 2010 to develop a custom task form. SharePoint uses the following three forms for each content type:

- *New*. Form used when creating a new item
- *Display*. View-only form used to display an item
- *Edit*. Form used to modify an item

Content types support inheritance, which means you can derive a new content type from an existing one. The new content type will inherit the columns and properties of its parent content type. The base content type is Item, and all other contents are derived (directly or indirectly) from Item. The Document content type, which is derived from Item, is the root type for all document libraries.

Lists and Libraries

If content types represent the *things* in a SharePoint site, lists are the *containers* they are stored in.

■ **Tip** A document library is just a special type of list, so I will often use the term *list* to refer to both.

Supporting Content Types

One thing that is somewhat unique about SharePoint and different from traditional databases is that a list can contain items of different types. For example, the standard Tasks list created by the Team Site template allows the content types shown in Figure 3-10.

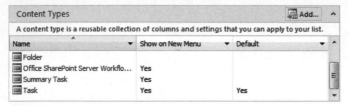

Figure 3-10. Content types supported by the Tasks list

This is a really handy feature. For instance, a document library can contain different types of documents. In several projects in this book, you will add new content types to the Tasks list. This allows you to have a single Tasks list that contains different types of tasks.

You can also create a new list and add columns to it without using content types. In this case, a content type definition is inferred from the list definition. This is a quick way to create a custom list, which you'll use in the next chapter.

Views

You can define any number of views for each list. A view usually includes a filter to define a subset of the items in the list. The Tasks list, for example, provides views to show only active tasks or only tasks assigned to the current user. Views can also define a subset of columns that are to be displayed.

Figure 3-11 shows a collapsed version of a view definition page.

Name	
Type a name for this view of the list. Make the name descriptive, such as "Sorted by Author", so that site visitors will know what to expect when they click this link.	View Name: `All Tasks` Web address of this view: http://omega5/Part3/Lists/Tasks/ `AllItems` .aspx This view appears by default when visitors follow a link to this list. If you want to delete this view, first make another view the default.
⊞ **Columns**	
⊞ **Sort**	
⊞ **Filter**	
⊟ **Inline Editing** Choose whether an edit button on each row should be provided. This button allows users to edit the current row in the current view, without navigating to the form.	☐ Allow inline editing
⊟ **Tabular View** Choose whether individual checkboxes for each row should be provided. These checkboxes allow users to select multiple list items to perform bulk operations.	☑ Allow individual item checkboxes
⊞ **Group By**	
⊞ **Totals**	
⊞ **Style**	
⊞ **Folders**	
⊞ **Item Limit**	
⊞ **Mobile**	

Figure 3-11. Edit View page

As you can see from the Edit View page, you can configure a lot of options using a view, including sorting, grouping, and subtotals.

Subsites

You can create subsites on a SharePoint server. Site columns and content types are inherited by all subsites. All the columns and content types that are defined by the home site are also available to any subsite. However, any custom column or content type defined on a subsite is not available on the home site. For that reason, it is best to define site columns and content types at the home (or root) site. Subsites can have their own subsites, creating a hierarchy of sites. Lists are not inherited, however. A Tasks list on one site, for example, is not available to child (or sibling) sites.

■ **Note** Column, content types, forms, and permissions are inherited from the parent site. Lists and content are not inherited. As you'll see later in this book, reusable workflows are also inherited.

When creating a SharePoint site for a large organization, each department will often have their own subsite so they can manage their own lists and libraries. Keep in mind that column and content type definitions are shared across all the subsites. This is why you should give some thought when defining them.

You can create columns and content types at each subsite as well. If a need is unique to a particular department, you may want to consider creating it at that level. If you do, it will not be available to other subsites. If you think other sites may want to use it, create it in the home site.

Templates

SharePoint provides templates for creating commonly used types of sites and lists. Templates are a convenient way of creating sites and adding site content.

Site Templates

When creating a new site (or subsite), you'll be presented with the dialog box shown in Figure 3-12, where you can choose an existing site template.

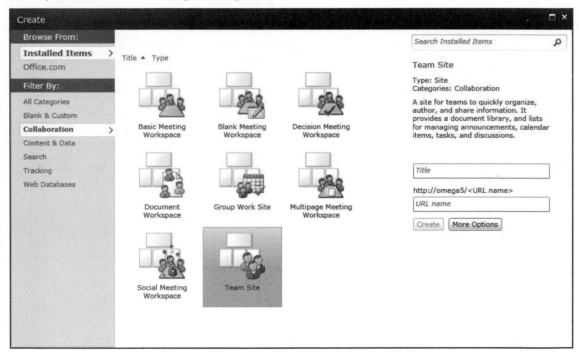

Figure 3-12. Using the Team Site template

The template will create the lists and other content based on the template definition. One that you'll use in some of the projects in this book is the Team Site template. It will create a `Tasks` list, a `Calendar`, a

`Shared Documents` library, and other lists. Quite a few templates are available, which should make it easy to get a basic site created quickly.

List Templates

You can also use templates to create commonly used lists. When creating a new list, you'll be presented with the dialog box shown in Figure 3-13 where you can choose an existing list template.

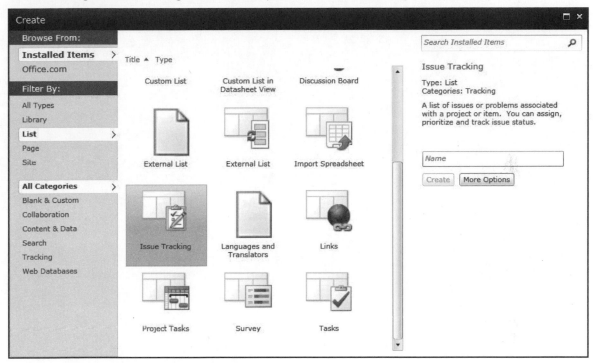

Figure 3-13. Using the Issue Tracking list template

On the left side of this dialog you can filter the templates that are displayed. By selecting the type such as List or Library and choosing the category, you can narrow down the search to find an appropriate template. You can also browse the Internet to find other templates that may be available there. You can choose the Blank template, if none of these suits your needs, and create a custom list. In Chapter 13, you will create your own list template that you can use for creating the same list on multiple sites.

■ **Note** List templates reside at the home site, and you can use them at any level in the site hierarchy.

Summary

SharePoint provides some very useful constructs for building office automation solutions. The column (or field) is the basic building block, defining a single piece of information. The content type defines a reusable collection of columns and can have custom forms defined for each. Content types define the *things* stored in SharePoint, and lists (and document libraries) are the containers for those *things*.

PART 2

■■■

Using Workflows

In this section you'll create several no-code workflows using a variety of tools. In Chapter 4 you'll configure an out-of-the-box workflow to track a list of work items. In Chapter 5 I'll show you how to use Office applications as workflow participants in a document library workflow. Chapters 6 and 7 will demonstrate the workflow editor in the SharePoint Designer. The solution presented in Chapter 6 uses Visio to design a workflow, which is then implemented in the SharePoint Designer. Chapter 7 provides a more detailed explanation of the SharePoint Designer's workflow editor and implements both a reusable list workflow and a site workflow.

■■■

CHAPTER 4

Three-state Workflow

Your first workflow will use the built-in Three-state workflow. As its name suggests, this workflow supports three states, which can be any three states and are referred to as the *initial*, *middle*, and *final* states. This is a good example of designing a generic process that you can reuse in a lot of different scenarios. For this exercise, you'll associate this workflow to a list of work requests.

Creating a New Site

First you should create a new site. You could use the default site that was created when SharePoint was installed. However, putting your test solutions into separate sites will help keep things organized. Creating a site is easy. Launch the SharePoint site, which will be the following URL (if installed on a server):

```
http://<Your computer name>/sites/<site name>/default.aspx
```

or the following (if installed on a client machine):

```
http://<Your computer name>/default.aspx
```

■ **Tip** If you installed SharePoint on a server, you can do most of the site administration from a client browser. You don't have to be logged into the server. Everything in this chapter can be done from the client. If you are doing this from a client PC, you will be prompted to install SharePoint Designer. Choose either 32-bit or 64-bit depending on the version of Office installed on your client machine.

Click the Site Actions menu on the top-left corner of the SharePoint page, and select the New Site option, as shown in Figure 4-1.

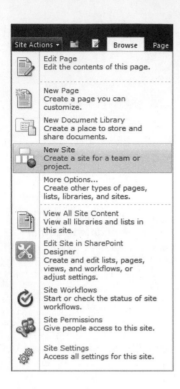

Figure 4-1. Creating a new site

Select the Blank Site template, and specify the name and location both as **Chapter04**, as shown in Figure 4-2. Then click the Create button.

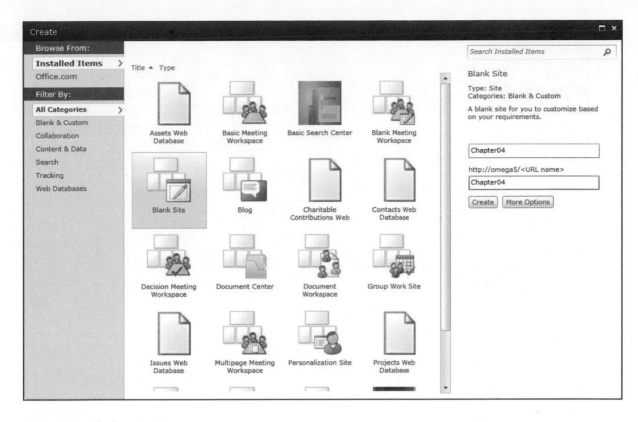

Figure 4-2. Configuring the new site

■ **Tip** If your client browser is running on a 64-bit OS, you should have both a 32-bit and a 64-bit version of Internet Explorer. You should use the 32-bit version. SharePoint and SharePoint Designer were intended to work with Silverlight, which is not available on the 64-bit platform. The pages will work on the 64-bit version, but you'll have a better user experience if you use the 32-bit version.

Creating a New List

On the new Chapter04 site, click the *Lists* link, which shows all the lists that have been created. This should be empty. Click the Create button. In the dialog box that appears, select List in the Filter By option, and then select the Custom List template. Enter the name as **Work Requests**, as shown in Figure 4-3. Then click the Create button.

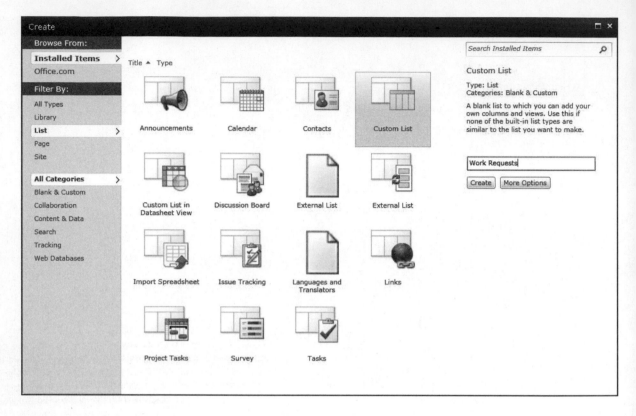

Figure 4-3. Creating a custom list

Understanding the Workflow Process

When someone wants to request some work to be done, they will add an item to the `Work Request` list. This person is referred to as the *initiator*. The items that are added to the list are assigned to someone to complete the request. Once completed, the item is then assigned to the initiator to review the work and provide feedback. Figure 4-4 illustrates this process.

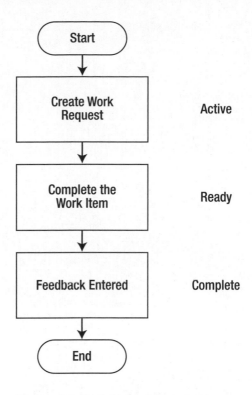

Figure 4-4. Work Request list process

The three states in the process (Active, Ready, and Complete) are shown alongside the task that will set that state. For example, when an item is created, it is put into Active status. When someone has completed the task, the status is changed to Ready. Finally, when the initiator has reviewed the work, the item is marked Complete.

Defining the List Columns

Now you'll need to define the columns for this list. Click the *Edit List* link near the top of the page. This will launch the SharePoint Designer that is shown in Figure 4-5.

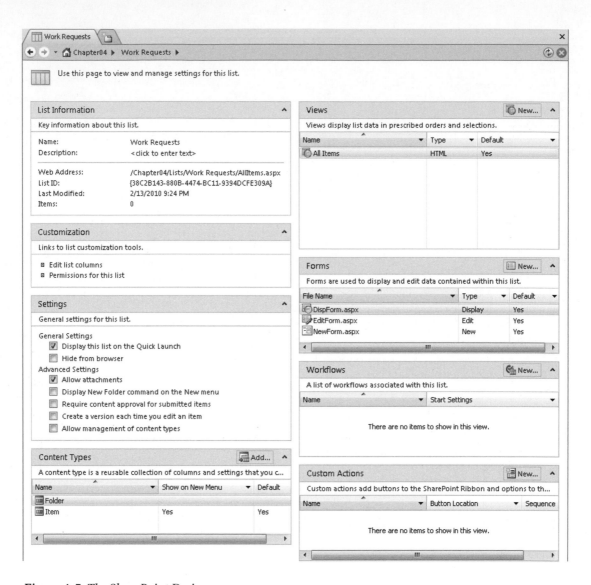

Figure 4-5. The SharePoint Designer

As you can see, the SharePoint Designer provides the ability to edit many aspects of this list. You can define various views of this list, modify the forms used to view and edit an item in the list, and so on. Click the *Edit list columns* link in the Customization section. This will display the column editor. Add the columns that are shown in Figure 4-6. Some of these columns (`Date Created`, `Assigned To`, and `Append-Only Comments`) already exist in the Site Columns collection. These are predefined columns that you can just add to your list. The other columns (`Description` and `Request Status`) must be added as a new column.

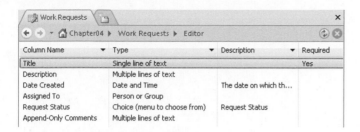

Figure 4-6. Adding columns to the list

The `Request Status` column is defined as a `Choice` type. This means that the allowed values are predefined. On the form, this can be presented as a drop-down list, radio buttons, or check boxes. When defining this column, enter the possible values as **Active**, **Ready**, and **Complete**, as shown in Figure 4-7. These values correspond to the states in the process described in Figure 4-4.

Figure 4-7. Defining the Choice values

Associating the Workflow

Now that you've set up the list, you can associate a workflow to it. Close the SharePoint Designer. On the SharePoint page, the `Work Requests` list should be displayed with the list currently empty. In the Settings sections of the List Tools ribbon, click the Workflow Settings button, as shown in Figure 4-8.

Figure 4-8. Selecting the workflow settings

The Workflow Settings page will be displayed (see Figure 4-9).

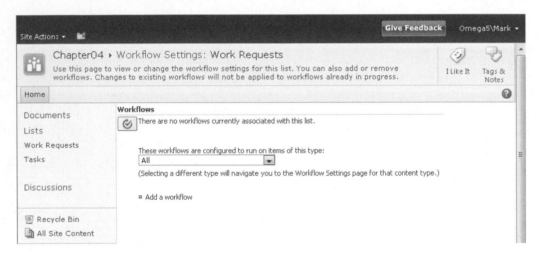

Figure 4-9. Associating a new workflow

No workflows are currently associated with this list. Click the *Add a workflow* link to associate a workflow to the `Work Requests` list.

■ **Note** In SharePoint, workflows are normally first *created* and then *associated* to a list or other object. The Three-state workflow that you are about to use already exists; it ships with SharePoint Foundation. You will *add* this workflow to the `Work Requests` list. On the SharePoint Designer page that you just used, there is a link in the Workflows section to *create* a workflow. This is used to design a new workflow, which you will do in Chapter 6. The terms *add* and *create* might seem synonymous, but they refer to two very different actions.

In the next dialog box, select the Three-state workflow, as shown in Figure 4-10.

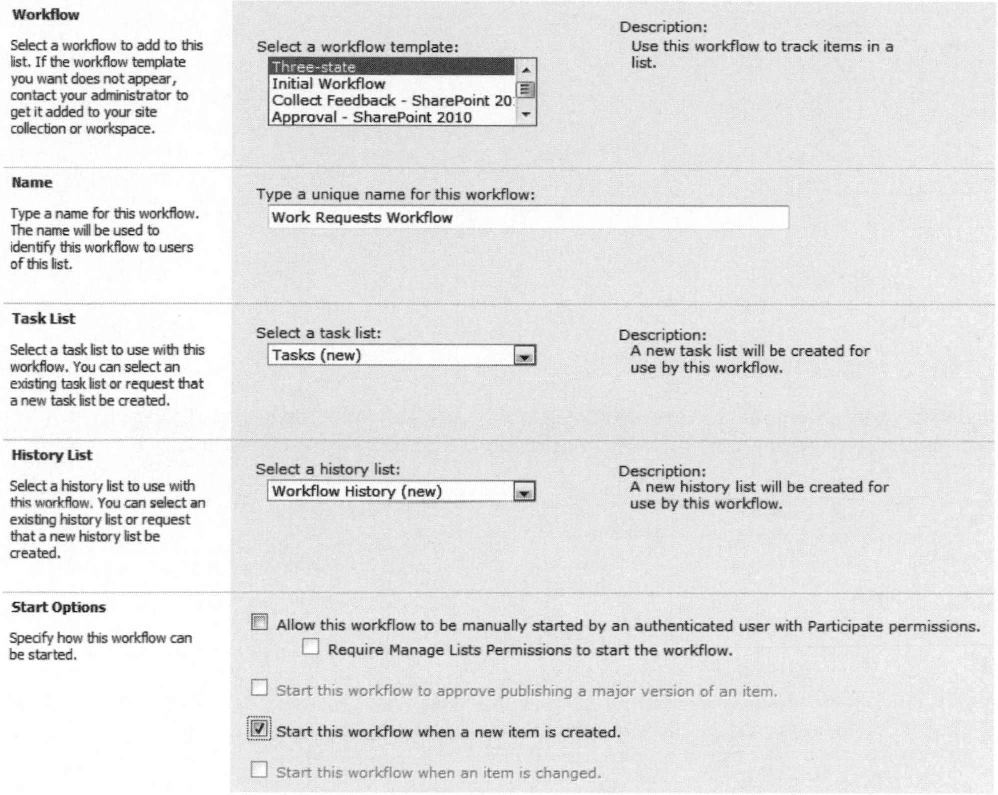

Workflow

Select a workflow to add to this list. If the workflow template you want does not appear, contact your administrator to get it added to your site collection or workspace.

Select a workflow template:

Three-state
Initial Workflow
Collect Feedback - SharePoint 20
Approval - SharePoint 2010

Description:
Use this workflow to track items in a list.

Name

Type a name for this workflow. The name will be used to identify this workflow to users of this list.

Type a unique name for this workflow:

Work Requests Workflow

Task List

Select a task list to use with this workflow. You can select an existing task list or request that a new task list be created.

Select a task list:

Tasks (new)

Description:
A new task list will be created for use by this workflow.

History List

Select a history list to use with this workflow. You can select an existing history list or request that a new history list be created.

Select a history list:

Workflow History (new)

Description:
A new history list will be created for use by this workflow.

Start Options

Specify how this workflow can be started.

☐ Allow this workflow to be manually started by an authenticated user with Participate permissions.
☐ Require Manage Lists Permissions to start the workflow.

☐ Start this workflow to approve publishing a major version of an item.

☑ Start this workflow when a new item is created.

☐ Start this workflow when an item is changed.

Figure 4-10. Adding the Three-state workflow

Select the Three-state workflow template, and enter a name for this workflow such as **Work Requests Workflow**. A task list and history list will be automatically created for you. You can select an existing list for these items. I'll explain how these are used later. For this project, use the default options, which is to create new lists.

For start options, select the option to start the workflow when a new item is added, and deselect all the other start options, as shown in Figure 4-10. Click the Next button. The next dialog box is driven by the options in the workflow template. In the first portion, you'll define the states. The template probably defaulted this correctly based on the list columns you defined. The `Request Status` column is the Choice field; the values in this column define the state of the list item. The state values are `Active`, `Ready`, and `Complete`, as shown in Figure 4-11.

Workflow states:

Select a 'Choice' field, and then
select a value for the initial, middle,
and final states. For an Issues list,
the states for an item are specified
by the Status field, where:
Initial State = Active
Middle State = Resolved
Final State = Closed
As the item moves through the
various stages of the workflow, the
item is updated automatically.

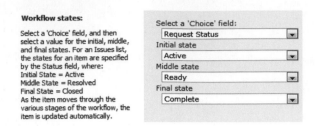

Select a 'Choice' field:
Request Status
Initial state
Active
Middle state
Ready
Final state
Complete

Figure 4-11. Specifying the state fields

Defining the First Transition

This workflow defines three states and two state transitions. In the next portion of this dialog box (see Figure 4-12), you'll define what happens in the first transition, when a new item is created.

Specify what you want to happen when a workflow is initiated:

For example, when a workflow is initiated on an issue in an Issues list, Microsoft SharePoint Foundation creates a task for the assigned user. When the user completes the task, the workflow changes from its initial state (Active) to its middle state (Resolved). You can also choose to send an e-mail message to notify the assigned user of the task.

Task Details:
Task Title:

Custom message: Request created:

The value for the field selected is concatenated to the custom message.

☑ Include list field: Title

Task Description:
Custom message: The following request ha

☑ Include list field: Description
☑ Insert link to List item

Task Due Date:
☐ Include list field: Date Created

Task Assigned To:
⦿ Include list field: Assigned To

○ Custom:

E-mail Message Details:

☑ Send e-mail message
To:
☑ Include Task Assigned To
Subject:
☑ Use Task Title
Body:
☑ Insert link to List item

Figure 4-12. Specifying workflow activities for the initial state

The workflow allows two actions:

- Create a task
- Send an e-mail

Creating a Task

When a request is added to the list, a task will be created. In this section, you'll specify how the task should be formatted. Some of the task properties can include fields from the work request. For example, the task title will be formatted as *Request created:* concatenated with the `Title` field of the work request.

Sending an E-mail

Similarly, the contents of the e-mail are configured based on a combination of fixed text and selected fields from the work request. In particular, the address that the e-mail is sent to is determined by the `Assigned To` user on the work request item.

Defining the Second Transition

The person who has been assigned this request will receive both an e-mail and a task in their task list. When the work has been performed, they will update this work request and change the status to `Ready`. This causes the second transition to occur. Figure 4-13 shows the configuration of this transition.

Specify what you want to happen when a workflow changes to its middle state:

For example, when an issue in an Issues list changes to Resolved status, it creates a task for the assigned user. When the user completes the task, the workflow changes from its middle state (Resolved) to its final state (Closed). You can also choose to send an e-mail message to notify the assigned user of the task.

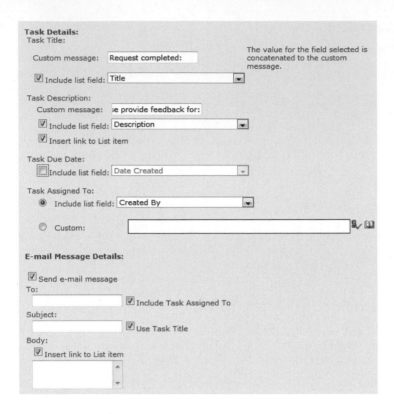

Figure 4-13. Specifying workflow activities for the middle state

A task is created for the initiator of the request, and an e-mail is sent to them as well. This is done in a similar manner as the first transition. Notice, however, that the e-mail is sent to the `Created By` field (the initiator) instead of the `Assigned To` field.

Using the Work Request Workflow

Now try the workflow. Go to the `Work Request` list, and click the *Add new item* link. The dialog box shown in Figure 4-14 will be displayed.

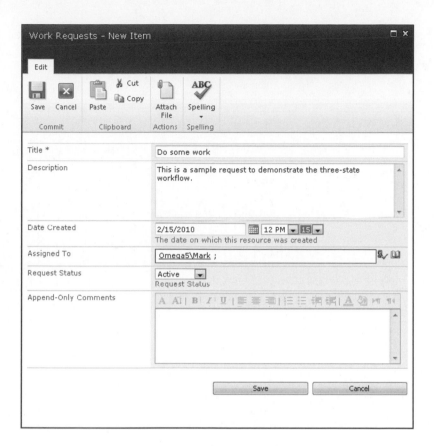

Figure 4-14. Creating a new work request

Enter a title and description, and set the `Date Created` field. For the `Assigned To` field, enter your Windows login (you do not need to specify the domain name). Click the Check Names button next to the `Assigned To` field. This will verify the name you entered can be resolved to a person or group defined in the SharePoint database. The `Request Status` should default to `Active`. Click the Save button to enter this request.

The `Work Request` list should now show the request that you just entered (see Figure 4-15). Notice that the last column (`Work Requests Workflow`) shows `In Progress`. This indicates that the workflow that you just set up is now being executed for this item.

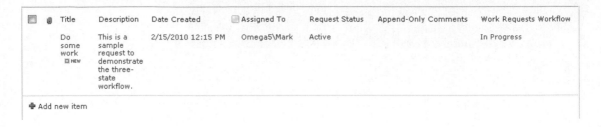

Figure 4-15. The Work Request *list with one item*

There are two ways to edit a list item. You can select Edit Item from the drop-down menu next to the Title field, as shown in Figure 4-16.

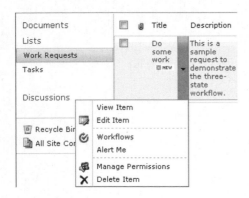

Figure 4-16. Editing the request using the drop-down menu

You can also click the Title field, which is a link that displays a view form. From there, you can click the Edit Item button, as shown in Figure 4-17.

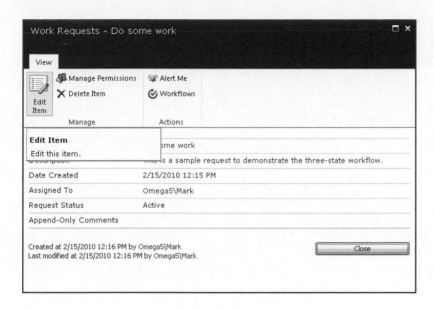

Figure 4-17. Editing the request using the view form

With either approach, you'll display the edit form for the selected item. Change the `Request Status` field to `Ready`, and enter a comment in the `Append-Only Comment` field (see Figure 4-18).

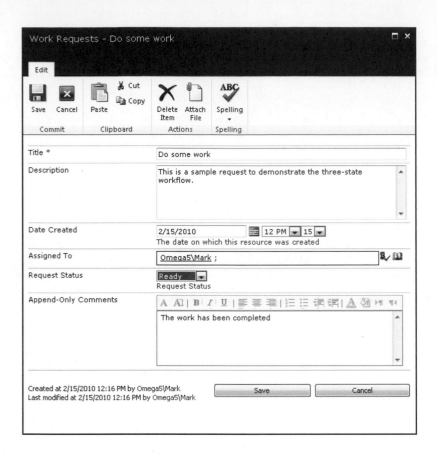

Figure 4-18. Using the edit form to complete the request

Workflow Tasks

When you associated the workflow to the `Work Request` list, a `Tasks` list was automatically created for you. The `Work Request` is sometimes referred to as the *payload*. It is the item being worked on. *Tasks* are the individual work items being performed to the payload. A complex workflow can have many steps that are performed by different people. Work is performed at the task level. A task is associated with a payload (in this case a `Work Request`).

Now select the `Tasks` list. There should be two items similar to the ones shown in Figure 4-19.

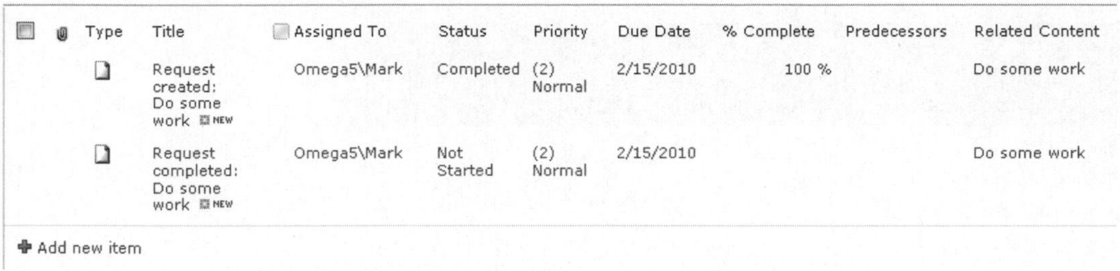

		Type	Title	Assigned To	Status	Priority	Due Date	% Complete	Predecessors	Related Content
☐	📎	📄	Request created: Do some work ☑NEW	Omega5\Mark	Completed	(2) Normal	2/15/2010	100 %		Do some work
		📄	Request completed: Do some work ☑NEW	Omega5\Mark	Not Started	(2) Normal	2/15/2010			Do some work

✚ Add new item

Figure 4-19. The Tasks list with both tasks listed

The first task is assigned to the person to whom the work request was assigned. This task was for them to do the actual work being requested. Notice that the status is set to `Completed`. When you edited the `Work Request` and changed its `Request Status` field to `Ready`, this first task was automatically marked complete.

The second task is assigned to the initiator. Their task is to review the work and provide any appropriate feedback. I realize that in this example these two are the same person, so this assignment logic may not be that obvious. Click the `Title` field of the second task. The display form for the task list will be displayed. Figure 4-20 shows a sample of this form.

Figure 4-20. Viewing a task item

The `Description` field includes the text `Please provide feedback for:` that you entered in the workflow definition. This will help clarify the purpose of this task. Also notice the statement at the top of the form. If you specified an e-mail address for this user, you should have received an e-mail for each of these tasks.

Summary

You created a `Work Request` list and associated a simple Three-state workflow to it. This didn't require any code and was fairly easy to set up. Even with this simple solution, however, you have started taking advantage of a workflow-enabled SharePoint solution. These are the two key features that you implemented:

- Tasks: A separate task was generated for each step in the workflow process.

- E-mail : The tasks are e-mailed to the appropriate person as they are generated.

■ ■ ■

CHAPTER 5

Office Applications as Workflow Participants

In this chapter, you'll see how you can use Office 2010 applications such as Word and Outlook in a workflow process. In Chapter 4, you associated a workflow on a list; in this chapter, you'll use the other primary SharePoint object—a document library. This site will have a document library that will contain design documents, and you will implement a workflow to automate the review process when a document is added or modified.

Creating a SharePoint Site

Create a new SharePoint site using the Blank Site template, as shown in Figure 5-1. Enter the site name as **Chapter05**.

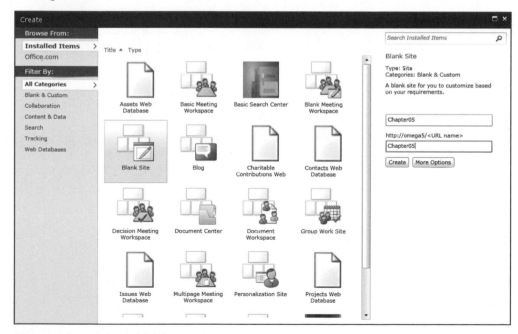

Figure 5-1. Creating a blank site

Once the site has been created, click the *Libraries* link. The page will look like the one shown in Figure 5-2 because there are no existing document libraries for this site.

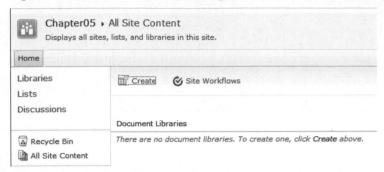

***Figure 5-2.** An empty document collection*

Creating a Document Library

Click the *Create* link to create a new document library. In the Create dialog box, filter by `Library`, and select the Document Library template, as shown in Figure 5-3. Enter the library name as **Design Docs**.

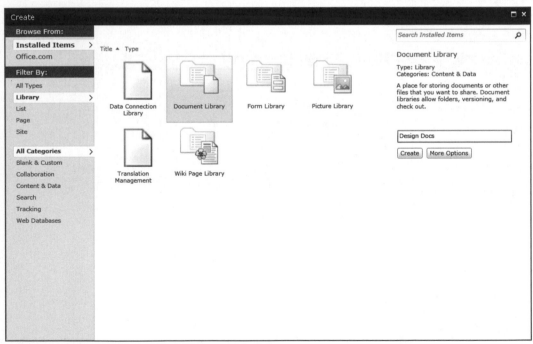

***Figure 5-3.** Creating a document library*

Associating a Workflow

From the Library Tools ribbon, click the Library Settings button, as shown in Figure 5-4.

Form Web Parts
Edit Library
New Quick Step
Customize Library
Library Settings
Settings
Library Settings
Go to the Library Settings page to manage settings such as permissions, columns, views and policy.

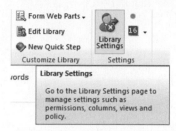

Figure 5-4. *The Library Settings button*

This will display the settings page for the document library. Figure 5-5 shows the top portion of this page.

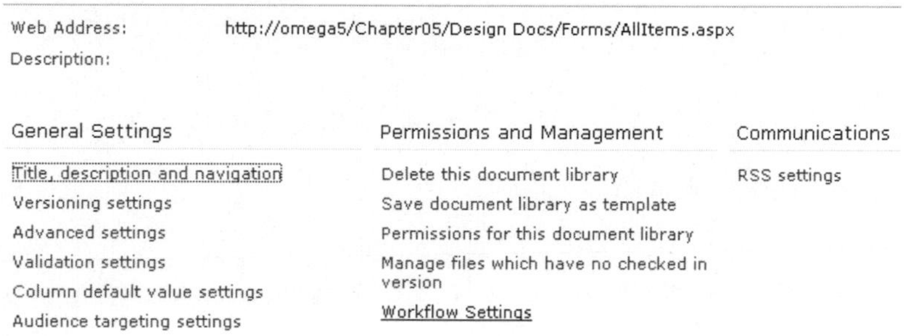

Web Address:
http://omega5/Chapter05/Design Docs/Forms/AllItems.aspx
Description:
General Settings
Title, description and navigation
Versioning settings
Advanced settings
Validation settings
Column default value settings
Audience targeting settings
Permissions and Management
Delete this document library
Save document library as template
Permissions for this document library
Manage files which have no checked in version
Workflow Settings
Communications
RSS settings

Figure 5-5. *The General Settings section for the Design Docs document library*

Click the *Workflow Settings* link, which will display the page shown in Figure 5-6.

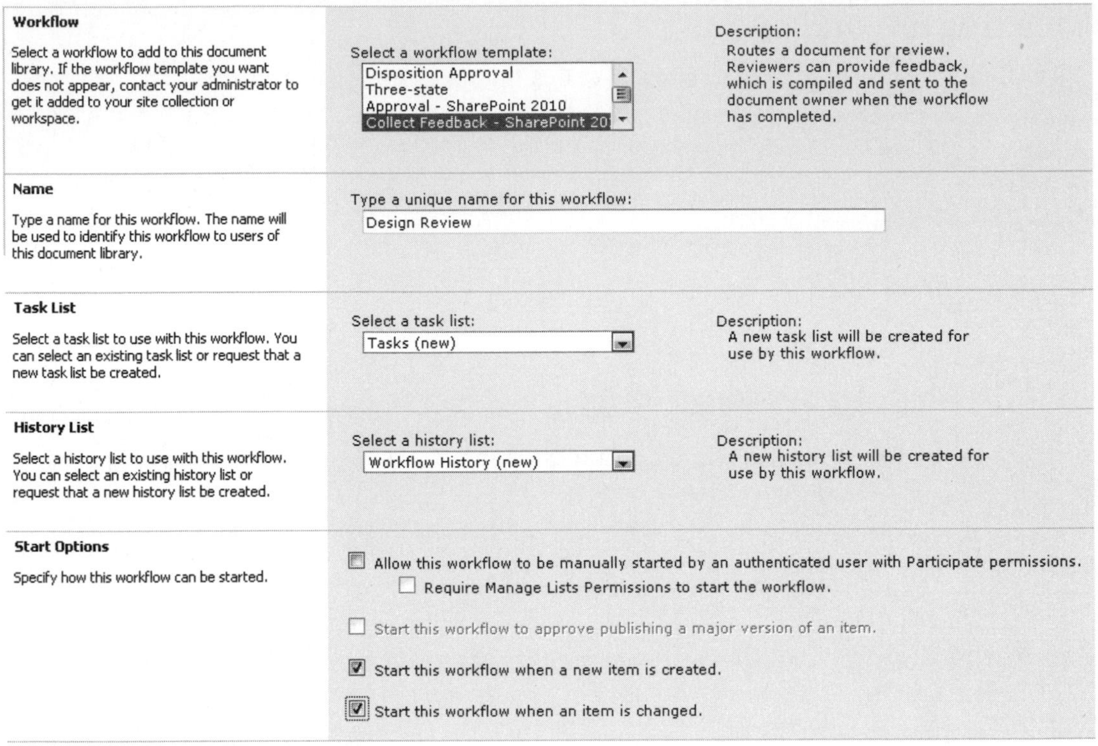

Workflow

Select a workflow to add to this document library. If the workflow template you want does not appear, contact your administrator to get it added to your site collection or workspace.

Select a workflow template:

Disposition Approval
Three-state
Approval - SharePoint 2010
Collect Feedback - SharePoint 201

Description:
Routes a document for review. Reviewers can provide feedback, which is compiled and sent to the document owner when the workflow has completed.

Name

Type a name for this workflow. The name will be used to identify this workflow to users of this document library.

Type a unique name for this workflow:

Design Review

Task List

Select a task list to use with this workflow. You can select an existing task list or request that a new task list be created.

Select a task list:

Tasks (new)

Description:
A new task list will be created for use by this workflow.

History List

Select a history list to use with this workflow. You can select an existing history list or request that a new history list be created.

Select a history list:

Workflow History (new)

Description:
A new history list will be created for use by this workflow.

Start Options

Specify how this workflow can be started.

☑ Allow this workflow to be manually started by an authenticated user with Participate permissions.
　☐ Require Manage Lists Permissions to start the workflow.

☐ Start this workflow to approve publishing a major version of an item.

☑ Start this workflow when a new item is created.

☑ Start this workflow when an item is changed.

Figure 5-6. Add a Workflow page

Select the Collect Feedback workflow, and enter the name as **Design Review**. Leave the task and history lists with their default options. Modify the start options so the workflow is started when an item is created or modified (see Figure 5-6). Click the Next button, which will display the page shown in Figure 5-7.

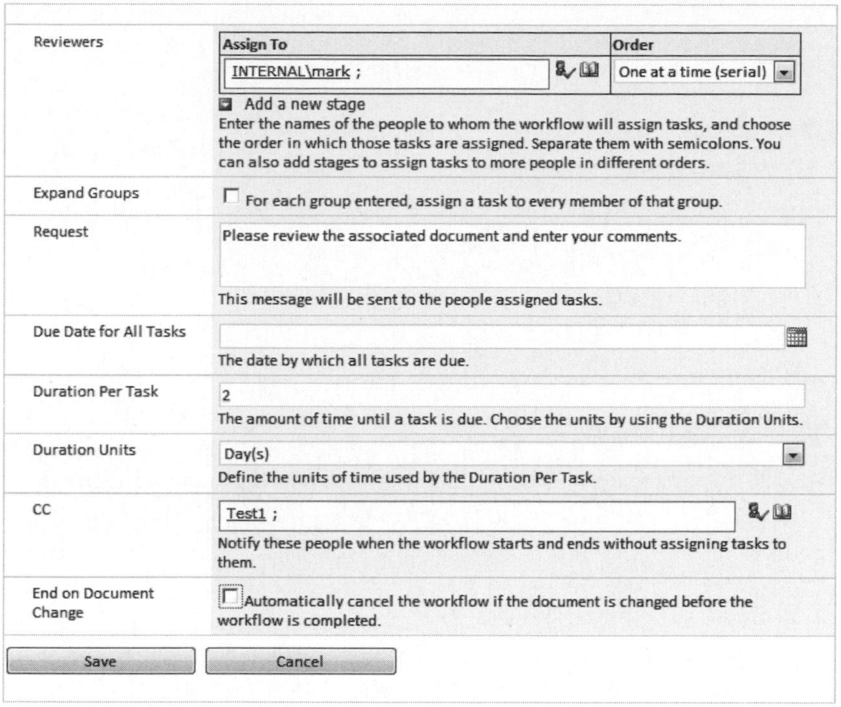

Figure 5-7. Entering the workflow parameters

This workflow will create a task for each person that you have set up as a reviewer. In the Reviewers section, select a person or group that you want to review a document in this library. If you select a group, the Expand Groups check box determines how the task should be assigned to the group. If Expand Groups is not selected, the task is assigned to the group, and anyone in the group can complete the task. If selected, a task is created for each person in the group. This means that every person in the group must review the document. If multiple tasks are created, the Order drop-down specifies whether they are assigned serially (one at a time) or in parallel (the reviews may be performed concurrently).

You can specify a due date for these tasks, either as a specific date or based on a duration from the time the task is assigned. I set this up for a duration of two days, which means that each reviewer will have two days to complete the task from the time it is assigned to them. Keep in mind that if you are using the serial option, the overall duration for the review process is compounded.

In the Reviewers section, you can also create additional stages. This allows you to fine-tune the review process. For example, you can have one person or group perform an initial review followed by a subsequent group once the first stage has completed.

Finally, click the Save button. The page should display the new Design Review workflow, as shown in Figure 5-8.

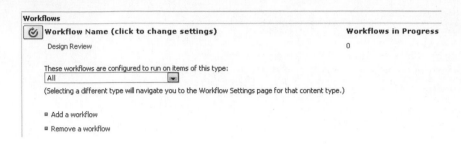

Figure 5-8. The workflow settings page

Using the Document Workflow

To test this workflow, open Word 2010, and create a new document; the content is immaterial. Save the document, and close Word.

Submitting a New Design Document

To start the workflow process, you'll need to add this document to the document library. Click the *Design Docs* link in the SharePoint navigation. You should see an empty document library, as shown in Figure 5-9.

Figure 5-9. Displaying an empty document library

Click the *Add new document* link, and the dialog box shown in Figure 5-10 will be displayed.

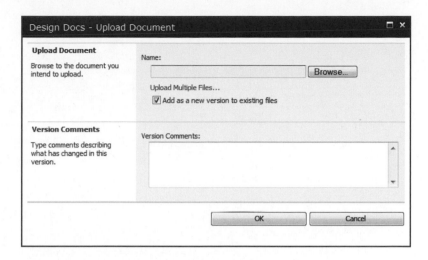

Figure 5-10. Uploaded the test document

Click the Browse button, navigate to the document you just created, and click OK. The dialog box shown in Figure 5-11 will then appear where you can fill in the details for this document.

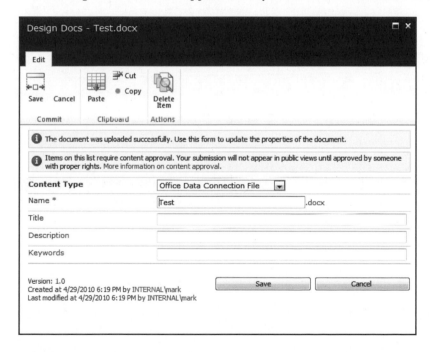

Figure 5-11. Document information form

After clicking the Save button, the document library should now look like the one shown in Figure 5-12.

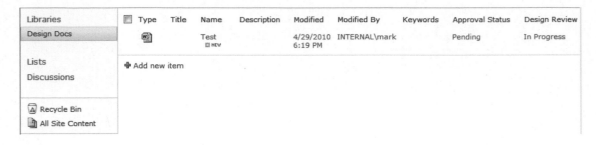

Figure 5-12. The document library with a new document loaded

Enabling Office

From the Library Tools ribbon, click the Connect to Office button, as shown in Figure 5-13.

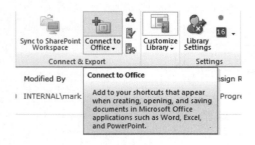

Figure 5-13. Connect to Office button

You should see a label appear to indicate that the library has been added. This will enable shortcuts to this document library from Office documents.

Receiving Workflow E-mail Notifications

You should have received two e-mails. One is sent to you as the initiator of the workflow because you submitted the new document to the library. The e-mail should look like the one shown in Figure 5-14.

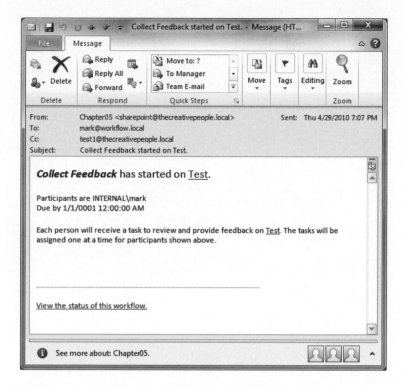

Figure 5-14. The workflow-started notification e-mail

Notice that the test1 user was copied on this e-mail because I added this e-mail address in the CC field. If you click the *View the status of this workflow* link, it will display the SharePoint page shown in Figure 5-15.

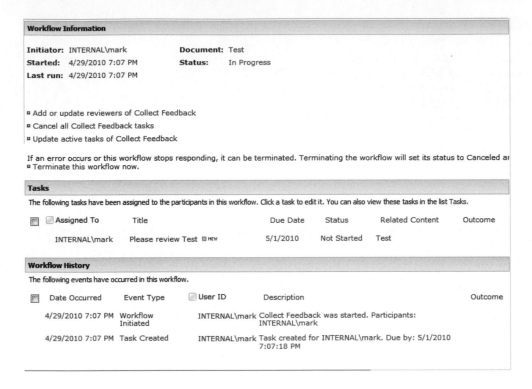

Figure 5-15. The Workflow Information page

This page shows that there is one task created for this document and it has not started yet.

Receiving a Task Notification

The other e-mail was sent to you because a task was assigned to you. It should look like the one shown in Figure 5-16.

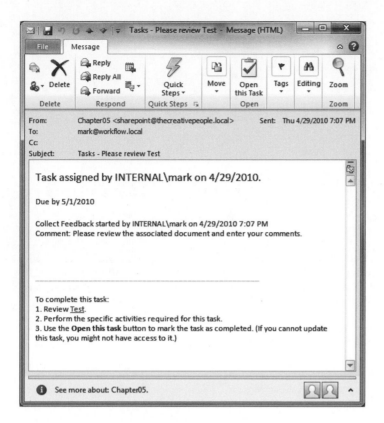

Figure 5-16. The task notification e-mail

This e-mail is sent only to you, the assignee. The due date should be two days in the future. In the task completion steps, step 1 contains a link to the document that needs to be reviewed. Click the *Test* link, and the Word document should open.

Using Office Shortcuts

When the document is opened, there should be two banners displayed at the top of the document, as shown in Figure 5-17

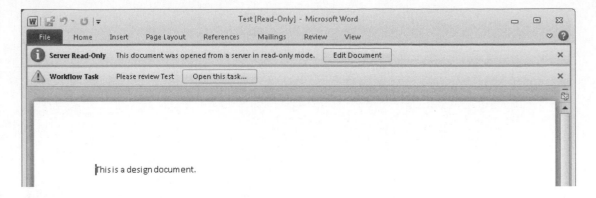

Figure 5-17. Office shortcuts

The first banner is letting you know that the document was opened in read-only mode. The second one is providing information about the workflow task on which you are working. Click the *Open this task* link on the second banner. This will open the task dialog box shown in Figure 5-18 directly on the Word document. Enter a comment, and click the Send Feedback button.

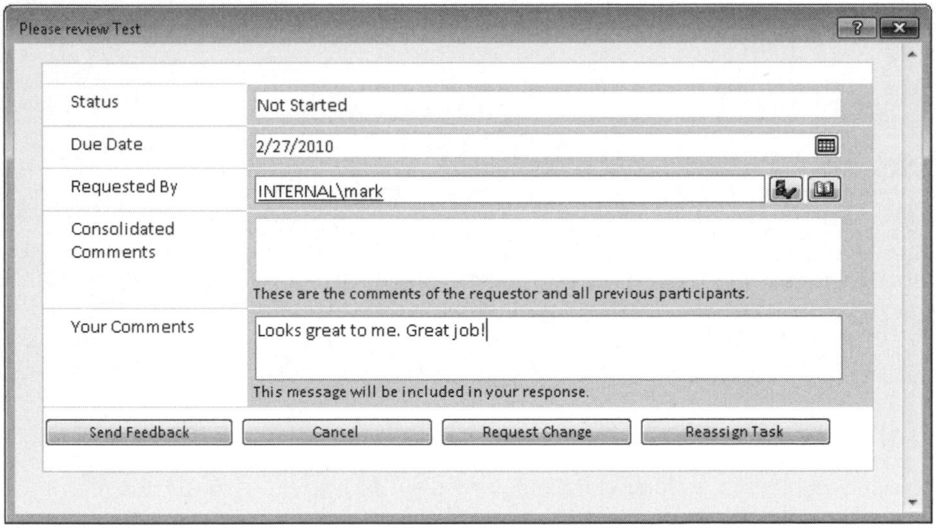

Figure 5-18. Displaying the task dialog box

Once you have sent the feedback, the banner should disappear because the task is now complete. You can close the Word document. If you refresh the Workflow Status page, it should look like Figure 5-19.

Figure 5-19. Updated workflow status page

The workflow is complete because the only task is completed. In the Workflow History section, you can see that the workflow was initiated, a task was created, the task was completed, and the workflow was completed. If you had set up other reviewers, there would be additional tasks, one for each reviewer. If you display the `Design Docs` library, you'll see that it indicates that the Design Review workflow for this document has been completed, as shown in Figure 5-20.

Type	Title	Name	Description	Modified	Modified By	Keywords	Approval Status	Design Review
📄		Test ⊠ NEW		4/29/2010 7:07 PM	INTERNAL\mark		Pending	Completed

✚ Add new item

Figure 5-20. The document library showing the workflow completed

Integrating the Task List

In this example so far, you responded to the e-mail notification to work on an assigned task. There is an even better way. Click the *Lists* link in the SharePoint navigation panel. You should see that a `Tasks` list has been set up for you when you created the workflow, as shown in Figure 5-21.

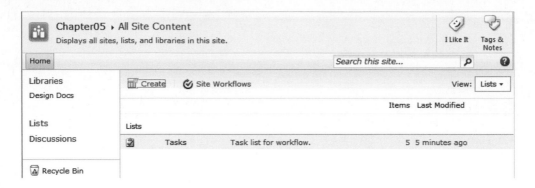

Figure 5-21. The existing lists

Click the *Tasks* link to display the **Tasks** list. You should see a single task that was completed when you reviewed the document (see Figure 5-22).

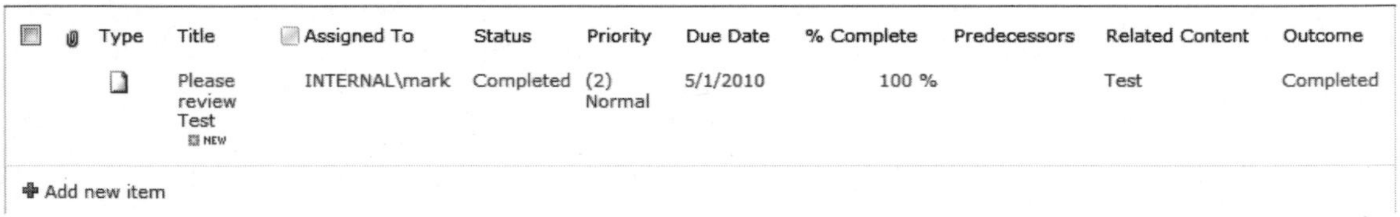

	🔗	Type	Title	Assigned To	Status	Priority	Due Date	% Complete	Predecessors	Related Content	Outcome
			Please review Test ☑ NEW	INTERNAL\mark	Completed	(2) Normal	5/1/2010	100 %		Test	Completed

✚ Add new item

Figure 5-22. Displaying the **Tasks** *list*

From the List Tools ribbon, click the Connect to Outlook button, as shown in Figure 5-23. This will create a task list in Outlook and automatically synchronize it with the SharePoint task list.

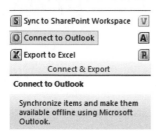

Figure 5-23. The Connect to Outlook button

■ **Note** When you click the Connect to Outlook button, you may receive one or more pop-up windows warning you about the access that is being requested. Click the appropriate button to allow the access.

A task list will be created in Outlook, as shown in Figure 5-24.

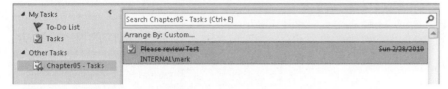

Figure 5-24. *A new tasks list added to Outlook 2010*

Notice that the only task has been crossed out. This is because the task has already been completed.

Executing the Workflow Again

Go back to the SharePoint site, and select the `Design Docs` list. Then check in a new document just like you did before. This should automatically start another workflow for the new document.

Displaying the Task in Outlook

Now go back to Outlook and look at your tasks. You should have a new task assigned to you, similar to the one shown in Figure 5-25.

Figure 5-25. *Listing your tasks in Outlook 2010*

If you double-click the new task, the window (shown in Figure 5-26) looks very similar to the e-mail you used to review the initial document.

Figure 5-26. Displaying the task details

Click the *Test.docx* link to open and review the modified document. Just like before, there should be a banner with a link to open the task. So, right from the Word document you can enter your comments and complete the task.

More About Tasks

When you link the Tasks list in SharePoint to your Outlook client, Outlook creates an offline copy of the task list. This is synchronized when you perform a Send and Receive. You can view and update your tasks while offline, and the SharePoint server will be updated automatically when you reconnect to the network.

Working with Multiple Task List

The SharePoint task list is added to Outlook as a separate task list. If you have multiple SharePoint sites that you use, you will need to connect each one of these individually. This will create separate lists in

Outlook that are all separate from the standard Outlook task list. For example, if you add a task to the standard list and select the standard list, those tasks are listed, but the tasks from all the other lists aren't, as demonstrated in Figure 5-27.

Figure 5-27. Displaying the standard Outlook task list

In some ways, this is a good thing. It allows you to keep the tasks organized by their source. But if you're like me (and I suspect like most people), you have tasks coming from multiple places, and you would like to combine them into one list. The solution is to use the To-Do bar. The To-Do bar (shown in Figure 5-28) shows you a combined view of all your tasks and gives you several options for categorizing and sorting them.

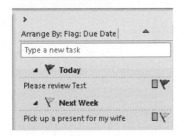

Figure 5-28. The To-Do bar

The SharePoint tasks are not automatically added to the To-Do bar, however. To add a SharePoint task to the To-Do bar, add a follow-up flag to it. You can do that by right-clicking the task and choosing Follow Up and then one of the available options, as shown in Figure 5-29.

Figure 5-29. *Adding a follow-up flag*

Deleting Tasks

In Outlook, you have the ability to delete a task. Simply select it and click the Delete button. When you do that, the task is also deleted from SharePoint when the synchronization occurs during a Send and Receive operation. You can try this by deleting the new task in Outlook, running Send and Receive, and then displaying the task list in SharePoint. You should see that the task is no longer there.

■ **Caution** Even though Outlook creates an offline copy of the task list, all changes you make locally are synchronized to the server. You should treat this as if you are actually modifying the tasks on the server. For example, if you have a task assigned to you that is due in five days and you add a follow-up flag on it for tomorrow, the SharePoint task will have tomorrow as the due date.

When a task is deleted, the workflow engine treats this as if the task was completed. The next task in the workflow will be created and assigned. Or, if this is the last task, the workflow will be completed. Because this was the only task, the workflow for this document should now show complete. The workflow history, however, will show that you deleted the task, as shown in Figure 5-30.

Workflow History

The following events have occurred in this workflow.

☐	Date Occurred	Event Type	☐ User ID	Description	Outcome
	4/29/2010 7:28 PM	Workflow Initiated	INTERNAL\mark	Collect Feedback was started. Participants: INTERNAL\mark	
	4/29/2010 7:28 PM	Task Created	INTERNAL\mark	Task created for INTERNAL\mark. Due by: 5/1/2010 7:28:02 PM	
	4/29/2010 7:32 PM	Task Deleted	INTERNAL\mark	Task assigned to INTERNAL\mark was deleted by INTERNAL\mark.	
	4/29/2010 7:32 PM	Task Completed	INTERNAL\mark	Task assigned to INTERNAL\mark was automatically completed because it was deleted by INTERNAL\mark.	Reviewed by INTERNAL\mark
	4/29/2010 7:32 PM	Task Completed	INTERNAL\mark	Task assigned to INTERNAL\mark was completed by INTERNAL\mark. Comments:	Reviewed by INTERNAL\mark
	4/29/2010 7:32 PM	Workflow Completed	INTERNAL\mark	Collect Feedback was completed.	Collect Feedback on Test2 has successfully completed. All participants have completed their tasks.

Figure 5-30. The workflow history with a deleted task

Summary

You created a document library and associated a review workflow process with it. This automatically assigned tasks to the desired people to review a document whenever it was added or modified. This is a fairly easy way to implement a no-code workflow process. The following are the two key features that you used in this chapter:

- Performing workflow tasks directly from an Office application such as Word

- Linking the SharePoint tasks to Outlook and using a follow-up flag to provide a combined view of all your task lists

▪▪▪

CHAPTER 6

Creating Workflows with SharePoint Designer

In the previous chapters, you built some fairly useful workflows using built-in templates. Often, however, you may need some processing that will require you to build a custom workflow. In this chapter, you'll create a custom workflow using Visio and the SharePoint Designer. This workflow will allow team members to submit a request for time off. This will generate a task for an individual to approve or request that request. Approved requests are then automatically added to the team's calendar.

Creating the Site

Start by creating a site named **Chapter06** using the Team Site template, as shown in Figure 6-1.

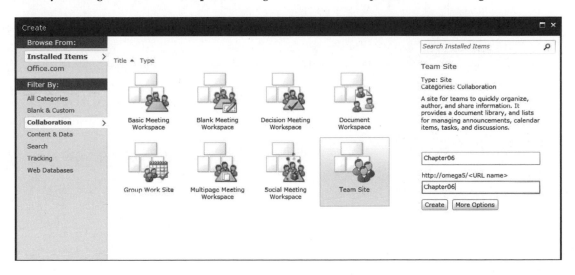

Figure 6-1. Create a Chapter06 site using the Team Site template.

The Team Site template will create a **Tasks** list and a **Calendar** that will be used by your workflow.

Creating a Custom List

Next, create a list named **TimeOff** using the Custom List template, as shown in Figure 6-2.

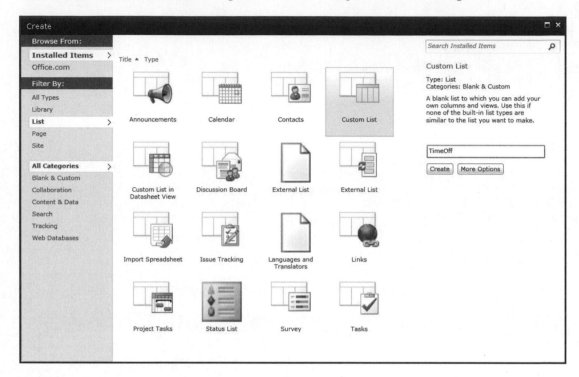

Figure 6-2. Creating a `TimeOff` list using the Custom List template

Defining the List Columns

Select the `TimeOff` list, and display the List Tools ribbon. Then click the Edit List button, which will launch the SharePoint Designer. Click the *Edit list columns* link, and define the columns like you did in Chapter 4. You'll need to create new columns for `Requested By`, `Request Status`, and `Approved By`. Add the columns shown in Figure 6-3.

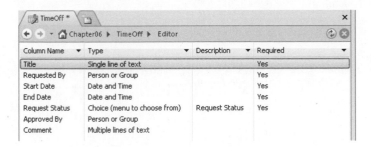

Figure 6-3. Adding the columns to the TimeOff list

The **Requested By** and **Approved By** columns use the **Person or Group** column type. These should be configured as **People Only** in the column editor, as shown in the Figure 6-4.

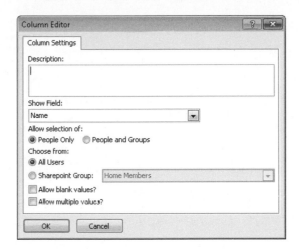

Figure 6-4. Configuring the Requested By column using the Column Editor

The **Request Status** column is defined as a **Choice** type. Enter the possible values using the options listed in Figure 6-5.

Figure 6-5. Entering the choice values for Request Status

Using Visio to Define a Workflow

Visio 2010 includes some enhancements that enable you to use it to visualize a SharePoint workflow. You will use Visio to design the steps of the workflow process and then import this design into the SharePoint Designer.

Designing a Workflow in Visio

Start Microsoft Visio 2010. From the File menu, choose New, and select the Microsoft SharePoint Workflow template. Then click the Create button. This template has custom shapes that are recognized by the SharePoint Designer. The shapes that you use are very important because they will determine the processing logic.

■ **Tip** If you don't have a template named Microsoft SharePoint Workflow, you can use the Basic template. Then add the SharePoint Workflow Actions and SharePoint Workflow Conditions stencils from the Flowchart group.

Each workflow starts with a `Start` shape and ends at a `Terminate` shape. You will find these shapes on the Quick Shapes collection. Drag a `Start` shape onto the diagram followed by an `Assign item for approval` shape. This shape represents the approval process for the request that has been submitted. Next, drag a `Compare data source` shape onto the diagram, and change the label to **Approved?**. This condition will evaluate whether the request was approved.

Now you'll need a shape that represents the action of adding the approved request to the calendar. From the SharePoint Workflow Actions collection, drag a `Create list item` shape to the diagram. Change its label to **Add to calendar**. Finally, drag a `Terminate` shape to the diagram. The **No** branch of the condition will go directly to the `Terminate` shape, and the `Yes` branch will go to the `Create list item` shape. Basically, denied requests will skip this step.

The completed diagram should look like Figure 6-6.

Figure 6-6. *A SharePoint Workflow diagram in Visio 2010*

Exporting a Visio Workflow

Now that you have designed the workflow, you'll need to export it to a file format that is usable to the SharePoint Designer. Go to the Process menu. Click the Check Diagram button. This will verify that the diagram is syntactically correct. Fix any issues that this reports.

Then click the Export button as shown in Figure 6-7, and select a location for the export file. Enter the file name as **Workflow**.

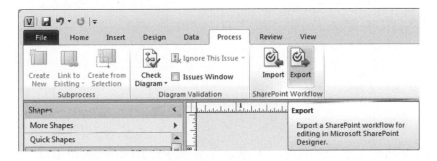

Figure 6-7. *Exporting a Visio workflow*

The Visio diagram is exported as a Visio Workflow Interchange file using a `*.vwi` extension. This is actually a `.cab` or `.zip` file. If you make a copy of the `Workflow.vwi` file and change the extension to `.zip`, you can inspect the contents using Windows Explorer. Figure 6-8 shows the contents.

Figure 6-8. Contents of the `Workflow.vwi` *file*

Importing a Visio Workflow

From the SharePoint Designer, click the Workflows link in the Site Objects list, as shown in Figure 6-9.

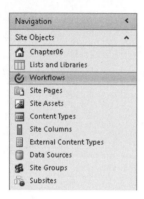

Figure 6-9. Selecting Workflows in SharePoint Designer

Click the Import from Visio button in the Workflows ribbon, and navigate to the `Workflow.vwi` file that you exported from Visio. The dialog box shown in Figure 6-10 should appear.

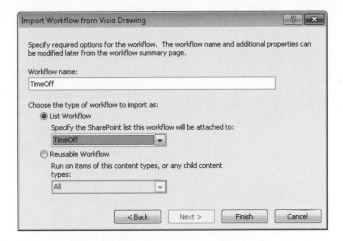

Figure 6-10. Associating the imported workflow

Enter the workflow name as **TimeOff**. The workflow that you create can be set up as a reusable workflow, which can be associated to multiple lists. For this project, however, make it a list-specific workflow, and associate it to the `TimeOff` list, as shown in Figure 6-10.

Entering the Workflow Definition

After you have imported this file, the workflow should look like the one shown in Figure 6-11.

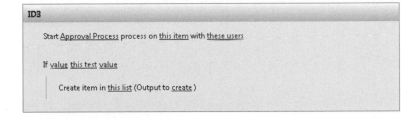

Figure 6-11. The initial workflow imported from Visio

The Visio diagram outlines the steps to be performed but without any details. The imported workflow has placeholders for the required information, which you'll now specify. In the workflow definition each line is either an *action* or a *condition*. The first action is specified as follows:

`Start `<u>`ApprovalProcess`</u>` process on `<u>`this item`</u>` with `<u>`these users`</u>

`ApprovalProcess` is a reusable mini workflow that implements a generic approval step. You'll use it, in this case, to approve the time-off request. This action will create an approval task, associate it to some list item, and assign it to one or more users.

■ **Note** The `Assign item for approval` shape in the Visio template is associated with this mini workflow. By adding that shape to your workflow design, this workflow is automatically included in your imported workflow.

Click the *this item* link, which will display the dialog box shown in Figure 6-12.

Figure 6-12. Selecting the item to associate the approval task with

The new task will be associated to the current item in the `TimeOff` list. This is the default response, so just click OK. Then click the *these users* link to specify to whom this task should be assigned. The dialog box shown in Figure 6-13 will be displayed.

Figure 6-13. Configuring the new task

For the `Title`, enter **Approve or Reject this TimeOff Request**. You can also define the allowed duration or a due date at the bottom of this dialog box, but you can leave this blank for this project. Click the icon next to the `Participants` field. The dialog box shown in Figure 6-14 will be displayed.

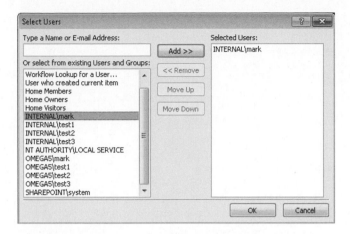

Figure 6-14. Selecting the user to assign the task to

Select the user to whom the approval task should be assigned. You can select a group such as Home Owners or an individual. You can assign this to your user account so you'll be able to access it.

Specifying a Condition

The next line in the workflow definition is a *condition* and is specified as follows:

If value this test value

You'll need to specify the two values that are being compared and this_test, which defines what type of comparison is to be used. Click the first *value* link, and you'll see that a text box is provided to enter the value, as shown in Figure 6-15.

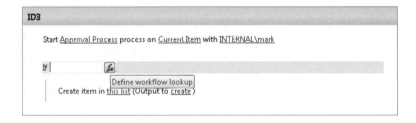

Figure 6-15. Specifying a value field

Notice there is a button with the *fx* text. This is used a lot when designing workflows in the SharePoint Designer. If you click this button, a dialog box will appear to help you build the expression for the associated field. Click this button, and the dialog box shown in Figure 6-16 will appear.

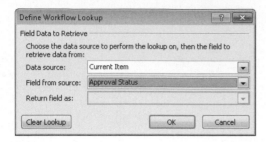

Figure 6-16. Entering an expression for the first value field

The purpose of this condition is to determine whether the request was approved. This will be indicated in the Approval Status field. Select the Current item as the data source, and select Approval Status for the field.

Click the *this test* link, and a drop-down will appear listing all the possible operations, as shown in Figure 6-17. Select the equals operation.

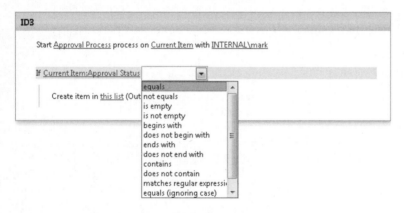

Figure 6-17. Selecting the operation for this condition

Select the second *value* link, and a drop-down will appear with the possible values that can be used, as shown in Figure 6-18.

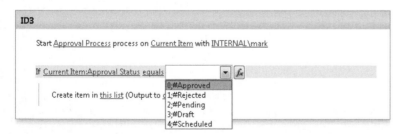

Figure 6-18. Selecting the Approved status

Because the column chosen in the first value field is defined as a `Choice` field, the possible values are listed in the drop-down. Choose 0;#Approved.

Creating a Calendar entry

The action that is executed (if the condition is true) is as follows:

`Create item in this list (Output to create)`

Click the *this list* link, and the dialog box shown in Figure 6-19 will be displayed.

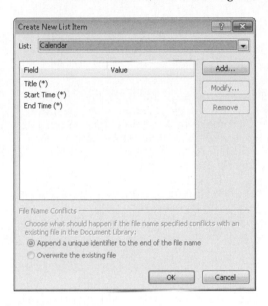

Figure 6-19. The initial Create New List Item dialog box

Select `Calendar` from the collection of lists provided in the drop-down. The `Calendar` list has three required fields (`Title`, `Start Time`, and `End Time`). Because they are required, in order to create an item in this list, you must specify values for these fields, and they are automatically listed in the dialog box for you. Select the `Title` field, and click the Modify button. The dialog box shown in Figure 6-20 will be displayed.

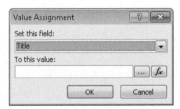

Figure 6-20. Specifying the value assignment

If the `Title` field is not already selected, select it. To enter the value for this field, click the fx button, and the dialog box shown in Figure 6-21 will be displayed.

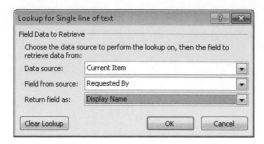

Figure 6-21. Specifying the value using an existing list column

The `Title` field (of the `Calendar` item being created) will contain the label that is displayed on the calendar. It should display the name of the person who has requested time off. The `Data source` specifies which list the value can be obtained from. In this case, it will be come from the current item, which is an item in the `TimeOff` list. Select `Current Item` if it's not already selected. Then choose the `Requested By` field. The third field allows you to define the format that this value should be returned as. Since this is a `Person or Group` field, several options are available such as User ID, Login, or Email. In this case, you'll want to use the `Display Name` option.

Specify the `Start Time` and `End Time` fields using the `Start Date` and `End Date` fields, respectively, from the `Current Item`. The completed dialog box should look like the one shown in Figure 6-22.

Figure 6-22. The Create New List Item dialog box with required fields

Now you'll add one nonrequired field. The `Description` field is shown when a `Calendar` item is viewed. You'll copy the `Title` field from the `TimeOff` request to the `Description` field so team members can see the reason for the time off when viewing the `Calendar` details.

Click the Add button, and the Value Assignment dialog box is displayed. Select the `Description` field, and then enter the value as **Current Item:Title**, as shown in Figure 6-23. Alternatively, you could click the *ƒx* button and specify the `Title` field the same way you did the other fields.

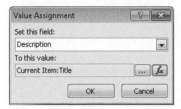

Figure 6-23. *Specifying the Description field*

Figure 6-24 shows the completed dialog box. Click OK to close it.

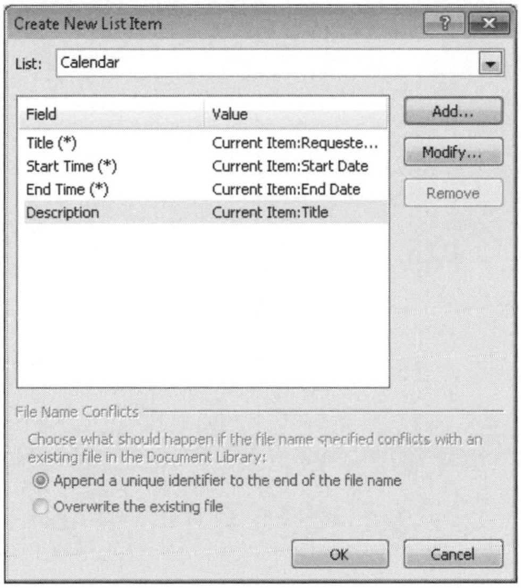

Figure 6-24. *The final Create New List Item dialog box*

The last piece of information that you'll need to specify is the variable that will store the ID of the new `Calendar` item. When the new item is created, its ID is stored in the variable you define so it can be used by the workflow. In this workflow, you don't need it, but you'll still need to specify a variable. Click the *create* link, and a drop-down is displayed, as shown in Figure 6-25.

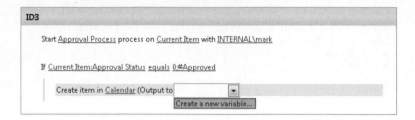

Figure 6-25. Showing the create new variable drop-down

Click the *Create a new variable* link in the drop-down list, and the dialog box shown in Figure 6-26 is displayed.

Figure 6-26. Specifying the output variable

Enter a name for the new variable, and click OK. The completed workflow specification should look like Figure 6-27.

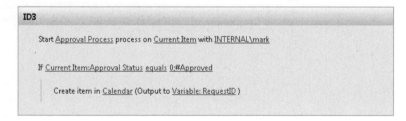

Figure 6-27. The completed workflow specification

Adding Workflow Details

You should add a few more details to the workflow to update the fields in the TimeOff list. You can create additional actions directly in the SharePoint Designer without going back to Visio. If you move the mouse around the workflow definition, you'll notice that an orange bar appears in various places. This gives you the opportunity to add an action or condition to the workflow.

Click the bar just below the **Create Item** action. A text box will appear for you to search for the desired action. Click the Action button in the Workflow ribbon, which will list all the available actions. Select the **Set Field in Current Item** action, as shown in Figure 6-28.

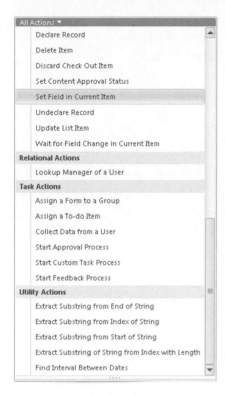

Figure 6-28. Selecting the Set Field in Current Item action

For the *field* link, select the **Request Status** field, and for the *value* link, select the **Approved** status. Add another **Set Field in Current Item** action, and for the *field* link, select **Approved By**. For the *value* link, select the same user that the approval task was assigned to.

You can also create an **Else** branch to the condition by clicking the orange bar where the **Else** would go and entering **Else** in the search box. In the **Else** branch, add a **Set Field in Current Item** action to set the **Request Status** to **Denied**. Figure 6-29 shows the final workflow definition.

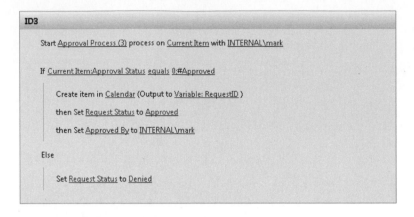

Figure 6-29. The completed workflow definition

Configuring the Workflow

In the SharePoint Designer, navigate to the workflow summary page shown in Figure 6-30.

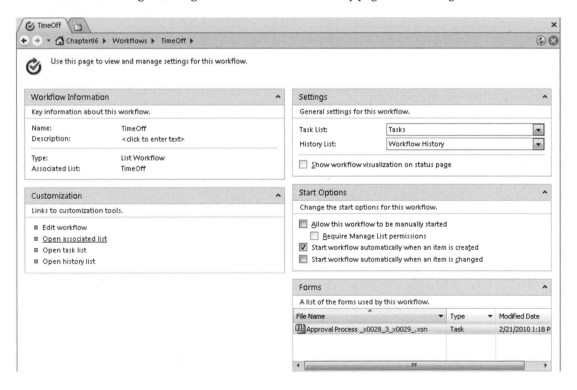

Figure 6-30. The TimeOff workflow summary

This page shows how this workflow is configured. For example, it is a List workflow and is associated with the `TimeOff` list. It uses the `Tasks` list when creating new tasks (approving the request), and history items are added to the `Workflow History` list. Modify the start options as shown in Figure 6-30. You'll want the workflow to start automatically when an item is created.

Click the *Edit workflow* link, which will take you to the Editor page that you just used to define the workflow. Click the *ApprovalProcess* link at the beginning of the workflow definition. This will display the workflow summary of the mini workflow used for the approval task. If you click the *Change the behavior of a single task* link, you'll see the page shown in Figure 6-31. This will give you an idea of how workflow actions are defined. This defines the actions such as recording workflow history and sending e-mail notifications related to the approval tasks.

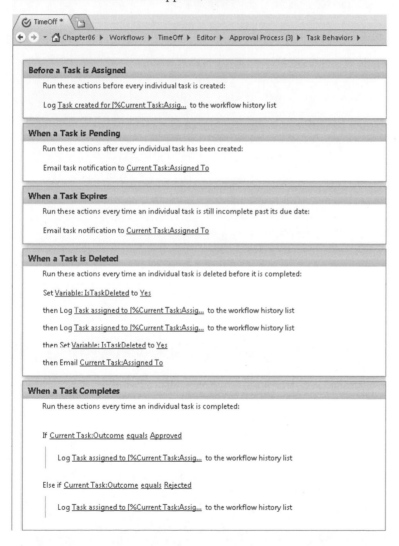

Figure 6-31. Task definitions for the ApprovalProcess workflow

Executing the Workflow

Now that the workflow has been created, let's try it. Close the SharePoint Designer, and go to the main SharePoint page. Navigate to the Chapter06 site, and select the TimeOff list, which should be empty.

Click the *Add new item* link, and enter a time-off request, as shown in Figure 6-32.

Figure 6-32. Entering a new time-off request

The TimeOff list should now have a single item. The Request Status should be Pending, and the TimeOff workflow should show In Progress like the one shown in Figure 6-33.

Figure 6-33. The TimeOff list with a pending item

Now select the Tasks list; it should also have a single item (see Figure 6-34), which is the approval task for the request you just submitted.

Figure 6-34. The Tasks list with a new task

Click the drop-down next to the Title field, and select Edit item. The dialog box shown in Figure 6-35 will be displayed.

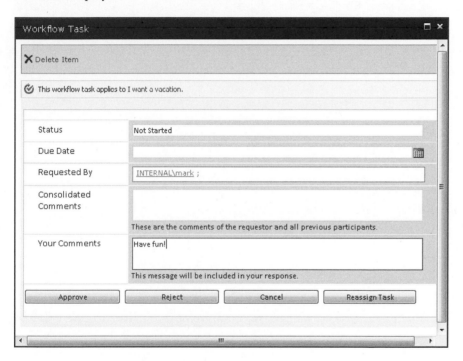

Figure 6-35. The approval task dialog box

Enter a comment, and click the Approve button. Select the TimeOff list, which should now display a completed request, as shown in Figure 6-36.

Figure 6-36. The TimeOff list with a completed request

The item in the `TimeOff` list should have a `Request Status` of `Approved`, and the TimeOff workflow should also show `Approved`. The `Approved By` field is also populated. Now, select the `Calendar` list. You should see the time-off request displayed in the calendar for the days requested. The person who requested the time off should show in the calendar, as shown in Figure 6-37.

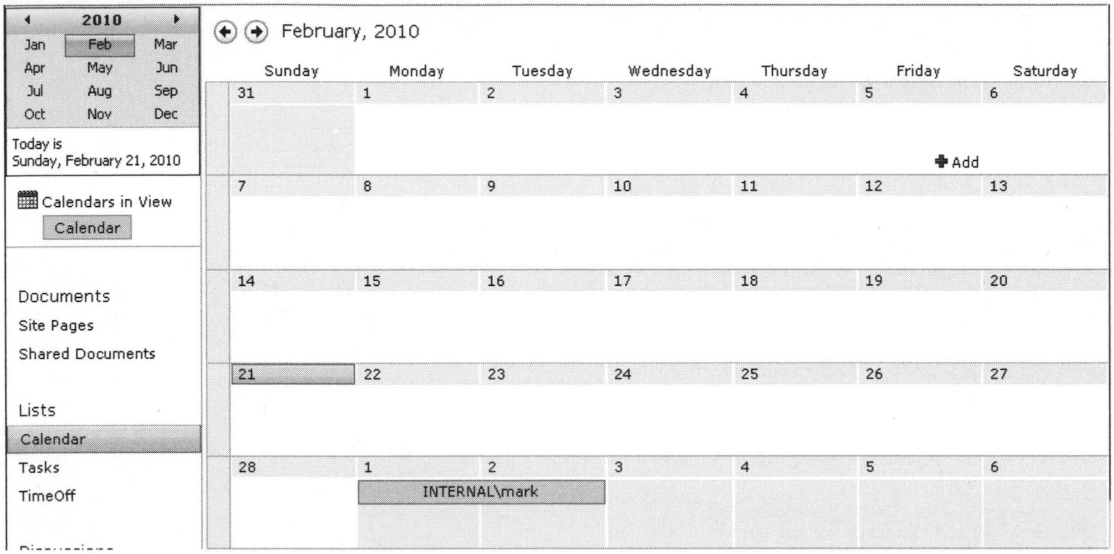

Figure 6-37. The `Calendar` *list showing the approved time-off request*

Double-click the calendar item, and the dialog box shown in Figure 6-38 should be displayed. Notice that the `Description` field shows the `Title` that was entered on the `TimeOff` request.

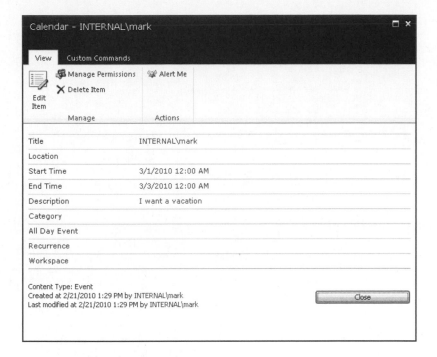

Figure 6-38. The Calendar item details

Exporting to Visio

To demonstrate the two-way Visio integration, you can export the final workflow definition and display it graphically in Visio. Go back to SharePoint Designer, and select the TimeOff workflow. Click the Export to Visio button in the Workflow Settings ribbon. Select a new file name so as to not overwrite the original `.vwi` file.

Start Visio 2010, and create a new document using the Microsoft SharePoint Workflow template. Click the Import button in the Process menu, and select the file you just exported. The workflow that will be displayed should be similar to the one shown in Figure 6-39.

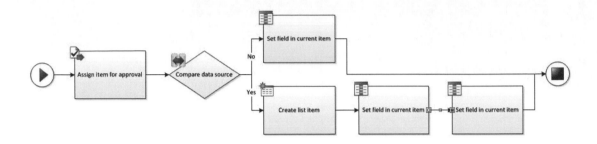

Figure 6-39. The final workflow displayed in Visio

Notice that the additional actions to set the fields are now displayed graphically.

Summary

In this chapter, you created a workflow to automate the processing of a request for time off. You used Visio 2010 to graphically design the workflow process and then used the SharePoint Designer to fill in the processing details. You also modified the workflow process in the SharePoint Designer and exported the design to display it graphically in Visio 2010. The combination of these tools provides a convenient way to design and build SharePoint workflows.

These two tools also are aligned with a typical division of labor. A business analyst can use Visio to design the basic workflow process. Then a developer or IT technician can use SharePoint Designer to fill in the details. The final implementation can then be passed back to the business analyst for review and documentation.

Your workflow employed the use of a built-in workflow for approving a list item. You used the expression builder to extract field values from several SharePoint lists. You also used some of the basic workflow actions such as creating a new list item or updating existing items.

■ ■ ■

CHAPTER 7

Creating Reusable and Site Workflows

To round out this section on using the SharePoint Designer, you'll create two more workflows. First, you will create a *reusable* workflow that can be associated to multiple lists or document libraries. Finally, you'll create a *site* workflow that is not associated with any list but is invoked at the site level.

Reusable Workflows

You have already used reusable workflows that are provided out of the box such as the Three-state workflow. These are referred to as a *globally reusable workflow* since they are available on all sites. You can also create your own reusable workflow that, once published to a site, can be associated to multiple lists and document libraries.

When you create a reusable workflow, the most significant decision that you'll need to make is which *content type* to base the workflow on. Among other things, the content type defines the items that are contained in a list or library. You will be allowed to associate a reusable workflow only with lists that are based on that content.

In light of this, you might be tempted to use the `All` option (as you will in this project). This will allow your workflow to be associated with any list or library. However, your workflow will only have access to the columns of the type you select. If you use the `All` option, you will be limited to the `Title` field (plus the created by and modified by fields). As you plan your workflow, decide what columns it will need and what types it would likely to be used with.

Creating a New Site

As with the previous chapters, start by creating a new site for the projects in this chapter. Use the Team Site template, and enter the site name as **Chapter07**, as shown in Figure 7-1.

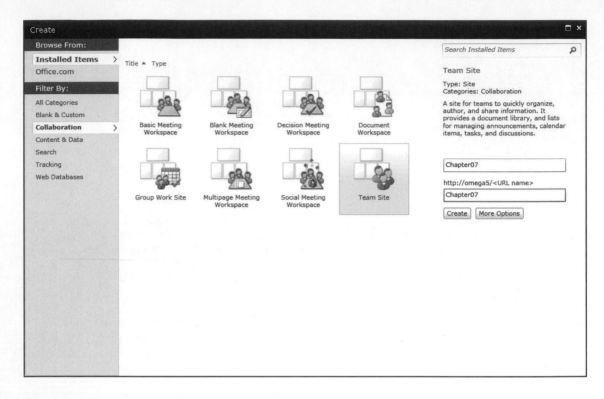

Figure 7-1. *Creating a new site*

For this project, you'll create the workflow using only the SharePoint Designer. To launch the SharePoint Designer, click the *Edit Site in SharePoint Designer* link in the Site Actions menu, as shown in Figure 7-2.

Figure 7-2. Launching the SharePoint Designer

■ **Tip** You can also launch the SharePoint Designer from the Start menu in Windows and then navigate to the desired site.

In the Navigation pane, select Workflows. You should see the three globally reusable workflows that are provided with SharePoint (see Figure 7-3).

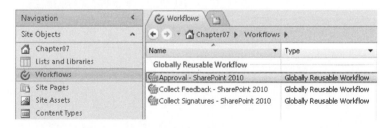

Figure 7-3. The initial workflow list

There are three types of workflows that can be created, as illustrated in the Workflows ribbon, which is shown in Figure 7-4. You created a list workflow in the previous chapter; in this chapter, you will create the other two workflow types: reusable and site.

Figure 7-4. Workflow types available in the ribbon

Creating a Reusable Workflow

Click the Reusable Workflow button. A dialog box will appear where you will specify the name of the workflow and enter a description. You must also choose a content type as I mentioned earlier. Select `All` as the content type, and enter the name as **Review and Approve**, as shown in Figure 7-5.

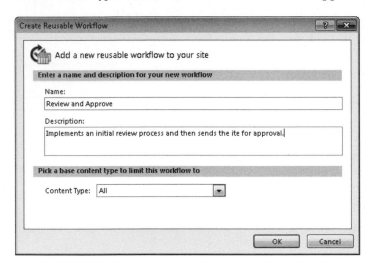

Figure 7-5. Specifying the name and content type

A blank workflow definition is displayed in the designer (see Figure 7-6).

Figure 7-6. A blank workflow

Workflow Editor Overview

In the previous chapter, you imported a workflow from Visio, which created the workflow structure for you, leaving only the details to be filled in. Now you'll use the SharePoint Designer to create the *actions* and *conditions* that define your workflow. Before getting started, I'll give a basic overview of the workflow editor.

Actions

Actions are the things your workflow will do such as create a task, send an e-mail, or update a variable. Figure 7-7 shows a partial list of the actions that are available to you.

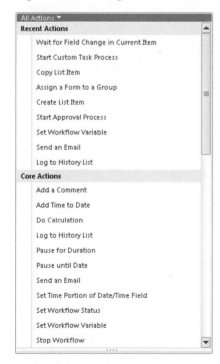

Figure 7-7. Available actions

The actions are grouped into categories to help you find the one you need. The first group, called Recent Actions, contains the actions you have used recently. These same actions are also listed in their normal groups. Listing them here makes it easier for you to find actions that you use frequently.

Conditions

Conditions give you the ability to execute actions based on the outcome of previous actions or input parameters. For example, if an item was approved, you may want to perform different actions than if it was rejected. Figure 7-8 shows the list of conditions that you can use.

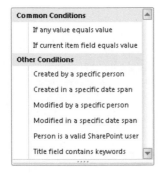

Figure 7-8. Available conditions

When you insert a condition, the designer creates a line in the workflow starting with If and followed by the condition. Subsequent actions are indented to show that they are performed only if the condition is true. You can also add an Else block, which will be executed if the condition is false.

Steps

Steps are simply a way of organizing your workflow into blocks that are easy to visualize. You'll notice that the initial workflow contains Step 1. You can add all of your actions and conditions into this step. However, for longer workflows, creating additional steps will make your workflow easier to read. Steps can also be nested so a single step can contain other, substeps.

Figure 7-9 shows the buttons available on the ribbon for inserting elements.

Figure 7-9. Insert section in the Workflows ribbon

I've explained the Condition, Action, and Step buttons, but there are a few smaller buttons that provide some interesting features. The Else-If Branch button will create an Else block for an existing condition, as I explained earlier. Clicking this button while on a condition will create the corresponding `Else` block.

The Parallel Block button allows you to create a group of actions that are performed simultaneously. The default logic is to perform actions sequentially (one at a time). As you start entering actions, you'll notice that the wording on the workflow will indicate how the actions are executed. For example, the second action will be prefixed with the word **then**, implying that the second action is started after the first action is completed. However, in parallel blocks, the word **and** is used, indicating they are being started at the same time.

The Impersonation Step button creates a new step just like the Step button with one important difference. The actions performed in this step are run as the user who designed the workflow (you) instead of the person who started the workflow (the end user). You will usually have more permission granted to you than most users, so this allows you to perform some actions that the end user might not otherwise have access to. Figure 7-10 shows the help text associated with this button.

Figure 7-10. The Impersonation Step button

Insertion Point

I'm sure you've noticed the flashing orange bar, which indicates the insertion point. This indicates where actions, conditions, or steps will be inserted when you click one of the buttons in the ribbon. The flashing orange bar indicates the current insertion point. You can move the insertion point by hovering the mouse pointer to where you want to insert an action, condition, or step. If this is a suitable location, a solid faint orange bar will appear where the mouse pointer is. This is demonstrated in Figure 7-11.

Figure 7-11. Moving the insertion point

The flashing orange bar (insertion point) is inside step 1. If you hover the mouse just below step 1, a faint orange bar will appear. If you click it, it will start flashing, indicating that this is now the current insertion point. You can generally move the insertion point to any of the following:

- Between existing actions (to insert a new action or condition)

- After the actions for a condition (to create an Else branch)

- After the last action in a step (to add an action or condition)

- Between existing steps (to insert a new step)

- After the last step (to add a new step)

When you click the insertion point, it will open a search box where you can search for the desired action or condition. For example, click the insertion point, and enter **email**. The designer should look like the one shown in Figure 7-12.

Figure 7-12. Searching for the e-mail action

■ **Tip** You don't have to click the current insertion point. If you just start typing, it will automatically open up the search box.

This is a really handy feature! As you started typing and entered **em**, it would show that it found 12 actions or conditions. If you press Enter at that point, it would list them for you to select one. By the time you typed **ema**, the search was narrowed down to a single result, and it told you to press Enter to select the matching action. So, by only typing **ema** and pressing Enter, you can add an action to send an e-mail.

Initiation Form Parameters

Now let's create the workflow that will perform an initial review of the item and then send an e-mail to someone else for approval.

The first step in designing a reusable workflow is to define the *initiation form parameters*. If you recall from the previous chapters, when you associated a workflow to a list or library, you were presented with a form to specify the workflow parameters. This is called the *association* form. Along with designing workflow actions, you must also define the parameters that will be included on this form.

There are actually two places where these parameters are used. The first, as you've already seen, is when a workflow is associated to a list (or library). The second is when a new workflow instance is started. The workflows you've used so far have been started automatically when an item is created or modified. It is possible to also manually start a workflow on an item. When started manually, an *initiation* form is presented to allow you to enter or modify the parameters.

When defining these parameters, you can supply default values. As you associate the workflow, the default values can be overridden. When the workflow is initiated, the current values are displayed, which are based on what was entered (or updated) on the association form. These can then be adjusted, if necessary. When a workflow is started automatically, the initiation form is not used, and the parameters entered on the associated form are used. When defining the parameters, you can decide which parameters will be included on the association form, the initiation form, or both.

From the Workflows ribbon, click the Initiation Form Parameters button. The dialog shown in Figure 7-13 will be displayed.

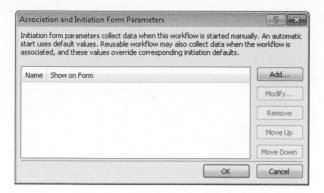

Figure 7-13. An empty Association and Initiation Form Parameters dialog box

Click the Add button to create a new parameter. For the `Field name`, enter **Reviewer**, and for the `Description` enter **The user who will perform the initial review**. Select the type of `Person or Group`, and select the `Both initiation and association` option, as shown in Figure 7-14.

Figure 7-14. Adding the `Reviewer` parameter

In the next dialog box, you'll configure how the people picker control will handle this field. Fill out this dialog box as shown in Figure 7-15.

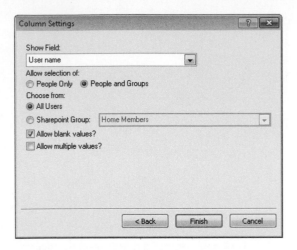

Figure 7-15. Person or Group column settings

Click the Finish button. Add an **Approver** parameter just like the **Reviewer** parameter. For the **Description** field, however, enter **The user who will perform the formal review**. Add a third parameter to specify the contents of the e-mail that will be sent to the approver, as shown in Figure 7-16. Make sure you change the type to be **Multiple lines of text**.

Figure 7-16. Adding the Message parameter

For the **Message** parameter, enter some suitable text for the default value. The completed dialog box should look like the one shown in Figure 7-17.

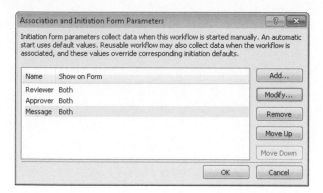

Figure 7-17. The completed Association and Initiation Form Parameters dialog box

Entering the Workflow Definition

For the first action, you'll add an entry to the history log.

Adding a Log to the History List

If the insertion point is not already in step 1, move it there. Type **log**, and press Enter. The designer should look like the one shown in Figure 7-18.

Figure 7-18. Adding a log action

Click the *this message* link to specify the text that should be written to the log. The display will change as shown in Figure 7-19.

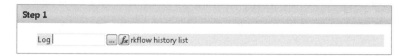

Figure 7-19. Editor changed to accept input

The link has changed into a text box and two buttons. This provides three ways for this information to be entered. For fixed text, you can simply type it in the text box. If you want to use a column, parameter or variable defined in SharePoint, use the *fx* button to provide a Lookup dialog box, as shown in Figure 7-20.

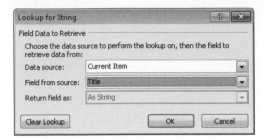

Figure 7-20. The Lookup dialog box

This third option is to click the button with the ellipsis. Click this button, and the String Builder dialog box will appear. Type **The workflow has been started on**, and then click the Add or Change Lookup button. Select the `Title` field from the `Current Item` data source, as shown in Figure 7-21.

Figure 7-21. Using the String Builder dialog box

Click OK, and the final string should look like the one shown in Figure 7-22.

Figure 7-22. The completed string

Click OK to close the String Builder dialog box.

Adding an Approval Process

Hover the mouse pointer just below this action until an insertion point appears, and then click it. Click the Action button in the ribbon, and select the *Approval* link. The action will have one blue link, *these users*, which indicates that more information is required (see Figure 7-23).

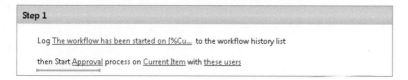

Figure 7-23. *The initial Start Approval Process action*

Click the *these users* link, and the Select Task Process Participants dialog box will appear. The participant for this task will be the **Reviewer** who was specified in the association or initiation form. Click the lookup icon to the right of the **Participants** field. In the Select Users dialog box, select the **Workflow Lookup for a User** option, as shown in Figure 7-24, and click the Add button.

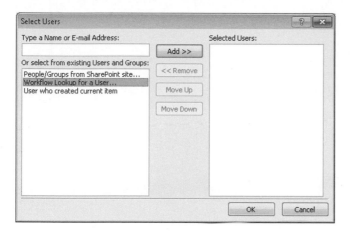

Figure 7-24. *Selecting the workflow lookup option*

In the Lookup dialog box, select the **Workflow Variables and Parameters** data source, and then select the **Reviewer** parameter, as shown in Figure 7-25.

Figure 7-25. Selecting the `Reviewer` *parameter*

In the Start Task Process Participants dialog box, enter **Please review this item** in the `Title` field. The completed dialog box should look like the one shown in Figure 7-26.

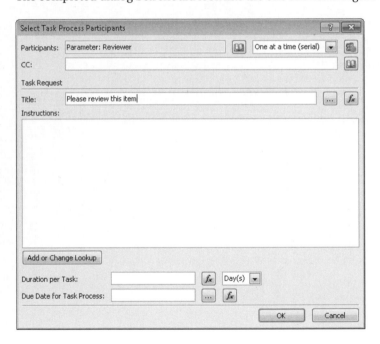

Figure 7-26. The completed Select Task Process Participants dialog box

Click OK to close this dialog box. In the workflow editor, click the insertion point below this task, type **log**, and press Enter. This action will log another entry into the history list. Click the *this message* link, and click the ellipsis button. Enter **This item has been reviewed by**, and then click the Add or Change Lookup button. Select the `Reviewer` parameter, as shown in Figure 7-27.

Figure 7-27. Selecting the Reviewer parameter

The workflow definition should look like the one shown in Figure 7-28.

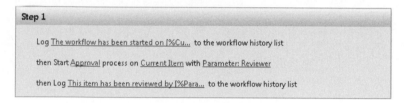

Figure 7-28. Completed step 1 definition

Checking the Review Outcome

To determine whether the review action approved this item, you will need to create a variable to store this and then modify the approval process to set the variable. Click the *Approval* link on the second action of the workflow. This will allow you to view and modify the approval process. In the Customization section, click the *Change the behavior of a single task process* link. This will show you the workflow actions that are performed by the approval process

Go to the last section labeled When a Task Completes. The If condition determines whether the outcome was approved. Put the insertion point below the If line, as shown in Figure 7-29.

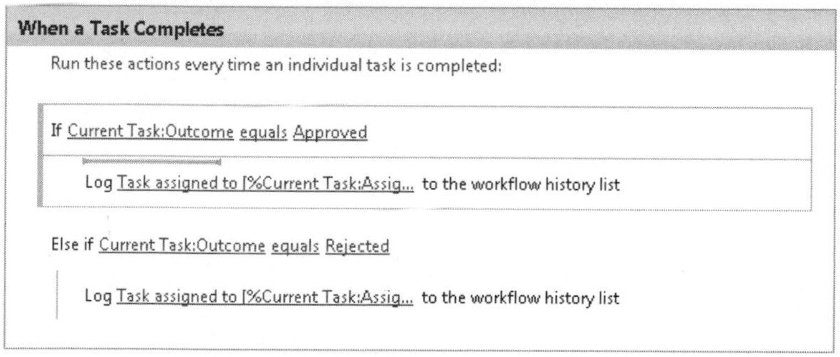

Figure 7-29. Selecting the insertion point

Click this insertion point, type **vari**, and press Enter. This will insert an action to set a workflow variable. Click the *workflow variable* link, which will display a list of variables that are already defined. Scroll to the bottom of the list, and select *Create a new variable*, as shown in Figure 7-30.

Figure 7-30. *Choosing to create a new variable*

In the Edit Variable dialog box that is displayed, enter the **Name** as **ItemApproved**, and set the **Type** list to **Boolean**, as shown in Figure 7-31.

Figure 7-31. *Creating the* **ItemApproved** *variable*

Click OK to close the dialog box. In the workflow editor, click the *value* link, and choose **Yes**. Put the insertion point below the **Else** line, and insert another set variable action. This time, the **ItemApproved** variable will be in the list presented; just select it instead of creating a new variable. Click the *value* link, and select **No**. The completed workflow section should look like the one shown in Figure 7-32.

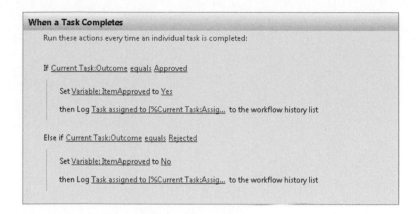

Figure 7-32. The completed workflow section

There is a navigation bar at the top of the workflow editor that is sometimes referred to as *breadcrumbs*. It shows you the path that you traversed in getting to the page you are currently on, as shown in Figure 7-33.

Figure 7-33. Workflow editor breadcrumbs

As this figure shows, you are several layers deep. Click the *Editor* link to get you back to the workflow editor where you started.

Adding a Second Step

Put the insertion point after the Step 1 box, and click it. Then click the Step button in the ribbon. This will create a Step 2 box. In Step 2, you will send an email to the approver if the review task was approved.

Adding a Condition

The insertion point should already be inside Step 2. Click the Condition button, and click the *If any value equals value* link, as shown in Figure 7-34.

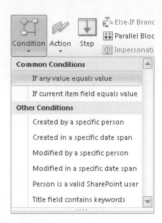

Figure 7-34. Adding an if any value equals value *condition*

Step 2 should now look like the one shown in Figure 7-35.

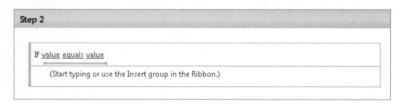

Figure 7-35. Step 2 showing an initial condition

Click the first *value* link, and the click the fx button. Select the `ItemApproved` variable from the `Workflow Variables and Parameters` data source, as shown in Figure 7-36.

Figure 7-36. Selecting the `ItemApproved` *variable*

For the second *value* link, choose `Yes`.

Sending an E-mail

The insertion point should be inside the sequence of activities to be executed when the condition is true (just below the If line). If it's not, move it there. Enter **email**, and press Enter. You just added an action to send an e-mail. Now click the *these users* link to configure the e-mail. This will display the Define E-mail Message dialog box that is shown in Figure 7-37.

Figure 7-37. The initial Define E-mail Message dialog box

For the To field, click the lookup icon to the right of the text box, and select the **Approver** parameter, as shown in Figure 7-38.

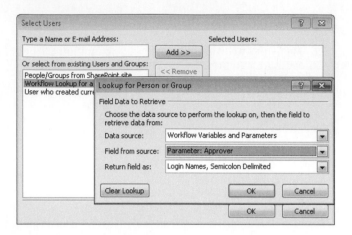

Figure 7-38. Selecting the Approver parameter

You can add a fixed user to be copied on this email, if you want. To do that, enter a user in the CC field. For the Subject, enter **Please review this item**. Put the cursor in the message box, and click the Add or Change Lookup button. Select the Message parameter, as shown in Figure 7-39.

Figure 7-39. Selecting the Message parameter

The completed dialog box should look similar to the one shown in Figure 7-40.

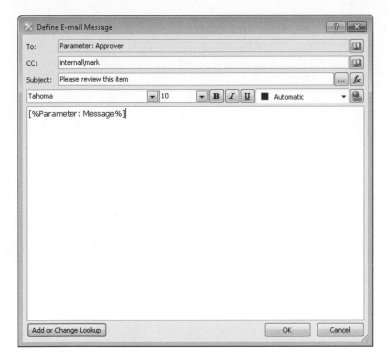

Figure 7-40. The completed Define E-mail Message dialog box

Click OK to close the dialog box. Put the insertion point after this action, click it, type **log**, and press Enter. This will create an action to log to the history list. Click the *this message* link, and then click the ellipsis. Enter **An email has been sent to**, click the Add or Change Lookup button, and select the **Approver** parameter. The final workflow definition should look like the one shown in Figure 7-41.

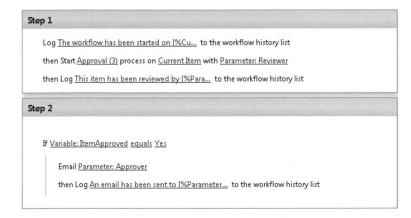

Figure 7-41. The final workflow definition

Publishing the Workflow

The last step of creating a reusable workflow is to publish it. This makes it available to be associated to lists and libraries on this site. The Save section of the Workflow ribbon has three buttons that are shown in Figure 7-42.

Figure 7-42. The Save section of the Workflow ribbon

The Publish button will also save the workflow and check for errors but the other buttons are available for you. Click the Publish button. A dialog box will appear showing the processing that is being done. If any errors are found, they will be shown in red. You'll need to fix these and then click the Publish button again.

Associating the Workflow

Now you're ready to associate this workflow. The SharePoint Designer is probably on the workflow editor page. Select the *Review and Approve* link on the breadcrumb strip to display the workflow settings page.

Click the Associate to List button in the ribbon, which should show the available lists and libraries that the workflow can be associated with, as shown in Figure 7-43.

Figure 7-43. Associating the workflow to a list

Select the Shared Documents library from this list. This will display the same association page that you've used before in previous chapters. You can use all the default values (see Figure 7-44).

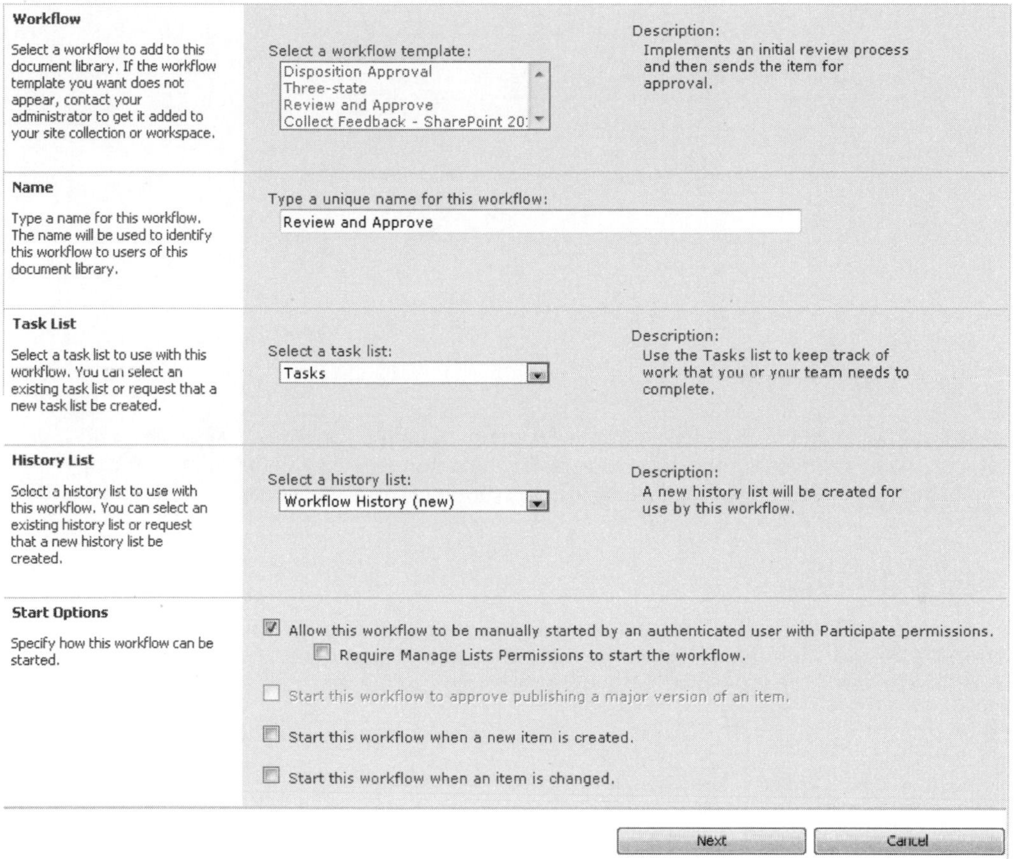

Workflow

Select a workflow to add to this document library. If the workflow template you want does not appear, contact your administrator to get it added to your site collection or workspace.

Select a workflow template:

Disposition Approval
Three-state
Review and Approve
Collect Feedback - SharePoint 201

Description:
Implements an initial review process and then sends the item for approval.

Name

Type a name for this workflow. The name will be used to identify this workflow to users of this document library.

Type a unique name for this workflow:

Review and Approve

Task List

Select a task list to use with this workflow. You can select an existing task list or request that a new task list be created.

Select a task list:

Tasks

Description:
Use the Tasks list to keep track of work that you or your team needs to complete.

History List

Select a history list to use with this workflow. You can select an existing history list or request that a new history list be created.

Select a history list:

Workflow History (new)

Description:
A new history list will be created for use by this workflow.

Start Options

Specify how this workflow can be started.

☑ Allow this workflow to be manually started by an authenticated user with Participate permissions.
    ☐ Require Manage Lists Permissions to start the workflow.

☐ Start this workflow to approve publishing a major version of an item.

☐ Start this workflow when a new item is created.

☐ Start this workflow when an item is changed.

[Next]   [Cancel]

Figure 7-44. The association page

Notice that because the Workflow History list doesn't currently exist, it is shown with (new) after the name. This indicates that this list will be created when the association is made. The default start options will only allow the workflow to be started manually. That will be fine for this project. Click the Next button, which will display the association form (see Figure 7-45).

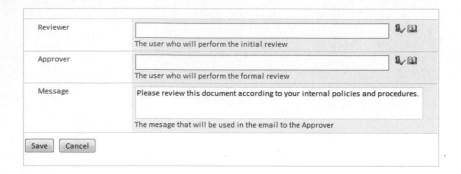

Figure 7-45. The empty association form

The association form contains the three parameters that you defined: **Reviewer**, **Approver**, and **Message**. Enter a user for the **Reviewer** and **Approver** parameters. You can use the default text for the **Message** or change it, if you want. Click the Save button to complete the association.

Testing the Workflow

To test this workflow, you'll need to first add a document to the Shared Documents library. Go to the Shared Documents list, and add a document (any type will work). To start a workflow on this document, select the *Workflows* link on the drop-down next to the document name, as shown in Figure 7-46.

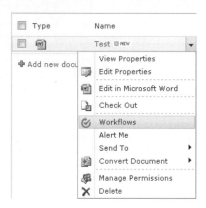

Figure 7-46. Selecting the Workflow link on a list item

The Workflows page shows the workflows that may be started on this document and the workflow instances that are currently running or have completed. Click the *Review and Approve* link, which will show the initiation form, as shown in Figure 7-47.

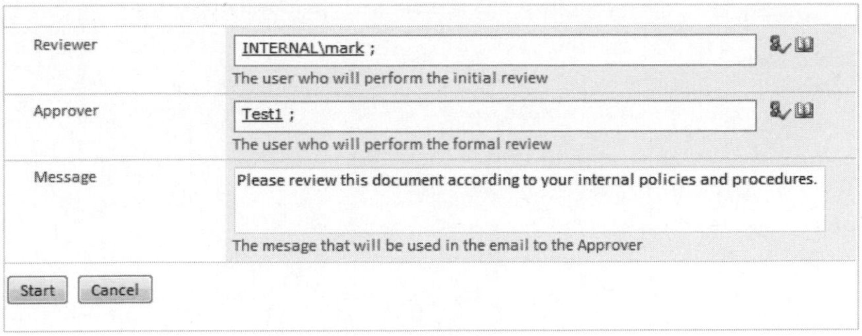

Reviewer	INTERNAL\mark ; The user who will perform the initial review	
Approver	Test1 ; The user who will perform the formal review	
Message	Please review this document according to your internal policies and procedures. The mesage that will be used in the email to the Approver	

Start   Cancel

Figure 7-47. The workflow initiation form

Because you choose the Both option when setting up the initiation form parameters, the association form and the initiation form are identical. You can set this option to control which parameters are on each form. Notice however, that this form has values filled in for all three parameters. The initiation form defaults to the values supplied during the association. You can leave these default values and click the Start button.

The workflow should now show `In Progress`. If you go to the task list, there should be a new task for the review step. Edit this task, and click the Approve button.

Go to the Shared Documents list, and select the Workflows link again from the drop-down menu. The Workflows page should now show that there is one completed workflow with a status of `Approved`. Click the *Approved* link, which will show the history of this workflow. The Workflow Status page should look similar to the one shown in Figure 7-48.

Figure 7-48. The Workflow Status page

This page shows all the details of the activities related to this workflow. The last two comments in the Workflow History section are the ones you logged from the workflow definition. Note that these are logged from the system account.

Site Workflows

Now you'll create a simple site workflow that will generate a task assigned to the specified user, requesting them to submit their status report. From the SharePoint Designer, click the *Workflows* link in the Navigation window, as shown in Figure 7-49.

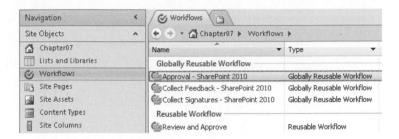

Figure 7-49. The Workflows page in SharePoint Designer

Notice that, in addition to the globally reusable workflows, there is now a reusable workflow named Review and Approve, which you just created. Click the Site Workflow button in the ribbon. This will display the Create Site Workflow dialog box shown in Figure 7-50.

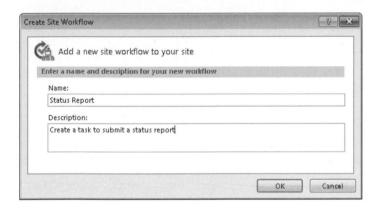

Figure 7-50. The Create Site Workflow dialog box

For the Name, enter **Status Report**, and for the Description, enter **Create a task to submit a status report**.

Initiation Form Parameters

As with a reusable workflow, you'll start with defining the parameters for this workflow. The difference, however, is that there is no association form; the parameters can only be set by the initiation form. You will need three parameters: the person that task should be assigned to, the due date for the assignment, and the message to be included in the task description.

Click the Initiation Form Parameters button on the ribbon, which will display the Association and Initiation Form Parameters dialog box. Click the Add button. Fill in the Add Field dialog box as shown in Figure 7-51.

Figure 7-51. Creating the `Assignee` *parameter*

■ **Note** This dialog box is identical to the one you used in the reusable workflow except that there is no option for choosing which form to display this in (association or initiation). Again, site workflows have no association form, so all parameters must be supplied during initiation.

Click the Next button. Leave the `Default value` blank, and click the Finish button. In similar fashion, create `DueDate` and `Message` parameters. For `DueDate`, use the `Date and Time` type, and for `Message`, use the `Multiple line of text` type. When adding a date field, there are some additional options that can be given for this parameter. Figure 7-52 shows the suggested settings. You can choose other options if you prefer. This will control how the initiation form will work.

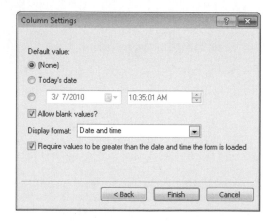

Figure 7-52. Date and time options

The completed dialog box should look like the one shown in Figure 7-53.

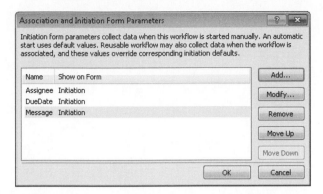

Figure 7-53. The completed Association and Initiation Form Parameters dialog box

Designing the Workflow

The initial workflow design will look like the one shown in Figure 7-54.

Figure 7-54. The initial workflow design

Click the insertion point, type **create**, and press Enter. This inserted an action to create a list item. Click the *this list* link to configure the item that will be created. Select **Tasks** from the drop-down list. The Create New List Item dialog box should look like the one shown in Figure 7-55.

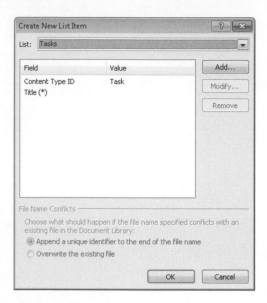

Figure 7-55. The initial Create New List Item dialog box

■ **Caution** The first option in the drop-down is `Association: Task List`, and for reusable workflows, this is normally the preferred choice. Recall that when you associate a workflow to a list, the first association page is standard for all workflows. It contains the name and description of the workflow and the start options. It also lets you specify the associated task and history lists. The `Association: Task List` option resolves to whichever list was selected on the first association page. For site workflows, however, there is no association and therefore no associated task list. So, this option will not work. Instead, you'll need to select the appropriate task list directly.

The `Title` field is automatically added to the dialog box and has (*) appended to it, indicating that this is a required field. Select this field, and click the Modify button, which will display the Value Assignment dialog box. For the `To` field, enter **Submit Status Report**, and click OK, as shown in Figure 7-56.

Figure 7-56. The Value Assignment dialog box

When creating a list item, the fields that are available to be set will depend on the list that was selected. The `Calendar` list, for example, will have different fields than the `Tasks` list. Which fields are required are also determined by the list that is being used. Click the Add button, and then open the field list drop-down to get a list of the fields that are available. Figure 7-57 shows a partial list.

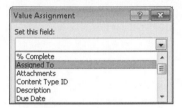

Figure 7-57. Partial list of available fields

Select the `Assigned To` field. For the `To` property, click the *fx* button, and select the `Assignee` parameter, as shown in Figure 7-58.

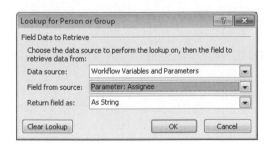

Figure 7-58. Selecting the `Assignee` parameter

In a similar fashion, add the `Due Date` field using the `DueDate` parameter, and add the `Description` field using the `Message` parameter. The completed dialog box should look like the one shown in Figure 7-59.

Figure 7-59. The completed Create New List Item dialog box

The last step is to publish the workflow. Click the Publish button, and fix any errors that it may report.

Testing the Workflow

To test your new site workflow, you'll need to go to the Chapter07 SharePoint site. From the Site Actions menu, click the *View All Site Content* link, as shown in Figure 7-60.

Figure 7-60. Selecting the View All Site Content link

There is a *Site Workflows* link on the All Site Content page, shown in Figure 7-61.

Figure 7-61. The All Site Content page

Click the *Site Workflows* link. The Workflows page (shown in Figure 7-62) will list the site workflows that can be started as well as any running or completed instances.

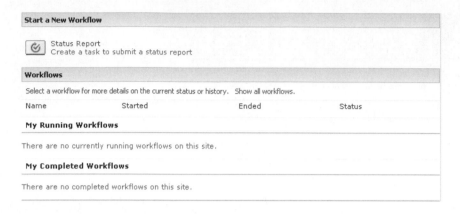

Figure 7-62. The Workflows page

Click the *Status Report* link, which will display the initiation form, shown in Figure 7-63.

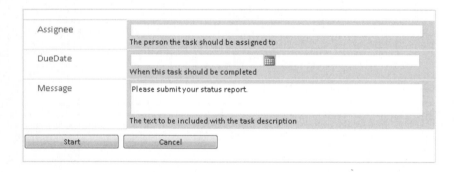

Figure 7-63. The Status Report initiation form

Specify a valid user, enter a due date, and click the Start button. The workflow should show `Completed`. Click the *Completed* link to see a history of this workflow instance. If you go to the `Tasks` list, there should be a new task that will be similar to the one shown in Figure 7-64.

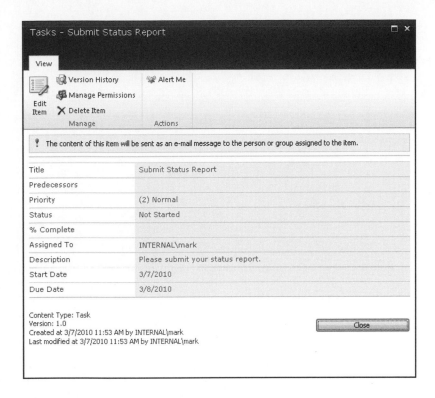

Figure 7-64. *The task that was created*

Summary

In this chapter, you created both a reusable workflow and a site workflow. A reusable workflow can be associated to any list or library on the site that contains items with the same content type that the workflow was designed for. A site workflow is not associated with any list and is manually initiated at the site level.

You also used many of the features of the workflow editor provided by the SharePoint Designer. Once you get the hang of it, the workflow editor makes it fairly easy to create simple, no-code workflows.

PART 3

■ ■ ■

Workflows in Visual Studio 2010

So far you have created some pretty useful workflows using several no-code approaches, including "out-of-the-box" workflows and the workflow editor in the SharePoint Designer. In this part of the book, you'll use Visual Studio 2010 to build more advanced workflows. In some ways, you'll probably notice some familiarity with workflows you have created so far.

If you have used previous versions of Visual Studio to develop SharePoint solutions, I think you will be pleasantly surprised to see how much it has been improved to make this a much easier process.

Chapter 8 will be deliberately simple because the goal of this chapter is to help you familiarize yourself with the development tools and the process of deploying and debugging workflows. In subsequent chapters, you will explore the SharePoint object model (giving you direct access to your site objects), create custom ASP.NET forms, handle various SharePoint events, and more.

CHAPTER 8

■■■

Creating a Simple Site Workflow

You'll use the same SharePoint site for all the projects in this part of the book. Create a new site named **Part3** using the Team Site template, as shown in Figure 8-1.

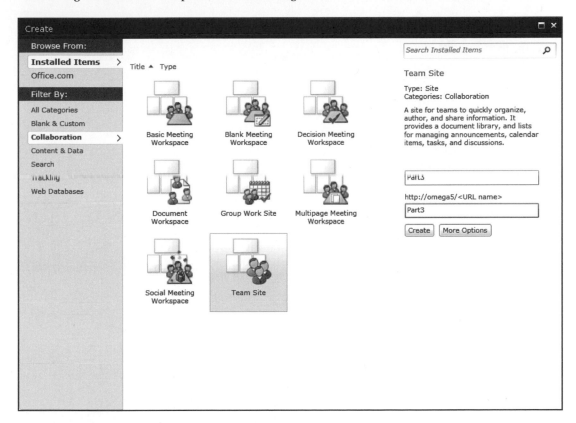

Figure 8-1. Creating a new SharePoint site

Using Visual Studio 2010

■ **Tip** The easiest way to deploy your workflows and debug them through Visual Studio is to install Visual Studio on the same computer that is also running SharePoint Server. The examples in this book will assume that you are running Visual Studio on the SharePoint desktop (or server).

Creating a SharePoint Project

From the Start page, click the *New Project* link. In the New Project dialog box, select SharePoint ▶ 2010. The dialog box should look like the one shown in Figure 8-2.

Figure 8-2. Creating a new workflow project

As you can see, Visual Studio 2010 provides templates to create many of the SharePoint components such as sites, lists, content types, and web parts. Choose the Sequential Workflow template, and enter the name as **WF_Chapter08**.

Running as Administrator

When working with a SharePoint project, Visual Studio must be started with administrator privileges. If you're not already running as administrator, the dialog box shown in Figure 8-3 will be displayed.

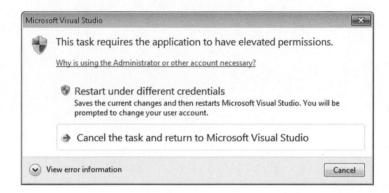

Figure 8-3. Action requires running as administrator

If you choose the restart option, Visual Studio will be restarted and run with administrator privileges. To save you this trouble in the future, you can modify the shortcut that you use to start Visual Studio. Right-click the shortcut, and choose Properties. Then select the Shortcut tab, as shown in Figure 8-4.

Figure 8-4. The Shortcut tab

In the Advanced Properties dialog box, select the "Run as administrator" check box (see Figure 8-5).

Figure 8-5. Setting the shortcut to run as administrator

Configuring the SharePoint Project

After you select the workflow template, you'll be prompted with a series of dialog boxes that allow you to configure the workflow. The first dialog box, shown in Figure 8-6, allows you to specify the SharePoint site that will be used for debugging. Enter the URL for the Part3 site that you just created.

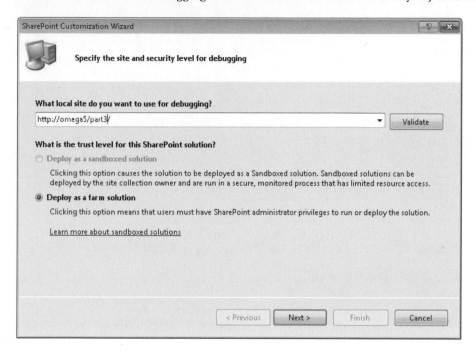

Figure 8-6. Specifying the SharePoint site

The dialog box has an option to deploy the project as a sandboxed solution. However, you cannot run a Visual Studio workflow in a sandbox environment, so this option is disabled. The next dialog box, shown in Figure 8-7, allows you to specify the type of workflow. Choose the Site Workflow option, and enter the name as **WF_Chapter08**.

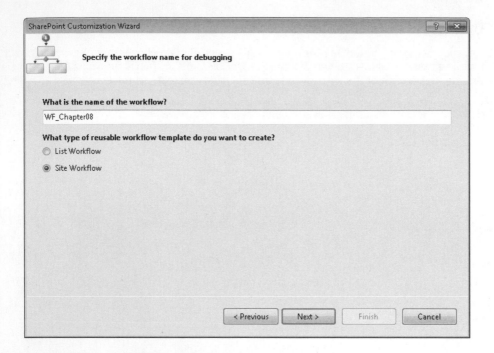

Figure 8-7. Selecting the workflow type

Visual Studio can automatically associate the workflow for you, which will save you some extra steps. Because this is a site workflow, it is not associated to any list, and this option is disabled. However, you can still associate the history list and task list that the workflow will use. Leave the default options shown in Figure 8-8, and click Next.

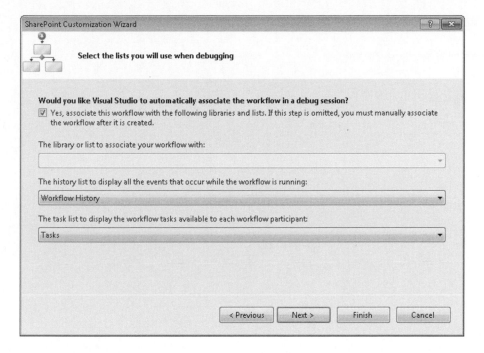

Figure 8-8. *The associated SharePoint lists*

The last dialog box allows you to specify the start options. Because this is a site workflow, the only allowable option is to start the workflow manually, as shown in Figure 8-9.

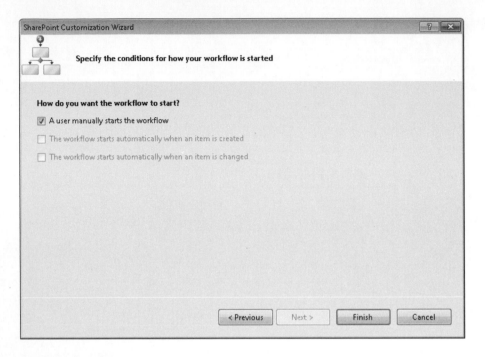

Figure 8-9. Selecting the start options

These dialog boxes provide you with the same basic workflow options that you used to configure the no-code workflows you created in the previous chapters.

SharePoint Support in Visual Studio 2010

Visual Studio will start with the Workflow Designer. Figure 8-10 shows a typical Integrated Development Environment (IDE).

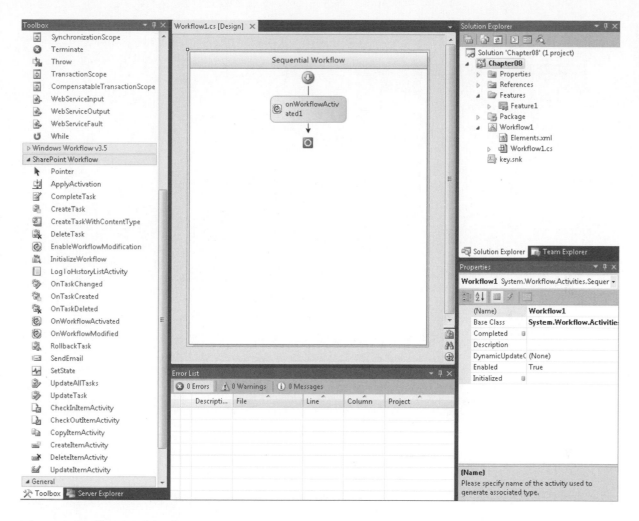

Figure 8-10. *The Visual Studio IDE*

The Toolbox is on the left and contains the standard workflow activities provided by .NET 3.0 and .NET 3.5. Because this workflow will be hosted by SharePoint, some of these activities are not supported. In addition, a special set of activities is provided specifically for SharePoint workflows, including activities such as `CreateTask`, `SendEmail`, and `LogtoHistoryListActivity`. Some of these such as `OnWorkflowActivated` and `OnTaskCreated` listen for specific events. (I'll cover these in Chapter 11.)

The Solution Explorer is shown in the top-right corner. Notice that the project template created a feature for you. This workflow will be installed on the SharePoint server as a feature. I'll explain that later in this chapter. The standard output windows are at the bottom, and a Properties window is at the bottom right.

The Workflow Designer is in the middle and provides a graphical view of your workflow activities. By default, the workflow starts with the `OnWorkflowActivated` activity, which listens for this event, triggering the start of the workflow instance.

The Server Explorer is also provided as a second tab in the left window. If you select the Server Explorer tab (see Figure 8-11), you'll see that Visual Studio is very nicely integrated with SharePoint 2010.

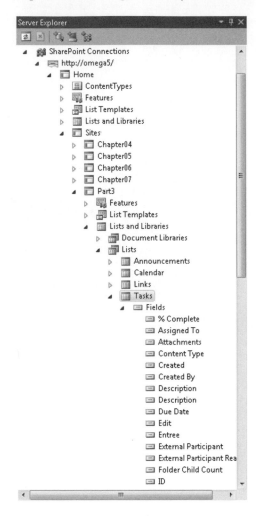

Figure 8-11. The Server Explorer navigating the SharePoint site

Visual Studio allows you to browse the objects in a SharePoint server in much the same way as previous versions allowed you to browse the contents of a database server. There is a new node, called SharePoint Connections. Because your project is already connected to a SharePoint server, it is already displayed in the Server Explorer. Notice the sites that were created for the previous chapters. You can right-click the SharePoint Connections node and attach other SharePoint servers as well.

If you click one of the objects in this tree, its properties are shown in the Properties window. For example, a partial list of the Tasks list properties are shown in Figure 8-12.

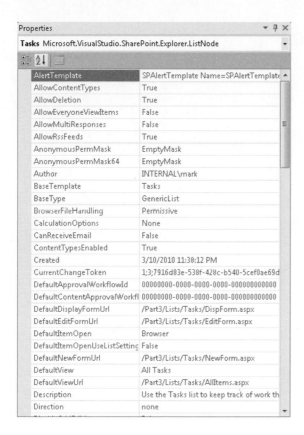

Figure 8-12. The Tasks list Properties window

Notice that the properties are all grayed. This browsing feature is for read-only use. You cannot use this to modify any of the SharePoint objects.

■ **Note** The instructions in this book assume that you're using the standard keyboard shortcuts, such as F5 to debug, F6 to build, and so on. It is possible to configure these differently, however. If you have different shortcuts, you'll need to translate these instructions accordingly. I believe that is will be fairly clear from the context what the appropriate action should be.

Designing a SharePoint Workflow

Now you'll use the Workflow Designer to construct a really simple workflow.

Logging to the History List

Start by dragging a `LogToHistoryListActivity` from the Toolbox onto the design pane, just below the existing `OnWorkflowActivated` activity. In the Properties window, set the `Name` to **logStarted**. Enter the `HistoryDescription` as **The workflow has started**, and enter the `HistoryOutcome` as **OK**. When you're done, the Properties window should look like the one in Figure 8-13.

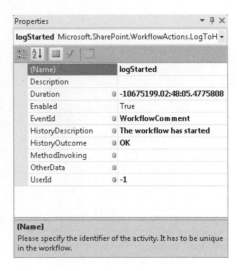

Figure 8-13. *The Properties window of* `LogToHistoryListActivity`

This workflow activity performs the same function as the Log to History list action in the workflow editor in the SharePoint Designer.

Creating a New Task

The workflow for this chapter will create a new task in the `Tasks` list using some hard-coded values. Drag a `CreateTask` activity from the Toolbox to the design pane, just below the `logStarted` activity.

Defining the Activity's Properties

In the Properties window, for the `CorrelationToken`, enter **taskToken**. Then expand that property and select `Workflow1` for the `OwnerActivityName` property.

For `TaskId` and `TaskProperties`, you'll need to create new dependency properties. To do that, select the `TaskId` property in the Properties window, and click the ellipsis next to the property value. In the dialog box that is displayed, select the second tab (labeled Bind to a new member), and enter the member name as **taskID**, as shown in Figure 8-14.

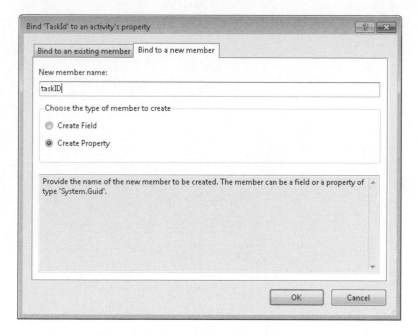

Figure 8-14. Creating a new **taskID** *property*

In the same way, click the ellipsis next to the `TaskProperties` property, and create a new member named **taskProperties**, as shown in Figure 8-15.

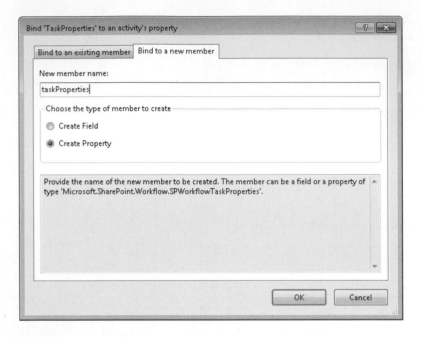

Figure 8-15. Creating a new `taskProperties` property

The completed Properties window should look like the one shown in Figure 8-16.

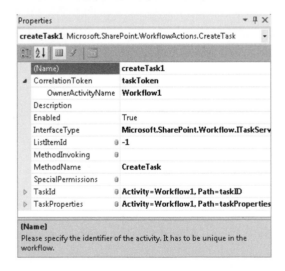

Figure 8-16. Completed Properties window for `CreateTask` activity

Entering Code in the Code-Beside Class

Double-click the `createTask1` activity, which will create an event handler for the `MethodInvoking` event and open the code-behind file. For the implementation of this event handler, enter the following code:

```
taskID = Guid.NewGuid();

taskProperties = new Microsoft.SharePoint.Workflow.SPWorkflowTaskProperties();
taskProperties.PercentComplete = (float)0.0;
taskProperties.AssignedTo = System.Threading.Thread.CurrentPrincipal.Identity.Name;
taskProperties.DueDate = DateTime.Now.AddDays(1);
taskProperties.Title = "Submit Status Report";
taskProperties.Description = "Please submit your status report ASAP";
```

When this activity is executed, its `MethodInvoking` event handler is called. This is your opportunity to perform whatever initialization code is necessary. First, the `taskID` property holds the `Guid` that defines the identifier of the task. `Guid.NewGuid()` is called to generate a new `Guid`. Then a `SPWorkflowTaskProperties` class is created, and its various members are populated. These two properties, `taskID` and `taskProperties` are defined as a `DependencyProperty`. If you scroll up in the code-beside class, you'll see where they are declared and where the public properties associated with them are implemented. These properties are bound to the `CreateTask` activity so they are available when the activity is executed.

Deploying the Workflow

Your workflow is complete and ready to be deployed. Press F6 to build the solution, and fix any build errors you may have. Right-click the Chapter08 project to view the context menu (shown in Figure 8-17).

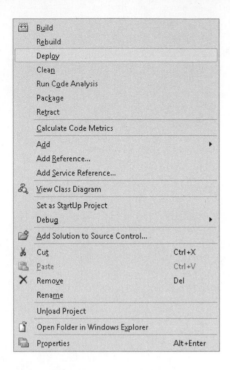

Figure 8-17. *SharePoint project context menu*

You may have noticed that there are a few actions that are not normally included in other Visual Studio projects. Deploy is used to install this workflow as a feature on the configured SharePoint site, and Retract is used to remove it. The Package command is used to build a package that can be installed on other sites.

Select the Deploy command and then look in the Output window. The contents should look like this:

```
------ Deploy started: Project: WF_Chapter08, Configuration: Debug Any CPU ------

Active Deployment Configuration: Default

Run Pre-Deployment Command:

  Skipping deployment step because a pre-deployment command is not specified.

Recycle IIS Application Pool:

  Skipping application pool recycle because no matching package on the server was found.

Retract Solution:

  Skipping package retraction because no matching package on the server was found.

Add Solution:

  Adding solution 'WF_Chapter08.wsp'...

  Deploying solution 'WF_Chapter08.wsp'...

Activate Features:

  Activating feature 'Feature1' ...

  Associating workflow template for Workflow1...

  Successfully associated the workflow template with a Microsoft SharePoint site.

Run Post-Deployment Command:

  Skipping deployment step because a post-deployment command is not specified.

========== Build: 1 succeeded or up-to-date, 0 failed, 0 skipped ==========

========== Deploy: 1 succeeded, 0 failed, 0 skipped ==========
```

The Deploy process performs the following steps:

1. The IIS application pool for the SharePoint web application is recycled.

2. The existing solution is removed (skipped because one was not found).

3. The solution is installed.

4. The feature is activated.

5. The workflow is associated with the site.

Running the Workflow

Now press F5 to debug the workflow. Notice that the application is rebuilt (as you would normally expect when debugging), and it is also redeployed. Whenever you debug the workflow, the current version is redeployed to the SharePoint site.

■ **Note** When you debug for the first time, Visual Studio may prompt you to enable the web for debugging. If you choose yes (and you should), it will update the `web.config` file to enable custom error messages. This will help you determine the source of a problem should you encounter any.

The debugger should launch the SharePoint site in a browser window. From the Site Actions menu, select *All Site Content* and the page should look like Figure 8-18.

Figure 8-18. The All Site Content page

Click the *Site Workflows* link and the Workflows page (see Figure 8-19) is displayed, showing the existing site workflows that can be started.

Figure 8-19. *The site workflows page*

Click the *WF_Chapter08* link, and the processing page will display for a few seconds. When it is finished, go to the **Tasks** list. You should see a new task similar to the one shown in Figure 8-20.

Figure 8-20. *The new task that was created*

Visual Studio Cleanup

Close the browser, which should end the debugging session. Now look at the Output window in Visual Studio. You should see text similar to this:

```
Active Deployment Configuration: Default

Recycle IIS Application Pool:

  Recycling IIS application pool 'SharePoint - 80'...

Retract Solution:

  Removed workflow association for Workflow1

  Deactivating feature 'WF_Chapter08_Feature1' ...

  Retracting solution 'wf_chapter08.wsp'...

  Deleting solution 'wf_chapter08.wsp'...
```

When debugging has finished, the solution is automatically removed from the SharePoint site.

Resolving Retract Issues

As you've seen, whenever Visual Studio deploys a feature, it first must retract the previous version. You might occasionally run into a scenario where Visual Studio tries to retract the feature but it doesn't exist. When this happens, you'll see an error similar to the one shown in Figure 8-21.

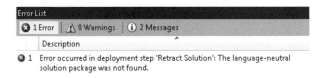

Figure 8-21. *Error retracting workflow*

This can happen when an error occurs while debugging and Visual Studio does not perform the normal cleanup logic. Once you're in this state, it won't let you deploy or debug the workflow. You can usually resolve this issue by deploying the workflow and skipping the retraction step.

SharePoint Deployment Configuration

Right-click the `WF_Chapter08` project, and choose Properties. Then select the SharePoint tab. You should see a window similar to the one shown in Figure 8-22.

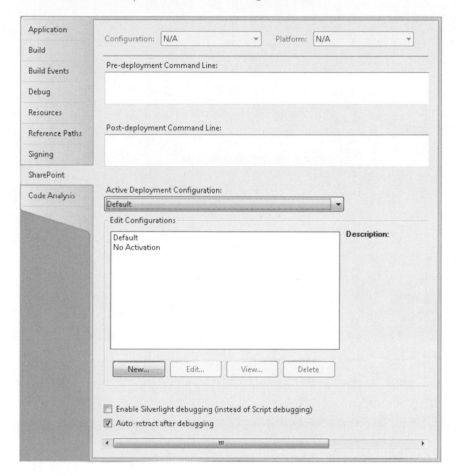

Figure 8-22. *The existing build configurations*

■ **Tip** Notice the "Auto-retract after debugging" check box. If you deselect this, the workflow is not automatically removed when debugging stops. There are times that you will want to do this. One of the side effects of removing a workflow is that all history of that workflow is also deleted. For example, if you go back to the Part3 site and look in the `Tasks` list, you'll find that the new task is no longer there.

The project template created two deployment configurations: Default and No Activation. You will create a third called No Retraction. Click the New button near the bottom of the window, which will display the Add New Deployment Configuration dialog box shown in Figure 8-23.

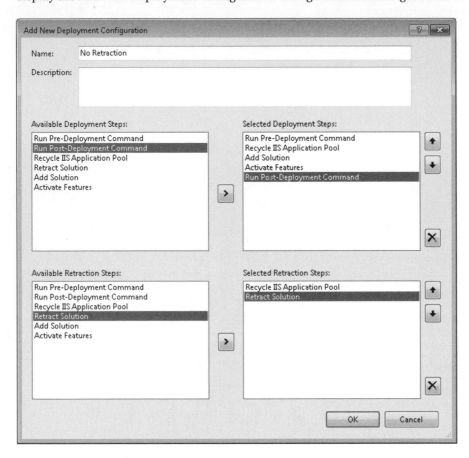

Figure 8-23. Creating a new configuration

Enter the name as **No Retraction**. Select all the steps in the top-left pane except Retract Solution, and click the arrow button to copy them to the pane on the right. Make sure the steps on the right are ordered in the same way shown in Figure 8-23. In the bottom pane, select the Recycle IIS Application Pool and Retract Solution steps, and copy them to the pane on the right. The completed dialog box should look like the one shown in Figure 8-23. Click OK.

Selecting the Active Configuration

Whenever you need to use this to resolve a retraction error, go to the project's property page, and select No Retraction as the active configuration, as shown in Figure 8-24.

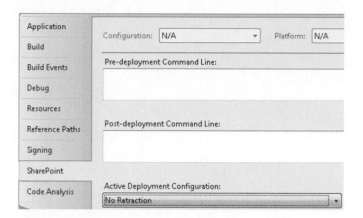

Figure 8-24. Specifying the build configuration

Then execute the Deploy command from the Project's context menu. Once the feature has been deployed, make sure you change the active configuration back to Default. If you don't, the next time you try to deploy or debug the workflow, the deploy step will fail because the feature will already be installed.

Summary

You have created a simple workflow using Visual Studio 2010. Visual Studio takes care of deploying, activating, and associating your workflow , making it pretty easy to test. We will get into more complex workflows in subsequent chapters. The purpose in this one was to learn the mechanics of creating, deploying, and debugging a SharePoint workflow using Visual Studio 2010. We hope you've seen that most of this work is done for you.

CHAPTER 9

■ ■ ■

Exploring the SharePoint Object Model

In this chapter you'll use the SharePoint object model to access lists and list items from code. There are hundreds of classes in the object model, so I won't be able to cover all of them. However, I'll explain some of the more commonly used classes.

Creating a SharePoint Project in Visual Studio

To demonstrate the flexibility of Visual Studio, you'll create the project differently than you did in the previous chapter. Create an empty SharePoint project as shown in Figure 9-1. Enter the project name as **WF_Chapter09**.

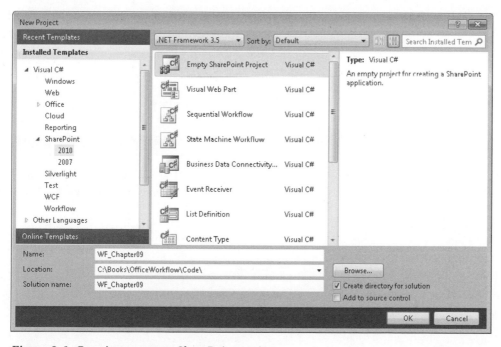

Figure 9-1. Creating an empty SharePoint project

■ **Tip** As I explained in the previous chapter, you will need to run Visual Studio 2010 with administrator privileges. If you did not set up the shortcut to automatically do this, make sure you right-click the shortcut or menu item and choose "Run as administrator."

After you click OK, the SharePoint Customization Wizard shown in Figure 9-2 will be displayed.

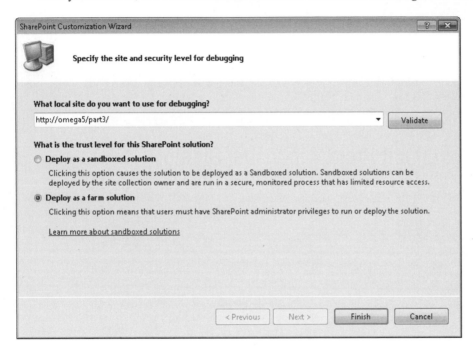

Figure 9-2. Deploying as a farm solution

This is the same dialog box that was used in the previous chapter. Notice, however, that the option to deploy as a sandboxed solution is now available. In the previous project it was grayed out because you cannot deploy a workflow feature as a sandboxed solution. Because this is an empty project, there is nothing in the project, yet, that would prevent this option.

■ **Caution** Make sure you change the default option and select "Deploy as a farm solution." If you don't, you will not be able to add a workflow to this project.

Adding a Workflow

In the Solution Explorer, right-click the WF_Chapter09 project, and choose Add ▶ New Item, as shown in Figure 9-3.

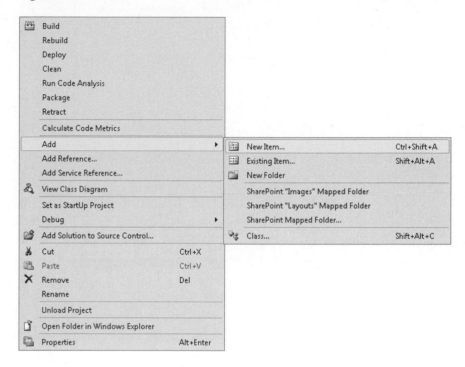

Figure 9-3. Adding an item to the project

In the Add New Item dialog box, select the SharePoint ▶ 2010 template folder. Then select the Sequential Workflow template, as shown in Figure 9-4. Enter the workflow name as **CheckTasksWorkflow**.

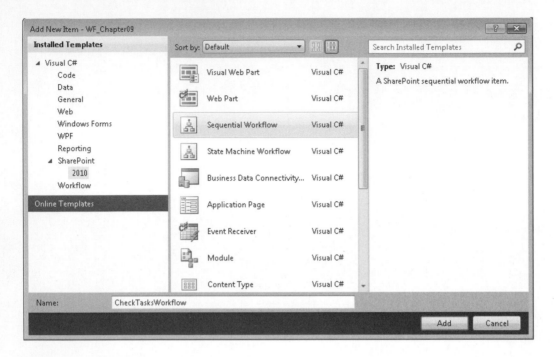

Figure 9-4. Selecting a sequential workflow

SharePoint Customization Wizard

When you add this workflow to the project, the SharePoint Customization Wizard will present a series of dialog boxes, which are identical to the ones you saw in the previous chapter. In the first dialog box, enter the name as **WF_Chapter09**, and select the Site Workflow option, as shown in Figure 9-5.

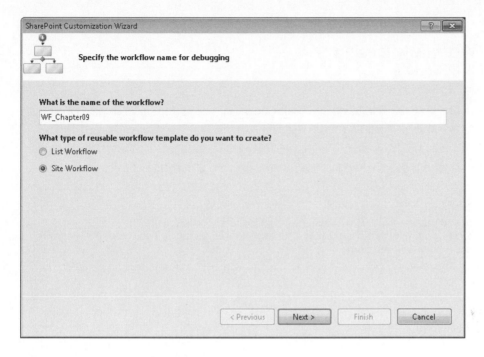

Figure 9-5. Creating a site workflow

For the remaining dialog boxes, accept the default options. You can refer to Chapter 8 if you want an explanation of these dialog boxes.

The template created an initial workflow with an `OnWorkflowActivated` event handler. This starts your workflow activities when SharePoint initiates a new workflow instance. The workflow that you'll create will have two parts. The first part will gather some details about the SharePoint site and write them to the history log. The second part will scan the Tasks list and report tasks that need someone to take action on them.

Writing SharePoint Details to the History List

Now you'll add activities to the workflow to gather some site details.

Creating the Workflow Design

■ **Tip** As I pointed out in Chapter 8, the activities in the Toolbox are organized into three main sections: Windows Workflow v3.0, Windows Workflow v3.5, and SharePoint Workflow. The Windows Workflow groups contain the standard activities shipped with .NET 3.0 and 3.5. The SharePoint Workflow group contains the activities that are specific to SharePoint. You can design workflows that use activities from any combination of these groups.

Drag a `CodeActivity` to the workflow, and rename it as **getDetails**. Then drag a `LogToHistoryListActivity` just below **getDetails**, and rename it as **logDetails**. The workflow diagram should look like the one shown in Figure 9-6.

Figure 9-6. Initial workflow design

■ **Tip** Notice the red circle with the exclamation point. This is used by the workflow designer to indicate there is an error in the workflow design. In this case, it is because you have not yet provided an event handler for the `CodeActivity`. You will take care of that shortly.

You used the `LogToHistoryListActivity` in Chapter 8 to write some static text to the history list. For this project, you'll bind the `HistoryDescription` property to a `DependencyProperty` and use the `CodeActivity` to format the text that should be logged. Click the `logDetails` activity. In the Properties window, enter the `HistoryOutcome` as **OK**. Then select the `HistoryDescription` property, and click the ellipsis next to it. In the dialog box that appears, select the second tab, and enter the new member name as **Details**, as shown in Figure 9-7.

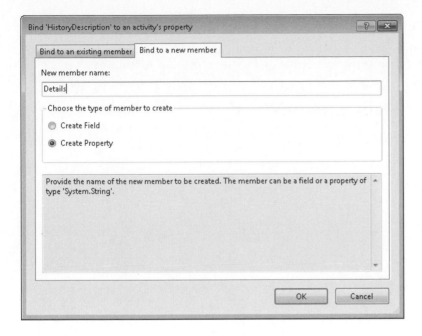

Figure 9-7. Creating a new `DependencyProperty`

The completed Properties window should look like the one shown in Figure 9-8.

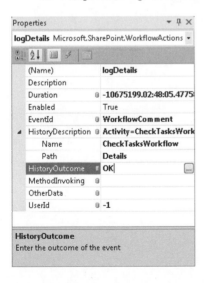

Figure 9-8. The properties window for `logDetails`

Accessing the Object Model

Double-click the getDetails activity, which will generate the event handler for this activity and open the code-behind window. Listing 9-1 shows the implementation for the getDetails_ExecuteCode() event handler.

Listing 9-1. Implementation of getDetails_ExecuteCode()

```
using (SPWeb web = SPContext.Current.Web)
{
    Details = "";

    try
    {
        // SPWeb
        Details += string.Format("URL: {0} \r\n", web.Url);

        // SPList
        SPList list = web.Lists["Tasks"];
        Details += string.Format("The task list has {0} views \r\n",
            list.Views.Count);

        // SPListItem
        if (list.ItemCount > 0)
        {
            SPListItem item = list.Items[0];
            Details += string.Format("The title of first task is {0} \r\n",
                item.Title);

            // SPField
            SPField field = item.Fields["Created"];
            Details += string.Format("The field name is {0} \r\n",
                field.StaticName);
        }
        else
            Details += "The Tasks list is empty\r\n";

        // SPDocumentLibrary
        list = web.Lists["Shared Documents"];
        if (list.BaseType == SPBaseType.DocumentLibrary)
        {
            SPDocumentLibrary lib = (SPDocumentLibrary)list;
            Details += string.Format("The template is {0}\r\n",
                lib.DocumentTemplateUrl);
            Details += string.Format("The library contains {0} documents \r\n",
                lib.ItemCount);

            // SPContentType
            SPContentType type = lib.ContentTypes[0];
            Details += string.Format
                ("The library supports the {0} content type \r\n",
```

```
                type.Name);
        }

        // SPGroup
        SPGroup group = web.Groups[0];
        Details += string.Format("The {0} group has {1} users \r\n",
            group.Name, group.Users.Count);

        // SPUser
        SPUser user = group.Users[0];
        Details += string.Format("The first user's email is {0} \r\n",
            user.Email);

    }
    catch (Exception ex)
    {
        Details += "Exception occurred: " + ex.Message;
    }
}
```

This code in Listing 9-1 uses several classes from the SharePoint object model. They're easy to spot because they always start with SP.

SPContext

SPContext is often your starting point when accessing the object model. This is a static class; notice that you do not create an instance of it. SPContext.Current provides the context of the current operation. You can use it to access the SPWeb object as we did here. In a similar manner, you can use it to get information about the current user, the current list, or the current list item. These properties may not always have values, however, depending on the current state of the workflow.

SPWeb

The SPWeb object represents a SharePoint site such as the Part3 site that you created in Chapter 8. You can use this object to access all of the lists and document libraries on the site. You can also use it to list the available workflows and the workflow associations. This project uses the Url property. It also uses the Lists property to get a specific list.

■ **Tip** The SPWeb class implements the IDispose interface, and it is important you dispose of it when you are finished using it. You should not keep a reference to it. Basically, you should obtain the SPWeb object, use it, and dispose of it. If you need it again, get another instance from the SPContext class. The easiest way to do this is by putting your code inside a using block, as demonstrated in the code in Listing 9-1. As soon as that block of code goes out of scope, the SPWeb object is automatically disposed.

■ **Note** The SharePoint object model also provides an `SPSite` object. This is actually a site collection and has an `AllWebs` property that you can use to enumerate all the web sites. `SPSite` is used for configuring and administering the SharePoint server and requires a higher level of security access to use it.

SPList

`SPList` represents a list or document library. You can get access to a list using the `Lists` property of the `SPWeb` object. A list is a table with rows and columns. Use the `Items` property to access the rows and the `Fields` property to access the columns. This project uses the `Views` property and reports the number of views that have been defined for the `Tasks` list.

SPListItem

`SPListItem` defines a row within a list. You get an `SPListItem` from the `Items` property of an `SPList` object or by calling one of its `GetItems` methods such as `GetItemsById()`. You can get and set the values of specific fields by referencing them by a name indexer as follows:

```
string Description = item["Description"].ToString();
item["Description"] = "Some description";
```

■ **Caution** You will need to make sure that you are passing an appropriate data type when setting field values. The compiler does not perform type checking for you and invalid data types will generate runtime exceptions. It is also a good practice to wrap your code inside a `try-catch` block to catch any exceptions that may be thrown.

SPDocumentLibrary

`SPDocumentLibrary` is derived from `SPList`. You obtain an `SPDocumentLibrary` from the `Lists` property, which returns an `SPList` object. You then need to cast that into an `SPDocumentLibrary` object. Notice that the code first checks to verify that the list has a `BaseType` of `DocumentLibrary` before performing the cast. This is a good practice because the cast will fail if the object is not actually a document library.

An `SPDocumentLibrary` acts just like an `SPList` object except that is has a few additional properties and methods, such as the `DocumentTemplateUrl` property referenced in the sample code.

SPContentType

You can get a list of all defined content types by using the `ContentTypes` property of the `SPWeb` object. Likewise, you can find out what content types are supported by a list (or document library) by accessing the `ContentTypes` property of an `SPList` object (or objects derived from it such as `SPDocumentLibrary`).

SPField

SPField represents a column definition and is used in a number of places. For example, the Fields property of an SPList or SPListItem object specifies the fields that have been defined for that list. SPContentType has a Fields property to specify the fields defined for that content type. SPWeb also has a Fields property that contains all the fields that have been defined on this site. (You might recall from Chapter 4 that when creating a new list, you used columns that had already been defined. This list is obtained from the Fields property of the SPWeb object.)

It is important to understand that SPField provides the column definition, not the actual contents of that column. The following code illustrates this point:

```
SPField f = item.Fields["Created"];
string sz1 = field.ToString();
string sz2 = item["Created"].ToString();
```

The SPField object represents the definition of the Created column for an SPListItem. Its ToString() method returns the name of the column, in this case Created. The second string will contain the value of the column. Its ToString() method will format the date stored in the Created column. Just remember that item["Created"] returns the value of the column, while item.Fields["Created"] returns the field definition.

SPGroup

SPGroup represents a user group that has been defined in SharePoint. You can access the list of defined groups by using the Groups property of the SPWeb object. SPGroup has a Users property that lists all of the users who are members of this group. You can also use the ContainsCurrentUser property to see whether the current user is in this group. In addition, you can use the Groups property of an SPUser object to see what groups a particular user is in.

SPUser

SPUser represents a specific user. You can use it to obtain details about a user such as name and e-mail address. You can obtain the current user with the CurrentUser property of the SPWeb object. SharePoint supports several authentication providers such as Active Directory. Depending on which one is used for a given scenario, you could have different set of fields available.

You can also determine the user that the current thread is running as by using the following code:

```
string szName = System.Threading.Thread.CurrentPrincipal.Identity.Name;
SPUser u = web.SiteUsers[szName];
```

The name of the user associated with the current thread is used to look up the SharePoint user from the SiteUsers property of the SPWeb object.

■ **Tip** Both SPGroup and SPUser are derived from SPPrincipal, and in many places users and groups can be used interchangeable. For example, you can assign a task either to a specific user or to a group.

Testing the Workflow

Press F6 to build the project and fix any compiler errors. Then press F5 to debug the workflow, which will launch the SharePoint site. From the Site Actions menu, select All Site Content and then click the *Site Workflows* link. There should be a link for your workflow similar to the one shown in Figure 9-9. Click this link to start the workflow.

Figure 9-9. *Starting the site workflow*

After the workflow has finished, go back to the Site Workflows page. It should now show a completed workflow, as shown in Figure 9-10.

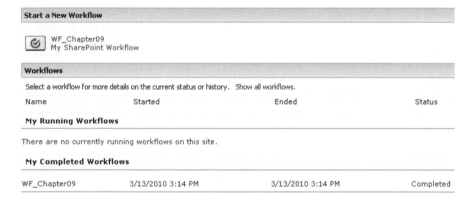

Figure 9-10. *Showing the completed workflow*

Click the link for this workflow (you can click either the *WF_Chapter09* link or the *Completed* link; either one will display the Workflow History page. Your results should be similar to the one shown in Figure 9-11. The details that are logged will be different depending on your configuration.

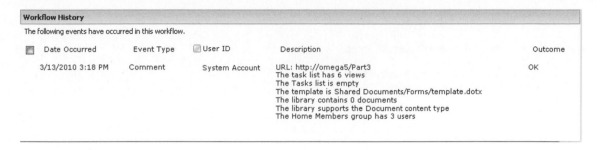

Workflow History

The following events have occurred in this workflow.

☐	Date Occurred	Event Type	☐ User ID	Description	Outcome
	3/13/2010 3:18 PM	Comment	System Account	URL: http://omega5/Part3 The task list has 6 views The Tasks list is empty The template is Shared Documents/Forms/template.dotx The library contains 0 documents The library supports the Document content type The Home Members group has 3 users	OK

Figure 9-11. The History list record

Scanning the Tasks List

I hope the previous example gave you a sense of how to use the SharePoint objects. Now let's do some real work with them.

Adding an Activity to Check the Tasks List

Go back to your workflow designer, and drag a `CodeActivity` to the workflow just below `logDetails`. Change the name to **checkTasks**. The workflow diagram should look like the one shown in Figure 9-12.

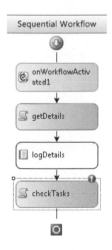

Figure 9-12. Workflow diagram

Implementing Check Tasks Logic

Double-click the `checkTasks` activity, and enter the implementation shown in Listing 9-2.

Listing 9-2. Implementation of checkTasks_ExecuteCode()

```
using (SPWeb web = SPContext.Current.Web)
{
    SPList tasks = web.Lists["Tasks"];
    foreach (SPListItem i in tasks.Items)
    {
        bool bSend = false;
        string szMessage = "";

        // Get the field values that we'll need
        DateTime dtDueDate;
        try
        {
            dtDueDate = DateTime.Parse(i["Due Date"].ToString());
        }
        catch (Exception)
        {
            dtDueDate = DateTime.MinValue;
        }

        string szAssigned = "";
        string szTitle = "";
        string szDesc = "";
        string szStatus = "";

        try
        {
            szStatus = i["Status"].ToString();
            szTitle = i.Title;
            szDesc = i["Description"].ToString();
            szAssigned = i["Assigned To"].ToString();
        }
        catch (Exception)
        {
        }

        if (szStatus == "Active" || szStatus == "Not Started")
        {
            if (szAssigned == "")
            {
                bSend = true;
                szMessage = "Task is not assigned";
            }

            if (!bSend && dtDueDate == DateTime.MinValue)
            {
                bSend = true;
                szMessage = "No due date set";
            }
```

```
        if (!bSend && dtDueDate < DateTime.Now)
        {
            bSend = true;
            szMessage = "Task is overdue";
        }

        if (bSend)
        {
            try
            {
                // Create a new task
                SPListItem newTask = workflowProperties.TaskList.AddItem();

                string szName =
                    System.Threading.Thread.CurrentPrincipal.Identity.Name;
                SPUser u = web.SiteUsers[szName];

                newTask["Title"] = szMessage + " - " + szTitle;
                newTask["Created"] = DateTime.Now;
                newTask["PercentComplete"] = (float)0.0;
                newTask["AssignedTo"] = u.ID;
                newTask["DueDate"] = DateTime.Now.AddDays(1);
                newTask["Description"] = szDesc;

                // Complete the updates in the database
                newTask.Update();
            }
            catch (Exception)
            {
            }
        }
    }
  }
}
```

The first part of this code gets an `SPList` object for the `Tasks` list. It then iterates through the `SPListItems` (in the `Items` property). For each task, it gets several field values including `Due Date`, `Assigned To`, and `Status`. If the task is `Active` or `Not Started`, it checks that task for several conditions. It verifies the task has been assigned, that task has a due date, and the due date is not overdue. If any of these conditions is false, the `bSend` flag is set to true, and the `szMessage` property is set to the appropriate text.

■ **Tip** When getting or setting field values through a name indexer, spaces are ignored. So, using "Due Date" or "DueDate" is equivalent.

Finally, if `bSend` is true, a new task is created, which is assigned to the person who started the workflow. The task is added to the list defined by `workflowProperties.TaskList`. The class member

workflowProperties is an instance of the **SPWorkflowActivationProperties** class and was created for you by the workflow template. Its **TaskList** property represents the task list specified in the SharePoint Customization Wizard dialog box.

Testing the Workflow

Press F6 to build the project and fix any compiler errors. To test this workflow, you'll need to make sure there are some tasks in the **Tasks** list. Make sure there is at least one task that is not assigned, one that has no due date, and one that is overdue, so you can verify the logic for each of these conditions.

Once you have the tasks setup, close the browser. From Visual Studio, press F5, which should launch the SharePoint site. As you did earlier, from the All Site Content page, select Site Workflows. From the Site Workflows page, start the WF_Chapter09 workflow. When it has finished, go to the **Tasks** list. Figure 9-13 shows what one of the new tasks should look like.

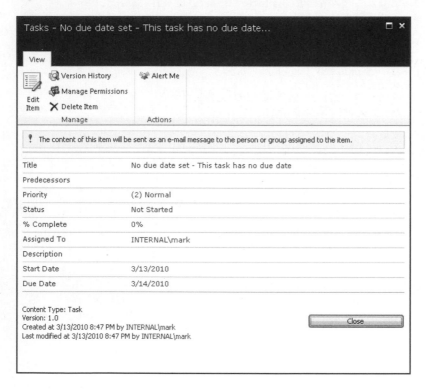

Figure 9-13. One of the new tasks created by the workflow

More About Content Types

A single list can contain items that have different content types. The `AddItem()` method creates an `SPListItem` using the default content type. In this case, the default content type is `Task`. Notice on the bottom left of the task form shown in Figure 9-13 that it has a content type of `Task`.

You can change the content type, however. Add the following code to the `checkTasks_ExecuteCode` event handler, just before the `newTask.Update()` call:

```
// Set the Content Type
SPContentType wfType = tasks.ContentTypes["Workflow Task"];
newTask["ContentTypeId"] = wfType.Id;

// Set the Workflow Name
newTask["Workflow Name"] = workflowProperties.TemplateName;
```

This code first gets the `SPContentType` object using its name, `Workflow Task`. The `ContentTypeId` of the task is then set using the `Id` of the `SPContentType` object. The `Workflow Name` property is also set using the `TemplateName` property of the `workflowProperties` object.

Press F5 to rerun the workflow. This time, the new tasks should look like the one shown in Figure 9-14.

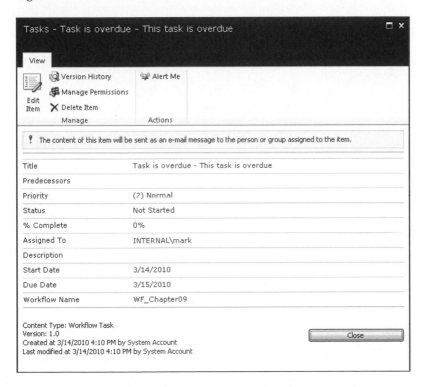

Figure 9-14. A new task using the Workflow Task content type

197

Notice that the `Workflow Name` field is now displayed, and the content type is now `Workflow Task` instead of `Task`.

Summary

With this fairly brief introduction into the SharePoint object model, you should have an idea of the power and flexibility it provides. Almost every aspect of a SharePoint solution can be accessed through this object model.

In this project, your code was executed in a workflow that was initiated by SharePoint. However, the SharePoint object model can be used by non-SharePoint application. This gives you a great deal of flexibility when integrating line-of-business (LOB) applications into SharePoint. I will demonstrate other ways to do this later in this book.

CHAPTER 10

■ ■ ■

Custom Workflow Forms

In this chapter you'll create custom forms for your workflow. First, you'll create an initiation form to allow the user to pass in data when starting a site workflow. Then, you will use a custom content type to define the data to be entered by a task. Finally, you will use InfoPath 2010 to create a custom form for displaying and updating an assigned task. The workflow that you'll implement will be used to coordinate a lunch meeting. It will create a task for each of the specified attendees, requesting them to submit their lunch order.

Creating a Sequential Workflow

Launch Visual Studio 2010, and create a new Sequential Workflow project, as shown in Figure 10-1. Enter the name **WF_Chapter10**.

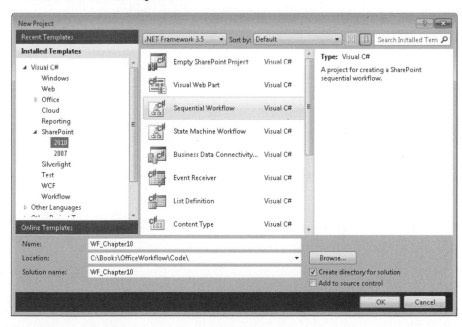

Figure 10-1. Creating a Sequential Workflow project

You can use the same Part3 SharePoint site that you used for the previous two chapters. You'll need to specify this site when the SharePoint Customization Wizard (shown in Figure 10-2) starts.

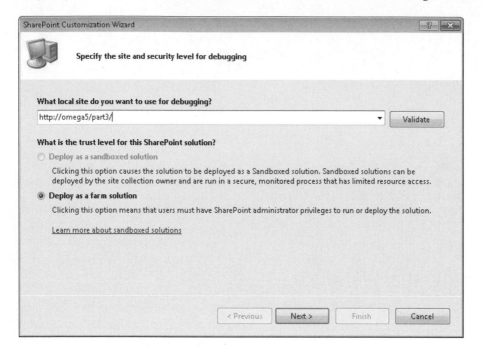

Figure 10-2. Specifying the Part3 SharePoint site

In the next dialog box, enter the workflow name **WF_Chapter10**, and choose the Site Workflow option.

Adding an Initiation Form

Association and initiation forms are used to provide configuration information to a workflow. An *association* form is used when associating a workflow to a list or library, and an *initiation* form is used when starting a workflow. Since this is a site workflow, only the initiation form can be used.

Adding an initiation or association form is pretty easy. From the Solution Explorer, right-click the Workflow1 item, and select Add ▶ New Item. Then select the Workflow Initiation Form template, as shown in Figure 10-3. Enter the name **Chapter10Initiation.aspx**.

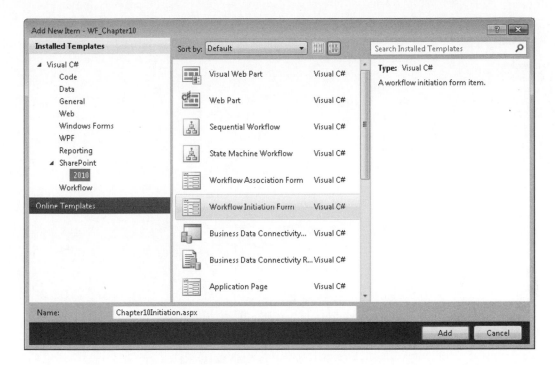

Figure 10-3. Adding an initiation form

■ **Caution** Make sure you right-click the Workflow1 element in the project, not the Chapter10 project, so that the form will be associated with this workflow.

The Solution Explorer should look like Figure 10-4.

Figure 10-4. The contents of the Solution Explorer

Notice that the `Chapter10Initiation.aspx` form is included with the `Workflow1` feature item along with the `Elements.xml` file and the workflow definition (`Workflow1.cs`). If you double-click the `Feature1` item, the contents of the feature should look like Figure 10-5.

Figure 10-5. The contents of the project feature

Customizing the Initiation Form

Open the `Chapter10Initiation.aspx` file. You will add a `TextBox` to collect three pieces of information:

- The list of people to be invited

- A description of the event

- The URL where the menu can be viewed

Listing 10-1 shows the complete implementation. The code that you'll need to add to the generated code is shown in bold.

Listing 10-1. Implementation of Chapter10Initiation.aspx

```
<%@ Assembly Name="$SharePoint.Project.AssemblyFullName$" %>
<%@ Assembly Name="Microsoft.Web.CommandUI, Version=14.0.0.0, Culture=neutral,
                   PublicKeyToken=71e9bce111e9429c" %>
<%@ Import Namespace="Microsoft.SharePoint" %>
<%@ Import Namespace="Microsoft.SharePoint.ApplicationPages" %>
<%@ Register Tagprefix="SharePoint"
             Namespace="Microsoft.SharePoint.WebControls"
             Assembly="Microsoft.SharePoint, Version=14.0.0.0, Culture=neutral,
                       PublicKeyToken=71e9bce111e9429c" %>
<%@ Register Tagprefix="Utilities"
             Namespace="Microsoft.SharePoint.Utilities"
             Assembly="Microsoft.SharePoint, Version=14.0.0.0, Culture=neutral,
                       PublicKeyToken=71e9bce111e9429c" %>
<%@ Register Tagprefix="asp"
             Namespace="System.Web.UI"
             Assembly="System.Web.Extensions, Version=3.5.0.0, Culture=neutral,
                       PublicKeyToken=31bf3856ad364e35" %>

<%@ Page Language="C#"
    DynamicMasterPageFile="~masterurl/default.master"
    AutoEventWireup="true"
    Inherits="WF_Chapter10.Workflow1.Chapter10Initiation"
    CodeBehind="Chapter10Initiation.aspx.cs" %>

<asp:Content ID="Main" ContentPlaceHolderID="PlaceHolderMain" runat="server">
    <!-- Add your custom content here -->
    <asp:Label ID="Label1" runat="server"
               Text="Invitees (separate names with a semi-colon)"></asp:Label>
    <br />
    <asp:TextBox ID="txtInvitees" Width="300px" runat="server"></asp:TextBox>
    <br />
    <asp:Label ID="Label2" runat="server" Text="Event Description"></asp:Label>
    <asp:TextBox ID="txtEventName" runat="server"></asp:TextBox>
    <br />
    <asp:Label ID="Label3" runat="server" Text="Menu URL"></asp:Label>
    <asp:TextBox ID="txtMenuUrl" runat="server"></asp:TextBox>
    <br />
```

```
    <!-- End of custom content -->
    <asp:Button ID="StartWorkflow" runat="server" OnClick="StartWorkflow_Click"
                Text="Start Workflow" />
          
    <asp:Button ID="Cancel" runat="server" OnClick="Cancel_Click" Text="Cancel" />
</asp:Content>

<asp:Content ID="PageTitle" ContentPlaceHolderID="PlaceHolderPageTitle"
            runat="server">
    Workflow Initiation Form
</asp:Content>

<asp:Content ID="PageTitleInTitleArea" runat="server"
            ContentPlaceHolderID="PlaceHolderPageTitleInTitleArea">
    Workflow Initiation Form
</asp:Content>
```

Now open the code-behind file, Chapter10Initiation.aspx.cs. You will need to implement the GetInitiationData() method. When the workflow is started, this method is called to retrieve the data from the form. The initiation data must be supplied to the workflow as a single string. The best way to accomplish this, especially with complex data elements, is to put all the data into an XML-formatted string.

Functional composition with LINQ to XML makes this a trivial task. Enter the following code for the GetInitiationData() method:

```
string[] szInvitees = txtInvitees.Text.Split(';');

XElement data = new XElement("InitiationData",
    new XElement("EventName", txtEventName.Text),
    new XElement("MenuUrl", txtMenuUrl.Text),
    new XElement("Invitees",
                from x in szInvitees
                select new XElement("Name", x)));

return data.ToString();
```

You will also need to add the following namespaces to this file so you can use the LINQ to XML classes:

```
using System.Linq;
using System.Xml.Linq;
```

■ **Tip** You can initialize the form with default values by adding code in the Page_Load() event handler.

Getting the Initiation Data in the Workflow

Open the `Workflow1.cs` file in design mode. It should have an `OnWorkflowActivated` event handler activity just like the previous projects. Double-click it to generate the event handler, and open the code-behind class. Add the following namespaces to this file:

```
using System.Collections.Generic;
using System.Xml.Linq;
```

Then add the following class members just before the `onWorkflowActivated1_Invoked()` event handler. These members will store the data that is provided by the initiation form.

```
private string _eventName;
private string _menuUrl;
private List<string> _invitees;
```

You used the `workflowProperties` member in the previous chapter to get the associated task list. This class also has an `InitiationData` property that contains the string data that is supplied by the initiation form. Add the following implementation for the `onWorkflowActivated1_Invoked()` method:

```
XElement data = XElement.Parse(workflowProperties.InitiationData);

_eventName = data.Elements().Single(x => x.Name == "EventName").Value;
_menuUrl = data.Elements().Single(x => x.Name == "MenuUrl").Value;

_invitees = new List<string>();

foreach (XElement x in data.Element("Invitees").Elements())
{
    _invitees.Add(x.Value);
}
```

This code creates an `XElement` class using the initiation data. It then extracts the data elements using LINQ queries and stores the data in the private members that you defined.

Listing 10-2 shows the complete implementation for this class.

Listing 10-2. Implementation of Workflow1.cs Class

```
using System;
using System.ComponentModel;
using System.ComponentModel.Design;
using System.Collections;
using System.Drawing;
using System.Linq;
using System.Workflow.ComponentModel.Compiler;
using System.Workflow.ComponentModel.Serialization;
using System.Workflow.ComponentModel;
using System.Workflow.ComponentModel.Design;
using System.Workflow.Runtime;
using System.Workflow.Activities;
using System.Workflow.Activities.Rules;
```

```
using Microsoft.SharePoint;
using Microsoft.SharePoint.Workflow;
using Microsoft.SharePoint.WorkflowActions;

using System.Collections.Generic;
using System.Xml.Linq;

namespace WF_Chapter10.Workflow1
{
    public sealed partial class Workflow1 : SequentialWorkflowActivity
    {
        public Workflow1()
        {
            InitializeComponent();
        }

        public Guid workflowId = default(System.Guid);
        public SPWorkflowActivationProperties workflowProperties =
            new SPWorkflowActivationProperties();

        private string _eventName;
        private string _menuUrl;
        private List<string> _invitees;

        private void onWorkflowActivated1_Invoked
            (object sender, ExternalDataEventArgs e)
        {
            XElement data = XElement.Parse(workflowProperties.InitiationData);

            _eventName = data.Elements().Single(x => x.Name == "EventName").Value;
            _menuUrl = data.Elements().Single(x => x.Name == "MenuUrl").Value;

            _invitees = new List<string>();

            foreach (XElement x in data.Element("Invitees").Elements())
            {
                _invitees.Add(x.Value);
            }
        }
    }
}
```

Implementing the Workflow

This workflow will execute the CreateTask activity that you used in previous projects. However, it will need to be executed multiple times, once for each person who is invited to the event. The ideal way to accomplish this is with the Replicator activity.

Replicator Activity

The **Replicator** activity allows you to generate multiple instances of an activity. Each instance can be configured with its own input data. In the workflow designer, drag a **Replicator** activity to the workflow, and change the name to **createTasks**. Figure 10-6 shows how the diagram should look.

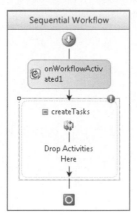

Figure 10-6. Adding a Replicator activity

You can place only a single activity onto the **Replicator** activity. However, that single activity can be a composite activity, such as a **Sequence** activity, which will allow you drag multiple activities onto it. Figure 10-7 shows the Properties window of the **Replicator** activity.

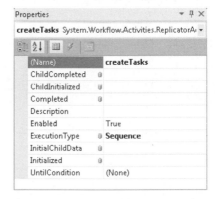

Figure 10-7. The Replicator Properties window

The **InitialChildData** property contains a collection of data structures. The collection object can be any type of collection that supports the **IList** interface. The child activities are executed for each element in this collection. Typically, the configured child activities are executed, and the **Replicator** activity completes when all of its children have completed. The **UntilCondition** property can be used to stop the execution before all the elements are processed. The child activities are executed as long as this condition resolves to false. The UntilCondition is optional and is normally not used.

As you can see from this property list, you can use a number of event handlers. ChildCompleted and ChildInitialized are raised as each child activity is started and completed, respectively. Similarly, Completed and Initialized are raised when the Replicator activity is started and completed.

The ExecutionType property indicates whether the child activities are executed one at a time (Sequence) or simultaneously (Parallel). For this project, you'll need to use the default value of Sequence.

Setting Up the Replicator Activity

Select the InitialChildData property, and click the ellipsis next to it. Go to the second tab in the dialog box, and create a new property named ChildData, as shown in Figure 10-8.

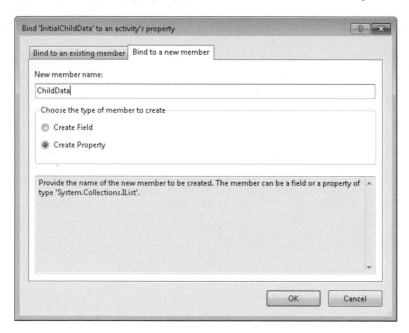

Figure 10-8. Creating the ChildData DependencyProperty

Open the Workflow1.cs code-behind file, and modify the onWorkflowActivated1 event handler, as shown in Listing 10-3. The additional code is shown in bold.

Listing 10-3. Modified Implementation of onWorkflowActivated1_Invoke()

```
private void onWorkflowActivated1_Invoked(object sender, ExternalDataEventArgs e)
{
    XElement data = XElement.Parse(workflowProperties.InitiationData);

    _eventName = data.Elements().Single(x => x.Name == "EventName").Value;
```

```
    _menuUrl = data.Elements().Single(x => x.Name == "MenuUrl").Value;

    _invitees = new List<string>();
    ChildData = new ArrayList();

    foreach (XElement x in data.Element("Invitees").Elements())
    {
        _invitees.Add(x.Value);
        ChildData.Add(x.Value);
    }
}
```

This code will create the `ChildData` collection and populate it with the people to be invited.

CreateTask Activity

Drag a **Sequence** activity onto the **Replicator** activity, and change its name to **createTask**. Then drag a **CreateTask** activity onto the **Sequence** activity, and change its name to **lunchOrder**. The workflow should look like Figure 10-9.

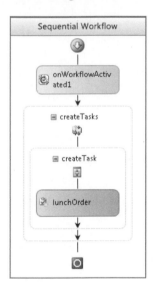

Figure 10-9. Workflow diagram with CreateTask activity

In the Properties window, select the `CorrelationToken` property, and enter **TaskToken**. Then expand this property, and select the `OwnerActivityName` as **createTask**.

■ **Caution** The OwnerActivityName property defines the scope of the correlation token. By limiting the scope to the createTask Sequence activity, you will ensure that each instance of this sequence will have its own token. If you select a different owner such as the createTasks Replicator activity or the main sequence, Workflow1, this token will be shared by all the tasks that are created. This will cause the workflow to fail after the first task is created.

Select the TaskID property, and click the ellipsis next to it. On the second tab of the dialog box that is displayed, enter the member name **TaskID**, and click OK. This will create a DependencyProperty and bind it the TaskID property. Likewise, select the TaskProperties property, and click the ellipsis. Create a new property named **TaskProperties**. The completed Properties window should look like Figure 10-10.

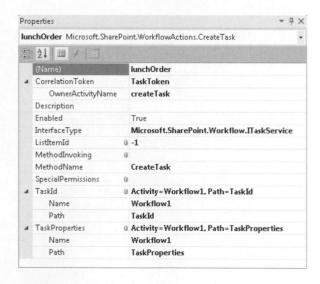

Figure 10-10. The CreateTask Properties window

Right-click the **createTasks Replicator** activity, and choose Generate Handlers, as shown in Figure 10-11.

Figure 10-11. Generating the event handlers for the `Replicator` *activity*

This will create an empty method for each of the event handlers. In the code-behind class, implement the `ChildInitiated` event using the code shown in Listing 10-4.

Listing 10-4. Implementation of the `ChildInitialized` *Event*

```
private void createTasks_ChildInitialized
    (object sender, ReplicatorChildEventArgs e)
{
    TaskId = Guid.NewGuid();

    TaskProperties = new Microsoft.SharePoint.Workflow.SPWorkflowTaskProperties();
    TaskProperties.PercentComplete = (float)0.0;
    TaskProperties.AssignedTo = e.InstanceData.ToString();
    TaskProperties.DueDate = DateTime.Now.AddDays(1);
    TaskProperties.Title = "Enter your lunch order";
    TaskProperties.Description = _eventName;
}
```

This event will be raised for each element in the `ChildData` collection. The `ReplicatorChildEventArgs` parameter contains the data element, which is obtained through the `InstanceData` property. This is copied to the `AssignedTo` property of the `SPWorkflowTaskProperties` object.

Testing the Workflow

Press F6 to build the application, and fix any errors that are reported. Then press F5, which will deploy the workflow and launch the SharePoint site. From the All Site Content page, go to the Site Workflows page, which is shown in Figure 10-12.

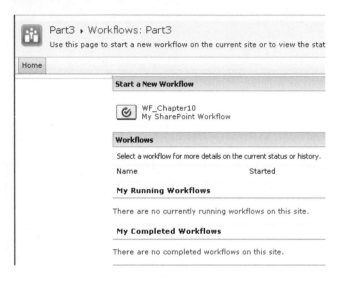

Figure 10-12. The Site Workflows page

Click the *WF_Chapter10* link, and your initiation page should be displayed. Enter several user names, an event description, and a URL, as shown in Figure 10-13.

Figure 10-13. Your initiation page

Click the Start Workflow button, which will run the workflow. The Site Workflows page will be displayed showing the completed workflow (see Figure 10-14).

Figure 10-14. The Site Workflows page showing a completed workflow

Click the completed workflow to see the workflow details. The workflow information page should show a task for each person you invited, similar to the one shown in Figure 10-15.

Figure 10-15. The workflow details showing the tasks that were created

Click one of these tasks to see the task details. You should see a form like Figure 10-16.

Figure 10-16. A sample task form

As you can see, the list of people to include and the event description were passed in to the workflow to configure the tasks that were created.

Content Types

The purpose of this workflow was to collect lunch orders from the people who are invited. So far, we have generated tasks for this, but there's no place to actually enter the orders. What we need now is a content type that is designed to hold the details of each person's preferences. If you've done much work with SharePoint, you're probably already familiar with using content types. If not, that's fine; I'll explain everything you'll need to know.

Creating a Content Type

From the Solution Explorer, right-click the WF_Chapter10 project, and choose Add ▶ New Item. In the Add New Item dialog box, select the Content Type template, as shown in Figure 10-17. Enter the name **LunchOrderTask**.

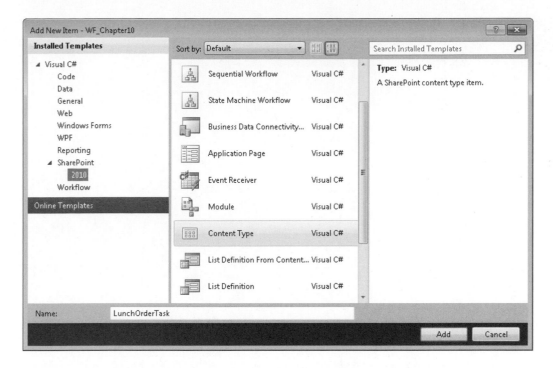

Figure 10-17. Adding a new content type

Click the Add button, and the SharePoint Configuration Wizard shown in Figure 10-18 will display, prompting you for the content type that this one should inherit from. By default, tasks created by workflows use the Workflow Task content type. You can verify this by looking at the task form in Figure 10-16. Near the bottom of the form it displays the content type that is used.

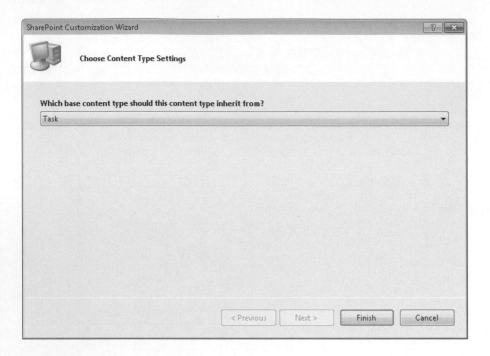

Figure 10-18. Selecting the parent content type

Your new content type should be derived from `Workflow Task`. Unfortunately, this content type is listed in a hidden group and is not available to you. Instead, choose the `Task` content type; you will fix this later. Click the Finish button.

The template created an `Elements.xml` file, as shown in Listing 10-5.

Listing 10-5. The Initial `Elements.xml` File

```
<?xml version="1.0" encoding="utf-8"?>
<Elements xmlns="http://schemas.microsoft.com/sharepoint/">
  <!-- Parent ContentType: Task (0x0108) -->
  <ContentType ID="0x0108000da2ad56f41a465bbaa3311519728c2c"
               Name="WF_Chapter10 - LunchOrderTask"
               Group="Custom Content Types"
               Description="My Content Type"
               Inherits="TRUE"
               Version="0">
    <FieldRefs>
    </FieldRefs>
  </ContentType>
</Elements>
```

Content Type Inheritance

The ID of a content type defines its inheritance tree. For example, the Item content type (of which all other content types are derived from) is 0x01. The ID of the Task content type is 0x0108. The first two digits (01) indicate that it is derived from Item. The custom content type that was just generated begins with 0x0108, indicating the parent type is Task. The remaining portion of the ID, for custom types, is a unique identifier generated by the template (yours will have a different ID from the one shown here).

The ID of the Workflow Task content type is 0x010801. As you might have deduced, it inherits from the Task type. To modify your custom content type to inherit from Workflow Task, simply insert 01 after the 0x0108 prefix. You should also modify the comment to indicate the new parent. The modified lines should look like this (the inserted text is shown in bold):

```
<!-- Parent ContentType: Workflow Task (0x010801) -->
<ContentType ID="0x010801000da2ad56f41a465bbaa3311519728c2c"
```

You can also change the Description to something more meaningful like **Lunch Order Details**.

■ **Note** The Inherits attribute is not supported; you'll need to delete this line.

Adding Field Definitions

This new content type will add some additional columns to the Workflow Task content type to store the details of the lunch order. However, before you can add them to the content type, you'll need to define the columns. SharePoint ships with quite a few columns already predefined, and you can use these by simply referencing them in your content type. However, no existing columns match the columns needed, so you'll need to create some new columns.

To define new fields (columns), add the code shown in Listing 10-6 to the Elements.xml file *before* the ContentType definition.

Listing 10-6. New Field Definitions

```
<Field
  ID="{4E4628C2-80DE-454A-ABCC-C34C8BA60CCA}"
  Type="Text"
  Name="MenuUrl"
  DisplayName="MenuUrl"
  Sealed="TRUE"
  StaticName="MenuUrl">
</Field>
<Field
  ID="{17AABD7C-AB2D-429E-8AAD-CF039E0CC0EB}"
  Type="Text"
  MaxLength="50"
  Name="Entree"
  DisplayName="Entree"
  Sealed="TRUE"
```

```
    StaticName="Entree">
</Field>
<Field
  ID="{A2997F75-A827-4346-B8FA-113A14B25DCE}"
  Type="Text"
  MaxLength="50"
  Name="Sides"
  DisplayName="Sides"
  Sealed="TRUE"
  StaticName="Sides">
</Field>
<Field
  ID="{B258A417-2F62-4D58-9286-798D340AC048}"
  Type="Note"
  Name="SpecialInstructions"
  DisplayName="SpecialInstructions"
  Sealed="TRUE"
  StaticName="SpecialInstructions">
</Field>
<Field
  ID="{44E3D93E-5743-4471-AE45-3D58217AEFD1}"
  Type="Boolean"
  Name="NoThanks"
  DisplayName="NoThanks"
  Sealed="TRUE"
  StaticName="NoThanks">
</Field>
```

The new fields are as follows:

- **MenuUrl**: The URL where the menu can be viewed

- **Entree**: The main entree selected

- **Sides**: The selected side dishes

- **SpecialInstructions**: Any special instructions that may be needed

- **NoThanks**: A Boolean value used to indicate that no lunch is requested

Adding the Field References

Now you'll need to include these new fields in the content type. To do that, include the **FieldRef** entries shown in Listing 10-7 to the **Elements.xml** file. (These must be inside the **ContentType** definition.)

Listing 10-7. The FieldRef Definitions

```
<FieldRefs>
  <FieldRef
    ID="{4E4628C2-80DE-454A-ABCC-C34C8BA60CCA}"
    Name="MenuUrl"
```

```
      Required="FALSE"
      ShowInNewForm="FALSE"
      ShowInDisplayForm="TRUE"
      ShowInEditForm="TRUE"/>
   <FieldRef
      ID="{17AABD7C-AB2D-429E-8AAD-CF039E0CC0EB}"
      Name="Entree"
      Required="FALSE"
      ShowInNewForm="FALSE"
      ShowInDisplayForm="TRUE"
      ShowInEditForm="TRUE"/>
   <FieldRef
      ID="{A2997F75-A827-4346-B8FA-113A14B25DCE}"
      Name="Sides"
      Required="FALSE"
      ShowInNewForm="FALSE"
      ShowInDisplayForm="TRUE"
      ShowInEditForm="TRUE"/>
   <FieldRef
      ID="{B258A417-2F62-4D58-9286-798D340AC048}"
      Name="SpecialInstructions"
      Required="FALSE"
      ShowInNewForm="FALSE"
      ShowInDisplayForm="TRUE"
      ShowInEditForm="TRUE"
      NumLines="2"/>
   <FieldRef
      ID="{44E3D93E-5743-4471-AE45-3D58217AEFD1}"
      Name="NoThanks"
      Required="FALSE"
      ShowInNewForm="FALSE"
      ShowInDisplayForm="TRUE"
      ShowInEditForm="TRUE"
      DefaultValue="FALSE"/>
</FieldRefs>
```

■ **Note** You can change the Guid used here and generate your own if you want. Just be sure that the same Guid used for the Field definition is also used in the associated FieldRef definition.

Notice that the Field definitions focus primarily on storage requirements such as data type and maximum length. The FieldRef definitions, on the other hand, focus more on display requirements such as if it is required and which forms should display it. This illustrates the hierarchical nature of SharePoint objects. To maximize reuse, only the minimum necessary details are provided at one level, deferring other details to subsequent layers. Fields can be reused in other lists and content types, allowing each to define its specific usage requirements.

Listing 10-8 shows the final implementation of Elements.xml.

Listing 10-8. Implementation of Elements.xml

```xml
<?xml version="1.0" encoding="utf-8"?>
<Elements xmlns="http://schemas.microsoft.com/sharepoint/">

  <!-- Define the new fields that are needed -->
  <Field
   ID="{4E4628C2-80DE-454A-ABCC-C34C8BA60CCA}"
   Type="Text"
   Name="MenuUrl"
   DisplayName="MenuUrl"
   Sealed="TRUE"
   StaticName="MenuUrl">
  </Field>
  <Field
    ID="{17AABD7C-AB2D-429E-8AAD-CF039E0CC0EB}"
    Type="Text"
    MaxLength="50"
    Name="Entree"
    DisplayName="Entree"
    Sealed="TRUE"
    StaticName="Entree">
  </Field>
  <Field
    ID="{A2997F75-A827-4346-B8FA-113A14B25DCE}"
    Type="Text"
    MaxLength="50"
    Name="Sides"
    DisplayName="Sides"
    Sealed="TRUE"
    StaticName="Sides">
  </Field>
  <Field
    ID="{B258A417-2F62-4D58-9286-798D340AC048}"
    Type="Note"
    Name="SpecialInstructions"
    DisplayName="SpecialInstructions"
    Sealed="TRUE"
    StaticName="SpecialInstructions">
  </Field>
  <Field
    ID="{44E3D93E-5743-4471-AE45-3D58217AEFD1}"
    Type="Boolean"
    Name="NoThanks"
    DisplayName="NoThanks"
    Sealed="TRUE"
    StaticName="NoThanks">
  </Field>

  <!-- Parent ContentType: Workflow Task (0x010801) -->
  <ContentType ID="0x010801000da2ad56f41a465bbaa3311519728c2c"
```

```
                Name="WF_Chapter10 - LunchOrderTask"
                Group="Custom Content Types"
                Description="Lunch Order Details"
                Version="0">

    <!-- Include the new fields in this content type -->
    <FieldRefs>
      <FieldRef
        ID="{4E4628C2-80DE-454A-ABCC-C34C8BA60CCA}"
        Name="MenuUrl"
        Required="FALSE"
        ShowInNewForm="FALSE"
        ShowInDisplayForm="TRUE"
        ShowInEditForm="TRUE"/>
      <FieldRef
        ID="{17AABD7C-AB2D-429E-8AAD-CF039E0CC0EB}"
        Name="Entree"
        Required="FALSE"
        ShowInNewForm="FALSE"
        ShowInDisplayForm="TRUE"
        ShowInEditForm="TRUE"/>
      <FieldRef
        ID="{A2997F75-A827-4346-B8FA-113A14B25DCE}"
        Name="Sides"
        Required="FALSE"
        ShowInNewForm="FALSE"
        ShowInDisplayForm="TRUE"
        ShowInEditForm="TRUE"/>
      <FieldRef
        ID="{B258A417-2F62-4D58-9286-798D340AC048}"
        Name="SpecialInstructions"
        Required="FALSE"
        ShowInNewForm="FALSE"
        ShowInDisplayForm="TRUE"
        ShowInEditForm="TRUE"
        NumLines="2"/>
      <FieldRef
        ID="{44E3D93E-5743-4471-AE45-3D58217AEFD1}"
        Name="NoThanks"
        Required="FALSE"
        ShowInNewForm="FALSE"
        ShowInDisplayForm="TRUE"
        ShowInEditForm="TRUE"
        DefaultValue="FALSE"/>
    </FieldRefs>
  </ContentType>
</Elements>
```

If you look at the Feature1 definition, shown in Figure 10-19, you'll see that in addition to the workflow, there is now a Content Type that will be deployed with this feature.

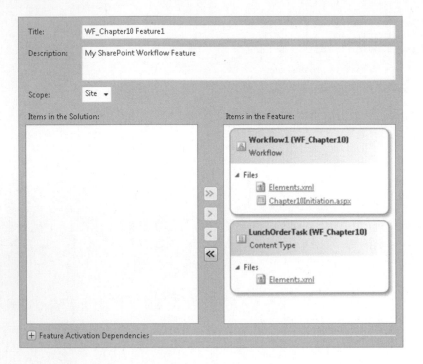

Figure 10-19. *Feature including a workflow and a content type*

Using the New Content Type

The next step is to modify the workflow to use the new content type. This can be done fairly easily by replacing the `CreateTask` activity with the `CreateTaskWithContentType` activity. This works just like the `CreateTask` activity except that it allows you to specify the content type to use.

Open the `Workflow1.cs` file in the workflow designer. Delete the `lunchOrder` task, and in its place drag a `CreateTaskWithContentType` activity. Change the name to **lunchOrder**. For the `CorrelationToken` property, enter **TaskToken**, expand the property, and select `createTask` for the `OwnerActivityName`. For the `TaskId` property, click the ellipsis, and select the existing `TaskId` property. Likewise, click the ellipsis next to the `TaskProperties` property, and select the existing `TaskProperties` property.

Select the `ContentTypeID` property, and click the ellipsis next to this property. On the second tab, create a new property named `ContentTypeId`, as shown in Figure 10-20.

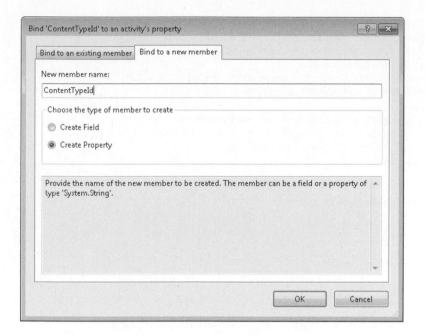

Figure 10-20. Adding a ContentTypeId *property*

Open the Workflow1.cs code-behind file, and modify the OnWorkflowActivated event handler as shown in Listing 10-9 (the additional lines are shown in bold).

Listing 10-9. Modified Implementation of the OnWorkflowActivated *Event Handler*

```
private void onWorkflowActivated1_Invoked(object sender, ExternalDataEventArgs e)
{
    XElement data = XElement.Parse(workflowProperties.InitiationData);

    _eventName = data.Elements().Single(x => x.Name == "EventName").Value;
    _menuUrl = data.Elements().Single(x => x.Name == "MenuUrl").Value;

    _invitees = new List<string>();
    ChildData = new ArrayList();

    foreach (XElement x in data.Element("Invitees").Elements())
    {
        _invitees.Add(x.Value);
        ChildData.Add(x.Value);
    }

    // Get the content type ID
    try
    {
```

```
            SPContentTypeId contentTypeId =
                new SPContentTypeId("0x010801000da2ad56f41a465bbaa3311519728c2c");
            workflowProperties.TaskList.ContentTypesEnabled = true;
            SPContentTypeId matchContentTypeId =
                workflowProperties.TaskList.ContentTypes.BestMatch(contentTypeId);
            if (matchContentTypeId.Parent.CompareTo(contentTypeId) != 0)
            {
                SPContentType ct = workflowProperties.TaskList.ParentWeb
                    .AvailableContentTypes[contentTypeId];
                workflowProperties.TaskList.ContentTypes.Add(ct);
                workflowProperties.TaskList.Update();
            }

            ContentTypeId = contentTypeId.ToString();
        }
        catch (Exception)
        {
        }
}
```

■ **Caution** The ID passed to the SPContentTypeId constructor should be the same value used in your Elements.xml file, which will be different from the value shown here.

This code ensures that the associated task list allows this content type. If it doesn't, this content type is added to the task list using the ContentTypes.Add() method. Finally, the ContentTypeID property is set with the value of the new content type's ID so the CreateTaskWithContentType activity can access it.

There's one more minor change that you'll need to make. When creating the task, you should populate the MenuUrl column with the value specified in the initiation form. You couldn't do this before because there was no field available to store it. However, the new content type defines a column for this. Modify the createTasks_ChildInitialized() event handler, and add the code shown here in bold:

```
private void createTasks_ChildInitialized
    (object sender, ReplicatorChildEventArgs e)
{
    TaskId = Guid.NewGuid();

    TaskProperties = new Microsoft.SharePoint.Workflow.SPWorkflowTaskProperties();
    TaskProperties.PercentComplete = (float)0.0;
    TaskProperties.AssignedTo = e.InstanceData.ToString();
    TaskProperties.DueDate = DateTime.Now.AddDays(1);
    TaskProperties.Title = "Enter your lunch order";
    TaskProperties.Description = _eventName;
    TaskProperties.ExtendedProperties["MenuUrl"] = _menuUrl;
}
```

The `SPWorkflowTaskProperties` class knows only about the columns provided by the `Workflow Task` content type. It doesn't have a `MenuUrl` property that you can set directly. Instead, you'll need to store it in the `ExtendedProperties` collection.

Testing the Workflow

Press F6 to build the application, and fix any build errors. Then right-click the WF_Chapter10 project, and choose Deploy. This will deploy this feature to the SharePoint site. Open the SharePoint site, and start the WF_Chapter10 workflow just like you did before.

■ **Tip** You may get an error the first time you run the workflow because the new content type is not added to the list until the workflow has executed. Subsequent instances should work correctly once this has been added.

Open one of tasks that was generated; it should be similar to Figure 10-21.

Figure 10-21. Sample task form showing custom columns

Notice that the new columns are included on the task form, including the MenuUrl supplied in the initiation form, and there are places to enter the lunch selection. Also, notice that the content type is now showing the new WF_Chapter10 - LunchOrderTask content type.

■ **Note** You may have some tasks in the task list from the previous chapter. If not, manually add a task to the list. Notice that when you display this task, it does not include the new columns. The task list can contain items with different content types, and the display and edit forms will include different columns depending on the content type of the item.

Creating Custom Task Forms with InfoPath 2010

You now have the new fields available so the lunch order can be entered. However, you don't really want all the other columns displayed. For example, you don't want the user to reassign the task or change the due date. Also, they shouldn't have to mark the task complete. Ideally, they should use a form that allows them to just enter their lunch order.

Connecting to SharePoint

To accomplish that, you'll use InfoPath 2010 to create a custom form specifically for the new content type. Start the InfoPath 2010 application. Select File ▶ New, and then select the SharePoint List template. Click the Design this Form button, as shown in Figure 10-22.

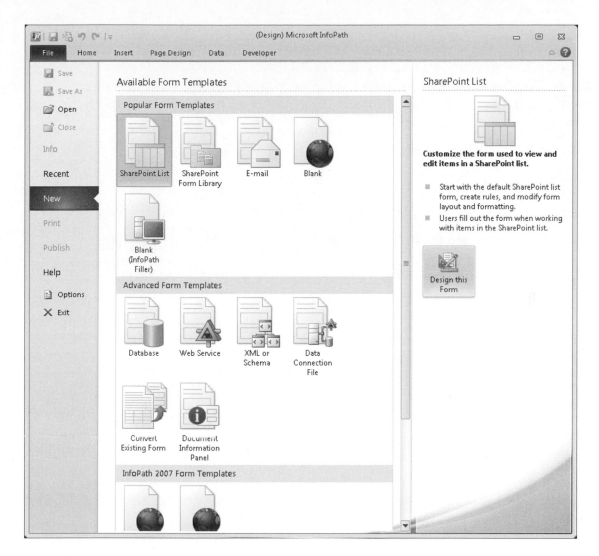

Figure 10-22. Creating an InfoPath template

■ **Tip** If you get an error message indicating that the Microsoft Office Forms Services 2010 is not available, you will need to activate this feature in the SharePoint server. Unfortunately, it is not listed as a configurable feature in SharePoint's Central Administration tool. Instead, you'll need to use the PowerShell utility. From the Windows Start menu, select the Microsoft SharePoint 2010 Products folder, and then run the SharePoint 2010 Management Shell application.

Then execute the following commands:

Install-SPFeature -path "IPFSSiteFeatures" - force

Install-SPFeature -path "IPFSWebFeatures" - force

Enable-SPFeature -Identity c88c4ff1-dbf5-4649-ad9f-c6c426ebcbf5 -URL <your site's URL> - force

Executing these commands will activate the InfoPath Forms Services and should resolve this error.

This will display the Data Connection Wizard shown in Figure 10-23.

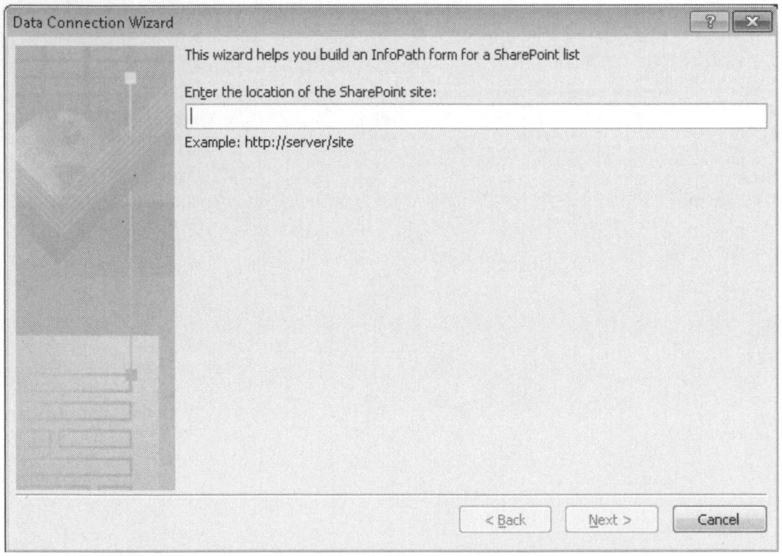

Figure 10-23. *The Data Connection Wizard*

Enter the URL for your site, such as **http://omega5/part3**, and click the Next button. In the next dialog box, choose the option to customize an existing list, and select the **Tasks** list, as shown in Figure 10-24.

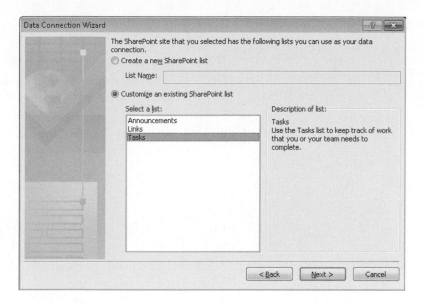

Figure 10-24. Selecting the existing Tasks list

The next dialog box, shown in Figure 10-25, lists the content types that are supported by the Tasks list. Select the custom LunchOrderTask content type, and click the Next button.

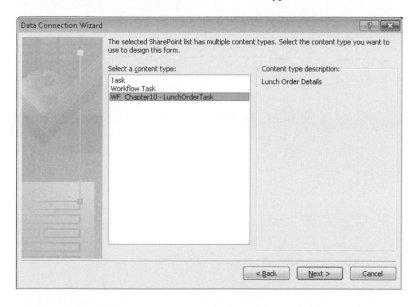

Figure 10-25. Selecting the LunchOrderTask content type

For the final dialog box, leave the default options as shown in Figure 10-26.

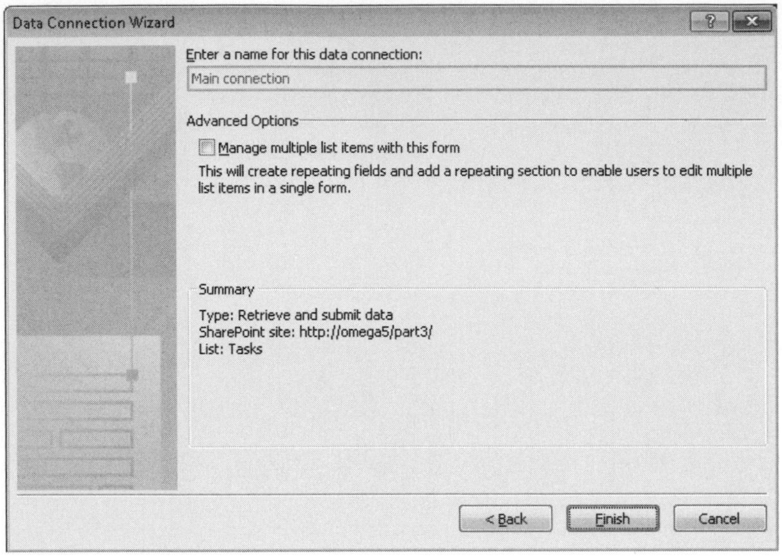

Figure 10-26. Using the default options for the final dialog box

Modifying the Form Layout

The InfoPath designer will then display the existing form that was retrieved from the SharePoint site, which should be similar to the one shown in Figure 10-27.

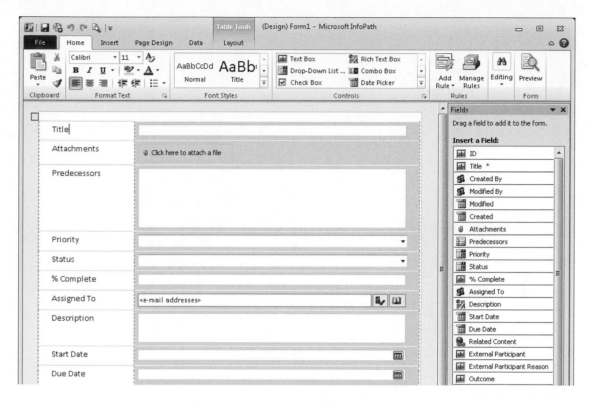

Figure 10-27. *The initial InfoPath form*

The list of fields in the Field Navigation window was obtained from the content type definition. The current form is roughly based on how the standard form is formatted. You'll need to delete most of the rows on this form. To delete a row, right-click the row label, and choose Delete ▶ Rows in the context menu, as shown in Figure 10-28.

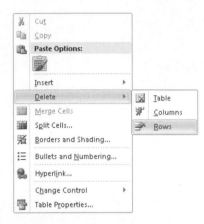

Figure 10-28. Deleting rows from the form

Delete all the rows except the **Description** field and the new fields (starting with **MenuUrl**). Change the label for **MenuUrl** to **For menu choices:**, and insert a space in the labels for the **SpecialInstructions** and **NoThanks** fields. To the right of the **NoThanks** check box, add (**I'll bring my own**). The form should look like Figure 10-29.

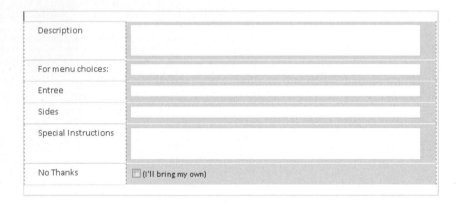

Figure 10-29. Updated form definition

Select the Control Tools ribbon. Click the **Description** field, and select the Read-Only check box, as shown in Figure 10-30.

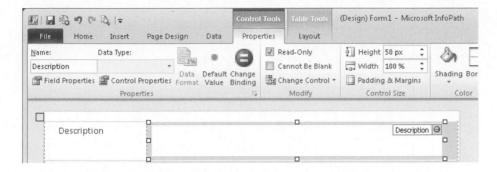

Figure 10-30. Using the Control Tools ribbon to make the description read-only

Select the `MenuUrl` field, and make it read-only as well. The user should not be able to modify these fields.

Defining Rules

InfoPath allows you to define rules for validating input and updating fields. You'll use that feature to automatically update the task status when the user has submitted their lunch order. Select the Data ribbon, and click the Submit Options button, which will display the Submit Options dialog box shown in Figure 10-31.

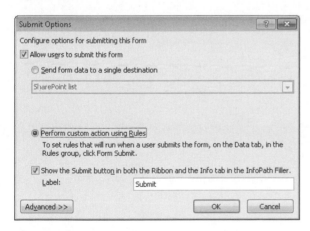

Figure 10-31. The Submit Options dialog box

The default option is to write the changes directly to the list item. Instead, select the `Perform custom action using Rules` option, as shown in Figure 10-31, and click the OK button. The Rules window will then be displayed with a default Rule 1. Click the condition, which will display the Condition editor. In the first drop-down list, choose `Select a field or group`, which will then display the list of available fields. Complete the Condition editor, as shown in Figure 10-32.

Figure 10-32. Defining the rule condition

This condition will be true if they have entered an entree *or* selected the `NoThanks` check box. Click the Add button to select the action that should be taken when this condition is true. Figure 10-33 shows the possible actions.

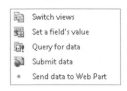

Figure 10-33. Allowable actions

Select `Set a field's value`. In the Rule Details dialog box, click the button next to the `Field` property, which will provide the list of available fields. Select the `Status` field. Then enter the value **Completed**. The dialog box should look like the one shown in Figure 10-34.

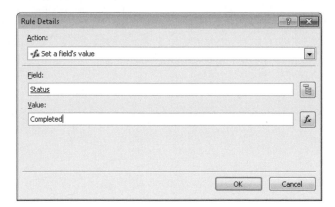

Figure 10-34. The completed Rule Details dialog box

In the same way, add another action to set the `% Complete` field to 1. Select the `Submit using a data connection` action, and in the drop-down list beside it, select `Move Down`, as shown in Figure 10-35.

Figure 10-35. Moving the first action down in the list

Do this twice to make this the last action. The completed rule should look like Figure 10-36.

Figure 10-36. The completed rule definition

Publishing the Form

Because you started with an existing list form, InfoPath knows exactly where to publish the new form. From the File menu, click the Quick Publish button, as shown in Figure 10-37.

Figure 10-37. Using the Quick Publish feature

When the form has been published, you'll see a confirmation dialog box shown in Figure 10-38.

Figure 10-38. Publish confirmation dialog box

Testing the Custom Form

Open the SharePoint site, and select one of the generated tasks. It should now display using the custom form, as shown in Figure 10-39.

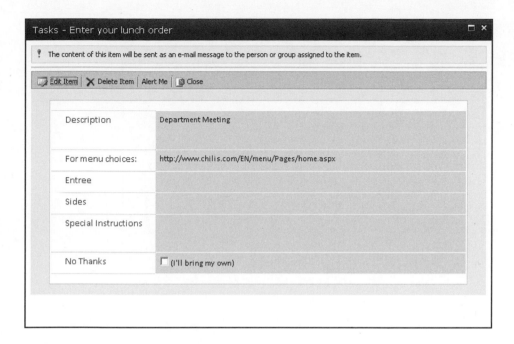

Figure 10-39. The custom display form

If you click the Edit Item button, the edit form should be displayed, as shown in Figure 10-40.

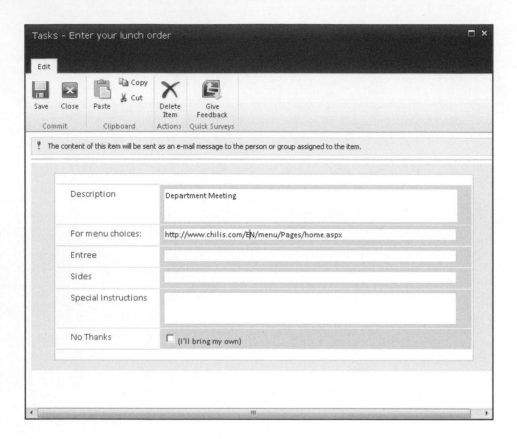

Figure 10-40. *The custom edit form*

Enter your lunch order, and click the Save button. The dialog box will close, and the task should be marked as complete.

Try displaying a task that is not one of the generated lunch order tasks. It should use the standard form rather than the custom InfoPath form.

Summary

In this chapter you created a workflow initiation form using Visual Studio. The data from the form was passed into the workflow using an XML-formatted string. To create multiple identical tasks, you used the `Replicator` workflow activity.

To provide columns for entering a lunch order, you created a custom content type using an `Element.xml` file and deployed it to SharePoint as part of the Visual Studio feature. You used the `CreateTaskWithContentType` activity to create the tasks using this custom content type.

Finally, you used InfoPath 2010 to create a custom form specifically for this content type. You added a rule to automatically complete the task when a lunch order was submitted. You used the Quick Publish feature publish the new form to the SharePoint server.

Using a combination of tools including Visual Studio 2010, Windows Workflow, and InfoPath 2010, you created a custom SharePoint application with a rich user interface.

CHAPTER 11

■ ■ ■

Handling Events

In the previous chapter you created a site workflow that generated tasks for a list of people requesting them to submit their orders for lunch. In this chapter, you will add logic to wait for each of these tasks to be completed and then create a final task once the orders have been submitted. Instead of creating a site workflow, however, you'll create a list workflow and associate it to the Calendar list. After a lunch event has been added to the calendar, you can initiate the workflow to gather the lunch orders.

Modifying the Calendar List

In the previous chapter, you used an initiation form to pass in the information needed by the workflow such as the list of people who were invited, the URL of the menu, and so on. In this implementation, this information will be stored in the Event item. The person organizing the event will enter this information when adding the item to the Calendar list. When the workflow is initiated, this data will be obtained from the event item that the workflow instance is associated with.

Adding the MenuUrl Column

Open the SharePoint Designer, and navigate to the Part3 site. You should already have the custom columns and content type that you created in Chapter 10.

■ **Tip** When debugging workflows with Visual Studio, when the debugging session ends, the feature is retracted from the SharePoint site. So, it's possible that the feature, which includes the custom columns and content type, has been removed. If this is the case, you'll need to open the WF_Chapter10 project in Visual Studio. From the Solution Explorer, right-click the project, and choose the Deploy command. This will deploy the feature to the SharePoint site. You can close the WF_Chapter10 Visual Studio project once the feature is deployed.

In the Navigation window, click the *List and Libraries* link, and then select the Calendar list. In the Customization section, click the *Edit list columns* link. The list of existing columns will be displayed; the columns should be similar to those shown in Figure 11-1.

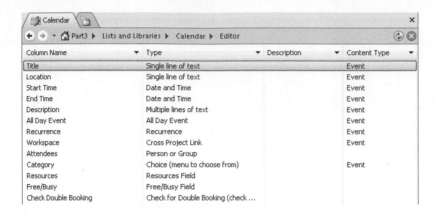

Figure 11-1. Existing Calendar columns

Click the Add Existing Site Column button. In the Site Columns Picker dialog box, select the `MenuUrl` column, which should be in the Custom Columns group. (This was one of the new columns deployed by the Chapter 10 feature.) Save the changes, and close the SharePoint Designer.

Adding the Attendees Column

Next, you'll need a column to store the list of people who are invited. In the initiation form for the previous chapter, this was implemented as a text field with the names separated by semicolons. In this chapter, you'll use the people picker control to provide a better user experience.

The `Event` content type includes a column called `Attendees`, but this column is not currently displayed on the form. Launch SharePoint, and open the Part3 site. Click the *Calendar* link in the navigation window. In the Calendar Tools ribbon, click the List Settings button, as shown in Figure 11-2.

Figure 11-2. Modifying the list settings

On the List Settings page, scroll down to the Content Type section. This shows that the `Event` content type is associated to this list (see Figure 11-3).

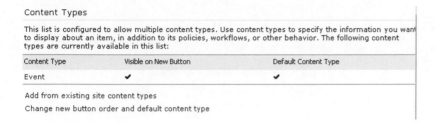

Content Types

This list is configured to allow multiple content types. Use content types to specify the information you want to display about an item, in addition to its policies, workflows, or other behavior. The following content types are currently available in this list:

Content Type	Visible on New Button	Default Content Type
Event	✔	✔

Add from existing site content types

Change new button order and default content type

Figure 11-3. Modifying the Event content type

Click the *Event* link, which will display the details of thc **Event** content type. The list of existing columns should look like the one shown in Figure 11-4.

Columns

Name	Type	Status	Source
Title	Single line of text	Required	Item
Location	Single line of text	Optional	Event
Start Time	Date and Time	Required	Event
End Time	Date and Time	Required	Event
Description	Multiple lines of text	Optional	Event
Category	Choice	Optional	Event
All Day Event	All Day Event	Optional	Event
Recurrence	Recurrence	Optional	Event
Workspace	Cross Project Link	Optional	Event
MenuUrl	Single line of text	Optional	

▪ Add from existing site or list columns

▪ Column order

Figure 11-4. The existing Calendar columns

Click the *Add from existing site or list columns* link, which will display the page shown in Figure 11-5.

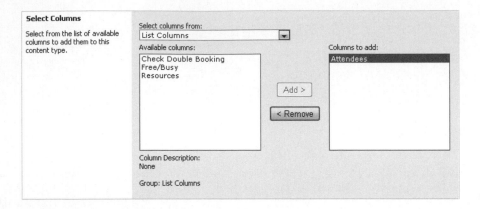

Figure 11-5. *Adding the* `Attendees` *column*

Select the `Attendees` column, and click the Add button. After you click the OK button, the list of columns will be updated showing the two new columns: `MenuUrl` and `Attendees`.

Creating a New Event

From the Navigation pane, click the *Calendar* link to display the site calendar. Hover the mouse over one of the days in the calendar, and an *Add* link should appear. Click it to create a new event for that day. Fill in the information for the event. The completed form should be similar to the one shown in Figure 11-6.

Figure 11-6. *Adding a lunch event to the calendar*

Notice that the two additional columns are included in the New Item form. You can put anything you want in the `MenuUrl` field. For the `Attendees` field, enter one or more users. You can use the people picker control to find a user or enter the user names and then click the Check Names button to verify that the names are valid. After you save the form, you should see an entry on the calendar like the one shown in Figure 11-7.

Figure 11-7. The calendar showing the new event

Designing the Workflow

Now you're ready to design a list workflow that will process the lunch orders. As I mentioned earlier, this workflow will not only create the tasks for submitting lunch orders but will also wait for each of them to complete and then create a final task.

Creating the Workflow Project

Start Visual Studio 2010, and create a new project named **WF_Chapter11** using the Sequential Workflow template, as shown in Figure 11-8.

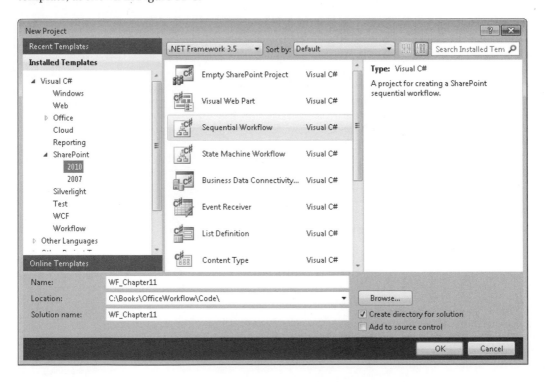

Figure 11-8. Creating a new Sequential Workflow project

The SharePoint Customization Wizard will then display a series of dialog boxes. In the first dialog box, specify the same Part3 site that you used in the previous chapter, as shown in Figure 11-9.

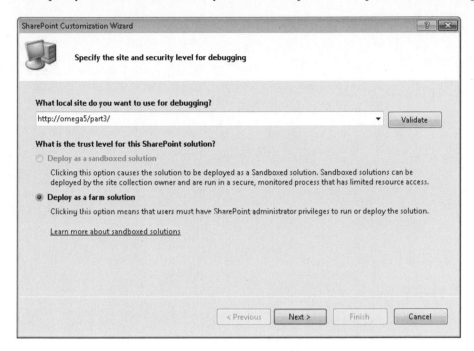

Figure 11-9. Selecting the SharePoint site to use for debugging

In the next dialog box, enter the name of the workflow as **WF_Chapter11**, and make sure the List Workflow radio button is selected, as shown in Figure 11-10.

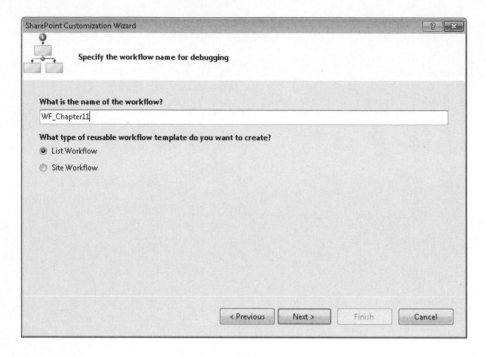

Figure 11-10. Specifying the workflow name and type

Since you selected to create a list workflow, you can then select what list the workflow should be associated with. In the next dialog box, select the `Calendar` list. You can use the default selections for the history and tasks list (see Figure 11-11).

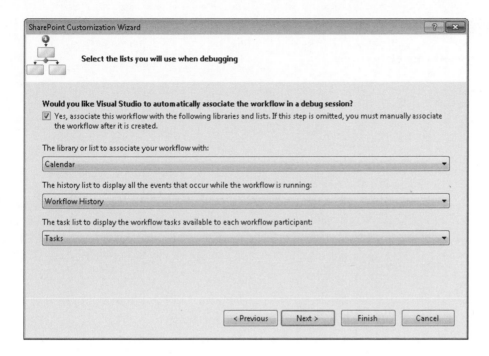

Figure 11-11. Associating the workflow with the `Calendar` *list*

In the final dialog box, deselect all the start options except for manual start, as shown in Figure 11-12.

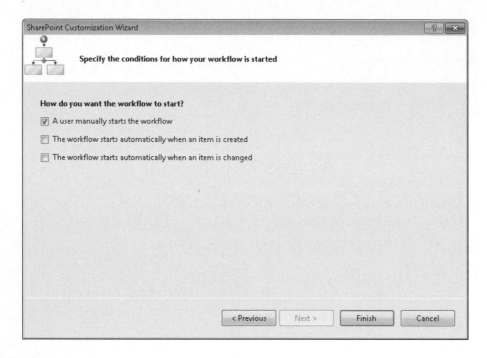

Figure 11-12. Deselecting all start options except manual

Managing the Tasks

In this project, you will need to keep track of the tasks that have been created and know when each has been completed. The easiest way to do that is to define a class that will store information about the task. Then define a collection of these classes, one for each task.

Open the code-behind class, `Workflow1.cs`, and add the following namespaces (you will need these later):

```
using System.Collections.Generic;
using System.Threading;
```

Then add the class definition shown in Listing 11-1 before the `Workflow1` class definition but inside the `Chapter11.Workflow` namespace.

Listing 11-1. Invitee Class Definition

```
[Serializable]
public class Invitee
{
    public string AssignedTo { get; set; }
    public Guid TaskId { get; set; }
    public bool Complete { get; set; }
```

```
    public Invitee(string assignedTo)
    {
        AssignedTo = assignedTo;
        Complete = false;
    }
}
```

This class defines three members:

- `AssignedTo`: The person the task is being assigned to, specified by the `Event` item
- `TaskId`: The ID of the task, which is generated at the time the task is created
- `Complete`: A flag indicating if the task has finished

The class also provides a constructor that initializes the `Complete` flag and allows you to set the `AssignedTo` member.

The `Serializable` attribute is very important. It could take hours, perhaps days, for all the tasks to complete. To save on system resources, once the workflow is idle (waiting on user input), the workflow engine will automatically persist the current state of the workflow to a database. When the user has updated a task, the workflow engine will load the workflow from the database and resume processing. This is all transparent to you. However, in order for the workflow engine to persist the class members, it must be able to serialize them.

Getting the Workflow Parameters

As I mentioned earlier, instead of using an initiation form, the parameters needed by the workflow will come from the list item that the workflow was started on. You can obtain this item through the `SPWorkflowActivationProperties` class. You used this in Chapter 9 to get access to the current SharePoint site. It also provides an `Item` property that specifies the current list item.

The initial workflow should have an `OnWorkflowActivated` activity. Double-click this to generate the handler for this event. The code-behind file that is generated for you provides the `SPWorkflowActivationProperties` class for you in a class member called `workflowProperties`. In the `Workflow1.cs` file, add the following class members to store the parameters you'll obtain from the event:

```
private string _eventName;
private string _menuUrl;
public List<Invitee> ChildData = new List<Invitee>();
private int _task = 0;
```

The `ChildData` member is a collection of the `Invitee` class that you just defined, each one representing a person who is invited to the event. It is declared `public` because it will be accessed by the `ReplicatorActivity` later. The `_task` member will be used later to determine the next `Invitee` object. Also add the following members that you'll need to define the custom content type (your content `typeID` may be different from the one listed here):

```
public SPContentTypeId contentTypeId =
    new SPContentTypeId("0x01080100211c4a0fc8144c7eb270141b81e38a8a");
public string contentTypeIdString = "";
```

Finally, in the event handler, add the following code:

```
SPListItem item = workflowProperties.Item;
_eventName = item.Title;
_menuUrl = item["MenuUrl"].ToString();

List<SPFieldUserValue> l = (List<SPFieldUserValue>)item["Attendees"];
foreach (SPFieldUserValue u in l)
{
    ChildData.Add(new Invitee(u.User.LoginName));
}
```

As you can see, the Item property of workflowProperties contains the SPListItem object that corresponds to the event item that the workflow is executing for. The Title property can be obtained directly and stored in the _eventName member. The other columns, MenuUrl and Attendees, must be accessed from the field collection using the column name. You can refer to Chapter 9 for a review of how field values are obtained from a list item.

The Attendees column allows for multiple people and is therefore implemented as a collection of SPFieldUserValue objects. This code obtains that collection and iterates the collection, storing the LoginName property in the ChildData collection using the Invitee class.

In addition, add the code shown in Listing 11-2 to the event handler to set up the custom content type (the code is identical to the code you wrote in the previous chapter).

Listing 11-2. Setting Up the Custom Content Type

```
try
{
    workflowProperties.TaskList.ContentTypesEnabled = true;
    SPContentTypeId matchContentTypeId = workflowProperties.TaskList
        .ContentTypes.BestMatch(contentTypeId);
    if (matchContentTypeId.Parent.CompareTo(contentTypeId) != 0)
    {
        SPContentType ct = workflowProperties.TaskList.ParentWeb
            .AvailableContentTypes[contentTypeId];
        workflowProperties.TaskList.ContentTypes.Add(ct);
        workflowProperties.TaskList.Update();
    }

    contentTypeIdString = contentTypeId.ToString();
}
catch (Exception)
{
}
```

Listing 11-3 shows the complete implementation of Workflow1.cs. The code you added manually is shown in bold.

Listing 11-3. Initial Implementation of Workflow1.cs

```csharp
using System;
using System.ComponentModel;
using System.ComponentModel.Design;
using System.Collections;
using System.Drawing;
using System.Linq;
using System.Workflow.ComponentModel.Compiler;
using System.Workflow.ComponentModel.Serialization;
using System.Workflow.ComponentModel;
using System.Workflow.ComponentModel.Design;
using System.Workflow.Runtime;
using System.Workflow.Activities;
using System.Workflow.Activities.Rules;
using Microsoft.SharePoint;
using Microsoft.SharePoint.Workflow;
using Microsoft.SharePoint.WorkflowActions;

using System.Collections.Generic;
using System.Threading;

namespace WF_Chapter11.Workflow1
{
    [Serializable]
    public class Invitee
    {
        public string AssignedTo { get; set; }
        public Guid TaskId { get; set; }
        public bool Complete { get; set; }

        public Invitee(string assignedTo)
        {
            AssignedTo = assignedTo;
            Complete = false;
        }
    }

    public sealed partial class Workflow1 : SequentialWorkflowActivity
    {
        public Workflow1()
        {
            InitializeComponent();
        }

        public Guid workflowId = default(System.Guid);
        public SPWorkflowActivationProperties workflowProperties =
            new SPWorkflowActivationProperties();

        public SPContentTypeId contentTypeId =
```

```
        new SPContentTypeId("0x01080100211c4a0fc8144c7eb270141b81e38a8a");
    public string contentTypeIdString = "";

    private string _eventName;
    private string _menuUrl;
    public List<Invitee> ChildData = new List<Invitee>();
    private int _task = 0;

    private void onWorkflowActivated1_Invoked(object sender,
        ExternalDataEventArgs e)
    {
        SPListItem item = workflowProperties.Item;
        _eventName = item.Title;
        _menuUrl = item["MenuUrl"].ToString();

        List<SPFieldUserValue> l = (List<SPFieldUserValue>)item["Attendees"];
        foreach (SPFieldUserValue u in l)
        {
            ChildData.Add(new Invitee(u.User.LoginName));
        }

        try
        {
            workflowProperties.TaskList.ContentTypesEnabled = true;
            SPContentTypeId matchContentTypeId = workflowProperties.TaskList
                .ContentTypes.BestMatch(contentTypeId);
            if (matchContentTypeId.Parent.CompareTo(contentTypeId) != 0)
            {
                SPContentType ct = workflowProperties.TaskList.ParentWeb
                    .AvailableContentTypes[contentTypeId];
                workflowProperties.TaskList.ContentTypes.Add(ct);
                workflowProperties.TaskList.Update();
            }

            contentTypeIdString = contentTypeId.ToString();
        }
        catch (Exception)
        {
        }
    }
}
}
```

Using the Replicator Activity

■ **Note** I'd like to apologize right up front. In the previous chapter, I showed you how to use the ReplicatorActivity to create multiple tasks. However, I made some shortcuts and didn't implement this in the "correct" way. It still worked, obviously, for the specific application needed in Chapter 10, but it won't work for this chapter. The focus in the previous chapter was on creating custom workflow forms, and I didn't want to spend too much time on this; the chapter was already long enough. Now I'll show you how to use the ReplicatorActivity in what we like to call "the right way."

The ReplicatorActivity is a really useful way to create multiple instances of an activity or sequence of activities. Basically, you provide a collection (any collection that supports the IList interface), and the defined activities are executed for each item in the collection.

The activities that you place in the ReplicatorActivity are considered *template* activities. As the ReplicatorActivity is executed, a copy of its child activities is created. For example, if you had three items in the collection and a single CodeActivity in the ReplicatorActivity, the workflow would create three instances of the CodeActivity object. All the properties that you define at design time are also copied to each of the instances. When you define the method to handle the ExecuteCode event, for example, all three instances will execute the same method. However, each will have their own copy of the local variables. It is equivalent to three different threads calling the same method. The code is shared; the data is not.

The CreateTask (and the CreateTaskWithContentType) activity has properties such as TaskId and TaskProperties that need to be different for each instance. If you specify these in the workflow designer, then all copies will have the same value. We worked around this in the previous chapter because the ReplicatorActivity was executed sequentially, and before each instance, the bound members, taskId and taskProperties, were modified.

Drag a ReplicatorActivity to the workflow, and change the name to **createTasks**. In the Properties window, select the InitialChildData property, and click the ellipsis. In the dialog box that is displayed, select the existing ChildData property, as shown in Figure 11-13.

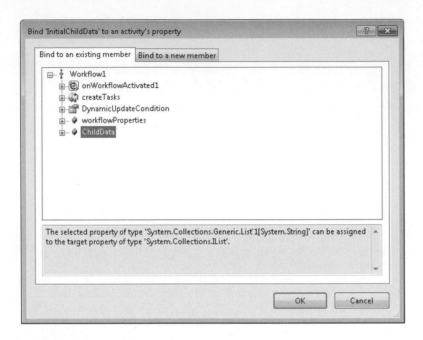

Figure 11-13. Selecting the `ChildData` *property*

Change the `ExecutionType` to `Parallel`. The completed Properties window should look like Figure 11-14.

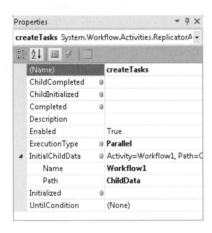

Figure 11-14. Completed `ReplicatorActivity` *Properties window*

■ **Caution** Note that none of the event handlers is implemented. In Chapter 10, you used the `ChildInitialized` event to pass in the instance data, which contained the person who the task was to be assigned to. When you're working with a single instance of each task, you can have one method set a class member, and then a subsequent method can access it. The `ChildInitialized` handler could store the `AssignedTo` value, and the `CreateTask_Invoking` handler could then read it. This does *not* work when dealing with multiple instances. The instance data passed in to the `ChildInitialized` handler is not useful in this scenario.

Task Activities

Drag a `SequenceActivity` onto the `createTasks` activity. Drag a `CreateTaskWithContentType` activity onto the `SequenceActivity`, and rename it to **createTask**. Drag a `WhileActivity` below this, and then drag an `OnTaskChanged` activity onto the `WhileActivity`. The workflow diagram should look like Figure 11-15.

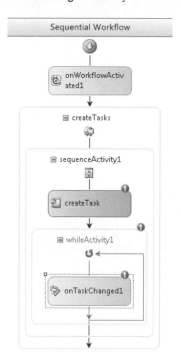

Figure 11-15. The workflow diagram

The red circles indicate errors because the activities are not configured yet; you'll get to that shortly. This pattern is a typical one that you will undoubtedly use often. You create a task and then put an `OnTaskChanged` handler inside a `while` loop, waiting for the appropriate conditions to exit the loop. In this case, you're waiting for the task to be completed.

Correlation Tokens

Correlation tokens allow you to associate activities that need to be performed on the same object instance. For example, in Figure 11-15, the `createTask` activity and the `onTaskChanged1` activity should operate on the same task instance. You ensure this by assigning the same correlation token to both. If you had other `CreateTask/OnTaskChanged` activity pairs in your workflow, you would assign a different correlation token to them.

There are generally two types of correlation tokens. You'll use one at the workflow level and one at the task level. The project template already set up a token at the workflow level called `workflowToken`, as shown in Figure 11-16.

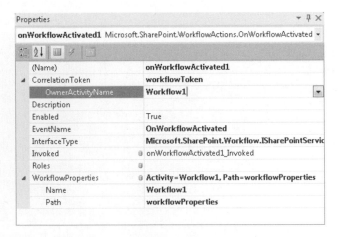

Figure 11-16. `OnWorkflowActivated` *Properties window*

If you expand the `CorrelationToken` property, the `OwnerActivityName` property is used to define the scope of the token. In this case, it is defined for `Workflow1`, which is the workflow level.

Since your tasks are being executed inside a `ReplicatorActivity`, it is important that you set the scope appropriately. If you set the scope at the `createTasks` (`ReplicatorActivity`) or `Workflow1` level, the same token will be used for all task instances. This will not work because you won't be able to match the `OnTaskChanged` event with the corresponding task.

They must be set with the `sequenceActivity1` as the owner. Recall that activities within a `ReplicatorActivity` are copied for each instance in the `ChildData` collection. This means that a separate instance of the `sequenceActivity1` will be created for each object in the collection. Consequently, a separate correlation token will be created for each as well. And this is exactly how you want this to work. Each `createTask/onTaskChanged1` activity pair will have their own correlation token.

■ **Caution** Since the project template already generated a `workflowToken` for you, there is a temptation to use it everywhere that an activity requires a `CorrelationToken`. Be careful about doing that. There are situations like I just described where this will not work like you want it to work.

Select the **createTask** activity, and in the Properties window enter the `CorrelationToken` as **taskToken**. Then expand this property, and select the `OwnerActivityName` as `sequenceActivity1`. Then select the **onTaskChanged1** activity. In the `CorrelationToken` property, you should be able to select the `taskToken` from the drop-down.

Setting the ContentTypeID

Select the **createTask** activity. In the Properties window, select the `ContentTypeID` property, and click the ellipsis. In the dialog box, select the existing `contentTypeIdString` member, as shown in Figure 11-17.

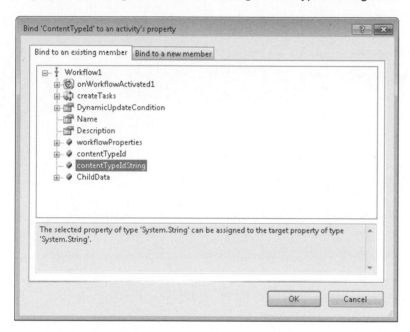

Figure 11-17. Selecting the `contentTypeIdString` *member*

The completed Properties window should look like Figure 11-18.

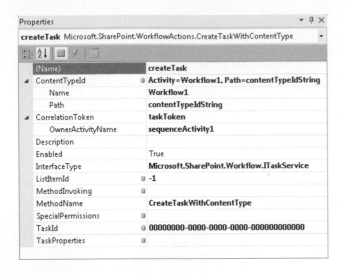

Figure 11-18. The createTask Properties window

Implementing the createTask Event Handler

Double-click the **createTask** activity, which will generate the event handler for the **MethodInvoking** event and display the method in the code-behind class. Listing 11-4 shows the implementation of this method.

Listing 11-4. The createTask MethodInvoking Handler Implementation

```
// Get the task object from the sender parameter
CreateTaskWithContentType task = sender as CreateTaskWithContentType;

// Assign a new TaskId
task.TaskId = Guid.NewGuid();

// Safely get the next Invitee
Mutex m = new Mutex(false);
Invitee i = (Invitee)ChildData[_task++];
m.Close();

// Setup the task properties
SPWorkflowTaskProperties wtp = new SPWorkflowTaskProperties();
wtp.PercentComplete = (float)0.0;
wtp.AssignedTo = i.AssignedTo;
wtp.TaskType = 0;
wtp.DueDate = DateTime.Now.AddDays(1);
wtp.Title = "Enter your lunch order";
wtp.Description = _eventName;
wtp.ExtendedProperties["MenuUrl"] = _menuUrl;
```

```
task.TaskProperties = wtp;

// Store the taskID in the Invitee object
i.TaskId = task.TaskId;

// Store the taskID on the OnTaskChanged activity
Activity seq = task.Parent;
if (seq != null)
{
    Activity w = seq.GetActivityByName("whileActivity1");
    if (w != null)
    {
        OnTaskChanged tc =
            (OnTaskChanged)w.GetActivityByName("onTaskChanged1");
        if (tc != null)
            tc.TaskId = task.TaskId;
    }
}
```

By convention, event handlers usually have two parameters. The first, named sender, is the object that raised the event. The second is a class derived from EventArgs that passes in data that is appropriate for the particular event. For this event, the sender is the CreateTaskWithContentType activity. The sender parameter can be cast to a variable of that type. Then you will be able to access the properties of that object.

Most importantly for our purposes, the sender object is the actual activity instance, not the template class that you configured in the workflow designer. The TaskProperties and TaskId properties of the activity instance can be set directly in code. The TaskId property can be set easily enough by calling the static NewGuid() method of the Guid class.

The ChildInitialized event of the ReplicatorActivity supplies the specific data object for this instance. However, as I discussed earlier, that's not very helpful because there's no easy way to supply it to the correct instance of the createTask activity. Instead, you'll simply access the next ChildData object from the collection. The _task member maintains the current index in the collection. The Invitee object at this index is obtained, and the _task member is incremented. Because you are executing the instances in parallel, you must wrap this logic with a Mutex object to ensure that only one instance is doing this at a time.

The event handler then creates an SPWorkflowTaskProperties object and sets the appropriate properties. The AssignedTo property is set using the value in the Invitee object. TaskId is then stored in the Invitee object. This will be used later to find the associated task.

The last part of this code stores the TaskId on the onTaskChanged1 activity instance that is associated with this task. This will be needed later when responding to OnTaskChanged events. Getting to the onTaskChanged1 activity may seem a bit circuitous. You might want to refer to Figure 11-15. The sequence1Activity contains a createTask activity and a whileActivity1 activity. The task object is the createTask activity. Its Parent property will be the sequenceActivity1 object. All activities are derived from the base Activity class, so you can either use the Activity class or cast it to the appropriate derived class.

You then call the GetActivityByName() method of the sequenceActivity1 object. This method will look for a child activity with the specified name and will return the whileActivity1 object. The WhileActivity has a single child activity, which is the OnTaskChanged activity. You can obtain this by calling the GetActivityByName() method on the whileActivty1 object. This is cast to an OnTaskChanged class and then used to store the TaskId.

Setting the While Condition

Add the notCompleted() method shown in Listing 11-5.

Listing 11-5. Implementation of the notCompleted Method

```
private void notCompleted(object sender, ConditionalEventArgs e)
{
    WhileActivity w = sender as WhileActivity;
    OnTaskChanged tc = (OnTaskChanged)w.GetActivityByName("onTaskChanged1");

    e.Result = true;

    foreach (Invitee i in ChildData)
    {
        if (i.TaskId == tc.TaskId)
        {
            e.Result = !i.Complete;
            break;
        }
    }
}
```

This method will be called by the **WhileActivity** to determine whether the **while** loop can exit or whether it needs to continue to wait. The answer is returned in the second parameter, which is a **ConditionalEventArgs** class. It has a **Result** property. You'll set this to **true** if the **while** loop needs to continue waiting. For your purposes, it will wait until the task is complete.

Just like with the **createTask** event handler, you'll need to make sure you're dealing with the actual object instance, not the template classes. And to do that, you'll again use the **sender** parameter. In this case, the sender is a **WhileActivity**. By itself, that's not really helpful. However, you can obtain any of its child activities by calling its **GetActivityByName()** method. The child you'll want to get is the **OnTaskChanged** activity. Once you have that, you can iterate through the **Invitee** objects looking for the one that has a matching **TaskId**. You then check to see whether that task has completed and set the **Result** property accordingly.

From the workflow designer, select **whileActivity1**, and in the Properties window, for the **Condition** property choose **Code Condition**. Then expand the property, and select the **notCompleted** method that you just implemented. The completed Properties window should look like Figure 11-19.

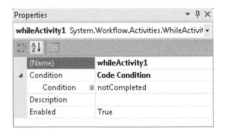

Figure 11-19. The WhileActivity Properties window

Handling the OnTaskChanged Event

You're probably wondering how the `Complete` flag on the `Invitee` object ever gets set. The answer to that is the `OnTaskChanged` event. Double-click the `onTaskChanged1` activity, which will generate the handler for this event. Listing 11-6 shows the implementation for this method.

Listing 11-6. Implementation of the OnTaskChanged Event Handler

```
SPTaskServiceEventArgs args = (SPTaskServiceEventArgs)e;

// Find this Invitee and mark it complete
foreach (Invitee i in ChildData)
{
    if (i.TaskId == args.taskId)
    {
        i.Complete = true;
        break;
    }
}
```

The second parameter is passed as an `ExternalDataEventArgs` class; however, the actual object that is provided is an `SPTaskServiceEventArgs` class. By casting this to the appropriate object type, you can access the important properties. For your purposes, you'll use the `taskId` property to find the matching `Invitee` object and set its `Complete` flag.

■ **Tip** The `SPTaskServiceEventArgs` class provides `beforeProperties` and `afterProperties` members. These are both instances of the same `SPWorkflowTaskProperties` class that you used to configure the task. These two properties give you a before and after snapshot of the task. Using them, you can determine exactly what has changed. You can also test various properties of the task to see whether you should mark the task complete.

Adding a Final Step

The last step on the workflow is to create a task to signal that all the lunch orders have been submitted. This would trigger the necessary actions such as calling the order in and picking it up.

From the Workflow Designer, drag a `CreateTask` activity to the bottom of the workflow (after the `createTasks` (`ReplicatorActivity`) activity). In the Properties window, enter the `CorrelationToken` as `finalTaskToken`. Expand the property, and select the `OwnerActivityName` as `Workflow1`. The completed Properties window should look like Figure 11-20.

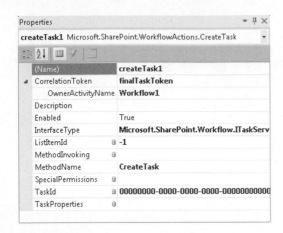

Figure 11-20. The Properties window for the final **createTask1** *activity*

Double-click the **createTask1** activity to generate the event handler. Listing 11-7 shows the implementation for this.

Listing 11-7. Implementation of createTasks1 MethodInvoking *Event*

```
CreateTask task = sender as CreateTask;
task.TaskId = Guid.NewGuid();

SPWorkflowTaskProperties wtp = new SPWorkflowTaskProperties();
wtp.PercentComplete = (float)0.0;
wtp.TaskType = 0;
wtp.DueDate = DateTime.Now.AddDays(1);
wtp.Title = "Lunch orders are complete";

task.TaskProperties = wtp;
```

Although you don't have to in this case because there's only one instance, you're already in that mode, so you will bind the **TaskProperties** and **TaskId** properties in code using the **sender** object. Figure 11-21 shows the final workflow design.

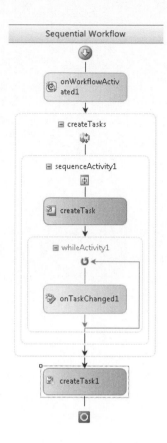

Figure 11-21. The final workflow design

Listing 11-8 shows the complete code listing of the code-behind class.

Listing 11-8. Complete Implementation of the Code-Behind Class

```
using System;
using System.ComponentModel;
using System.ComponentModel.Design;
using System.Collections;
using System.Drawing;
using System.Linq;
using System.Workflow.ComponentModel.Compiler;
using System.Workflow.ComponentModel.Serialization;
using System.Workflow.ComponentModel;
using System.Workflow.ComponentModel.Design;
using System.Workflow.Runtime;
using System.Workflow.Activities;
using System.Workflow.Activities.Rules;
```

```
using Microsoft.SharePoint;
using Microsoft.SharePoint.Workflow;
using Microsoft.SharePoint.WorkflowActions;

using System.Collections.Generic;
using System.Threading;

namespace WF_Chapter11.Workflow1
{
    [Serializable]
    public class Invitee
    {
        public string AssignedTo { get; set; }
        public Guid TaskId { get; set; }
        public bool Complete { get; set; }

        public Invitee(string assignedTo)
        {
            AssignedTo = assignedTo;
            Complete = false;
        }
    }

    public sealed partial class Workflow1 : SequentialWorkflowActivity
    {
        public Workflow1()
        {
            InitializeComponent();
        }

        public Guid workflowId = default(System.Guid);
        public SPWorkflowActivationProperties workflowProperties =
            new SPWorkflowActivationProperties();

        public SPContentTypeId contentTypeId =
            new SPContentTypeId("0x010801000da2ad56f41a465bbaa3311519728c2c");
        //("0x01080100211c4a0fc8144c7eb270141b81e38a8a");
        public string contentTypeIdString = "";

        private string _eventName;
        private string _menuUrl;
        public List<Invitee> ChildData = new List<Invitee>();
        private int _task = 0;

        private void onWorkflowActivated1_Invoked(object sender,
            ExternalDataEventArgs e)
        {
            SPListItem item = workflowProperties.Item;
            _eventName = item.Title;
            _menuUrl = item["MenuUrl"].ToString();

            List<SPFieldUserValue> l = (List<SPFieldUserValue>)item["Attendees"];
```

```
        foreach (SPFieldUserValue u in l)
        {
            ChildData.Add(new Invitee(u.User.LoginName));
        }

        try
        {
            workflowProperties.TaskList.ContentTypesEnabled = true;
            SPContentTypeId matchContentTypeId = workflowProperties.TaskList
                .ContentTypes.BestMatch(contentTypeId);
            if (matchContentTypeId.Parent.CompareTo(contentTypeId) != 0)
            {
                SPContentType ct = workflowProperties.TaskList.ParentWeb
                    .AvailableContentTypes[contentTypeId];
                workflowProperties.TaskList.ContentTypes.Add(ct);
                workflowProperties.TaskList.Update();
            }

            contentTypeIdString = contentTypeId.ToString();
        }
        catch (Exception)
        {
        }
    }

    private void createTask_MethodInvoking(object sender, EventArgs e)
    {
        // Get the task object from the sender parameter
        CreateTaskWithContentType task = sender as CreateTaskWithContentType;

        // Assign a new TaskId
        task.TaskId = Guid.NewGuid();

        // Safely get the next Invitee
        Mutex m = new Mutex(false);
        Invitee i = (Invitee)ChildData[_task++];
        m.Close();

        // Setup the task properties
        SPWorkflowTaskProperties wtp = new SPWorkflowTaskProperties();
        wtp.PercentComplete = (float)0.0;
        wtp.AssignedTo = i.AssignedTo;
        wtp.TaskType = 0;
        wtp.DueDate = DateTime.Now.AddDays(1);
        wtp.Title = "Enter your lunch order";
        wtp.Description = _eventName;
        wtp.ExtendedProperties["MenuUrl"] = _menuUrl;

        task.TaskProperties = wtp;

        // Store the taskID in the Invitee object
        i.TaskId = task.TaskId;
```

```
        // Store the taskID on the OnTaskChanged activity
        Activity seq = task.Parent;
        if (seq != null)
        {
            Activity w = seq.GetActivityByName("whileActivity1");
            if (w != null)
            {
                OnTaskChanged tc =
                    (OnTaskChanged)w.GetActivityByName("onTaskChanged1");
                if (tc != null)
                    tc.TaskId = task.TaskId;
            }
        }
    }

    private void notCompleted(object sender, ConditionalEventArgs e)
    {
        WhileActivity w = sender as WhileActivity;
        OnTaskChanged tc = (OnTaskChanged)w.GetActivityByName("onTaskChanged1");

        e.Result = true;

        foreach (Invitee i in ChildData)
        {
            if (i.TaskId == tc.TaskId)
            {
                e.Result = !i.Complete;
                break;
            }
        }
    }

    private void onTaskChanged1_Invoked(object sender, ExternalDataEventArgs e)
    {
        SPTaskServiceEventArgs args = (SPTaskServiceEventArgs)e;

        // Find this Invitee and mark it complete
        foreach (Invitee i in ChildData)
        {
            if (i.TaskId == args.taskId)
            {
                i.Complete = true;
                break;
            }
        }
    }

    private void createTask1_MethodInvoking(object sender, EventArgs e)
    {
        CreateTask task = sender as CreateTask;
        task.TaskId = Guid.NewGuid();
```

```
            SPWorkflowTaskProperties wtp = new SPWorkflowTaskProperties();
            wtp.PercentComplete = (float)0.0;
            wtp.TaskType = 0;
            wtp.DueDate = DateTime.Now.AddDays(1);
            wtp.Title = "Lunch orders are complete";

            task.TaskProperties = wtp;
        }
    }
}
```

Testing the Workflow

Now you're ready to try it. Press F5 to deploy the workflow and launch the SharePoint site. This should display the Calendar list on the Part3 site. Double-click the event that you set up earlier, and click the Workflows button at the top of the form. The Workflows page shown in Figure 11-22 should be displayed.

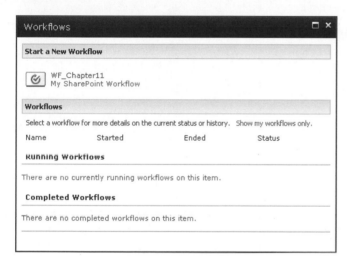

Figure 11-22. The Workflows page

Click the *WF_Chapter11* link to start the workflow on this event. When it finishes, close the Event item, and select the Tasks list. You should have a lunch order task for each person you added to the Attendees property. The Tasks list should be similar to the one shown in Figure 11-23.

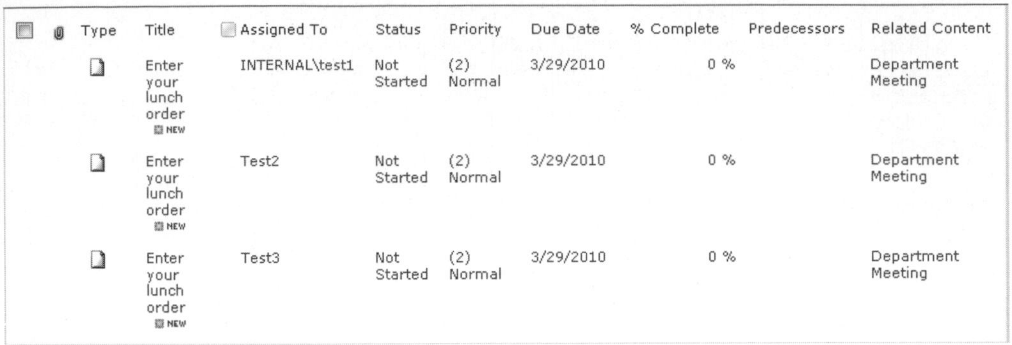

Type
Title
Assigned To
Status
Priority
Due Date
% Complete
Predecessors
Related Content
Enter your lunch order NEW
INTERNAL\test1
Not Started
(2) Normal
3/29/2010
0 %
Department Meeting
Enter your lunch order NEW
Test2
Not Started
(2) Normal
3/29/2010
0 %
Department Meeting
Enter your lunch order NEW
Test3
Not Started
(2) Normal
3/29/2010
0 %
Department Meeting

Figure 11-23. The `Tasks` *list with the lunch order tasks*

Go back to the `Calendar` list, and double-click the `Event` item again. Click the Workflows button, and the Workflows page (shown in Figure 11-24) should show that the workflow is in progress.

Workflows
Start a New Workflow
There are no workflows currently available to start on this item.
Workflows
Select a workflow for more details on the current status or history. Show my workflows only.
Name
Started
Ended
Status
Running Workflows
WF_Chapter11
3/28/2010 12:24 AM
In Progress
Completed Workflows
There are no completed workflows on this item.

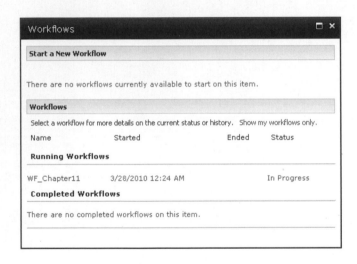

Figure 11-24. The Workflows page showing status In Progress

Now, go back to the `Tasks` list, and edit one of the tasks. You should see the custom form (see Figure 11-25) that you created in the previous chapter. Enter your lunch order, and click the Save button.

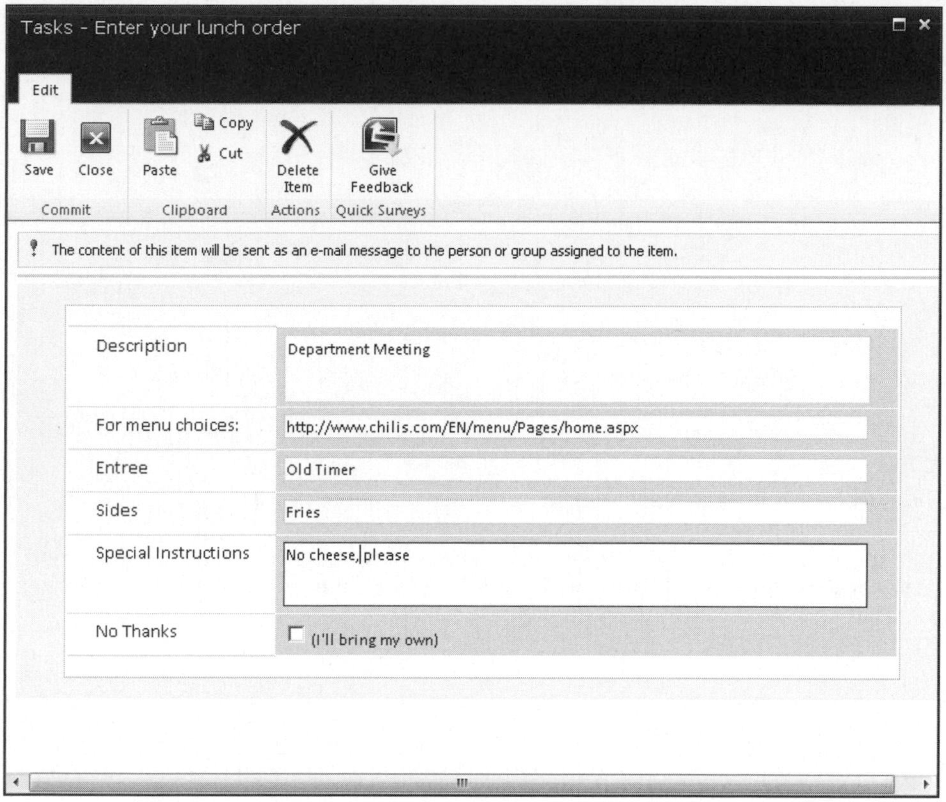

Figure 11-25. The custom lunch order form

Edit the remaining tasks, entering a lunch order or selecting the No Thanks check box. When you have completed the last task, a new task should appear, as shown in Figure 11-26.

		Type	Title	Assigned To	Status	Priority	Due Date	% Complete	Predecessors	Related Cont
☐	🔘			☑						
		🗋	Enter your lunch order ☒ NEW	INTERNAL\test1	Completed	(2) Normal	3/29/2010	100 %		Department Meeting
		🗋	Enter your lunch order ☒ NEW	Test2	Completed	(2) Normal	3/29/2010	100 %		Department Meeting
		🗋	Enter your lunch order ☒ NEW	Test3	Completed	(2) Normal	3/29/2010	100 %		Department Meeting
		🗋	Lunch orders are complete ☒ NEW		Not Started	(2) Normal	3/29/2010	0 %		Department Meeting

Figure 11-26. The Tasks list with the final task

The final task is to let you know that all the orders have been submitted. If you view this task, you'll see that it uses the standard task form (see Figure 11-27). This is because the task was created using the `CreateTask` activity and did not use the custom content type.

Figure 11-27. The final task details

Summary

In this chapter, you used the `OnTaskChanged` activity inside a `WhileActivity`. This design pattern allows you to monitor a task and wait for a user to complete it. The workflow then performed a final step once all the tasks were complete.

You also used the `sender` parameter to access the appropriate activity instance. You used the `ReplicatorActivity` in parallel mode and implemented a structure to keep track of multiple simultaneous tasks.

■ ■ ■

CHAPTER 12

LINQ to SharePoint

Language Integrated Query (LINQ) is one of the really useful technologies that Microsoft has provided in the .NET platform. It offers a convenient and consistent method for manipulating complex data structures. LINQ to Objects, LINQ to SQL, LINQ to XML, and now LINQ to SharePoint all work the same way; they just work against different types of data sources. If you've used LINQ before, you will really enjoy LINQ to SharePoint; even if you haven't, you'll quickly see just how useful it is.

■ **Tip** This chapter will provide an example of how you can use LINQ to SharePoint, but I won't try to explain LINQ in any depth. If you're new to LINQ, you might want to read a good book on LINQ that covers the fundamentals of the technology. One that I found particularly helpful is *Pro LINQ: Language Integrated Query in C# 2008* by Joseph C. Rattz, Jr. Read the first five chapters. After that, the book covers the specific implementations such as LINQ to XML and LINQ to SQL. These are interesting but not germane to the SharePoint implementation.

Setting Up the Project

In this chapter, you'll start with the solution you developed in Chapter 11 and add some functionality. In the previous chapter, the workflow generated a task for each person who was invited and waited for all tasks to complete. Each task used a custom form to allow the user to enter their lunch order. Now that these are complete, it would be really nice to do something with that data. You will now add an extra step to the workflow to collect the lunch orders and send a consolidated order to the person responsible for placing the order.

Start Visual Studio 2010, and create an empty solution. Enter the solution name **WF_Chapter12**, as shown in Figure 12-1.

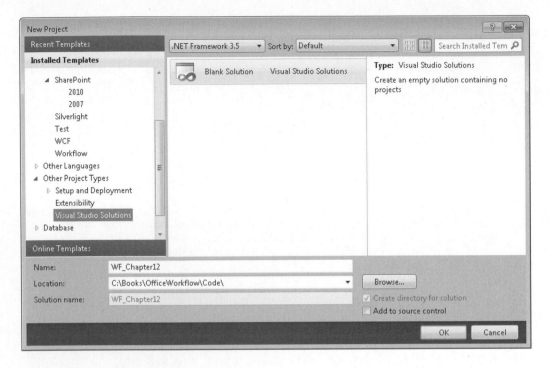

Figure 12-1. Creating an empty solution

Copying the Chapter 11 Project

Next, copy the project folder highlighted in Figure 12-2 from the WF_Chapter11 folder to the WF_Chapter12 folder.

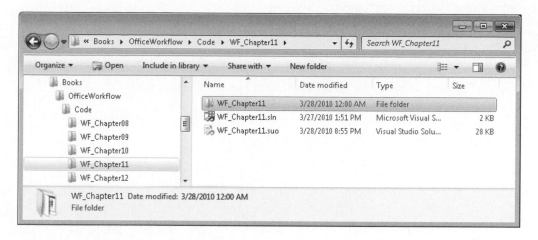

Figure 12-2. Copying the project from Chapter 11

Back in Visual Studio, from the Solution Explorer, right-click the solution, and choose Add ▸ Existing Project. In the Add Existing Project dialog box, navigate to the `WF_Chapter12\WF_Chapter11` folder, and select the `WF_Chapter11.csproj` file, as shown in Figure 12-3.

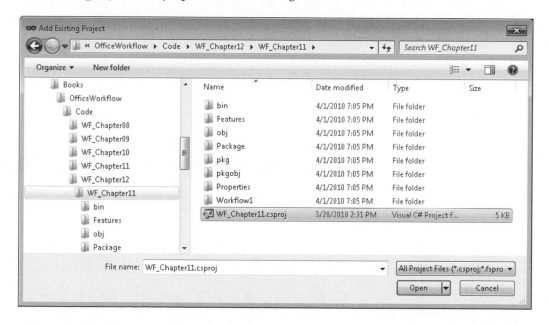

Figure 12-3. Selecting the WF_Chapter11 project

Configuring the Debugging Site

When you first create a SharePoint project in Visual Studio, the template prompts you with a series of dialog boxes called the SharePoint Customization Wizard. These allow you to enter the name of the workflow and associate it to a list or library. You can also modify these settings after the project has been created.

In the Solution Explorer, select the **Workflow1** folder, as shown in Figure 12-4.

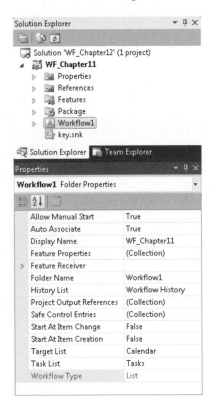

Figure 12-4. Workflow properties

The Properties window contains all the values that were entered in these dialog boxes. If you select the **History List**, **Target List**, or **Task List** properties, an ellipsis will appear for each. When you click the ellipsis, the SharePoint Customization Wizard will start. It doesn't matter which property you select; all dialog boxes will display just like they did when creating a new project. The existing values will be displayed in the dialog boxes, and you can make the desired changes.

Click the ellipsis on one of these properties to start the SharePoint Customization Wizard. In the first dialog box, change the workflow name to **WF_Chapter12**, as shown in Figure 12-5.

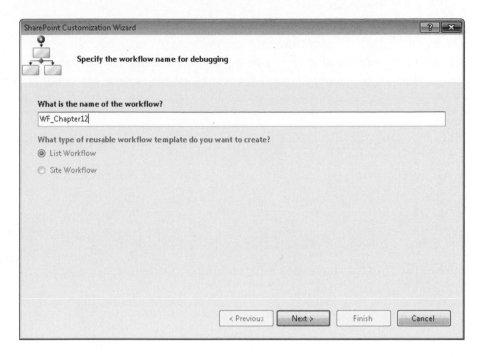

Figure 12-5. Changing the workflow name

For the remaining pages, just leave the existing values.

Testing the Workflow

At this point, it is a good idea to run the workflow and verify that everything is still working. Press F5 to debug the application. This will start the Part3 site and display the `Calendar` list. Select the event you created in the previous chapter, and start the workflow. Manually complete each of the tasks that were created, and a final task should be created when you're done.

SPMetal

In Chapter 9, I introduced the extensive object model that enables you to access the various SharePoint objects. For example, you can obtain an `SPList` object that represents a list or document library and then iterate through the `SPListItem` objects that represent items in this list. However, as I mentioned, these generic objects provide no compile-time type checking. You access a particular field value using its field name. If the field name is not valid or you try to store a variable in it of the wrong type, the compiler cannot detect this, and the error is not generated until runtime.

One of the best features of LINQ to SharePoint is that it provides strongly typed classes. The available fields, for example, are provided by IntelliSense, and the compiler will tell you if you try to store a text string into an integer. To do this, SharePoint provides a utility called `SPMetal` that will create strongly typed classes that are specific to your SharePoint objects.

■ **Note** This is roughly equivalent to the `SQLMetal` utility provided in earlier versions of Visual Studio. `SQLMetal` connects to the specified database and creates a class for each table with properties for each column. It also generates associations between classes based on foreign key constraints in the database schema. In a similar fashion, `SPMetal` generates classes that correspond to your lists and content types with properties that map to the columns defined for each.

Running SPMetal

`SPMetal` is located in the `BIN` folder where SharePoint is installed. If you installed SharePoint in the default location, this will be as follows:

```
C:\Program Files\Common Files\Microsoft Shared\Web Server Extensions\14\BIN\SPMetal.exe
```

It is run from a command line. If you run it with no parameters, the following instructions are returned:

```
Microsoft (R) SharePoint LINQ Code Generator 2008

for Microsoft (R) .NET Framework version 3.5

Copyright (C) Microsoft Corporation. All rights reserved.


SPMetal [options]


Options
/web:<url>                 Specifies absolute URL of the web-site. Host address can be
local, in

                           which case Server OM will be used to connect to the server.
/useremoteapi              Specifies that the web-site URL is remote.
/user:<name>               Specifies logon username (or domain).
/password:<password>       Specifies logon password.
/parameters:<file>         Specifies XML file with code generation parameters.
/code:<file>               Specifies output for generated code (default: console).
/language:<language>       Specifies source code language. Valid options are "csharp" and
"vb"
```

	(default: inferred from source code file name).
/namespace:<namespace>	Specifies namespace that is used for source code (default: no namespace).
/serialization:<type>	Specifies serialization type. Valid options are "none" and "unidirectional" (default: none).

Generate C# source code from a local SharePoint site:

```
SPMetal /web:http://localserver:5555/localsite /namespace:nwind /code:nwind.cs
```

Generate VB source code from a local SharePoint site with specified parameters:

```
SPMetal /web:http://localserver:5555/localsite /namespace:nwind /code:nwind.vb
 /parameters:parameters.xml
```

Generate C# source code from a remote SharePoint site using default credentials:

```
SPMetal /web:http://remoteserver:5555/remotesite /useremoteapi /namespace:nwind
/code:nwind.cs
```

Generate C# source code from remote SharePoint server using Client OM with specified credentials:

```
SPMetal /web:http://remoteserver:5555/remotesite /user:domain\username /password:password

/namespace:nwind /code:nwind.cs
```

These are the primary arguments that you'll need to supply:

- /web:<url>: url is the path to your SharePoint site.
- /namespace:<namespace>: namespace specifies the namespace used in the code file.
- /code:<file>: file is the filename of the output file.

The namespace argument specifies the namespace that the generated classes will be contained by. SPMetal can generate the output classes in either C# or Visual Basic, and you can specify this with the

/language:<language> argument. The allowed values are **csharp** and **vb**. However, you don't generally need to use this because it will determine the language from the extension of the file name.

These additional parameters may be needed to connect to the site depending on your configuration:

- **/useremoteapi** (use this if the SharePoint site is not on the local machine)

- **/user:<user name>**

- **/password:<password>**

To run **SPMetal**, you can open a command window and execute **SPMetal** with the appropriate arguments. However, because of the lengthy paths and number of arguments, you might find it easier to create a command file. Then from Windows Explorer, you can double-click this file to start **SPMetal**. Create a text file in the **Workflow1** folder of the WF_Chapter12 solution, with the filename **SPMetal.cmd**. Enter the following text in this file (all on one line):

```
"C:\Program Files\Common Files\Microsoft Shared\Web Server Extensions\14\BIN\SPMetal"
/web:<url> /namespace:WF_Chapter12.Workflow1.SPPart3 /code:SPPart3.cs
```

The **<url>** text is a placeholder for the URL of the Part3 SharePoint site that you set up in Chapter 8. The contents of the **Workflow1** folder should look like Figure 12-6.

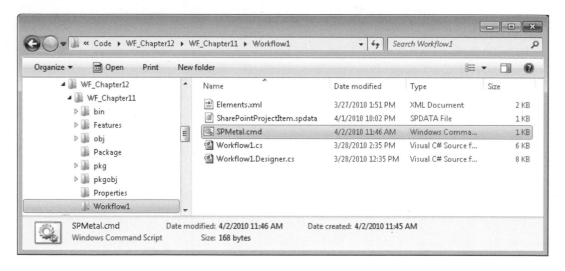

*Figure 12-6. The Workflow1 folder with **SPMetal.cmd***

Double-click the **SPMetal.cmd** file. A command window will appear for a few seconds while SPMetal is running. When it has finished, the window will close, and there should be an **SPPart3.cs** file in this folder. In Visual Studio, from the Solution Explorer, right-click the **Workflow1** folder, and choose Add ▶ Existing Item. In the Add Existing Item dialog box, select the **SPPart3.cs** file that was just generated.

■ **Note** To use LINQ to SharePoint, you'll need to add a reference to `Microsoft.SharePoint.Linq`. Right-click the WF_Chapter11 project, and choose Add Reference. On the .NET tab, select `Microsoft.SharePoint.Linq`, and click OK.

Default Generation Rules

As expected, the `SPPart3.cs` file contains several classes that define the objects in your SharePoint site.

DataContext Class

`SPMetal` generates a single class to represent the site. This class is named `SPPart3DataContext` and is derived from the `DataContext` class. By collapsing the code regions, you can get an overview of the contents of this class (see Figure 12-7).

```
public partial class SPPart3DataContext : Microsoft.SharePoint.Linq.DataContext {

    Extensibility Method Definitions

    public SPPart3DataContext(string requestUrl) :
            base(requestUrl) [...]

    /// <summary> ...
    [Microsoft.SharePoint.Linq.ListAttribute(Name="Announcements")]
    public Microsoft.SharePoint.Linq.EntityList<Announcement> Announcements [...]

    /// <summary> ...
    [Microsoft.SharePoint.Linq.ListAttribute(Name="Calendar")]
    public Microsoft.SharePoint.Linq.EntityList<CalendarEvent> Calendar [...]

    /// <summary> ...
    [Microsoft.SharePoint.Linq.ListAttribute(Name="Links")]
    public Microsoft.SharePoint.Linq.EntityList<Link> Links [...]

    /// <summary> ...
    [Microsoft.SharePoint.Linq.ListAttribute(Name="Shared Documents")]
    public Microsoft.SharePoint.Linq.EntityList<Document> SharedDocuments [...]

    /// <summary> ...
    [Microsoft.SharePoint.Linq.ListAttribute(Name="Site Assets")]
    public Microsoft.SharePoint.Linq.EntityList<Document> SiteAssets [...]

    /// <summary> ...
    [Microsoft.SharePoint.Linq.ListAttribute(Name="Site Pages")]
    public Microsoft.SharePoint.Linq.EntityList<WikiPage> SitePages [...]

    /// <summary> ...
    [Microsoft.SharePoint.Linq.ListAttribute(Name="Tasks")]
    public Microsoft.SharePoint.Linq.EntityList<Item> Tasks [...]

    /// <summary> ...
    [Microsoft.SharePoint.Linq.ListAttribute(Name="Team Discussion")]
    public Microsoft.SharePoint.Linq.EntityList<Item> TeamDiscussion [...]
}
```

Figure 12-7. SPPart3DataContext class

The constructor takes a URL as its only parameter. When you instantiate this class, you will supply the URL of the SharePoint site to which you want to connect.

This class then provides an `EntityList<>` property for each of the lists and libraries that are defined. You should recognize some of these lists such as `Calendar`, `Shared Documents`, and `Tasks`. The `EntityList<>` class is a template class, and the type of object that it contains is specified when the property is declared. The `Calendar` list, for example, contains `CalendarEvent` objects.

■ **Note** Class and property names cannot have spaces in them. Spaces in the corresponding SharePoint object name will be removed. Also, if the first character is not capitalized, the corresponding class or property name will use a capitalized letter instead.

Content Types

The list items, such as `CalendarEvent`, are defined by a content type. The `SPPart3.cs` file contains classes for each of these content types. These class definitions follow the same inheritance as their associated content types. For example, `CalendarEvent` is derived from `Event`, which is derived from `Item`.

If you create a custom list without using a content type, like you did in Chapter 4, `SPMetal` will generate a class for it as an *implied* content type. The list name will be used as the name of this implied content type.

Choice Columns

Some column definitions provide a fixed list of available values. These will be defined in the `SPPart3.cs` file as enumerations. For example, Listing 12-1 shows the `TaskStatus` column definition.

Listing 12-1. Definition of TaskStatus

```
public enum TaskStatus : int {

    None = 0,

    Invalid = 1,

    [Microsoft.SharePoint.Linq.ChoiceAttribute(Value="Not Started")]
    NotStarted = 2,

    [Microsoft.SharePoint.Linq.ChoiceAttribute(Value="In Progress")]
    InProgress = 4,

    [Microsoft.SharePoint.Linq.ChoiceAttribute(Value="Completed")]
    Completed = 8,

    [Microsoft.SharePoint.Linq.ChoiceAttribute(Value="Deferred")]
    Deferred = 16,
```

```
    [Microsoft.SharePoint.Linq.ChoiceAttribute(Value="Waiting on someone else")]
    WaitingOnSomeoneElse = 32,
}
```

Lookup Fields

Fields that are used as a lookup to another list are generated as an `EntryRef<T>`, where `T` is the content type of the related list. If the field supports multiple values, `EntrySet<T>` is used instead. This will allow your code to navigate the association using the standard dot notation. For example:

```
List1Item.LookupField.List2Property
```

If the class for the associated list is not included in the `SPMetal` output and the lookup field allows for multiple values, `SPMetal` will generate two properties using the `LookupList<>` class. The first will hold the ID values that have been selected; the second will hold the display values. A good example of this is the `Calendar Event` content type. The first portion of the class definition is as follows:

```
public partial class CalendarEvent : Event
    {
    private string _menuUrl;
    private Microsoft.SharePoint.Linq.LookupList<System.Nullable<int>> _attendeesId;
    private Microsoft.SharePoint.Linq.LookupList<string> _attendeesImnName;
```

Recall from Chapter 10 that you added two columns to this content type (`MenuUrl` and `Attendees`). The `_attendeesId` property holds the list of IDs for each person who has been invited to this event, and `_attendeesImnName` holds their names. These private members are each wrapped in a public property using the `IList<>` interface.

Configuring SPMetal

You can configure which objects are included by supplying an XML parameters file. This is specified using the `/parameters:<file>` argument. From the Solution Explorer, right-click thc Workflow1 folder, and choose Add ▶ New Item. In the Add New Item dialog box, from the Data group, select the XML File template, and enter the file name **SPMetal.xml**, as shown in Figure 12-8.

Figure 12-8. Adding an SPMetal.xml *file*

Including Hidden Content Types

You may have noticed that there were some content types missing from the SPPart3.cs file. By default, the hidden content types (such as Workflow Task) and any that are derived from hidden content types are not included.

Enter the following as the contents of the SPMetal.xml file:

```
<?xml version="1.0" encoding="utf-8"?>
<Web AccessModifier="Internal"
  xmlns="http://schemas.microsoft.com/SharePoint/2009/spmetal">
  <IncludeHiddenContentTypes/>
</Web>
```

The main node of this XML file is called Web. On this node, you can add instructions that apply at the site level. In this example, you added the IncludeHiddenContentTypes element. This will tell the SPMetal utility to include the hidden content types. Edit the SPMetal.cmd file, and add the following argument:

```
/parameters:SPMetal.xml
```

Now run the SPMetal.cmd file again. This will overwrite the existing SPPart3.cs file, and you will get a warning from Visual Studio that the file has been modified. If you reload the file in Visual Studio, you will notice that there are several additional content type classes including WorkflowTask and WF_Chapter10LunchOrderTask.

■ **Tip** If you run the `SPMetal.cmd` command file and the `SPPart3.cs` file is deleted or not updated, start a command window, navigate to the `Workflow1` folder, and run `SPMetal.cmd`. If there is an error in the XML file, it will output a message that indicates where the error is. The following message indicates there is an error on line 5 at column 4: `Error: There is an error in XML document (5,4)`.

Specifying Lists

You can use a `List` element to force a list to be included in the output file. To output the `Tasks` list, for example, you would add the following:

```
<List Name="Tasks" />
```

If you want only certain lists to be generated, add `List` elements to specify them, and then add an `ExcludeOtherLists` element. This will cause all other lists to be excluded. For example, to only generate the `Tasks` list, enter the following elements:

```
<List Name="Tasks" />
<ExcludeOtherLists />
```

The `ExcludeOtherLists` element must come after the List elements. You can also add an `IncludeHiddenLists` element, which will force any hidden lists to be generated.

■ **Caution** You can't use both `ExcludeOtherLists` and `IncludeHiddenLists`.

Specifying Content Types

You can force a particular content type to be included in the output file by adding a `ContentType` element. To force the `WorkflowTasks` list to be generated, for example, add the following:

```
<ContentType Name="Workflow Task" />
```

Similarly, you can also exclude a specific content type from being generated by adding an `ExcludeContentType` element such as the following:

```
<ExcludeContentType Name="Document" />
```

If you exclude a content type, all the content types derived from it are also excluded. Also, the classes for any lists that were based on that content type will now use its base class, in this case `Item`.

You can also use the `ContentType` element to change the class name that will be generated for that content type. The existing class `WF_Chapter10LunchOrderTask` is somewhat awkward. In Visual Studio, edit the `SPMetal.xml` by adding a `ContentType` element. Listing 12-2 shows the complete file, and the additional line is in bold.

Listing 12-2. Modified SPMetal.xml File

```xml
<?xml version="1.0" encoding="utf-8"?>
<Web AccessModifier="Internal"
  xmlns="http://schemas.microsoft.com/SharePoint/2009/spmetal">
  <ContentType Name="WF_Chapter10 - LunchOrderTask" Class="LunchOrderTask" />
  <IncludeHiddenContentTypes/>
</Web>
```

■ **Caution** The IncludeHiddenContentTypes element must come after any ContentType elements.

Open the SPPart3.cs file, and you should see the class for this custom content type declared as follows:

```
internal partial class LunchOrderTask : WorkflowTask
```

Just like with lists, you can cause only the specific content types to be generated by adding the ExcludeOtherContentTypes element. This prevents classes from being generated for any content type that is not specifically included using a ContentType element. You cannot use both this and IncludeHiddenContentTypes. Also, ExcludeOtherContentTypes must come after all ContentType elements in the XML file.

Specifying Columns

In the same way, you can force columns to be included or excluded from the class definition using the Column and ExcludeColumn elements. The Column element can also be used to override the property name and/or type in the generated class. For example, the following elements will change the NoThanks column to NotEating and exclude the Sides column from being generated:

```xml
<ContentType Name="WF_Chapter10 - LunchOrderTask" Class="LunchOrderTask" >
  <Column Name="NoThanks" Member="NotEating" />
  <ExcludeColumn Name="Sides" />
</ContentType>
```

■ **Caution** This code is just a sample. Do not add this to the SPMetal.xml file.

Using LINQ to SharePoint

Now that you have generated the strongly typed classes, you can use the power of LINQ to access data from your SharePoint site.

Adding a Collection Step

Open the `Workflow1.cs` file using the workflow designer. Drag a `CodeActivity` just before the final `createTask1` activity. Change the name to **collectOrders**. The workflow design should look like Figure 12-9.

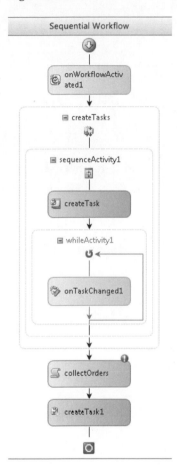

Figure 12-9. *Final workflow design*

Double-click the `collectOrders` activity to generate the event handler. This should open the code-behind file. Add the following namespace:

```
using WF_Chapter12.Workflow1.SPPart3;
```

This was the namespace passed in to the SPMetal utility. All the generated classes are in this namespace, so you'll need to include this namespace to be able to access them.

Add the following members to the `Workflow1` class:

```
private string _relatedItem = "";
private string _orders = "";
```

The _relatedItem member will store the ID of the Event item that generated this workflow. The _orders member will store the consolidated orders for this event. Go to the onWorkflowActivated_Invoked event handler, and add a line of code to store the event ID. The following code shows the beginning of this method with the added line in bold:

```
private void onWorkflowActivated1_Invoked(object sender,
    ExternalDataEventArgs e)
{
    SPListItem item = workflowProperties.Item;
    _eventName = item.Title;
    _menuUrl = item["MenuUrl"].ToString();
    _relatedItem = string.Format("ID={0},", item.ID);
```

This code takes the ID from the list item that this workflow was invoked on and stores it in a string. I'll explain how that is used later.

Writing a LINQ Query

The event handler for the collectOrders activity should be at the end of the code-behind file. Enter the code shown in Listing 12-3 for its implementation.

Listing 12-3. Implementation of collectOrders

```
private void collectOrders_ExecuteCode(object sender, EventArgs e)
{
  SPPart3DataContext dc = new SPPart3DataContext("http://omega5/part3");

  IQueryable<LunchOrderTask7> q
      = dc.Tasks.OfType<LunchOrderTask>()
          .Where(x => x.RelatedContent.Contains(_relatedItem));

  _orders = "The lunch orders are as follows:\r\n";

  foreach (LunchOrderTask i in q)
  {
      _orders += i.AssignedTo;

      if (i.NoThanks.HasValue && i.NoThanks.Value)
      {
          _orders += " - not eating";
      }
      else
      {
          _orders += string.Format
              ("\r\nEntree: {0}\r\nSides: {1}\r\nInstructions: {2}",
              i.Entree, i.Sides, i.SpecialInstructions);
```

```
        }
        _orders += "\r\n\r\n";
    }
}
```

This code creates an instance of the SPPart3DataContext class and passes in the URL of the SharePoint site.

■ **Note** You'll need to modify this code to use the correct URL for your environment.

The code then executes the following LINQ query:

```
IQueryable<LunchOrderTask> q
    = dc.Tasks.OfType<LunchOrderTask>()
        .Where(x => x.RelatedContent.Contains(_relatedItem));
```

The query returns an IQueryable collection of LunchOrderTask objects. The LunchOrderTask is the class generated by SPMetal representing your custom content type. Using dc.Tasks specifies that you are looking for items in the Tasks list. The OfType<T>() method filters the items in the Tasks list to only the ones that use the custom content type. This eliminates all the other tasks that may also be in the Tasks list.

The Where() method is used to further filter the results to only those that were generated for this event. The RelatedContent column of the Workflow Task content type (of which the custom content type is derived from) is provided by SharePoint as a URL to a form that will display the related item. In this case, it is the Event item that this workflow was invoked on. The ID of the specific event is passed in to this URL. The format of the URL will be as follows:

```
<form url>?ID=<event ID>,<other parameters>
```

Recall that the _relatedItem member was formatted as follows:

```
_relatedItem = string.Format("ID={0},", item.ID);
```

By using the Contains() method, this query returns only those tasks that have this specific event ID in their RelatedItem column. In other words, it returns the tasks associated with this event.

Collecting the Orders

The rest of this code formats the _orders string. Using a foreach block, it processes each of the tasks that is returned by the query. The AssignedTo property contains the login of the person the task was assigned to; this is the person who the lunch order is for.

It checks to see whether the No Thanks check box was selected. If not, it adds the Entree, Sides, and SpecialInstructions to the _orders string.

The last step is to include the _orders information in the final task description. Modify the createTask1_MethodInvoking() method by adding the code shown in bold in Listing 12-4.

Listing 12-4. Implementation of createTask1_MethodInvoking

```
CreateTask task = sender as CreateTask;
task.TaskId = Guid.NewGuid();

SPWorkflowTaskProperties wtp = new SPWorkflowTaskProperties();
wtp.PercentComplete = (float)0.0;
wtp.TaskType = 0;
wtp.DueDate = DateTime.Now.AddDays(1);
wtp.Title = "Lunch orders are complete";
wtp.Description = _orders;

task.TaskProperties = wtp;
```

Listing 12-5 shows the complete implementation of the `Workflow1.cs` code-behind class.

Listing 12-5. Implementation of Workflow1.cs

```
using System;
using System.ComponentModel;
using System.ComponentModel.Design;
using System.Collections;
using System.Drawing;
using System.Linq;
using System.Workflow.ComponentModel.Compiler;
using System.Workflow.ComponentModel.Serialization;
using System.Workflow.ComponentModel;
using System.Workflow.ComponentModel.Design;
using System.Workflow.Runtime;
using System.Workflow.Activities;
using System.Workflow.Activities.Rules;
using Microsoft.SharePoint;
using Microsoft.SharePoint.Workflow;
using Microsoft.SharePoint.WorkflowActions;

using System.Collections.Generic;
using System.Threading;

using WF_Chapter12.Workflow1.SPPart3;

namespace WF_Chapter11.Workflow1
{
    [Serializable]
    public class Invitee
    {
        public string AssignedTo { get; set; }
        public Guid TaskId { get; set; }
        public bool Complete { get; set; }

        public Invitee(string assignedTo)
        {
```

```
            AssignedTo = assignedTo;
            Complete = false;
        }
}

public sealed partial class Workflow1 : SequentialWorkflowActivity
{
    public Workflow1()
    {
        InitializeComponent();
    }

    public Guid workflowId = default(System.Guid);
    public SPWorkflowActivationProperties workflowProperties =
        new SPWorkflowActivationProperties();

    public SPContentTypeId contentTypeId =
        new SPContentTypeId("0x010801000da2ad56f41a465bbaa3311519728c2c");
    //("0x01080100211c4a0fc8144c7eb270141b81e38a8a");
    public string contentTypeIdString = "";

    private string _eventName;
    private string _menuUrl;
    public List<Invitee> ChildData = new List<Invitee>();
    private int _task = 0;
    private string _relatedItem = "";
    private string _orders = "";

    private void onWorkflowActivated1_Invoked(object sender,
        ExternalDataEventArgs e)
    {
        SPListItem item = workflowProperties.Item;
        _eventName = item.Title;
        _menuUrl = item["MenuUrl"].ToString();
        _relatedItem = string.Format("ID={0},", item.ID);

        List<SPFieldUserValue> l = (List<SPFieldUserValue>)item["Attendees"];
        foreach (SPFieldUserValue u in l)
        {
            ChildData.Add(new Invitee(u.User.LoginName));
        }

        try
        {
            workflowProperties.TaskList.ContentTypesEnabled = true;
            SPContentTypeId matchContentTypeId = workflowProperties.TaskList
                .ContentTypes.BestMatch(contentTypeId);
            if (matchContentTypeId.Parent.CompareTo(contentTypeId) != 0)
            {
                SPContentType ct = workflowProperties.TaskList.ParentWeb
                    .AvailableContentTypes[contentTypeId];
                workflowProperties.TaskList.ContentTypes.Add(ct);
```

```
            workflowProperties.TaskList.Update();
        }

        contentTypeIdString = contentTypeId.ToString();
    }
    catch (Exception)
    {
    }
}

private void createTask_MethodInvoking(object sender, EventArgs e)
{
    // Get the task object from the sender parameter
    CreateTaskWithContentType task = sender as CreateTaskWithContentType;

    // Assign a new TaskId
    task.TaskId = Guid.NewGuid();

    // Safely get the next Invitee
    Mutex m = new Mutex(false);
    Invitee i = (Invitee)ChildData[_task++];
    m.Close();

    // Setup the task properties
    SPWorkflowTaskProperties wtp = new SPWorkflowTaskProperties();
    wtp.PercentComplete = (float)0.0;
    wtp.AssignedTo = i.AssignedTo;
    wtp.TaskType = 0;
    wtp.DueDate = DateTime.Now.AddDays(1);
    wtp.Title = "Enter your lunch order";
    wtp.Description = _eventName;
    wtp.ExtendedProperties["MenuUrl"] = _menuUrl;

    task.TaskProperties = wtp;

    // Store the taskID in the Invitee object
    i.TaskId = task.TaskId;

    // Store the taskID on the OnTaskChanged activity
    Activity seq = task.Parent;
    if (seq != null)
    {
        Activity w = seq.GetActivityByName("whileActivity1");
        if (w != null)
        {
            OnTaskChanged tc =
                (OnTaskChanged)w.GetActivityByName("onTaskChanged1");
            if (tc != null)
                tc.TaskId = task.TaskId;
        }
    }
}
```

```csharp
private void notCompleted(object sender, ConditionalEventArgs e)
{
    WhileActivity w = sender as WhileActivity;
    OnTaskChanged tc =
        (OnTaskChanged)w.GetActivityByName("onTaskChanged1");

    e.Result = true;

    foreach (Invitee i in ChildData)
    {
        if (i.TaskId == tc.TaskId)
        {
            e.Result = !i.Complete;
            break;
        }
    }
}

private void onTaskChanged1_Invoked(object sender, ExternalDataEventArgs e)
{
    SPTaskServiceEventArgs args = (SPTaskServiceEventArgs)e;

    // Find this Invitee and mark it complete
    foreach (Invitee i in ChildData)
    {
        if (i.TaskId == args.taskId)
        {
            i.Complete = true;
            break;
        }
    }
}

private void createTask1_MethodInvoking(object sender, EventArgs e)
{
    CreateTask task = sender as CreateTask;
    task.TaskId = Guid.NewGuid();

    SPWorkflowTaskProperties wtp = new SPWorkflowTaskProperties();
    wtp.PercentComplete = (float)0.0;
    wtp.TaskType = 0;
    wtp.DueDate = DateTime.Now.AddDays(1);
    wtp.Title = "Lunch orders are complete";
    wtp.Description = _orders;

    task.TaskProperties = wtp;
}

private void collectOrders_ExecuteCode(object sender, EventArgs e)
{
    SPPart3DataContext dc = new SPPart3DataContext("http://omega5/part3");
```

```
IQueryable<LunchOrderTask> q
    = dc.Tasks.OfType<LunchOrderTask>()
        .Where(x => x.RelatedContent.Contains(_relatedItem));

_orders = "The lunch orders are as follows:\r\n";

foreach (LunchOrderTask i in q)
{
    _orders += i.AssignedTo;

    if (i.NoThanks.HasValue && i.NoThanks.Value)
    {
        _orders += " - not eating";
    }
    else
    {
        _orders += string.Format
            ("\r\nEntree: {0}\r\nSides: {1}\r\nInstructions: {2}",
            i.Entree, i.Sides, i.SpecialInstructions);
    }
    _orders += "\r\n\r\n";
}
            }
        }
}
```

Testing the Workflow

Press F6 to rebuild the solution, and fix any compiler errors. Then press F5 to debug the application. This should launch the SharePoint site and display the Calendar list. Select the event that you created in the previous chapter. If the event was deleted, refer to Chapter 11 for instructions on how to set it up. The event should look like the one shown in Figure 12-10.

Figure 12-10. The Event item

Click the *Workflows* link at the top of the event form, which will display the Workflows page shown in Figure 12-11.

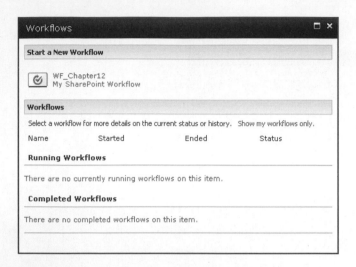

Figure 12-11. The Workflows page

The `WF_Chapter12` workflow should be listed as an available workflow. Click the *WF_Chapter12* link to start the workflow process. Once it has finished, close this window, and display the `Tasks` list. There should be a task for each person who was invited to the event. The `Tasks` list should look like Figure 12-12.

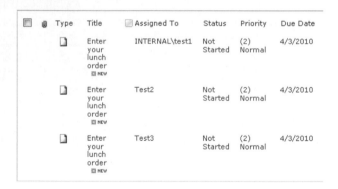

Figure 12-12. The Tasks list showing the lunch order tasks

Edit each of these tasks, entering a lunch order for that person. On at least one of these, select the **No Thanks** check box. When the last task has been completed, the workflow should create a final task.

■ **Note** You may have to refresh the page for the new task to appear in the `Tasks` list.

Click the final task to view its details. The form should look like the one shown in Figure 12-13.

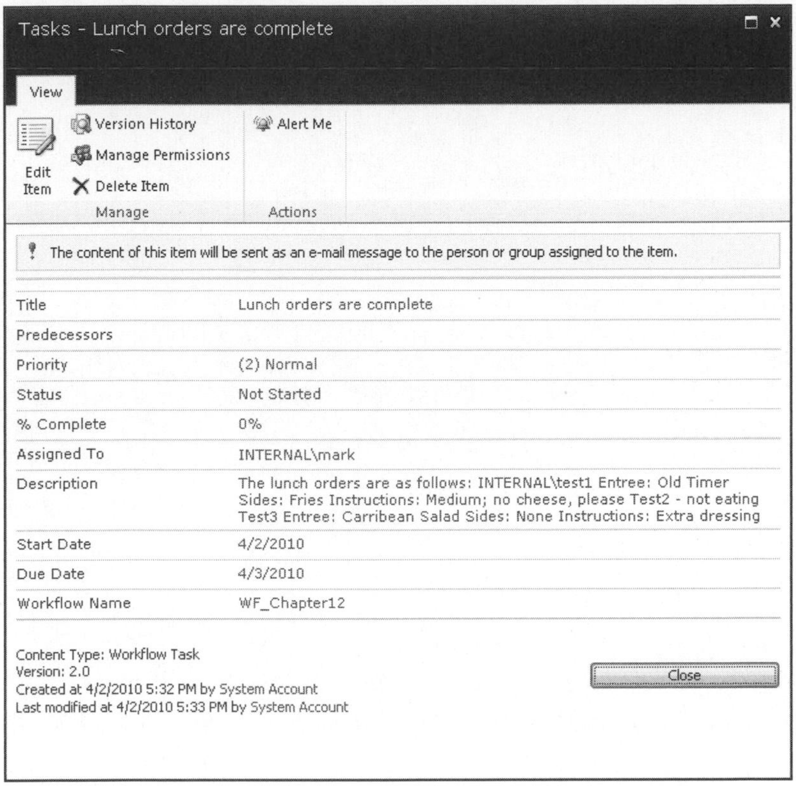

Figure 12-13. The final task form showing the consolidated lunch orders

The `Description` field contains the details of each of the orders that was entered.

Summary

In this chapter, you used the `SPMetal` utility to generate strongly types classes to represent your lists and content types. You provided an XML file to control which objects were included and what class names to use. The generated output file was then added to your Visual Studio project.

You then implemented code inside your workflow that used a LINQ to SharePoint query to collect the data from each of the tasks in this workflow. The consolidated data was then provided in the final workflow task.

In addition to being a very convenient way to access data, this approach also has the benefit of compile-time type checking and IntelliSense support.

CHAPTER 13

■ ■ ■

Using State Machine Workflows

Until now, you have used only sequential workflows. They are useful for fairly simple workflows and were adequate to demonstrate the features I have covered so far. If you're going to build any serious workflows, however, you will probably want to use a state machine workflow. They may take some getting used to, but once you get the hang of it, you'll find they can simplify your design and often more closely model the real-world scenarios.

The problem with sequential workflows is just that; they're sequential. They perform step A, then B, then C. You can use conditional branches and `while` loops, but you can't really step backward. For example, in the Three-state workflow you used in Chapter 4, the item was created, worked, and then submitted for feedback. What if the initiator wasn't satisfied? There was no way to put the item back in the assigned status to be reworked.

Creating the Sample Project

In this chapter, you'll build a bug-tracking system. An initiator will submit a bug, and an admin person will review and assign it to a developer. The developer will fix the bug, and a tester will be notified to verify the fix. That's the normal path anyway. The system will also allow the reviewer (and developer) to indicate that the system is "working as designed" and send the bug back to the initiator. The developer can also push this back to the initiator if clarification is needed. Finally, the tester can send it back to the developer if the fix is not working.

Start Visual Studio 2010, and create a blank solution as shown in Figure 13-1. Enter the solution name **WF_Chapter13**.

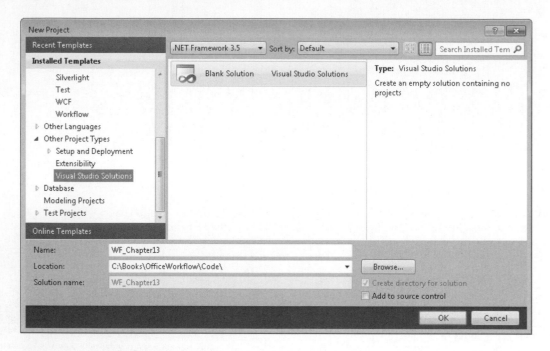

Figure 13-1. *Creating a blank solution*

The first step in creating this solution is to define the list and content types that will be used by the workflow. You'll put these into a separate project. This will keep the workflow logic separate from the list definition and allow you to deploy them independently.

■ **Tip** You may have noticed in the previous projects that Visual Studio deploys the workflow to the home site. You can specify a child site for debugging, but the workflow feature is still deployed to the home site and is available to all sites on that server. More importantly, other elements of the feature such as content types are also added to the home site. By putting these definitions in a separate project, you can add them to the subsite, Part3 in this case, instead of the root.

Creating the BugList

From the Solution Explorer, right-click the WF_Chapter13 solution, and choose Add ▶ New Project. In the Add New Project dialog box, select the Content Type template from the SharePoint 2010 group. Enter the name **BugList**, as shown in Figure 13-2.

Figure 13-2. Creating a new Content Type project

In the SharePoint Customization Wizard, select the same Part3 SharePoint site that you have been using for the past few chapters. Select the `Deploy as a farm solution` option, as shown in Figure 13-3.

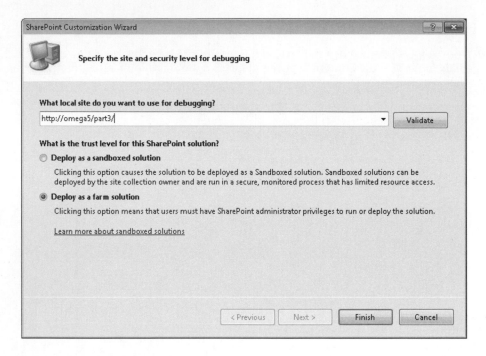

Figure 13-3. Specifying the target site

This is the same dialog box that you have used before. Notice however that the other dialog boxes are not shown because you are not defining a workflow, yet.

Defining the Bug Content Type

A dialog box will appear to select the base content type; just use the default value. The template will create a `ContentType1` content type. From the Solution Explorer, right-click the `ContentType1` item, and choose Delete. You will now create a new content type. Right-click the BugList project, and choose Add ▶ New Item. In the Add New Item dialog box, select the Content Type template from the SharePoint 2010 group. Enter the name **Bug**, as shown in Figure 13-4.

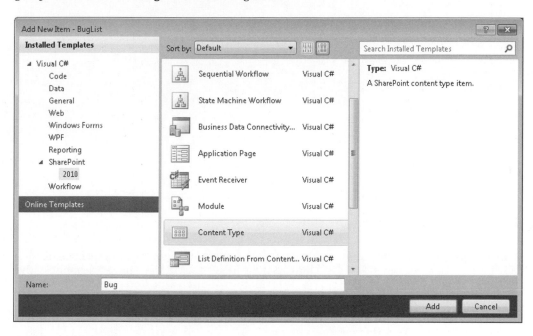

Figure 13-4. Adding a content type

The SharePoint Customization Wizard will then ask you which content type should be used as the base type for the new content type. Select **Item**, as shown in Figure 13-5.

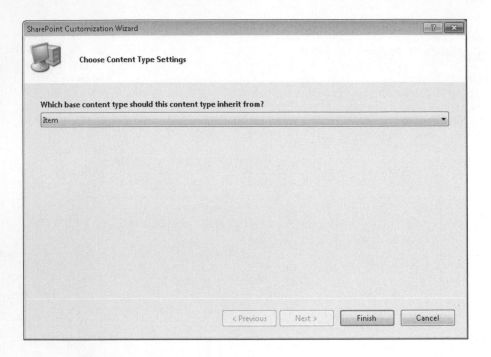

Figure 13-5. Specifying the base content type

You will first need to define the columns (or fields) that this content type will use. `Elements.xml` should already be open; if not, open it. Edit the contents of the `Elements.xml` file, change the name of the content type to **Bug**, and enter a description such as **Information about a reported bug**. Add the field definitions shown in Listing 13-1 to the `Elements.xml` file *before* the content type definition.

Listing 13-1. Field Definitions Needed for the Bug Content Type

```
<Field ID="{7B7EBD2E-F2D8-4B9E-8DBD-0CAB24521542}"
       Type="Choice"
       BaseType="Text"
       Name="BugStatus"
       DisplayName="BugStatus"
       Sealed="TRUE"
       StaticName="BugStatus">
  <CHOICES>
    <CHOICE>Pending</CHOICE>
    <CHOICE>Working As Designed</CHOICE>
    <CHOICE>Assigned</CHOICE>
    <CHOICE>Active</CHOICE>
    <CHOICE>Waiting</CHOICE>
    <CHOICE>Fixed</CHOICE>
    <CHOICE>Tested</CHOICE>
    <CHOICE>Closed</CHOICE>
```

```
    </CHOICES>
</Field>
<Field ID="{C61854FA-254F-4597-9A86-B0533185A288}"
        Type="Note"
        Name="Description"
        DisplayName="Description"
        Sealed="TRUE"
        StaticName="Description">
</Field>
<Field ID="{6805B891-76EE-4B22-9373-9D8C95CEE761}"
        Type="Note"
        Name="Resolution"
        DisplayName="Resolution"
        Sealed="TRUE"
        StaticName="Resolution">
</Field>
<Field ID="{6CFB14EE-7834-42DE-9E7B-9847D6ADA88A}"
        Type="Note"
        Name="Feedback"
        DisplayName="Feedback"
        Sealed="TRUE"
        StaticName="Feedback">
</Field>
```

This defines the following fields:

- BugStatus

- Description

- Resolution

- Feedback

The BugStatus field uses a CHOICES collection to define the allowable values for this field. These also correspond to the possible states that the workflow can be in. Add the FieldRef specifications shown in Listing 13-2 to the content type definition.

Listing 13-2. The Bug Content Type Definition

```
<FieldRefs>
  <FieldRef ID="{fa564e0f-0c70-4ab9-b863-0177e6ddd247}"
            Name="Title"
            Required="TRUE"
            ShowInNewForm="TRUE"
            ShowInDisplayForm="TRUE"
            ShowInEditForm="TRUE"/>
  <FieldRef ID="{9F8B4EE0-84B7-42c6-A094-5CBDE2115EB9}"
            Name="Date Created"
            Required="FALSE"
            ShowInNewForm="FALSE"
            ShowInDisplayForm="TRUE"
```

```
                    ShowInEditForm="TRUE"/>
    <FieldRef ID="{7B7EBD2E-F2D8-4B9E-8DBD-0CAB24521542}"
                    Name="BugStatus"
                    Required="TRUE"
                    ShowInNewForm="FALSE"
                    ShowInDisplayForm="TRUE"
                    ShowInEditForm="FALSE"/>
    <FieldRef ID="{C61854FA-254F-4597-9A86-B0533185A288}"
                    Name="Description"
                    Required="TRUE"
                    ShowInNewForm="TRUE"
                    ShowInDisplayForm="TRUE"
                    ShowInEditForm="TRUE"/>
    <FieldRef ID="{a8eb573e-9e11-481a-a8c9-1104a54b2fbd}"
                    Name="Priority"
                    Required="FALSE"
                    ShowInNewForm="FALSE"
                    ShowInDisplayForm="TRUE"
                    ShowInEditForm="TRUE"/>
    <FieldRef ID="{53101f38-dd2e-458c-b245-0c236cc13d1a}"
                    Name="AssignedTo"
                    Required="FALSE"
                    ShowInNewForm="FALSE"
                    ShowInDisplayForm="TRUE"
                    ShowInEditForm="TRUE"/>
    <FieldRef ID="{24BFA3C2-E6A0-4651-80E9-3DB44BF52147}"
                    Name="DateCompleted"
                    Required="FALSE"
                    ShowInNewForm="FALSE"
                    ShowInDisplayForm="TRUE"
                    ShowInEditForm="TRUE"/>
    <FieldRef ID="{6805B891-76EE-4B22-9373-9D8C95CEE761}"
                    Name="Resolution"
                    Required="FALSE"
                    ShowInNewForm="FALSE"
                    ShowInDisplayForm="TRUE"
                    ShowInEditForm="TRUE"/>
    <FieldRef ID="{6CFB14EE-7834-42DE-9E7B-9847D6ADA88A}"
                    Name="Feedback"
                    Required="FALSE"
                    ShowInNewForm="FALSE"
                    ShowInDisplayForm="TRUE"
                    ShowInEditForm="TRUE"/>
</FieldRefs>
```

■ **Tip** Some of the fields are the new fields that you just defined. However, many of them are existing site columns that are shipped with SharePoint. To include them in a content type, you need to specify the `Guid` assigned to them. This presents a bit of a problem because the `Guid` is not displayed anywhere on SharePoint or the SharePoint Designer. The following web site provides a list of the built-in site columns and their associated `Guids`: `http://www.johnholliday.net/downloads/fieldswss.htm`. This will come in handy when setting up content types in Visual Studio.

Defining the BugList

The next step is to define the list that will store the bugs that are reported. Visual Studio provides a template that lets you create a list using a content type definition. From Visual Studio, right-click the BugList project, and choose Add ▶ New Item. In the Add New Item dialog box, select the List Definition From Content Type template, as shown in Figure 13-6. Enter the name **BugList**.

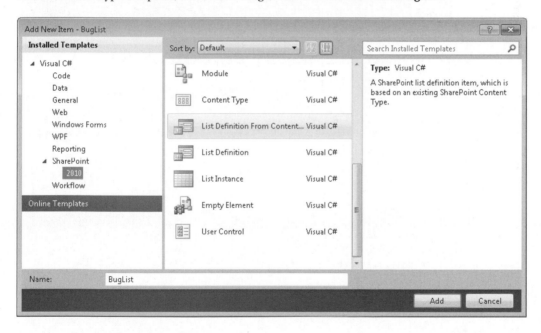

Figure 13-6. Adding a list definition

The SharePoint Customization Wizard will then display giving you some options for configuring the list. The new Bug content type that you just defined should be the default choice. Also, make sure you deselect the `Add a list instance for this list definition` check box, as shown in Figure 13-7.

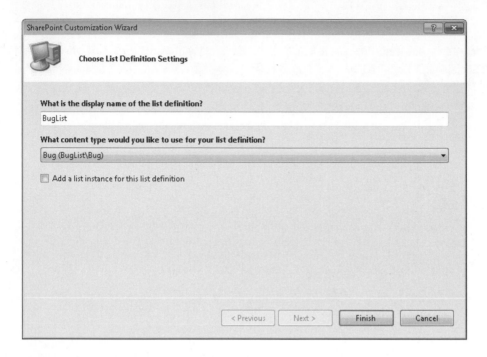

Figure 13-7. Configuring the new list

This feature will deploy this as a list template. This will allow the user to create their own list(s) from this template. The template creates a new `Elements.xml` file for the `BugList`. Edit the `Description` to give it a more meaningful value. The contents of the `Elements.xml` file should look like Listing 13-3.

Listing 13-3. The `Elements.xml` File for the BugList

```xml
<?xml version="1.0" encoding="utf-8"?>
<Elements xmlns="http://schemas.microsoft.com/sharepoint/">
    <!-- Do not change the value of the Name attribute below.
         If it does not match the folder name of the List Definition
         project item, an error will occur when the project is run. -->
    <ListTemplate
        Name="BugList"
        Type="10000"
        BaseType="0"
        OnQuickLaunch="TRUE"
        SecurityBits="11"
        Sequence="410"
        DisplayName="BugList"
        Description="Bugs needing resolution"
        Image="/_layouts/images/itgen.png"/>
</Elements>
```

■ **Note** In addition to the `Elements.xml` file, the template also creates a `Schema.xml` file. If you open it, you'll find that is has much of the same information that defined the content type but in a different format. It also includes view, query, and form definitions.

Creating Tasks List Content Types

Recall from Chapter 10 that different content types can be used to customize the SharePoint forms. As a bug works through the workflow, various tasks will be created to perform specific actions such as review, fix, test, and so on. You will need to define a content type for each task to control what fields are displayed and editable in each.

Defining Additional Fields

First, however, you will specify some additional field definitions. Open the first `Elements.xml` file (the one that defined the `Bug` content type), and add the field definitions from Listing 13-4 to the `Elements.xml` file *before* the content type.

■ **Note** You will put the extra field definitions here, in the first `Elements.xml` file, because many of them will be used by multiple content types. Putting them here is a convenient way to keep them all together, without duplicating them for each of the content types.

Listing 13-4. Additional Field Definitions

```
<!-- These fields will be used by the task content types -->
<Field ID="{E50B3B2E-93B3-4B30-BCE2-29A2168CB635}"
       Type="Boolean"
       Name="BugWAD"
       DisplayName="Working As Designed"
       Sealed="TRUE"
       StaticName="BugWAD">
</Field>
<Field ID="{79C98C47-B7AC-4CE8-96DE-13B1BEEC3E05}"
       Type="Boolean"
       Name="BugWaiting"
       DisplayName="Waiting"
       Sealed="TRUE"
       StaticName="BugWaiting">
</Field>
<Field ID="{AD4B49AC-8138-4825-962C-6D38536E09F1}"
       Type="Boolean"
       Name="BugStarted"
```

```
        DisplayName="Started"
        Sealed="TRUE"
        StaticName="BugStarted">
</Field>
<Field ID="{FC7781A6-150C-4CC6-BE72-55DFCF8EA5B2}"
        Type="Boolean"
        Name="BugFixed"
        DisplayName="Fixed"
        Sealed="TRUE"
        StaticName="BugFixed">
</Field>
<Field ID="{9FB079A4-28C7-411E-829C-5891C19DF702}"
        Type="Boolean"
        Name="BugTested"
        DisplayName="Tested"
        Sealed="TRUE"
        StaticName="BugTested">
</Field>
<Field ID="{4C1D9606-F044-4D43-AD00-AE3B912764FB}"
        Type="Boolean"
        Name="BugNotFixed"
        DisplayName="Not Fixed"
        Sealed="TRUE"
        StaticName="BugNotFixed">
</Field>
<Field ID="{3868124A-D162-4A99-8A61-C91E593D68A7}"
        Type="Boolean"
        Name="BugClosed"
        DisplayName="Closed"
        Sealed="TRUE"
        StaticName="BugClosed">
</Field>
<Field ID="{69E039E9-F4D9-4CBB-A4C2-346B79FA8F6A}"
        Type="Boolean"
        Name="BugReSubmit"
        DisplayName="Re-submit"
        Sealed="TRUE"
        StaticName="BugReSubmit">
</Field>
<Field ID="{E7C4ED6D-38DD-4A5C-A6EE-14791E7BCC14}"
        Type="Choice"
        BaseType="Text"
        Name="BugPriority"
        DisplayName="Priority"
        Sealed="TRUE"
        StaticName="BugPriority">
  <CHOICES>
    <CHOICE>High</CHOICE>
    <CHOICE>Normal</CHOICE>
    <CHOICE>Low</CHOICE>
  </CHOICES>
</Field>
```

```
<Field ID="{35A9F18D-6AA9-4580-838C-A9F4DCA2B85C}"
       Type="User"
       Name="BugAssign"
       DisplayName="Assign To"
       Sealed="TRUE"
       StaticName="BugAssign">
</Field>
```

Listing 13-5 shows the complete final implementation of the Elements.xml file (for the Bug content type).

Listing 13-5. Final Implementation of the Bug Content Type

```
<?xml version="1.0" encoding="utf-8"?>
<Elements xmlns="http://schemas.microsoft.com/sharepoint/">

  <Field ID="{7B7EBD2E-F2D8-4B9E-8DBD-0CAB24521542}"
         Type="Choice"
         BaseType="Text"
         Name="BugStatus"
         DisplayName="BugStatus"
         Sealed="TRUE"
         StaticName="BugStatus">
    <CHOICES>
      <CHOICE>Pending</CHOICE>
      <CHOICE>Working As Designed</CHOICE>
      <CHOICE>Assigned</CHOICE>
      <CHOICE>Active</CHOICE>
      <CHOICE>Waiting</CHOICE>
      <CHOICE>Fixed</CHOICE>
      <CHOICE>Tested</CHOICE>
      <CHOICE>Closed</CHOICE>
    </CHOICES>
  </Field>
  <Field ID="{C61854FA-254F-4597-9A86-B0533185A288}"
         Type="Note"
         Name="Description"
         DisplayName="Description"
         Sealed="TRUE"
         StaticName="Description">
  </Field>
  <Field ID="{6805B891-76EE-4B22-9373-9D8C95CEE761}"
         Type="Note"
         Name="Resolution"
         DisplayName="Resolution"
         Sealed="TRUE"
         StaticName="Resolution">
  </Field>
  <Field ID="{6CFB14EE-7834-42DE-9E7B-9847D6ADA88A}"
         Type="Note"
         Name="Feedback"
```

```
        DisplayName="Feedback"
        Sealed="TRUE"
        StaticName="Feedback">
</Field>

<!-- These fields will be used by the task content types -->
<Field ID="{E50B3B2E-93B3-4B30-BCE2-29A2168CB635}"
        Type="Boolean"
        Name="BugWAD"
        DisplayName="Working As Designed"
        Sealed="TRUE"
        StaticName="BugWAD">
</Field>
<Field ID="{79C98C47-B7AC-4CE8-96DE-13B1BEEC3E05}"
        Type="Boolean"
        Name="BugWaiting"
        DisplayName="Waiting"
        Sealed="TRUE"
        StaticName="BugWaiting">
</Field>
<Field ID="{AD4B49AC-8138-4825-962C-6D38536E09F1}"
        Type="Boolean"
        Name="BugStarted"
        DisplayName="Started"
        Sealed="TRUE"
        StaticName="BugStarted">
</Field>
<Field ID="{FC7781A6-150C-4CC6-BE72-55DFCF8EA5B2}"
        Type="Boolean"
        Name="BugFixed"
        DisplayName="Fixed"
        Sealed="TRUE"
        StaticName="BugFixed">
</Field>
<Field ID="{9FB079A4-28C7-411E-829C-5891C19DF702}"
        Type="Boolean"
        Name="BugTested"
        DisplayName="Tested"
        Sealed="TRUE"
        StaticName="BugTested">
</Field>
<Field ID="{4C1D9606-F044-4D43-AD00-AE3B912764FB}"
        Type="Boolean"
        Name="BugNotFixed"
        DisplayName="Not Fixed"
        Sealed="TRUE"
        StaticName="BugNotFixed">
</Field>
<Field ID="{3868124A-D162-4A99-8A61-C91E593D68A7}"
        Type="Boolean"
        Name="BugClosed"
        DisplayName="Closed"
```

```xml
          Sealed="TRUE"
          StaticName="BugClosed">
</Field>
<Field ID="{69E039E9-F4D9-4CBB-A4C2-346B79FA8F6A}"
       Type="Boolean"
       Name="BugReSubmit"
       DisplayName="Re-submit"
       Sealed="TRUE"
       StaticName="BugReSubmit">
</Field>
<Field ID="{E7C4ED6D-38DD-4A5C-A6EE-14791E7BCC14}"
       Type="Choice"
       BaseType="Text"
       Name="BugPriority"
       DisplayName="Priority"
       Sealed="TRUE"
       StaticName="BugPriority">
  <CHOICES>
    <CHOICE>High</CHOICE>
    <CHOICE>Normal</CHOICE>
    <CHOICE>Low</CHOICE>
  </CHOICES>
</Field>
<Field ID="{35A9F18D-6AA9-4580-838C-A9F4DCA2B85C}"
       Type="User"
       Name="BugAssign"
       DisplayName="Assign To"
       Sealed="TRUE"
       StaticName="BugAssign">
</Field>

<!-- Parent ContentType: Item (0x01) -->
<ContentType ID="0x0100f0f7844f4fd24c57946f5d88cab09e0e"
             Name="Bug"
             Group="Custom Content Types"
             Description="Information about a reported bug"
             Inherits="TRUE"
             Version="0">
  <FieldRefs>
    <FieldRef ID="{fa564e0f-0c70-4ab9-b863-0177e6ddd247}"
         Name="Title"
         Required="TRUE"
         ShowInNewForm="TRUE"
         ShowInDisplayForm="TRUE"
         ShowInEditForm="TRUE"/>
    <FieldRef ID="{9F8B4EE0-84B7-42c6-A094-5CBDE2115EB9}"
              Name="Date Created"
              Required="FALSE"
              ShowInNewForm="FALSE"
              ShowInDisplayForm="TRUE"
              ShowInEditForm="TRUE"/>
    <FieldRef ID="{7B7EBD2E-F2D8-4B9E-8DBD-0CAB24521542}"
```

```xml
                    Name="BugStatus"
                    Required="TRUE"
                    ShowInNewForm="FALSE"
                    ShowInDisplayForm="TRUE"
                    ShowInEditForm="FALSE"/>
        <FieldRef ID="{C61854FA-254F-4597-9A86-B0533185A288}"
                    Name="Description"
                    Required="TRUE"
                    ShowInNewForm="TRUE"
                    ShowInDisplayForm="TRUE"
                    ShowInEditForm="TRUE"/>
        <FieldRef ID="{a8eb573e-9e11-481a-a8c9-1104a54b2fbd}"
                    Name="Priority"
                    Required="FALSE"
                    ShowInNewForm="FALSE"
                    ShowInDisplayForm="TRUE"
                    ShowInEditForm="TRUE"/>
        <FieldRef ID="{53101f38-dd2e-458c-b245-0c236cc13d1a}"
                    Name="AssignedTo"
                    Required="FALSE"
                    ShowInNewForm="FALSE"
                    ShowInDisplayForm="TRUE"
                    ShowInEditForm="TRUE"/>
        <FieldRef ID="{24BFA3C2-E6A0-4651-80E9-3DB44BF52147}"
                    Name="DateCompleted"
                    Required="FALSE"
                    ShowInNewForm="FALSE"
                    ShowInDisplayForm="TRUE"
                    ShowInEditForm="TRUE"/>
        <FieldRef ID="{6805B891-76EE-4B22-9373-9D8C95CEE761}"
                    Name="Resolution"
                    Required="FALSE"
                    ShowInNewForm="FALSE"
                    ShowInDisplayForm="TRUE"
                    ShowInEditForm="TRUE"/>
        <FieldRef ID="{6CFB14EE-7834-42DE-9E7B-9847D6ADA88A}"
                    Name="Feedback"
                    Required="FALSE"
                    ShowInNewForm="FALSE"
                    ShowInDisplayForm="TRUE"
                    ShowInEditForm="TRUE"/>
    </FieldRefs>
  </ContentType>
</Elements>
```

Defining the Task Content Types

The next step is to define a content type for each type of task that will be created. You will need the following content types:

- BugActive
- BugAssigned
- BugFixed
- BugPending
- BugWad
- BugWaiting

From the Solution Explorer, right-click the BugList project, and choose Add ▶ New Item. In the Add New Item dialog box, select the Content Type template, and enter the name **BugActive**, as shown in Figure 13-8.

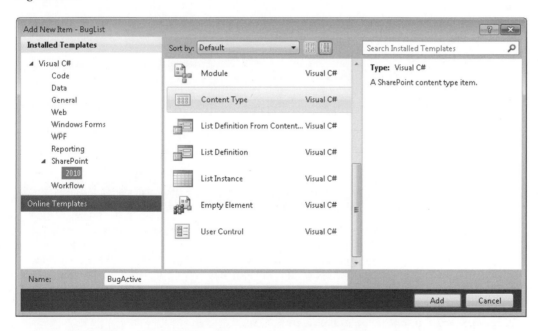

Figure 13-8. Adding a new content type

The SharePoint Customization Wizard will them prompt you for the base content type. These content types should be derived from the Workflow Task content type. However, because this is set up as a hidden type, it is not available in the drop-down list. Just select the `Task` content type, as shown in Figure 13-9, and you'll fix this later.

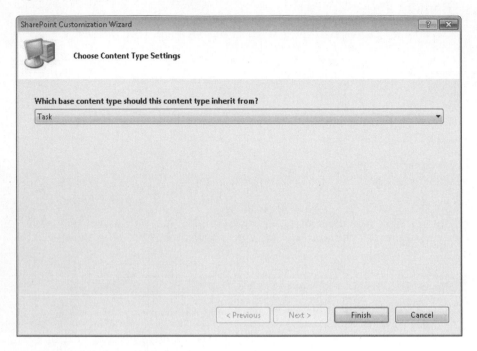

Figure 13-9. *Selecting the* `Task` *base content type*

The `Elements.xml` file for this content type should be displayed. The `ID` that is generated for you starts with `0x010800`. Insert a `01` after the `08`. The final prefix will be `0x01080100`.

■ **Note** You may want to refer to Chapter 10 for more information about content type ID conventions.

Change the `Name` to **BugActive** and the `Description` to **Bug – Active**. Add the `FieldRef` definitions from Listing 13-6. The contents of your `Elements.xml` file will look like Listing 13-6 but will have a different value for the `ID`.

Listing 13-6. `Elements.xml` *File for the* `BugActive` *Content Type*

```xml
<?xml version="1.0" encoding="utf-8"?>
<Elements xmlns="http://schemas.microsoft.com/sharepoint/">
  <!-- Parent ContentType: Workflow Task (0x010801) -->
  <ContentType ID="0x010801006f51849cf46b42939046cfd9cf6d3e0b"
               Name="BugActive">
```

```
                Group="Custom Content Types"
                Description="Bug - Active"
                Inherits="TRUE"
                Version="0">
    <FieldRefs>
      <FieldRef ID="{E50B3B2E-93B3-4B30-BCE2-29A2168CB635}"
                Name="BugWAD"
                Required="FALSE"
                ShowInNewForm="FALSE"
                ShowInDisplayForm="TRUE"
                ShowInEditForm="TRUE"/>
      <FieldRef ID="{79C98C47-B7AC-4CE8-96DE-13B1BEEC3E05}"
                Name="BugWaiting"
                Required="FALSE"
                ShowInNewForm="FALSE"
                ShowInDisplayForm="TRUE"
                ShowInEditForm="TRUE"/>
      <FieldRef ID="{FC7781A6-150C-4CC6-BE72-55DFCF8EA5B2}"
                Name="BugFixed"
                Required="FALSE"
                ShowInNewForm="FALSE"
                ShowInDisplayForm="TRUE"
                ShowInEditForm="TRUE"/>
      <FieldRef ID="{6805B891-76EE-4B22-9373-9D8C95CEE761}"
                Name="Resolution"
                Required="FALSE"
                ShowInNewForm="FALSE"
                ShowInDisplayForm="TRUE"
                ShowInEditForm="TRUE"/>
    </FieldRefs>
  </ContentType>
</Elements>
```

Tasks in the **Active** state will include the following fields:

- Working as Designed

- Waiting

- Fixed

- Resolution

The first three are check boxes that the developer can use to move the bug to another state. **Resolution** is a field where they will describe what was fixed.

Remaining Content Types

Repeat these steps to add the remaining content type definitions:

1. Right-click the BugList project, and choose Add ▶ New Item.

2. Select the Content Type template, and enter the content type name.

3. Select Task as the base content type.

4. Edit the content type ID, inserting an 01.

5. Modify the Name and Description .

6. Add the FieldRefs from the applicable code listing.

The following code listings, Listing 13-7 through Listing 13-11, are provided for each of the content types.

Listing 13-7. Elements.xml File for the BugAssigned Content Type

```xml
<?xml version="1.0" encoding="utf-8"?>
<Elements xmlns="http://schemas.microsoft.com/sharepoint/">
  <!-- Parent ContentType: Workflow Task (0x010801) -->
  <ContentType ID="0x01080100afbba42fb3c348f7923f08981f3546f9"
               Name="BugAssigned"
               Group="Custom Content Types"
               Description="Bug - Assigned"
               Inherits="TRUE"
               Version="0">
    <FieldRefs>
      <FieldRef ID="{E50B3B2E-93B3-4B30-BCE2-29A2168CB635}"
                Name="BugWAD"
                Required="FALSE"
                ShowInNewForm="FALSE"
                ShowInDisplayForm="TRUE"
                ShowInEditForm="TRUE"/>
      <FieldRef ID="{79C98C47-B7AC-4CE8-96DE-13B1BEEC3E05}"
                Name="BugWaiting"
                Required="FALSE"
                ShowInNewForm="FALSE"
                ShowInDisplayForm="TRUE"
                ShowInEditForm="TRUE"/>
      <FieldRef ID="{AD4B49AC-8138-4825-962C-6D38536E09F1}"
                Name="BugStarted"
                Required="FALSE"
                ShowInNewForm="FALSE"
                ShowInDisplayForm="TRUE"
                ShowInEditForm="TRUE"/>
      <FieldRef ID="{FC7781A6-150C-4CC6-BE72-55DFCF8EA5B2}"
                Name="BugFixed"
                Required="FALSE"
```

```
                    ShowInNewForm="FALSE"
                    ShowInDisplayForm="TRUE"
                    ShowInEditForm="TRUE"/>
        <FieldRef ID="{6805B891-76EE-4B22-9373-9D8C95CEE761}"
                    Name="Resolution"
                    Required="FALSE"
                    ShowInNewForm="FALSE"
                    ShowInDisplayForm="TRUE"
                    ShowInEditForm="TRUE"/>
      </FieldRefs>
    </ContentType>
</Elements>
```

Listing 13-8. Elements.xml File for the BugFixed Content Type

```
<?xml version="1.0" encoding="utf-8"?>
<Elements xmlns="http://schemas.microsoft.com/sharepoint/">
  <!-- Parent ContentType: Workflow Task (0x010801) -->
  <ContentType ID="0x0108010071aa11fb81d84de98ef7a53b1ee6ae38"
                    Name="BugFixed"
                    Group="Custom Content Types"
                    Description="Bug - Fixed"
                    Inherits="TRUE"
                    Version="0">
    <FieldRefs>
      <FieldRef ID="{9FB079A4-28C7-411E-829C-5891C19DF702}"
                    Name="BugTested"
                    Required="FALSE"
                    ShowInNewForm="FALSE"
                    ShowInDisplayForm="TRUE"
                    ShowInEditForm="TRUE"/>
      <FieldRef ID="{4C1D9606-F044-4D43-AD00-AE3B912764FB}"
                    Name="BugNotFixed"
                    Required="FALSE"
                    ShowInNewForm="FALSE"
                    ShowInDisplayForm="TRUE"
                    ShowInEditForm="TRUE"/>
      <FieldRef ID="{6CFB14EE-7834-42DE-9E7B-9847D6ADA88A}"
                    Name="Feedback"
                    Required="FALSE"
                    ShowInNewForm="FALSE"
                    ShowInDisplayForm="TRUE"
                    ShowInEditForm="TRUE"/>
    </FieldRefs>
  </ContentType>
</Elements>
```

Listing 13-9. Elements.xml File for the BugPending Content Type

```xml
<?xml version="1.0" encoding="utf-8"?>
<Elements xmlns="http://schemas.microsoft.com/sharepoint/">
  <!-- Parent ContentType: Workflow Task (0x010801) -->
  <ContentType ID="0x010801008fa5ff065e7e42e9b861eae33021c895"
               Name="BugPending"
               Group="Custom Content Types"
               Description="Bug - Pending"
               Inherits="TRUE"
               Version="0">
    <FieldRefs>
      <FieldRef ID="{E50B3B2E-93B3-4B30-BCE2-29A2168CB635}"
                Name="BugWAD"
                Required="FALSE"
                ShowInNewForm="FALSE"
                ShowInDisplayForm="TRUE"
                ShowInEditForm="TRUE"/>
      <FieldRef ID="{E7C4ED6D-38DD-4A5C-A6EE-14791E7BCC14}"
                Name="BugPriority"
                Required="FALSE"
                ShowInNewForm="FALSE"
                ShowInDisplayForm="TRUE"
                ShowInEditForm="TRUE"/>
      <FieldRef ID="{35A9F18D-6AA9-4580-838C-A9F4DCA2B85C}"
                Name="BugAssign"
                Required="FALSE"
                ShowInNewForm="FALSE"
                ShowInDisplayForm="TRUE"
                ShowInEditForm="TRUE"/>
    </FieldRefs>
  </ContentType>
</Elements>
```

Listing 13-10. Elements.xml File for the BugWad Content Type

```xml
<?xml version="1.0" encoding="utf-8"?>
<Elements xmlns="http://schemas.microsoft.com/sharepoint/">
  <!-- Parent ContentType: Workflow Task (0x010801) -->
  <ContentType ID="0x010801005c5fcc143af649f3bc1153474b637a7a"
               Name="BugWad"
               Group="Custom Content Types"
               Description="Bug - Wad"
               Inherits="TRUE"
               Version="0">
    <FieldRefs>
      <FieldRef ID="{3868124A-D162-4A99-8A61-C91E593D68A7}"
                Name="BugClosed"
                Required="FALSE"
                ShowInNewForm="FALSE"
                ShowInDisplayForm="TRUE"
```

```
                         ShowInEditForm="TRUE"/>
        <FieldRef ID="{69E039E9-F4D9-4CBB-A4C2-346B79FA8F6A}"
                         Name="BugReSubmit"
                         Required="FALSE"
                         ShowInNewForm="FALSE"
                         ShowInDisplayForm="TRUE"
                         ShowInEditForm="TRUE"/>
        <FieldRef ID="{6CFB14EE-7834-42DE-9E7B-9847D6ADA88A}"
                         Name="Feedback"
                         Required="FALSE"
                         ShowInNewForm="FALSE"
                         ShowInDisplayForm="TRUE"
                         ShowInEditForm="TRUE"/>
      </FieldRefs>
    </ContentType>
</Elements>
```

Listing 13-11. Elements.xml File for the BugWaiting Content Type

```
<?xml version="1.0" encoding="utf-8"?>
<Elements xmlns="http://schemas.microsoft.com/sharepoint/">
  <!-- Parent ContentType: Workflow Task (0x010801) -->
  <ContentType ID="0x01080100489237b45582435dbff019fbefb313bf"
                   Name="BugWaiting"
                   Group="Custom Content Types"
                   Description="Bug - Waiting"
                   Inherits="TRUE"
                   Version="0">
    <FieldRefs>
        <FieldRef ID="{3868124A-D162-4A99-8A61-C91E593D68A7}"
                         Name="BugClosed"
                         Required="FALSE"
                         ShowInNewForm="FALSE"
                         ShowInDisplayForm="TRUE"
                         ShowInEditForm="TRUE"/>
        <FieldRef ID="{69E039E9-F4D9-4CBB-A4C2-346B79FA8F6A}"
                         Name="BugReSubmit"
                         Required="FALSE"
                         ShowInNewForm="FALSE"
                         ShowInDisplayForm="TRUE"
                         ShowInEditForm="TRUE"/>
        <FieldRef ID="{6CFB14EE-7834-42DE-9E7B-9847D6ADA88A}"
                         Name="Feedback"
                         Required="FALSE"
                         ShowInNewForm="FALSE"
                         ShowInDisplayForm="TRUE"
                         ShowInEditForm="TRUE"/>
      </FieldRefs>
    </ContentType>
</Elements>
```

Feature Summary

After you have added all the content types, you should see them listed in the Solution Explorer. It should look like Figure 13-10.

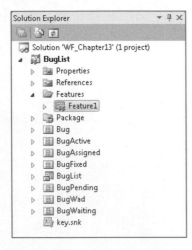

Figure 13-10. Solution Explorer showing all the SharePoint objects

Also, if you open the **Feature1** file, you should see all of these elements listed as well, similar to Figure 13-11.

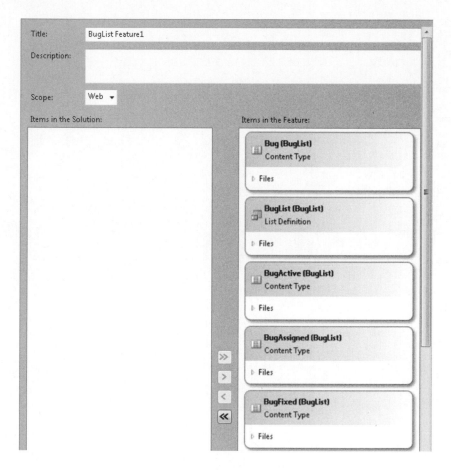

Figure 13-11. A partial listing of the Feature1 *file*

Deploying the BugList Project

Now you're ready to deploy this project to the SharePoint site. From the Solution Explorer, right-click the BugList project, and choose Deploy. You can verify that it was deployed correctly by starting the SharePoint Designer. You should see your custom content types listed in the Custom Content Types group similar to Figure 13-12.

Name	Group	Parent	Source	Description
Custom Content Types				
Bug	Custom Content Types	Item	http://omega5/part3	Information about a reported bug
BugActive	Custom Content Types	Workflow Task	http://omega5/part3	Bug - Active
BugAssigned	Custom Content Types	Workflow Task	http://omega5/part3	Bug - Assigned
BugFixed	Custom Content Types	Workflow Task	http://omega5/part3	Bug - Fixed
BugPending	Custom Content Types	Workflow Task	http://omega5/part3	Bug - Pending
BugWad	Custom Content Types	Workflow Task	http://omega5/part3	Bug - Wad
BugWaiting	Custom Content Types	Workflow Task	http://omega5/part3	Bug - Waiting

Figure 13-12. The SharePoint Designer showing the new content types

Creating a List Instance

Start the SharePoint site in a browser window, and navigate to the Part3 site. Click the *Lists* link to show the existing lists on this site. This should look like Figure 13-13.

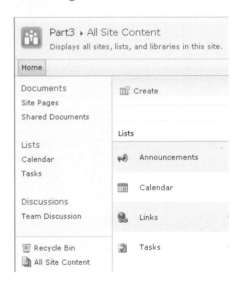

Figure 13-13. Displaying the existing lists

The `BugList` was deployed as a list template and not a list instance. Notice that there is no new list in your site. You'll create one now. Click the *Create* link. In the Create dialog box, select the Blank & Custom category, and then select the `BugList` template. Enter the name as **BugList**, as shown in Figure 13-14, and click the Create button.

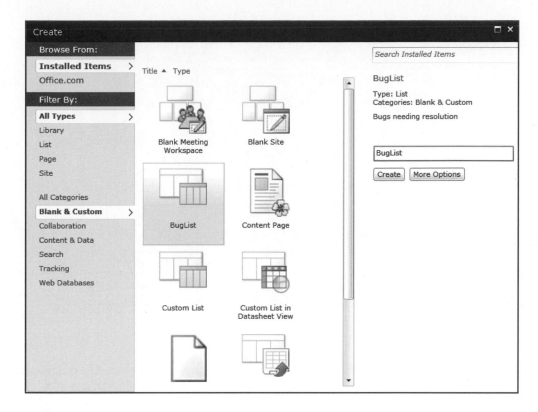

Figure 13-14. Selecting the BugList template

Creating the BugList Workflow

Now that you have the list set up as well as the custom content types, you're ready to build a state machine workflow. You'll start by creating a workflow project just like in previous projects except you'll use the State Machine Workflow template.

Creating the Workflow Project

In Visual Studio, from the Solution Explorer, right-click the WF_Chapter13 solution, and choose Add ▶ New Project. In the Add New Project dialog box, select the State Machine Workflow template, and enter the name **BugListWorkflow**, as shown in Figure 13-15.

Figure 13-15. Creating a State Machine Workflow project

In the first dialog box, the site should default to the Part3 site (the site you used for the first project, BugList); use this default value. In the second dialog box, enter the workflow name **BugListWorkflow**, and select the List Workflow type, as shown in Figure 13-16.

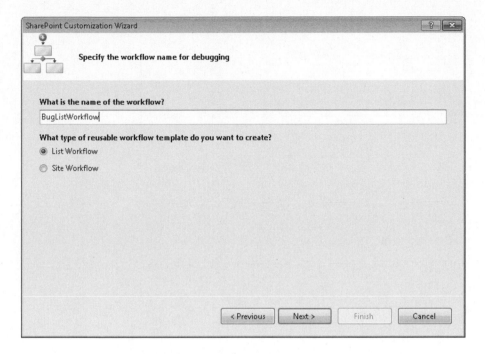

Figure 13-16. Configuring the workflow settings

In the third dialog box, select the new `BugList` to associate this workflow with, as shown in Figure 13-17.

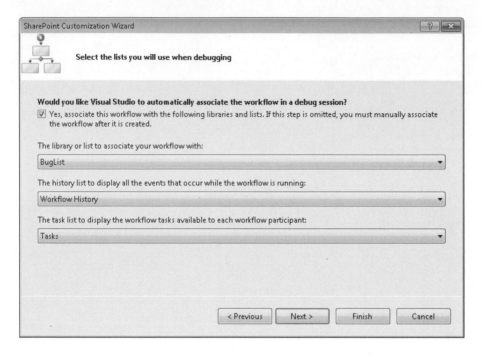

Figure 13-17. Associating the workflow with the new BugList

In the final dialog box, set the start options so the workflow is started when an item is added to the list. You should have only the middle check box checked, as shown in Figure 13-18.

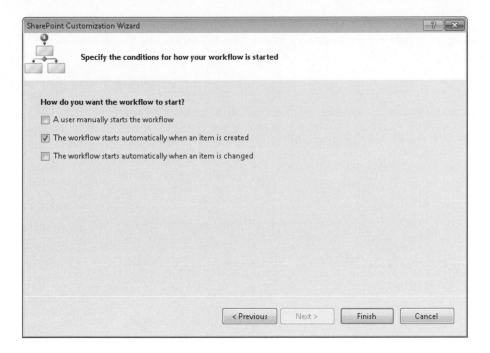

Figure 13-18. Selecting the start options

From the Solution Explorer, right-click the BugListWorkflow project, and choose *Set as StartUp Project*. When debugging the solution, you'll want to execute this project, not the BugList project.

State Machine Overview

Visual Studio should display the workflow designer with a single activity named `Workflow1InitialState`. This is a `StateActivity`, and it contains a single activity called `eventDrivenActivity1`.

Understanding States

As it name suggests, a state machine workflow is designed by specifying the states of a workflow. A state represents a stable condition of the workflow. Often a workflow will be idle, waiting for *something* to happen. That idle condition is represented by a *state*. When that *something* occurs, there is some activity, and the result is that the workflow becomes idle again, usually in a different state.

In the bug list scenario, when a bug is entered, it goes in to a pending state and waits. When the admin reviews the bug and assigns it, the bug then goes into an assigned state. Once again, the bug becomes idle waiting for the developer to work on it. The first step in designing a state machine workflow is to define these idle points, which you'll model using a `StateActivity`.

■ **Tip** The first step in designing a state machine workflow is to determine the idle points of the process. These will be modeled as states.

There are two special states that all workflows will have: an initial state and a completed state. The initial state is where the workflow will start. The completed state represents a workflow that has finished. No activity may be done on a completed state. It is simply a placeholder, indicating the end of the workflow.

Your workflow will have the following additional states:

- `Pending`
- `Assigned`
- `Active`
- `Fixed`
- `Working as Designed` (WAD)
- `Waiting`

EventDrivenActivity

The second step in designing a workflow is to define what the *something to happen* is. This is modeled as an event. You will define for each state what events it can expect and what activity should occur with each event. To do that, you'll use the `EventDrivenActivity`.

■ **Tip** The second step in designing a state machine workflow is to specify the *things* that can happen in each state. These will be modeled as events.

In Visual Studio, if you double-click the `EventDrivenActivity`, you'll see what looks like a mini-workflow similar to the one shown in Figure 13-19.

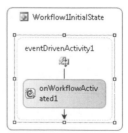

Figure 13-19. EventDrivenActivity sequence

This sequence contains the same OnWorkflowActivated activity that you've used on your previous workflows. The EventDrivenActivity is a special type of sequence; in fact, its parent class is SequenceActivity. So, like SequenceActivity, it can contain any number of child activities. But it has some unique rules. Essentially, the sequence can contain only one activity that handles events, and that must be the first child activity.

Activities that handle events include the HandleExternalEventActivity and activities that are derived from it. The workflow event activities such as OnWorkflowActivated and OnTaskChanged are derived from HandleExternalEventActivity. So, the workflow generated by the template satisfies that rule.

A state can have multiple EventDrivenActivity objects, but each one must respond to a different event. You could have one EventDrivenActivity that has OnWorkflowActivated for its first child activity, and the second EventDrivenActivity could use OnWorkflowModified. Which sequence is executed would depend on which event was raised.

Navigation

As you probably noticed, when you double-click a sequence to expand it, only that sequence is displayed. The rest of the workflow is hidden. With state machine workflows, you'll find yourself doing that a lot since all of the real "work" is done on sequences that are not visible from the top-level diagram. To help you find your way within the workflow, the top of the workflow designer includes a navigation bar, which is shown in Figure 13-20.

Figure 13-20. The workflow navigation bar

The main (or top-level) diagram is Workflow1. The state is called Workflow1InitialState; this is the second level. You are currently on the third level, which is the eventDriveActivity1 sequence. The top-level diagram displays both the first and second levels. That is, it displays the main workflow (level 1), which includes the states (level 2). If you click either link on the navigation bar, the top-level diagram will be displayed.

Initialization and Finalization

The StateActivity is also a special sequence activity. It can contain only four types of activities. The first you've already seen, which is the EventDrivenActivity. Navigate back to the top-level diagram, and right-click the Workflow1InitialState activity. Figure 13-21 displays the content menu.

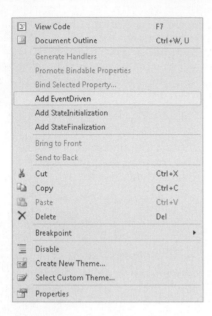

回	View Code	F7
📄	Document Outline	Ctrl+W, U
	Generate Handlers	
	Promote Bindable Properties	
	Bind Selected Property...	
	Add EventDriven	
	Add StateInitialization	
	Add StateFinalization	
	Bring to Front	
	Send to Back	
✂	Cut	Ctrl+X
📋	Copy	Ctrl+C
📋	Paste	Ctrl+V
✕	Delete	Del
	Breakpoint	▶
☰	Disable	
	Create New Theme...	
	Select Custom Theme...	
	Properties	

Figure 13-21. Context menu for a StateActivity

Two of your other choices of activities are included in this menu. In addition to the
EventDrivenActivity, you can also add a StateInitializationActivity and a
StateFinalizationActivity. These are also derived from SequenceActivity and can have multiple child
activities. The StateInitializationActivity contains activities that you want executed whenever the
workflow enters that state. Similarly, the StateFinalizationActivity contains activities that are
executed when the workflow leaves that state.

Both of these are optional, and you can have one without the other. But you cannot have more than
one of each. You should not put any event handlers in these sequences; the workflow should never
become idle during these activities. Their purpose is to perform initialization or cleanup activities for
this state.

Substates

The forth type of activity that can be included on a StateActivity is another StateActivity. These are
known as substates. In a complex workflow, you may want to model a mini-state machine for a
particular state.

In our bug list, for example, when a bug is in the Pending state, it is reviewed and assigned to a
developer. Suppose the review process requires several steps to complete, such as multiple reviewers or
developer feedback. You could model that review process as its own state machine. That would keep the
overall state machine more manageable.

To use substates, drag the substates onto the top-level state. Then define the events just like you
would for top-level states.

SetState

You will use the SetStateActivity to transition to another state. The SetStateActivity is normally used in an EventDrivenActivity. For example, when a bug is reviewed and assigned, this will trigger an OnTaskChanged event. The event handler will then use the SetStateActivity to move the workflow to the Assigned state.

■ **Caution** In the Toolbox there are two activities labeled SetState. The one in the Windows Workflow 3.0 section is the one I'm referring to here and is the one you will use throughout this chapter. The SetState activity in the "SharePoint Workflow" section is completely different and is used for setting workflow properties. Do not use this one.

You can also use the SetStateActivity in a StateInitializationActivity. You may want to do this if the initialization activities determine that this state is not required. The initialization sequence can immediately move the workflow to the next state, essentially skipping this state.

■ **Caution** You cannot use a SetStateActivity in a StateFinalizationActivity.

Designing the Workflow

Now you'll design the state machine for the bug list workflow.

Adding the States

Click the Workflow1InitialState activity, and in the Properties window, change the name to **stateInitial**. As I said, the first step in designing a state machine is to identify the states. Drag seven more StateActivity objects onto the workflow diagram, and change their names as follows:

- statePending
- stateAssigned
- stateWad
- stateActive
- stateWaiting
- stateFixed
- stateFinal

The diagram should look like Figure 13-22.

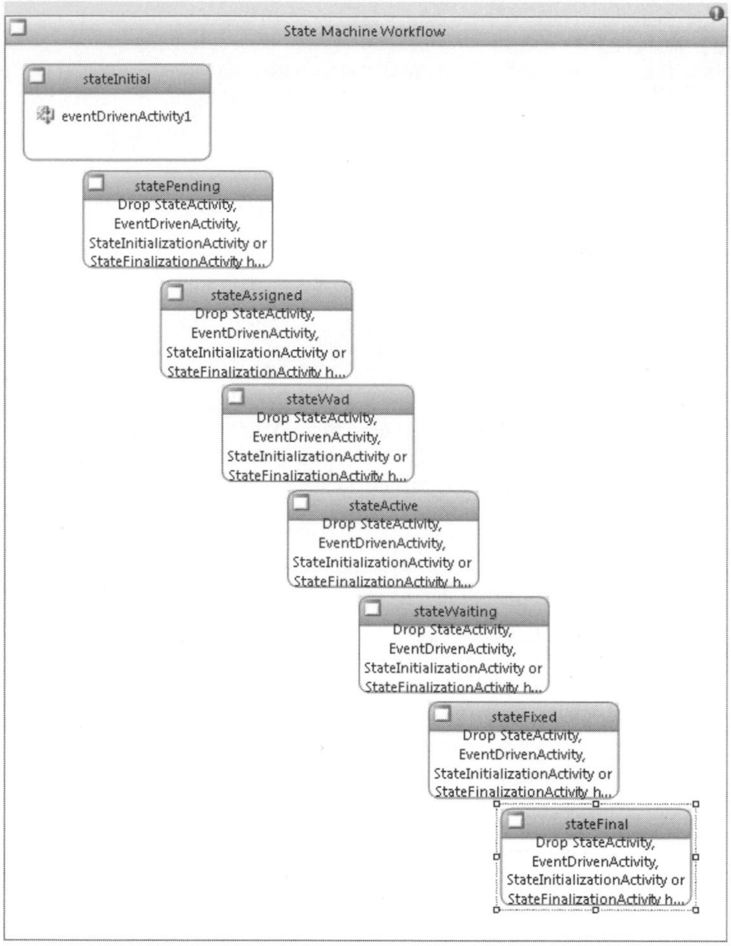

Figure 13-22. The workflow diagram with all the states

Notice the helper text that is displayed when you drag a **StateActivity** to the workflow. It is reminding you to include one of the four types of activities that are allowed on a **StateActivity**.

Initial and Completed States

Right-click the **stateInitial** activity, and choose Set as Initial State. Notice the icon in the activity has changed to a green circle indicating this is the initial state. Likewise, right-click the **stateFinal** activity and choose Set as Completed State. Notice the icon has changed to a red circle, and the helper text is gone. As I said, you cannot add activities to the completed state.

Setting Up the Workflow

There's some initial configuration work you'll need to do before you start implementing the state logic. The template created the **eventDrivenActivity1** in the initial state. Rename this to **eventInitial**. Then double-click it to display the sequence for this event. The sequence contains only the **onWorkflowActivated1** activity. Double-click this activity to generate the event handler, and open the **Workflow1.cs** file in code view. Add the following namespaces:

```
using System.Collections.Generic;
using System.Xml.Linq;
```

Add the following class members (these should go just after the **workflowProperties** member):

```
private string _admin = "internal\\test1";
private string _test = "internal\\test2";
private string _itemTitle;
private string _itemDescription;
```

The **_admin** and **_test** members will store the logon names of the users that the tasks will be assigned to. For now, just hard-code these. You'll add an association form later to allow these to be specified by the end users. The **_itemTitle** and **_itemDescription** members will store these values that are obtained from the **BugList** item. These will be used in setting the properties of the tasks that will be generated.

Enter the implementation for the **onWorkflowActivated1_Invoked** event handler using the code from Listing 13-12.

Listing 13-12. Implementation of onWorkflowActivated1_Invoked Event Handler

```
private void onWorkflowActivated1_Invoked(object sender, ExternalDataEventArgs e)
{
    // Get the details from the BugList item that we'll need later
    _itemTitle = workflowProperties.Item.Title;
    _itemDescription = workflowProperties.Item["Description"].ToString();

    // Make sure the Tasks lists supports all of our content types
    List<SPContentTypeId> types = new List<SPContentTypeId>();

    // BugActive
    types.Add(new SPContentTypeId("0x010801006f51849cf46b42939046cfd9cf6d3e0b"));

    // BugAssigned
    types.Add(new SPContentTypeId("0x01080100afbba42fb3c348f7923f08981f3546f9"));

    // BugFixed
    types.Add(new SPContentTypeId("0x0108010071aa11fb81d84de98ef7a53b1ee6ae38"));

    // BugPending
    types.Add(new SPContentTypeId("0x010801008fa5ff065e7e42e9b861eae33021c895"));

    // BugWAD
```

```
        types.Add(new SPContentTypeId("0x010801005c5fcc143af649f3bc1153474b637a7a"));

        // BugWaiting
        types.Add(new SPContentTypeId("0x01080100489237b45582435dbff019fbefb313bf"));

        foreach (SPContentTypeId type in types)
        {
            workflowProperties.TaskList.ContentTypesEnabled = true;
            SPContentTypeId matchContentTypeId
                = workflowProperties.TaskList.ContentTypes.BestMatch(type);
            if (matchContentTypeId.Parent.CompareTo(type) != 0)
            {
                SPContentType ct
                    = workflowProperties.TaskList.ParentWeb.AvailableContentTypes[type];
                workflowProperties.TaskList.ContentTypes.Add(ct);
                workflowProperties.TaskList.Update();
            }
        }

        // Set the Date Created
        SPListItem item = workflowProperties.Item;
        item["_DCDateCreated"] = DateTime.Now;
        item.Update();
}
```

This code first gets the `BugList` item using `Item` property of the `workflowProperties` member. The `Title` and `Description` properties are then stored in the class members.

The code then ensures that the `Tasks` list supports all the various content types that may be used for the workflow tasks. This code is identical to the code used in Chapter 10, except, since there are multiple content types, they are first put in a collection, which is processed with a `foreach` loop.

■ **Caution** The content type IDs that you use will be different that the ones shown here. Open the `Element.xml` file (for the corresponding content type feature) to determine the correct content type IDs to use.

The last step of this method is to update the `BugList` item to set the `DateCreated` field. Notice that the `Update()` method is used to commit this change to the database.

Adding State Initialization

For each of the states (except `stateInitial` and `stateFinal`), add a `StateInitializationActivity`. You can drag a `StateInitializationActivity` from the Toolbox, or you can right-click the state and choose Add StateInitialization. In either case, rename the activity to **init<state name>**. For example, on **statePending**, the activity should be named **initPending**.

■ **Tip** All of the activities in the workflow must have unique names. The workflow designer will automatically generate unique names for you by taking the name of activity type and adding a sequential number (such as eventDrivenActivity1). This is OK for simple workflows, but for complex workflows such as this one, more meaningful names will help you keep track better. As you start debugging, you may not remember which state eventDrivenActivity6 was for.

The BugList item is the payload of this workflow. As it works its way through the various states, a new task will be created for the work needed for that state. There will be a task to review the bug, a task to fix the bug, a task to test the fix, and so on. To accomplish this, the initialization sequence of each state will create the appropriate task. Double-click the initPending activity (the initialization sequence for the Pending state). Drag a CreateTaskWithContentType activity onto this sequence, and rename it **createPendingTask**.

In the Properties window, enter the appropriate content type ID for the BugPending content type. Again, make sure you use the same one that is specified in the associated Elements.xml file.

■ **Note** I explained in Chapter 11 how correlation tokens are used to associate events with the appropriate objects. In that chapter, you used a token for the workflow and a separate token for the task. In this workflow, you'll create a separate token for each state.

In the Properties window, enter the CorrelationToken as **pendingToken**. Then expand the property, and select the OwnerActivityName as the StateActivity, statePending. This will limit the scope of this token to activities in this state. That includes the initialization sequence and any event-driven sequences.

The Properties window should look like Figure 13-23.

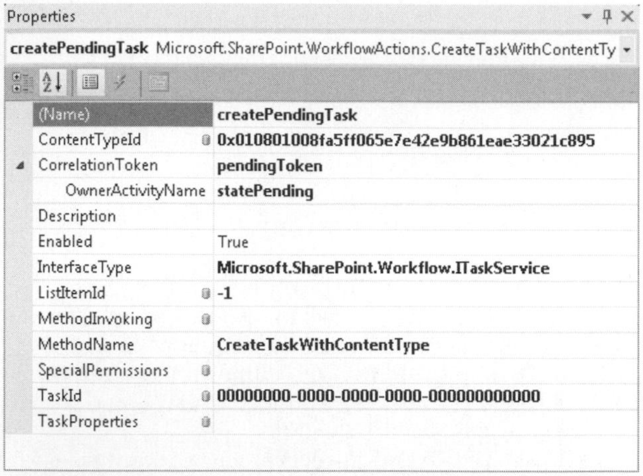

Figure 13-23. *The* CreateTaskWithContentType *Properties window*

Double-click the createPendingTask activity to generate the MethodInvoking event handler. For the implementation of this method, use the code shown in Listing 13-13.

Listing 13-13. *Implementation of* createPendingTask_MethodInvoking

```
CreateTaskWithContentType task = sender as CreateTaskWithContentType;
task.TaskId = Guid.NewGuid();

SPWorkflowTaskProperties wtp = new SPWorkflowTaskProperties();
wtp.PercentComplete = (float)0.0;
wtp.AssignedTo = _admin;
wtp.TaskType = 0;
wtp.DueDate = DateTime.Now.AddDays(1);
wtp.Title = "Pending: " + _itemTitle;
wtp.Description = _itemDescription;

task.TaskProperties = wtp;
```

This code should be familiar to you; it's basically the same code you used in previous chapters to initialize a task. The task will be assigned to the admin user with a due date of one day in the future. The Title for this task will use the Title of the BugList item prepended with "Pending:". The Description of the bug is copied to the task description.

There is one more action that is needed here. Go back to the workflow designer, and drag a CodeActivity just below createPendingTask. Rename this to **codeInitPending**. Double-click this activity to generate the event handler. Enter the following code for the implementation:

```
SPListItem item = workflowProperties.Item;
item["BugStatus"] = "Pending";
item.Update();
```

This code updates the `BugList` item to show that it is now in the `Pending` state. The initialization sequence should look like Figure 13-24.

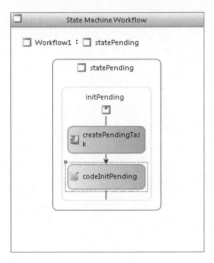

Figure 13-24. The initialization sequence for the Pending state

Adding Event Logic

Navigate the workflow designer back to the top-level diagram that shows all the states. Drag an `EventDrivenActivity` to the **statePending** activity, and rename it to **eventPending**. Double-click **eventPending** activity to display the sequence of activities, which should be empty. Remember that the first activity in an `EventDrivenActivity` sequence must be an event handler.

You will use the `OnTaskChanged` event to trigger the appropriate activities. Drag an `OnTaskChanged` activity onto the sequence, and rename it to **onPendingChanged**. In the Properties window, select the **pendingToken** as the `CorrelationToken`. You can leave the remaining properties with their default values. The Properties window should look like Figure 13-25.

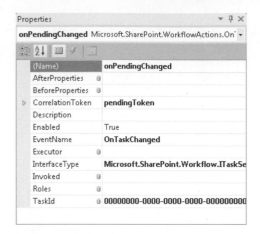

Figure 13-25. onPendingChanged Properties window

Double-click `onPendingChanged` to generate the event handler.

Gathering Task Details

In the first part of this chapter, you created a custom content type for each state with the specific fields that were allowed for that state. For example, the `BugPending` had the following fields:

- `BugAssign`: The developer that the task should be assigned
- `BugPriority`: The priority to be assigned to this task
- `BugWad`: A flag indicating the bug is "working as designed"

In the `OnTaskChanged` events handler, you will extract those fields from the task and store them in the workflow's class members. Subsequent workflow logic will then use these members to take the appropriate action(s). To facilitate this, add the following class members (these should go near the top of the `Workflow1.cs` file, just after the existing members that you added earlier):

```
private string _priority = "Normal";
private string _assign = "";
private string _resolution;
private string _feedback;
private bool _wad = false;
private bool _waiting = false;
private bool _started = false;
private bool _fixed = false;
private bool _closed = false;
private bool _reSubmit = false;
private bool _tested = false;
private bool _notFixed = false;

private Guid _taskId = Guid.Empty;
private Guid _workTaskId = Guid.Empty;
```

These members will support all the states that you will be implementing. The _taskId member is used to keep track of the task that was just changed. (I'll explain the _workTaskId member later.) Return to the onPendingChanged event handler, and enter the code shown in Listing 13-14.

Listing 13-14. Implementation of the onPendingChanged_Invoke Event handler

```
private void onPendingChanged_Invoked(object sender, ExternalDataEventArgs e)
{
    CreateTaskWithContentType task = sender as CreateTaskWithContentType;
    SPTaskServiceEventArgs args = (SPTaskServiceEventArgs)e;

    _taskId = args.taskId;

    SPWorkflowTaskProperties after = args.afterProperties;
    if (after != null)
    {
        _priority = after.ExtendedProperties[
            workflowProperties.TaskList.Fields.GetFieldByInternalName("BugPriority")
            .Id].ToString();
        _assign = after.ExtendedProperties[
            workflowProperties.TaskList.Fields.GetFieldByInternalName("BugAssign")
            .Id].ToString();
        _wad = bool.Parse(after.ExtendedProperties[
            workflowProperties.TaskList.Fields.GetFieldByInternalName("BugWAD")
            .Id].ToString());

        // Store the item's priority
        if (_priority.Length > 0)
        {
            SPListItem item = workflowProperties.Item;

            if (_priority.Length > 0)
                item["Priority"] = _priority;

            item.Update();
        }
    }
}
```

The second parameter to the event handler is an SPTaskServiceEventArgs class, and the parameter is cast to a variable of this type. From that, the taskId can be obtained and stored in the _taskId member. The afterProperties is also obtained, and the three custom fields are extracted from the ExtendedProperties collection. To do that, the field Id is needed, which can be determined by calling GetFieldByInternalName() method. This code will set the following class members:

- _priority
- _assign
- _wad

343

Finally, if the `BugPriority` field was specified, the `BugList` item is updated using this priority.

Specify the Event Activities

Return to the workflow designer. You'll now add activities that will take appropriate action depending on the values entered on the task form.

IfElseActivity

Drag an `IfElseActivity` just below `onPendingChanged`. The workflow diagram should look like Figure 13-26.

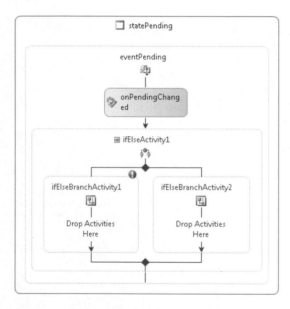

Figure 13-26. An initial IfElseActivity

An `IfElseActivity` can have any number of branches, and all except the last branch must specify a `boolean` condition. The processing goes from left to right until it finds a branch with a condition that is true. Each branch can contain a sequence of activities. The first branch with a true condition is then executed, and the activity is completed (no other branches are executed). If no true condition was found, the last branch is executed if it does *not* have a condition.

For a typical `if-then-else` scenario, use two branches. The left branch will have a condition, and the right will not. If the left branch's condition is true, the left branch is executed otherwise the right branch is executed.

You can also use the `IfElseActivtity` like a `switch` statement. Specify the appropriate `case` condition on each branch. Leave the condition blank on the last branch if you want an `else case`.

■ **Caution** If you specify a condition on all branches, then it is possible that none of the branches will be executed. In that case, the `IfElseActivity` is simply skipped, and processing will continue with the next activity.

For the `Pending` state, there are two possible actions:

- If "Working as Design" is checked, move to the `Wad` state.
- If a developer is assigned , move to the `Assigned` state.

■ **Note** If the admin specified both values—that is, the developer is assigned and they also select the Working as Designed check box—then we have an interesting dilemma. Ideally, the form logic should prevent this. For the workflow logic, we'll assume that Working as Design takes priority. You'll do that by putting that condition in the first branch of the `IfElseActivity`.

If neither is specified, then the workflow stays in the `Pending` state.

There are two ways that you can specify a condition. You can use a code condition by implementing an event handler that returns true or false in the event arguments. You used this in previous chapters. The other method is to define a declarative rule condition, which you'll use in this chapter.

In the workflow designer, select the left branch, and change the name to **ifPendingWad**. In the Properties window, for the `Condition` property, select `Declarative Rule Condition`, and then expand this property. Select the `ConditionName`, and click the ellipsis. This will display the Select Condition dialog box shown in Figure 13-27.

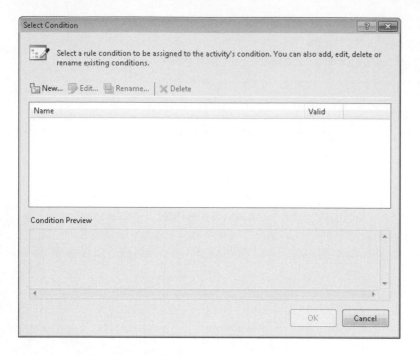

Figure 13-27. An empty Select Condition dialog box

This dialog box should be empty since you have not created any conditions yet. Click the *New* link to create one. In the Rule Condition Editor shown in Figure 13-28, enter **this._wad**.

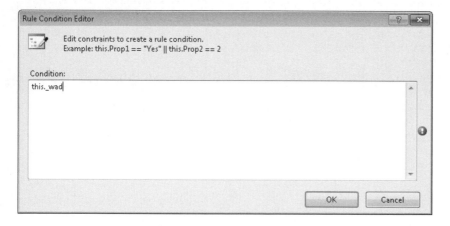

Figure 13-28. The Rule Condition Editor

■ **Tip** The `Condition` property uses standard C# syntax. You can access workflow members using the `this.` notation. You can also access static members such as `DateTime.Now`.

When you click the OK, button, the condition will be created but will be given the name `Condition1`. Click the *Rename* link, and change the name to **Working as Designed**. Click the OK button to update the Properties window. The completed Properties window should look like Figure 13-29.

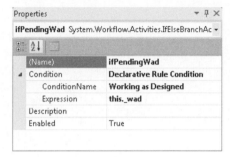

Figure 13-29. The completed Properties window for the `ifPendingWad` branch

Select the right branch of the `IfElseActivity`, and rename it to **ifPendingAssigned**. In the Properties window, select the `Condition` as a `Declarative Rule Condition`. Expand the property, select the `Condition` property, and click the ellipsis, just like you did for the left branch. In the Select Condition dialog box, click the *New* link to create a new condition, and enter the condition as **this._assign > ""**. Rename this condition to **Assigned**. The completed Properties window should look like Figure 13-30.

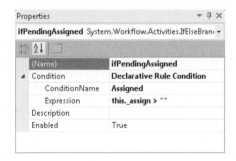

Figure 13-30. The completed Properties window for the `ifPendingAssigned` branch

CompleteTaskActivity

When the admin assigns this bug to a developer or marks it as Working as Designed, their work is done (for this task anyway), and the task should be marked complete. In Chapter 10, you implemented a custom form to enter a lunch order. When the form was submitted, you added a custom rule to mark the task complete. In this project, you'll accomplish the same thing using the `CompleteTaskActivity` in your workflow.

Drag a `CompleteTaskActivity` to the left branch (`ifPendingWad`), and rename it to **completePendingWad**. For the `CorrelationToken`, choose the existing `pendingToken`. Go to the `Workflow1.cs` code-behind file, and add the following method:

```
private void completeTask_MethodInvoking(object sender, EventArgs e)
{
    CompleteTask ct = (CompleteTask)sender;
    ct.TaskId = _taskId;
}
```

This code simply casts the `sender` parameter as a `CompleteTask` activity and updates the `TaskId` property using the `_taskId` class member. (Recall this was stored by the `OnTaskChanged` event handler). Go back to the workflow designer. In the Properties window, select `MethodInvoking` property, and select the `completeTask_MethodInvoking` method from the drop-down list. The completed Properties window should look like Figure 13-31.

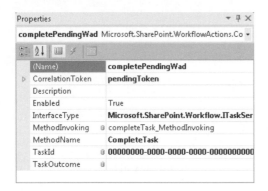

Figure 13-31. *The completed Properties window for the* `completePendingWad` *activity*

Now drag a `CompleteTaskActivity` to the `ifPendingAssigned` branch. This should be configured exactly like the first one, using the `pendingToken` and the `completeTask_MethodInvoking` method.

Using the SetStateActivity

The last thing you'll need to add to the event handler sequence is to move to the appropriate next step. Drag a `SetStateActivity` to each branch, just below the `CompleteTaskActivity`. Rename them as **setPendingWad** and **setPendingAssigned**. The only property that you'll need to set is the `TargetStateName`, which is the state that the workflow should transition to. For the left branch, select `stateWad` from the drop-down list. For the right branch, select `stateAssigned`.

The completed sequence should look like Figure 13-32.

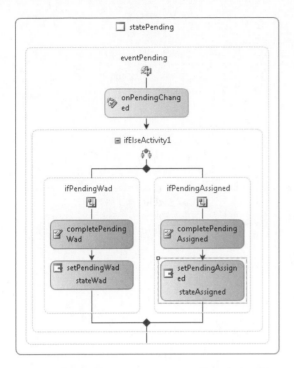

Figure 13-32. The completed event handler sequence for the Pending state

Navigate back to the top-level workflow diagram. Notice that the diagram now has arrows connecting the **Pending** state to the **Assigned** and **Wad** states, as shown in Figure 13-33. It is able to determine this from the **SetStateActivty** objects that you placed on the **eventPending** activity.

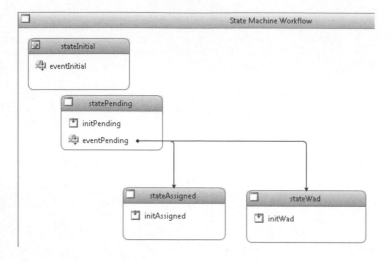

Figure 13-33. The top-level diagram showing state transitions

Handling the Work Task

The workflow is designed so every time it transitions to a different state, a new task is created. That also means that if a state is repeated, a second task for that state is created. For example, if the admin determines that the system is working as designed, the bug is moved to the Wad state, and the pending task is completed. The initiator can then update the bug and resubmit it. At that point, a second pending task is created.

There is one exception to this logic. The actual task that is assigned to the developer is not repeated. If the tester determined that the fix is not working, the bug goes back to the Assigned state, but the same task is used; another task is *not* created. The logic behind this approach is that any additional work that may be needed for this bug is an extension to the original task, not an independent work item. So when a developer has fixed a bug, that task (referred to as the *work task*) is kept open until the workflow completes.

■ **Note** I designed the workflow this way to give you an example of how you could implement this business rule. When you implement your own workflows, if this scenario does not fix your requirements, you don't have to implement it this way. It's actually easier to create a new task every time, and that may be a better design in some situations.

Implementing the Assign State Initialization Sequence

In the initialization sequence, you normally need to create a task for that state. For the Assigned state, however, you should only do this the first time the workflow enters this state. To do this, you'll use the _workTaskId workflow class member, which you added earlier.

Double-click the initAssigned activity, which is the initialization sequence for the Assigned state. Drag an IfElseActivity to this sequence. Rename the left branch to ifNotCreated. Select the Condition as a declarative rule condition and expand the property. Create a new condition like you did with the previous IfElseActivity. Specify the ConditionName as NotCreated, and for the Expression, use the following code:

```
this._workTaskId == System.Guid.Empty
```

The completed Properties window should look like Figure 13-34.

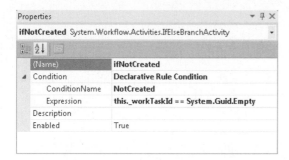

Figure 13-34. The completed Properties window for the ifNotCreated branch

Next, drag a CreateTaskWithContentType activity onto the left branch, and rename it to createAssignedTask. In the Properties window, enter the CorrelationToken as taskToken, expand the property, and select the OwnerActivityName as Workflow1. This task is different from the other tasks in that only one is created and it is global to the entire workflow. The other tasks are used only for the specific state and are no longer used once the workflow transitions to another state.

Enter the appropriate content type Id, which you can determine from the corresponding Element.xml file. The completed Properties window should look like Figure 13-35.

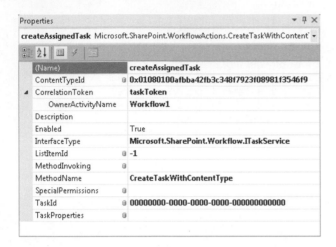

Figure 13-35. The completed properties window for `createAssignedTask`

Double-click the `createAssignedTask` activity to generate the event handler. Listing 13-15 shows the implementation.

Listing 13-15. Implementation of `createAssignedTask_MethodInvoking`

```
private void createAssignedTask_MethodInvoking(object sender, EventArgs e)
{
    CreateTaskWithContentType task = sender as CreateTaskWithContentType;
    task.TaskId = Guid.NewGuid();
    _workTaskId = task.TaskId;

    SPWorkflowTaskProperties wtp = new SPWorkflowTaskProperties();
    wtp.PercentComplete = (float)0.0;
    wtp.AssignedTo = _assign;
    wtp.TaskType = 1;
    wtp.DueDate = DateTime.Now.AddDays(1);
    wtp.Title = "Bug: " + _itemTitle;
    wtp.Description = _itemDescription;

    task.TaskProperties = wtp;

    // Update the item to show the assignee
    SPUser u = workflowProperties.Web.SiteUsers[_assign];
    SPListItem item = workflowProperties.Item;
    item["AssignedTo"] = u;
    item.Update();
}
```

This code stores the `TaskId` that was assigned to this task in the `_workTaskId` member. If the `Assigned` state is entered again, because this member has a value in it, another task will not be created.

In addition to setting up the task properties, the `BugList` item is also updated to show which developer is assigned to this bug. To update the `AssignedTo` property, however, an `SPUser` object is required. This is obtained by looking up the selected login name against the `SiteUsers` collection.

The last step in the initialization sequence is to update the `BugStatus` of the `BugList` item. Drag a `CodeActivity` to the sequence below the `IfElseActivity`, and rename it to `codeInitAssigned`. Double-click it to generate the event handler, and enter the following code for its implementation:

```
SPListItem item = workflowProperties.Item;
item["BugStatus"] = "Assigned";
item.Update();
```

This code simply sets the `BugStatus` property to `Assigned`. This activity is done outside the `IfElseActivity` because whether this is the first time entering this state, we should update the `BugList` item. The final initialization sequence should look like Figure 13-36.

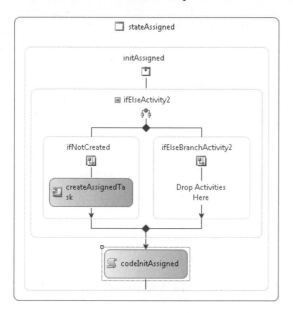

Figure 13-36. Final initAssigned sequence

Implementing the Active State Initialization Sequence

From the top-level workflow diagram, double-click the `initActive` activity, which is the state initialization sequence for the `Active` state. When entering the `Active` state, no task is necessary. The `Active` state indicates that the developer has started working on this bug. The developer will continue to use the work task that was created when the `Assigned` state was initialized.

Drag a `CodeActivity` to the sequence, and rename it to `codeInitActive`. Double-click this activity, and enter the following code for its implementation:

```
SPListItem item = workflowProperties.Item;
item["BugStatus"] = "Active";
item.Update();
```

This code updates the BugList item to change the state to Active. This is the only initialization sequence that does not create a new task.

Adding Additional State Processing

Now you'll need to implement the appropriate logic for all the other states. Start by defining the initialization sequences. So far, you have implemented the initialization sequence for the Pending, Assigned, and Active states. Now you'll implement the remaining states, which are as follows:

- Wad

- Waiting

- Fixed

For each of these, you will drag a CreateTaskWithContentType activity and a CodeActivity. Follow the same naming convention for these activities, which is **create**<state>**Task** and **codeInit**<state>, respectively.

Configuring CreateTaskWithContentType

For the CreateTaskWithContentType activities, you'll need to create a new CorrelationToken. Enter the name using the state name such as assignedToken. Expand the property, and select the OwnerActivityName as the StateActivity object (for example, stateWad).

You will also need to assign the appropriate content type Id. You can get this from the corresponding Elements.xml file that you created for the first project in this solution.

Lastly, double-click the activity to generate the event handler. Listing 13-16 shows the implementation for all three states.

Listing 13-16. Implementation of the CreateTaskWihContentType Event Handlers

```
private void createWadTask_MethodInvoking(object sender, EventArgs e)
{
    CreateTaskWithContentType task = sender as CreateTaskWithContentType;
    task.TaskId = Guid.NewGuid();

    SPWorkflowTaskProperties wtp = new SPWorkflowTaskProperties();
    wtp.PercentComplete = (float)0.0;
    wtp.AssignedTo = _test;
    wtp.TaskType = 2;
    wtp.DueDate = DateTime.Now.AddDays(1);
    wtp.Title = "Working As Designed: " + _itemTitle;
    wtp.Description = _itemDescription;

    task.TaskProperties = wtp;
```

```
}

private void createWaitingTask_MethodInvoking(object sender, EventArgs e)
{
    CreateTaskWithContentType task = sender as CreateTaskWithContentType;
    task.TaskId = Guid.NewGuid();

    SPWorkflowTaskProperties wtp = new SPWorkflowTaskProperties();
    wtp.PercentComplete = (float)0.0;
    wtp.AssignedTo = _admin;
    wtp.TaskType = 4;
    wtp.DueDate = DateTime.Now.AddDays(1);
    wtp.Title = "Waiting: " + _itemTitle;
    wtp.Description = _itemDescription;

    task.TaskProperties = wtp;
}

private void createFixedTask_MethodInvoking(object sender, EventArgs e)
{
    CreateTaskWithContentType task = sender as CreateTaskWithContentType;
    task.TaskId = Guid.NewGuid();

    SPWorkflowTaskProperties wtp = new SPWorkflowTaskProperties();
    wtp.PercentComplete = (float)0.0;
    wtp.AssignedTo = _test;
    wtp.TaskType = 3;
    wtp.DueDate = DateTime.Now.AddDays(1);
    wtp.Title = "Resolved: " + _itemTitle;
    wtp.Description = _itemDescription;

    task.TaskProperties = wtp;
}
```

The implementation of these event handlers is similar to the Pending state that you implemented initially.

Setting the BugStatus

On each of the three remaining initialization sequences, double-click the CodeActivity objects, and enter the implementation using the code from Listing 13-17.

Listing 13-17. Implementation of the Initialization CodeActivity Objects

```
private void codeInitWad_ExecuteCode(object sender, EventArgs e)
{
    SPListItem item = workflowProperties.Item;
    item["BugStatus"] = "Working As Designed";
    item.Update();
}
```

```
private void codeInitWaiting_ExecuteCode(object sender, EventArgs e)
{
    SPListItem item = workflowProperties.Item;
    item["BugStatus"] = "Waiting";
    item.Update();
}

private void codeInitFixed_ExecuteCode(object sender, EventArgs e)
{
    SPListItem item = workflowProperties.Item;
    item["BugStatus"] = "Fixed";
    item.Update();
}
```

Implementing the Event Handlers

Now you'll implement the `EventDrivenActivity` sequences for the remaining states, starting with the `Assigned` state.

Assigned State

From the top-level workflow diagram, drag an `EventDrivenActivity` to the `stateAssigned` activity, and rename it as **eventAssigned**. Double-click this activity to view the sequence. Drag an `OnTaskChanged` activity to the empty sequence, and rename it as **onAssignedChanged**. For the `CorrelationToken`, select the existing `taskToken` from the drop-down list. The Properties window should look like Figure 13-37.

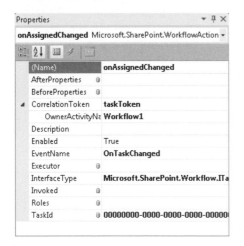

Figure 13-37. The Properties window for the onAssignedChanged *activity*

Double-click this activity to generate the event handler. Enter the implementation using the code in Listing 13-18.

Listing 13-18. Implementation of onAssignedChanged_MethodInvoking

```
CreateTaskWithContentType task = sender as CreateTaskWithContentType;
SPTaskServiceEventArgs args = (SPTaskServiceEventArgs)e;

_taskId = args.taskId;
SPWorkflowTaskProperties after = args.afterProperties;
if (after != null)
{
    if (after.ExtendedProperties[
        workflowProperties.TaskList.Fields.GetFieldByInternalName("Resolution")
        .Id] != null)
    {
        _resolution = after.ExtendedProperties[
            workflowProperties.TaskList.Fields.GetFieldByInternalName("Resolution")
            .Id].ToString();
        _wad = bool.Parse(after.ExtendedProperties[
            workflowProperties.TaskList.Fields.GetFieldByInternalName("BugWAD")
            .Id].ToString());
        _waiting = bool.Parse(after.ExtendedProperties[
            workflowProperties.TaskList.Fields.GetFieldByInternalName("BugWaiting")
            .Id].ToString());
        _started = bool.Parse(after.ExtendedProperties[
            workflowProperties.TaskList.Fields.GetFieldByInternalName("BugStarted")
            .Id].ToString());
        _fixed = bool.Parse(after.ExtendedProperties[
            workflowProperties.TaskList.Fields.GetFieldByInternalName("BugFixed")
            .Id].ToString());

        if (_resolution.Length > 0)
        {
            SPListItem item = workflowProperties.Item;
            item["Resolution"] = _resolution;
            item.Update();
        }
    }
    else
        _fixed = false;
}
```

This code is similar to the code you implemented for the onPendingChanged activity. It retrieves the values for the following properties:

- _resolution: A description of the fix entered by the developer

- _wad: A flag indicating that this is working as designed

- _waiting: A flag indicating that more information is needed

- _started: A flag to indicate that this bug is being worked on

- _fixed: A flag indicting that the bug has been fixed

If a resolution has been entered, the BugList item is updated with the resolution details. One thing that is different about this implementation is that the code is wrapped by an if statement verifying that the Resolution property is not null. I'll explain why that is necessary later.

Go back to the workflow designer, and drag an IfElseActivity below the onAssignedChanged activity. There are four check boxes on the assigned task form, and you will need four branches on the IfElseActivity, one for each check box. You can add branches by right-clicking the IfElseActivity and choosing Add Branch, as shown in Figure 13-38.

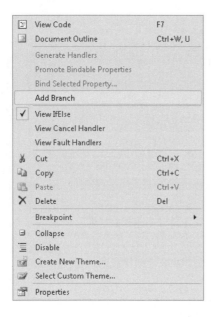

Figure 13-38. Adding an additional IfElseActivity branch

As I mentioned earlier, the order of the branches is important because multiple check boxes could be selected. The correct order is probably debatable, but the order I used is as follows:

1. Fixed

2. Wad

3. Waiting

4. Started

For each branch, rename the branch as **ifAssigned<state>**, as in **ifAssignedFixed**. Then set the condition using a declarative rule condition just like you have done previously. The Expression will simply check the flag set by the **onAssignedChange** activity. For example, the first one will be **this._fixed**. As you create these conditions, give them a meaningful name like **Fixed**.

Drag a `SetStateActivity` to each branch, and set the `TargetStateName` to the appropriate state. Rename each of these as **setAssigned<target state>**. The completed sequence should look like Figure 13-39.

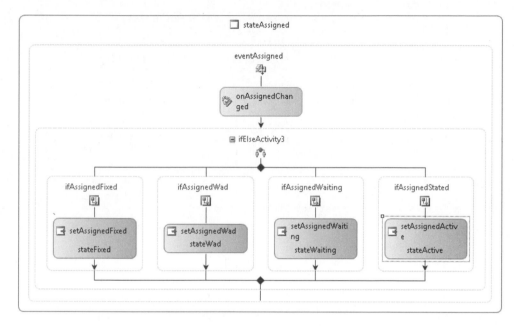

Figure 13-39. The eventAssigned *sequence*

Active State

From the top-level workflow diagram, drag an `EventDrivenActivity` to the **stateActive** activity, and rename it as **eventActive**. Double-click this activity to view the sequence. Drag an `OnTaskChanged` activity to the empty sequence, and rename it as **onActiveChanged**. For the `CorrelationToken`, select the existing `taskToken` from the drop-down list. Double-click this activity to generate the event handler. Enter the implementation using the code in Listing 13-19.

Listing 13-19. Implementation of onActiveChanged_MethodInvoking

```
private void onActiveChanged_Invoked(object sender, ExternalDataEventArgs e)
{
    CreateTaskWithContentType task = sender as CreateTaskWithContentType;
    SPTaskServiceEventArgs args = (SPTaskServiceEventArgs)e;

    _taskId = args.taskId;

    SPWorkflowTaskProperties after = args.afterProperties;
    if (after != null)
    {
```

```
    _resolution = after.ExtendedProperties[
        workflowProperties.TaskList.Fields.GetFieldByInternalName("Resolution")
        .Id].ToString();
    _wad = bool.Parse(after.ExtendedProperties[
        workflowProperties.TaskList.Fields.GetFieldByInternalName("BugWAD")
        .Id].ToString());
    _waiting = bool.Parse(after.ExtendedProperties[
        workflowProperties.TaskList.Fields.GetFieldByInternalName("BugWaiting")
        .Id].ToString());
    _started = bool.Parse(after.ExtendedProperties[
        workflowProperties.TaskList.Fields.GetFieldByInternalName("BugStarted")
        .Id].ToString());
    _fixed = bool.Parse(after.ExtendedProperties[
        workflowProperties.TaskList.Fields.GetFieldByInternalName("BugFixed")
        .Id].ToString());

    if (_resolution.Length > 0)
    {
        SPListItem item = workflowProperties.Item;
        item["Resolution"] = _resolution;
        item.Update();
    }
  }
}
```

This code is almost identical to the implementation of the **onAssignedChanged_Invoke()** method except that is doesn't need to be wrapped around an `if` statement to ensure the **Resolution** property is not null.

The activities in this workflow sequence will also be nearly identical as the **eventAssigned** sequence. The only difference will be with the last branch that checks the **_started** flag. In the **Assigned** event, the workflow moves to the **Active** state if the **_started** flag is true. In the **Active** state, the workflow will move back to the **Assigned** state if the **_started** flag is false. This will allow the developer to deselect this check box to indicate that they're no longer working on it.

The fourth branch should be renamed as **ifActiveNotStarted**, the **Expression** will be **!this._started**, and the **TargetStateName** of the **SetStateActivity** will be the **Assigned** state. Everything is identical, except for the activity names, which follow the same naming conventions you have been using. The complete sequence should look like Figure 13-40.

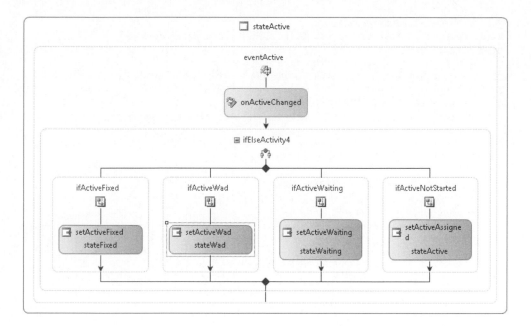

Figure 13-40. The eventActive sequence

Working as Designed State

Either the admin who performs the initial review or the developer assigned to the bug can indicate that this is working as designed and is not really a bug. This will put the workflow in the Wad state. In this state, the initiator has two options: they can either close the bug, which will end the workflow or they can resubmit it, with some feedback.

From the top-level workflow diagram, drag an EventDrivenActivity to the stateWad activity, and rename it **eventWad**. Double-click this activity to view the sequence. Drag an OnTaskChanged activity to the empty sequence, and rename it **onWadChanged**. For the CorrelationToken, select the existing wadToken from the drop-down list. Double-click this activity to generate the event handler. Enter the implementation using the code in Listing 13-20.

Listing 13-20. Implementation of onWadChanged_MethodInvoking

```
private void onWadChanged_Invoked(object sender, ExternalDataEventArgs e)
{
    CreateTaskWithContentType task = sender as CreateTaskWithContentType;
    SPTaskServiceEventArgs args = (SPTaskServiceEventArgs)e;

    _taskId = args.taskId;

    SPWorkflowTaskProperties after = args.afterProperties;
    if (after != null)
    {
```

```
    _feedback = after.ExtendedProperties[
        workflowProperties.TaskList.Fields.GetFieldByInternalName("Feedback")
        .Id].ToString();
    _closed = bool.Parse(after.ExtendedProperties[
        workflowProperties.TaskList.Fields.GetFieldByInternalName("BugClosed")
        .Id].ToString());
    _reSubmit = bool.Parse(after.ExtendedProperties[
        workflowProperties.TaskList.Fields.GetFieldByInternalName("BugReSubmit")
        .Id].ToString());

    if (_feedback.Length > 0)
    {
        SPListItem item = workflowProperties.Item;
        if (item["Feedback"] != null)
            item["Feedback"] += "\r\n";
        item["Feedback"] += _feedback;
        item.Update();
    }
}
}
}
```

This code retrieves the following values from the task form:

- **Feedback**: Feedback provided by the initiator

- **BugClosed**: A flag indicating to close the bug

- **BugReSubmit**: A flag indicating the bug should be resubmitted

If the Feedback property was populated, its contents are appended to the existing Feedback property of the BugList item.

In the workflow designer, drag an IfElseActivity just below the onWadChange activity. The first thing that needs to be determined is if the bug should be closed or resubmitted. Rename the left branch as **ifWadClosed**, and rename the right branch as **ifWadResubmit**. For the left branch, enter a new declarative rule condition, and set the Expression as **this._closed**. For the right branch, create a new condition, and enter the Expression as **this._reSubmit**. If neither of these flags is set, then no action is taken, and the workflow stays in the Wad state.

Processing the Closed Branch

In the closed (left) branch, you'll need to close the Wad task as well as the work task. Drag two CompleteTaskActivity objects to the left branch, and rename them as **completeWad** and **completeWadWork**. Set the CorrelationToken as wadToken and taskToken, respectively. For the MethodInvoking property of the completeWad activity, select the completeTask_MethodInvoking() method from the drop-down list. Drag a CodeActivity below these, and rename it as **codeWadClosed**.

Open the Workflow1.cs code-behind class, and add the methods shown in Listing 13-21.

Listing 13-21. Implementation of Completion Event Handlers

```
private void completeWorkTask_MethodInvoking(object sender, EventArgs e)
{
```

```
    CompleteTask ct = (CompleteTask)sender;
    ct.TaskId = _workTaskId;
}

private void codeSetClosed_ExecuteCode(object sender, EventArgs e)
{
    // Now set the BugStatus and the completed date
    SPListItem item = workflowProperties.Item;
    item["DateCompleted"] = DateTime.Now;
    item["BugStatus"] = "Closed";
    item.Update();
}
```

The first method will be used to close the work task (the task assigned to the developer). The second method will be used to set the BugStatus to closed and also set the DateCompleted property on the BugList item.

For the MethodInvoking property of the completeWadWork activity, select the completeWorkTask_MethodInvoking() method from the drop-down list. For the codeWadClosed activity, select the codeSetClosed_ExecuteCode() method. Finally, drag a SetStateActivity below the codeWadClosed activity, and rename it as **setWadClosed**. Set the TargetStateName as stateFinal.

Processing the Resubmit Branch

Drag a CompleteTaskActivity to the right branch, and rename it as **completeWadResubmit**. For the CorrelationToken, select the wadToken from the drop-down list. For the MethodInvoking property, select the completeTask_MethodInvoking() method from the drop-down list. This will complete the existing Wad task.

If the initiator has chosen to resubmit this bug, the workflow will be moved to either the Pending state or the Assigned state, depending on whether a work task has already been created. If it was put in the Wad state directly from the Pending state, then it needs to go back to the Pending state to be reviewed again and possibly assigned to a developer. If the developer put it in the Wad state, then a developer has been assigned, and a work task has already been created. In this case, it can go directly to the Assigned state.

In the workflow designer, drag an IfElseActivity to the right branch. Rename the left branch of the new IfElseActivity as **ifWadAssigned**, and rename the right branch as **ifWadNotAssigned**. For the condition of the left branch, select the existing Assigned declarative rule condition. The right branch does not need a condition. The Properties window for the left branch should look like Figure 13-41.

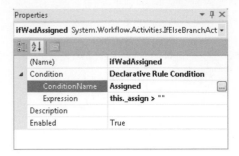

Figure 13-41. The Properties windows of the `ifWadAssigned` *branch*

Drag a `SetStateActivity` to both the left and right branches, and name them **setWadAssigned** and **setWadPending**, respectively. Set the `TargetStateName` property as `stateAssigned` and `statePending`, respectively. The completed sequence should look like figure 13-42.

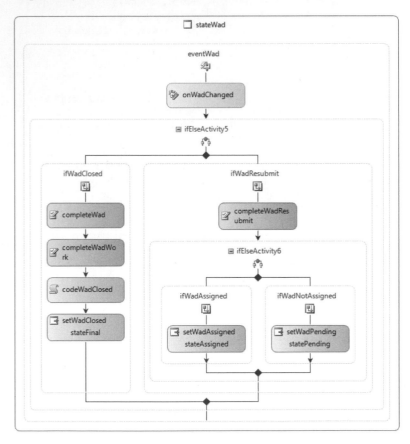

Figure 13-42. The completed `eventWad` *sequence*

Waiting State

The EventDrivenActivity sequence for the Waiting state is identical to the implementation of the Wad state. You can follow the same instructions that were given for the Wad state. The completed sequence should look like Figure 13-43.

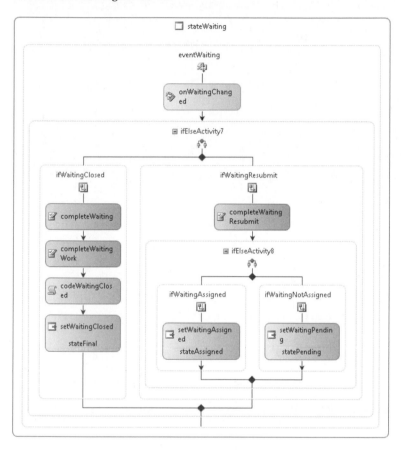

Figure 13-43. Completed eventWaiting sequence

Listing 13-22 shows the implementation of the onWaitingChanged event handler.

Listing 13-22. Implementation of onWaitingChanged_Invoked

```
private void onWaitingChanged_Invoked(object sender, ExternalDataEventArgs e)
{
    CreateTaskWithContentType task = sender as CreateTaskWithContentType;
    SPTaskServiceEventArgs args = (SPTaskServiceEventArgs)e;

    _taskId = args.taskId;
```

```
    SPWorkflowTaskProperties after = args.afterProperties;
    if (after != null)
    {
        _feedback = after.ExtendedProperties[
            workflowProperties.TaskList.Fields.GetFieldByInternalName("Feedback")
            .Id].ToString();
        _closed = bool.Parse(after.ExtendedProperties[
            workflowProperties.TaskList.Fields.GetFieldByInternalName("BugClosed")
            .Id].ToString());
        _reSubmit = bool.Parse(after.ExtendedProperties[
            workflowProperties.TaskList.Fields.GetFieldByInternalName("BugReSubmit")
            .Id].ToString());

        if (_feedback.Length > 0)
        {
            SPListItem item = workflowProperties.Item;
            if (item["Feedback"] != null)
                item["Feedback"] += "\r\n";
            item["Feedback"] += _feedback;
            item.Update();
        }
    }
}
```

Fixed State

The task for a bug in the Fixed state is assigned to the test user. The test user can enter feedback of the results of the tests and can mark the bug as either fixed or not fixed. A bug that is marked fixed will be closed. If not fixed, it will go back to the Assigned state.

From the top-level workflow diagram, drag an EventDrivenActivity to the stateFixed activity, and rename it as **eventFixed**. Double-click this activity to view the sequence. Drag an OnTaskChanged activity to the empty sequence, and rename it as **onFixedChanged**. For the CorrelationToken, select the existing fixedToken from the drop-down list. Double-click this activity to generate the event handler. Enter the implementation using the code in Listing 13-23.

Listing 13-23. Implementation of onFixedChanged_MethodInvoking

```
private void onFixedChanged_Invoked(object sender, ExternalDataEventArgs e)
{
    CreateTaskWithContentType task = sender as CreateTaskWithContentType;
    SPTaskServiceEventArgs args = (SPTaskServiceEventArgs)e;

    _taskId = args.taskId;

    SPWorkflowTaskProperties after = args.afterProperties;
    if (after != null)
    {
        _feedback = after.ExtendedProperties[
            workflowProperties.TaskList.Fields.GetFieldByInternalName("Feedback")
```

```
       .Id].ToString();
_tested = bool.Parse(after.ExtendedProperties[
    workflowProperties.TaskList.Fields.GetFieldByInternalName("BugTested")
    .Id].ToString());
_notFixed = bool.Parse(after.ExtendedProperties[
    workflowProperties.TaskList.Fields.GetFieldByInternalName("BugNotFixed")
    .Id].ToString());

if (_feedback.Length > 0)
{
    SPListItem item = workflowProperties.Item;
    if (item["Feedback"] != null)
        item["Feedback"] += "\r\n";
    item["Feedback"] += _feedback;
    item.Update();
}
    }
}
```

This code retrieves the values from the task form. If the Feedback property was entered, it is appended to the Feedback property of the BugList item.

In the workflow designer, drag an IfElseActivity below the onFixedChanged activity. Rename the left branch as **ifFixed**, and rename the right branch as **ifNotFixed**. For the left branch, the Expression property of the declarative code condition should be **this._fixed**, and for the right branch it should be **this._notFixed**.

■ **Caution** This is not an if-then-else expression; each branch evaluates different conditions. The left branch determines whether the bug was marked fixed, and the right branch determines if the bug was marked not fixed. These are not mutually exclusive. It is possible that neither was checked. In this case, it means that the testing is not complete and no action is taken. The feedback, if entered, is still appended to the BugList item, however.

If the bug was indeed fixed, the left branch will complete the fixed task and the work task as well as set the BugStatus and complete the workflow. Drag two CompleteTaskActivity objects to the left branch, and rename them as **completeFixed** and **completeFixedWork**. Set the CorrelationToken as fixedToken and taskToken, respectively. For the MethodInvoking property of the completeFixed activity, select the completeTask_MethodInvoking() method from the drop-down list. For the MethodInvoking property of the completeFixedWork activity, select the completeWorkTask_MethodInvoking() method from the drop-down list.

Drag a CodeActivity below these, and rename it as **codeFixedClosed**. For the ExecuteCode property, select the codeSetClosed_ExecuteCode() method from the drop-down list.

Finally, drag a SetStateActivity below the codeFixedClosed activity, and rename it as **setFixedClosed**. Set the TargetStateName as stateFinal.

If the bug was not fixed, you will need to put the workflow back to the Assigned state as well as update the task and the BugList item. Drag a CompleteTaskActivity to the right branch, and rename it as **completeFixedAssigned**. For the CorrelationToken, select the fixedToken from the drop-down list. For the MethodInvoking property, select the completeTask_MethodInvoking method from the drop-down list.

Drag a **CodeActivity** just below this, and rename it as **codeFixedNotFixed**. Drag a **SetStateActivity** below this, and rename it as **setFixedAssigned**. Set the **TargetStateName** to **stateAssigned**. The complete sequence should look like Figure 13-44.

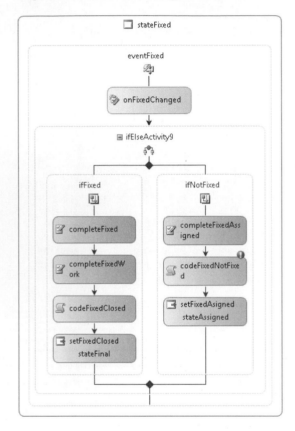

Figure 13-44. *The completed* **eventFixed** *sequence*

Using AlterTask

You still need to provide the implementation for the **codeFixedNotFixed** activity. Double-click it to generate the event handler. Enter the implementation shown in Listing 13-24.

Listing 13-24. Implementation of codeFixedNotFixed

```
private void codeFixedNotFixed_ExecuteCode(object sender, EventArgs e)
{
    SPListItem task = null;
    foreach (SPWorkflowTask t in workflowProperties.Item.Tasks)
    {
```

```
        if (t.DisplayName.Substring(0, 4) == "Bug:")
        {
            task = (SPListItem)t;
            break;
        }
    }

    if (task != null)
    {
        Hashtable ht = new Hashtable();
        ht["BugFixed"] = 0;
        SPWorkflowTask.AlterTask(task, ht, false);
    }
}
```

This code uses the static AlterTask method to modify the properties of an existing task. The developer checked the Fixed check box on the task form, which sets the BugFixed property. That is what caused the workflow to move to the Fixed state. Now the tester is stating that the fix is not working. Because we are reusing the work task, when the developer displays their work task, it will still show as fixed. So, this code is executed to clear the BugFixed property.

The first step is to find the work task. The WorkflowProperties.Item member represents the BugList item. Its Tasks property is a collection of all the tasks that have been created for this item. These are the tasks that are created in the initialization sequence of each state. You have been prepending the Title property with different text for each state. The work task is prepended with the "Bug:" text, so it's fairly easy to find it.

The next step is to create a hash table containing the property names and values that should be updated. There is only one, the BugFixed property, and it is being set to 0. Finally, the AlterTask() method is called, which will update the task.

The perhaps unexpected side effect, however, is that this will raise the OnTaskChanged event. Recall when you implemented the onAssignedChanged event handler that you wrapped the code by an if statement to verify that the Resolution property was not null. When the OnTaskChange event is raised because of an AlterTask command, it doesn't have the afterProperties populated. When the Resolution property is null, this is an indication that the event was not raised by the normal task form, so the code simply ignores this event.

Completing the Workflow

There's one last very important step. Double-click the eventInitial activity on the Initial state. Drag a SetStateActivity below the onWorkflowActivated1 activity, and change the name to setInitialPending. Set the TargetStateName to statePending. This will cause the workflow to move to the Pending state when it is activated.

The top-level workflow will look something like Figure 13-45.

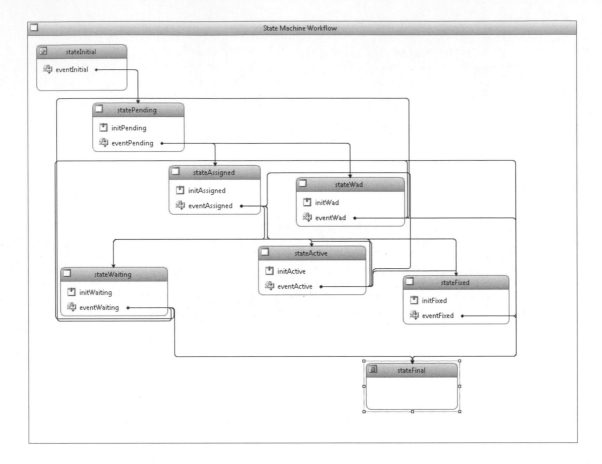

Figure 13-45. *The final top-level workflow*

Adding an Association Form

Now you'll add an association form that will allow the end users to configure the admin and test users. This workflow is configured to start automatically when an item is added to the `BugList`. An initiation form is not helpful here because it is used only when starting a workflow manually. However, the association form will allow the users to configure the workflow when it is associated to a list, `BugList` in this case.

An association form is implemented just like the initiation form that you implemented in Chapter 10. From the Solution Explorer, right-click the Workflow1 feature, and select Add ▶ New Item. In the Add New Item dialog box, select the Workflow Association Form template, and enter the name as `Chapter13Association.aspx`, as shown in Figure 13-46.

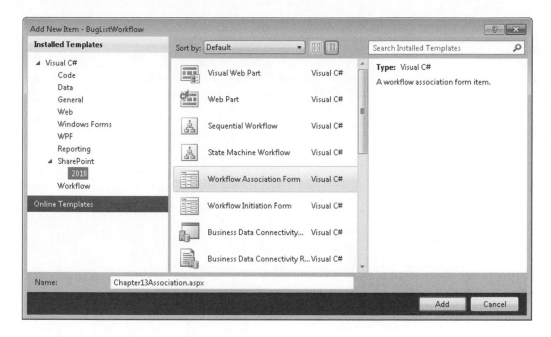

Figure 13-46. *Adding an association form*

Listing 13-25 shows the contents of the **Chapter13Association.aspx** file, with the lines that you'll need to add in bold.

Listing 13-25. *Implementation of Chapter13Association.aspx*

```
<%@ Assembly Name="$SharePoint.Project.AssemblyFullName$" %>
<%@ Assembly Name="Microsoft.Web.CommandUI, Version=14.0.0.0, Culture=neutral,
                   PublicKeyToken=71e9bce111e9429c" %>
<%@ Import Namespace="Microsoft.SharePoint" %>
<%@ Import Namespace="Microsoft.SharePoint.ApplicationPages" %>
<%@ Register Tagprefix="SharePoint"
            Namespace="Microsoft.SharePoint.WebControls"
            Assembly="Microsoft.SharePoint, Version=14.0.0.0, Culture=neutral,
                      PublicKeyToken=71e9bce111e9429c" %>
<%@ Register Tagprefix="Utilities"
            Namespace="Microsoft.SharePoint.Utilities"
            Assembly="Microsoft.SharePoint, Version=14.0.0.0, Culture=neutral,
                      PublicKeyToken=71e9bce111e9429c" %>
<%@ Register Tagprefix="asp"
            Namespace="System.Web.UI"
            Assembly="System.Web.Extensions, Version=3.5.0.0, Culture=neutral,
                      PublicKeyToken=31bf3856ad364e35" %>

<%@ Page Language="C#"
    DynamicMasterPageFile="~masterurl/default.master"
```

```
        AutoEventWireup="true"
        Inherits="BugListWorkflow.Workflow1.Chapter13Association"
        CodeBehind="Chapter13Association.aspx.cs" %>

<asp:Content ID="Main" ContentPlaceHolderID="PlaceHolderMain" runat="server">

    Admin User:  
    <SharePoint:PeopleEditor
        AllowEmpty="false"
        ValidatorEnabled="true"
        id="adminUser"
        runat="server"
        ShowCreateButtonInActiveDirectoryAccountCreationMode="true"
        SelectionSet="User" /> <br/><br/>

    Test User:  
    <SharePoint:PeopleEditor
        AllowEmpty="false"
        ValidatorEnabled="true"
        id="testUser"
        runat="server"
        ShowCreateButtonInActiveDirectoryAccountCreationMode="true"
        SelectionSet="User" /> <br/><br/>

<asp:Button ID="AssociateWorkflow"
            runat="server"
            OnClick="AssociateWorkflow_Click"
            Text="Associate Workflow" />
          
    <asp:Button ID="Cancel" runat="server" Text="Cancel" OnClick="Cancel_Click" />
</asp:Content>

<asp:Content ID="PageTitle"
            ContentPlaceHolderID="PlaceHolderPageTitle"
            runat="server">
    Workflow Association Form
</asp:Content>

<asp:Content ID="PageTitleInTitleArea"
            runat="server"
            ContentPlaceHolderID="PlaceHolderPageTitleInTitleArea">
    Workflow Association Form
</asp:Content>
```

This code adds two `PeoplePicker` controls to the form: one to select the admin user and the other to select the test user. Now open the `Chapter13Association.aspx.cs` code-behind file, and add the following namespaces:

```
using System.Linq;
using System.Xml.Linq;
using System.Collections.Generic;
```

Then provide the following implementation for the `GetAssociationData()` method:

```
private string GetAssociationData()
{
    XElement data = new XElement("InitiationData",
        new XElement("AdminUsers",
                    from PickerEntity x in adminUser.Entities.ToArray()
                    select new XElement("Name", x.Description)),
        new XElement("TestUsers",
                    from PickerEntity x in testUser.Entities.ToArray()
                    select new XElement("Name", x.Description)));

    return data.ToString();
}
```

This code creates an XML string that contains the values from the `PeoplePicker` controls. It allows for multiple users to be selected for each.

Finally, open the `Workflow1.cs` code-behind file, and add the code from Listing 13-26 to the `onWorkflowActivated1_Invoked()` method.

Listing 13-26. Code to Add to the onWorkflowActivated Event Handler

```
// Get the association data
if (workflowProperties.AssociationData != null)
{
    XElement data = XElement.Parse(workflowProperties.AssociationData);

    foreach (XElement x in data.Element("AdminUsers").Elements())
    {
        _admin = x.Value;
        break;  // just get the first one
    }
    foreach (XElement x in data.Element("TestUsers").Elements())
    {
        _test = x.Value;
        break;  // just get the first one
    }
}
```

This code takes the first user from the `AdminUser` collection and stores it in the `_admin` class member. Likewise, the `_test` member is set using the first user from the `TestUsers` collection. If no association data is available, the workflow will use the hard-coded values.

Testing the Workflow

Now you're ready to deploy and test the workflow. Press F6 to build the solution and fix any compiler errors. Then, from the Solution Explorer, right-click the BugListWorkflow project, and choose Deploy. Visual Studio should have already associated the workflow to the `BugList`. However, you'll now associate it manually so you can use the association form that you provided.

Go to the Part3 SharePoint site through a browser window, and select the `BugList`. From the List ribbon, click the Workflow Settings button as shown in Figure 13-47.

Figure 13-47. *Selecting the Workflow Settings page*

This will display the standard association page that you've used before. Everything on this page should default as shown in Figure 13-48. These are the settings you specified when setting up the project in Visual Studio.

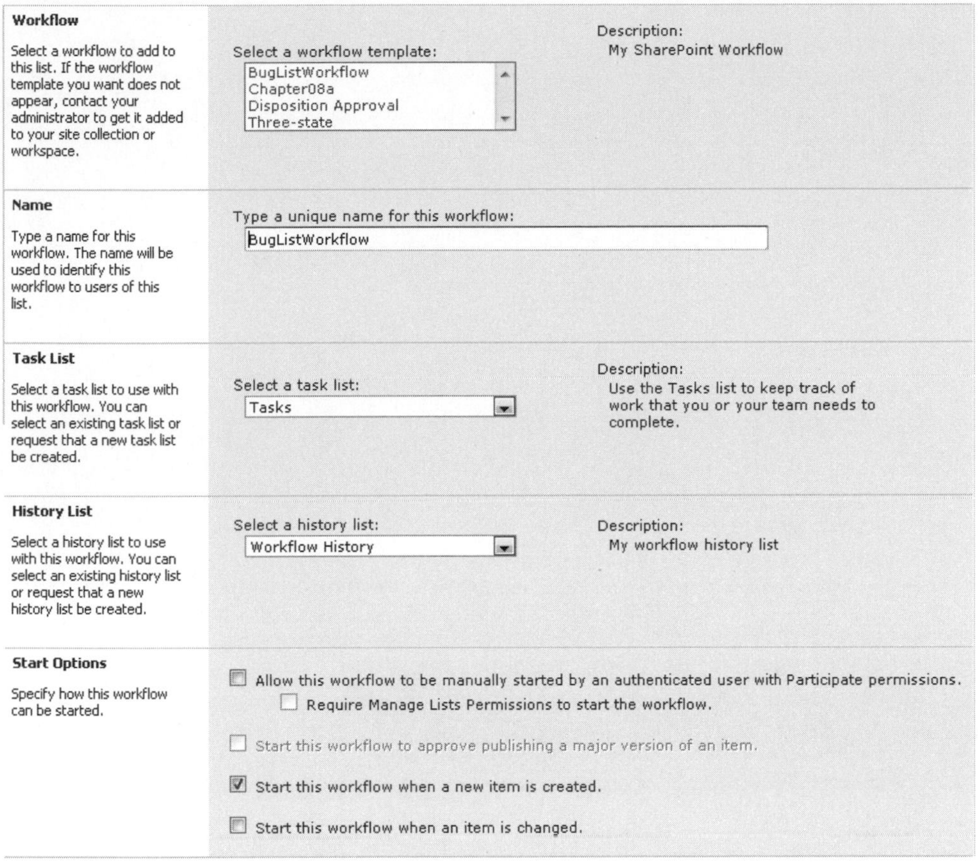

Workflow		
Select a workflow to add to this list. If the workflow template you want does not appear, contact your administrator to get it added to your site collection or workspace.	Select a workflow template: BugListWorkflow Chapter08a Disposition Approval Three-state	Description: My SharePoint Workflow
Name		
Type a name for this workflow. The name will be used to identify this workflow to users of this list.	Type a unique name for this workflow: BugListWorkflow	
Task List		
Select a task list to use with this workflow. You can select an existing task list or request that a new task list be created.	Select a task list: Tasks	Description: Use the Tasks list to keep track of work that you or your team needs to complete.
History List		
Select a history list to use with this workflow. You can select an existing history list or request that a new history list be created.	Select a history list: Workflow History	Description: My workflow history list
Start Options		
Specify how this workflow can be started.	☐ Allow this workflow to be manually started by an authenticated user with Participate permissions. 　☐ Require Manage Lists Permissions to start the workflow. ☐ Start this workflow to approve publishing a major version of an item. ☑ Start this workflow when a new item is created. ☐ Start this workflow when an item is changed.	

Figure 13-48. The standard workflow association page

The next page, shown in Figure 13-49, will be the custom page that you created. It has two `PeoplePicker` controls on it. Enter a user for the admin and test user fields, and click the Associate Workflow button.

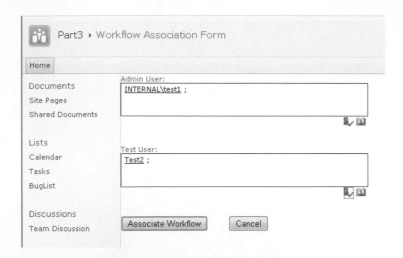

Figure 13-49. *The custom association page*

Go to the `BugList`, and add a new item to the list. The new item form only has two fields, `Title` and `Description`, as shown in Figure 13-50. Enter some appropriate text, and click the Save button.

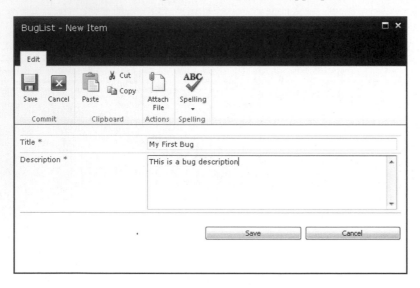

Figure 13-50. *The `BugList` New Item form*

Now go to the `Tasks` list. There should be a new task assigned to the admin user that you specified on the association form. Edit this task, which will display the form shown in Figure 13-51.

Figure 13-51. The Pending task form

Your custom fields are at the bottom of the form. Notice that there is a check box to mark this bug "working as designed." There is also a place to specify the priority and assign a developer. Select a Priority, enter a user for the Assign To field, and click the Save button.

■ **Tip** I showed you in Chapter 10 how you can develop custom task forms using InfoPath 2010. Ideally, these tasks should use custom forms that have only the fields that are appropriate for that state. I'll leave that for you to do using the instructions provided in Chapter 10.

The workflow will automatically generate a new task assigned to the developer you just selected. You may have to refresh the page to see the new task in the list. Edit the new task, which will display the form shown in Figure 13-52.

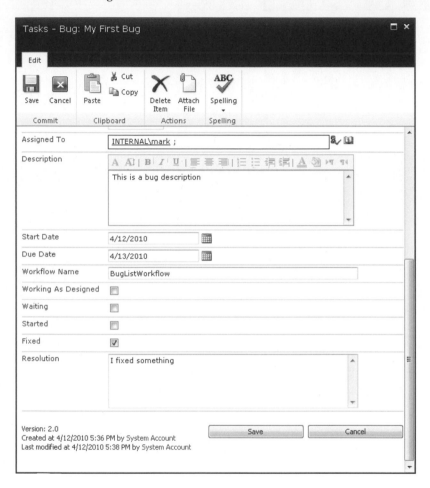

Figure 13-52. The Bug task form

The Bug task form is where the developer will record the fix that was made. There are also check boxes that will move this bug to the `Wad` or `Waiting` state. If the fix will take some time, the developer can select the `Started` check box now and then select the `Fixed` check box when the fix is complete.

Select the `Fixed` check box, enter some text in the `Resolution` field, and click the Save button. The workflow will now generate a task for the test user to verify the fix. Again, you may need to refresh the page for the new task to appear. Edit the new task, which will display the Resolved task form shown in Figure 13-53.

Figure 13-53. The Resolved task form

In the Resolved task form, check the Tested check box, enter some text in the Feedback field, and click the Save button. This will complete the workflow. All the tasks should be completed as shown in Figure 13-54.

	@	Type	Title	Assigned To	Status	Priority	Due Date	% Complete	Predecessors	Related Conte
		🗋	Pending: My First Bug ⊠NEW	INTERNAL\test1	Completed	(2) Normal	4/13/2010	100 %		My First Bug
		🗋	Bug: My First Bug ⊠NEW	INTERNAL\mark	Completed	(2) Normal	4/13/2010	100 %		My First Bug
		🗋	Resolved: My First Bug ⊠NEW	Test2	Completed	(2) Normal	4/13/2010	100 %		My First Bug

Figure 13-54. The updated task list

Now go to the `BugList` and display the item. The `BugList` form should look like Figure 13-55.

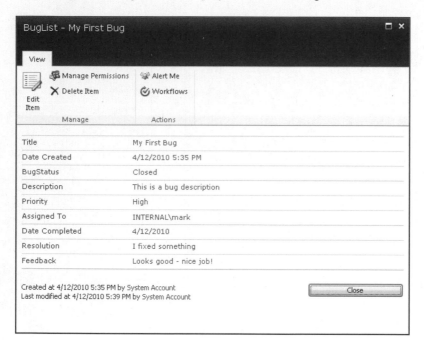

Figure 13-55. The completed `BugList` item

Notice that all of the fields have been filled in including the `Assigned To`, `Resolution`, and `Feedback` fields. You can click the Workflows button and see a history of all the tasks associated with this bug, which will show the same tasks listed in Figure 13-54.

Try all the other scenarios such as marking the bug as Working as Designed, and marking the bug as Not Fixed in the Resolved form.

Summary

In this chapter, you built a robust bug-tracking system using a state machine workflow. Also, as part of this project you did the following:

- Created and deployed fields, content types, and a list template using Visual Studio

- Used state initialization sequences to generate task-specific forms

- Updated the payload (`BugList` item) with task form data

- Used the `AlterTask` method to modify existing task properties

- Implemented an association form.

You should now have a sense for the power of this design model. Even complex workflow scenarios are more easily managed by breaking them down into the appropriate states and the events that each state must handle.

PART 4

■■■

Miscellaneous Topics

In this section I'll explain how to use several interesting features provided for Office workflows. In Chapter 14 you'll use a ConditionedActivityGroup to send reminder emails at regular intervals until an assigned task has been completed. In Chapter 15 you'll create a simple workflow using the SharePoint Designer and then import this workflow into Visual Studio. This allows you to start a workflow using a no-code approach and then transition to Visual Studio to add more complex capabilities. This will also give you a view into how no-code workflows are implemented "under-the-covers."

In Chapter 16 I'll show you how to build custom actions in Visual Studio and deploy them to the SharePoint server. These actions can then be used by the SharePoint Designer and included in no-code workflows. Finally, you'll implement a Pluggable Workflow Service in Chapter 17 that allows you to call external systems using asynchronous processing. This was not possible in prior releases and is one of the nice improvements in Office 2010.

CHAPTER 14

■■■

Using a ConditionedActivityGroup

Workflow provides an interesting activity called the ConditionedActivityGroup, often referred to as CAG. It contains a group of activities (or activity sequences) that are executed based on the defined conditions. There are three important rules to understand when using a CAG:

- There is an UntilCondition for the group. The child activities are executed, simultaneously, as long as the UntilCondition is false. If there is no UntilCondition, the CAG will execute until no children are executing.

- There is a WhenCondition for each child activity (or activity sequence). The child activity is executed repeatedly as long as its WhenCondition is true. If there is no WhenCondition, the activity is executed once.

- The conditions are evaluated (and the appropriate activities executed) when the CAG is first executed and as each child activity (or sequence) completes.

Setting Up the Project

In this chapter, I'll show you how you can use a ConditionedActivityGroup to implement logic to follow up on a task that is still outstanding.

Creating a Part4 Site

Start by creating a new site for the projects in Part 4. Open the SharePoint site in a browser window. From the Site Actions menu, click the *New Site* link. In the dialog box, select the Team Site template, and enter **Part4** for the name and URL, as shown in Figure 14-1.

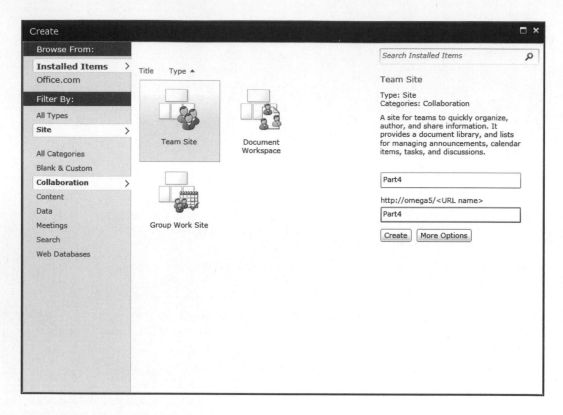

Figure 14-1. *Creating the Part4 site*

Creating the Visual Studio Project

Next, open Visual Studio 2010, and create a new project. Use the SharePoint 2010 Sequential Workflow template, as shown in Figure 14-2. For the project name, enter **WF_Chapter14**.

Figure 14-2. Creating a new Visual Studio project

The familiar SharePoint Customization Wizard dialog boxes will appear that you'll use to set up your debugging environment. In the first one, enter the URL for the Part4 site that you just created, as shown in Figure 14-3.

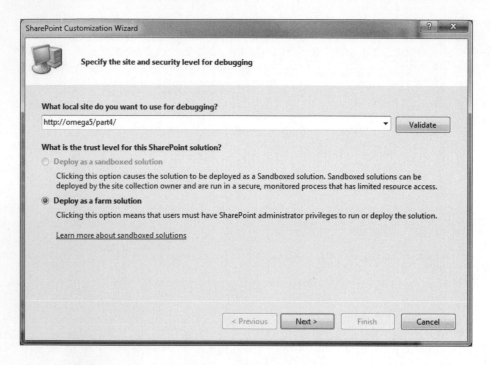

Figure 14-3. Specifying the Part4 site

Following the naming conventions used previously, enter **WF_Chapter14** for the workflow name. Also, this will be a site workflow, so make sure you select that option, as shown in Figure 14-4.

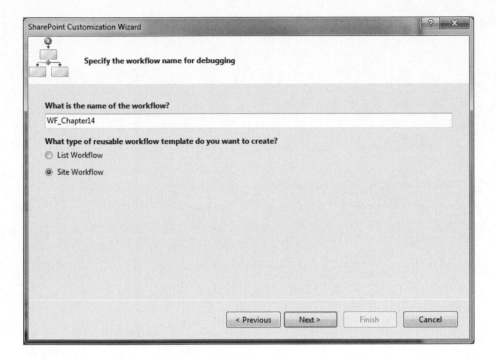

Figure 14-4. Entering the workflow name

In the third dialog box shown in Figure 14-5, associate the `Workflow History` and `Tasks` lists using the default options.

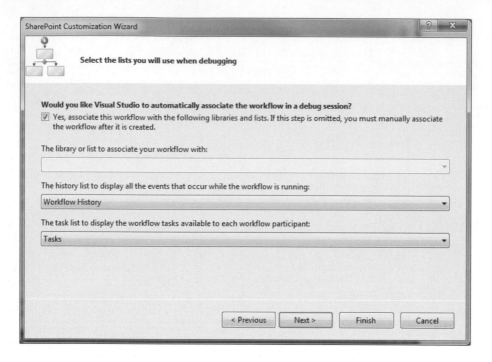

Figure 14-5. *Associating the task and history lists*

The final dialog box displays the start options, but there is only one allowed for site workflows, which is to start it manually. Just use the default value.

Designing the Workflow

Now you're ready to design the workflow, which will create a task and then wait for it to be completed. While it's waiting, it will send out reminder e-mails at specified intervals until the task is complete.

Creating the Task

The template should have generated a sequential workflow with the standard `OnWorkflowActivated` event handler. Drag a `CreateTaskActivity` just below this. In the Properties window, enter the `CorrelationToken` as `taskToken`. Expand the property, and select the `OwnerActivityName` as `Workflow1`. The Properties window should look like Figure 14-6.

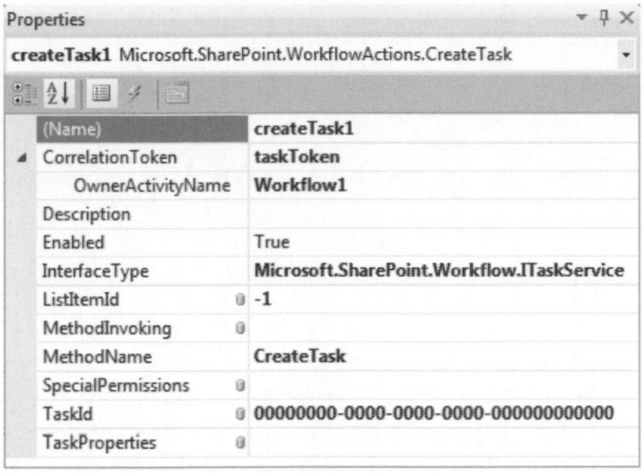

Figure 14-6. The `CreateTask1` *Properties window*

Double-click the **createTask1** activity to generate the event handler, and open the code-behind file. Add the following class members:

```
private Guid taskID = Guid.NewGuid();
private bool bTaskComplete = false;
```

These members will store the ID of the task and a flag that indicates whether the task has been completed. Then add the code from Listing 14-1 to implement the **createTask1_MethodInvoking** method. While in the code-behind file, also enter the **completed** and **notCompleted** methods (also included in Listing 14-1), which will be used as code conditions.

Listing 14-1. Implementation of `createTask1_MethodInvoking()`

```
private void createTask1_MethodInvoking(object sender, EventArgs e)
{
    CreateTask task = sender as CreateTask;
    task.TaskId = taskID;

    SPWorkflowTaskProperties wtp = new SPWorkflowTaskProperties();
    wtp.PercentComplete = (float)0.0;
    wtp.TaskType = 0;
    wtp.DueDate = DateTime.Now.AddDays(1);
    wtp.Title = "Perform some task";

    task.TaskProperties = wtp;
}

private void completed(object sender, ConditionalEventArgs e)
{
    e.Result = bTaskComplete;
}
```

```
private void notCompleted(object sender, ConditionalEventArgs e)
{
    e.Result = !bTaskComplete;
}
```

The `completed` method returns `True` if the task is complete, and `notCompleted` returns `True` if the task is *not* complete.

ConditionedActivityGroup Activity

Drag a `ConditionedActivityGroup` activity to the workflow, just below `createTask1`. In the Properties window, for the `UntilCondition`, select `Code Condition`, and then select the `completed` method. The `UntilCondition` will be false until the task has been completed. Until then, the child activities will continue to execute. The Properties window should look like Figure 14-7.

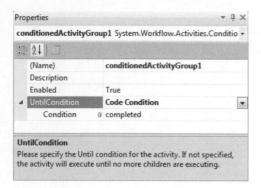

Figure 14-7. *The* `ConditionedActivityGroup` *Properties window*

Figure 14-8 shows a blank `ConditionedActivityGroup`.

Figure 14-8. *A blank* `ConditionedActivityGroup`

Using this activity may seem a bit odd at first. You drag child activities to the top portion of this activity, and the bottom portion shows a preview of the currently selected activity.

■ **Tip** If you want to execute a sequence of activities, then drag a SequenceActivity to the CAG. In the preview/edit pane, you'll be able to define the activities that make up the sequence.

Designing the First Child Activity

The first child activity will wait for the OnTaskChanged event. Drag a SequenceActivity onto the top portion of the CAG activity (where it says "Drop Activities Here"). Then double-click the bottom portion to switch from preview mode to edit mode. The CAG should look like Figure 14-9.

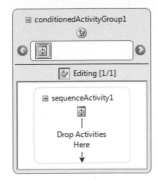

Figure 14-9. The CAG with a single SequenceActivity

Click the sequenceActivity1 activity. In the Properties window, set the WhenCondition using the notCompleted method, as shown in Figure 14-10.

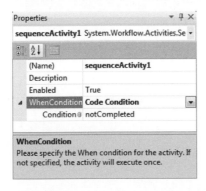

Figure 14-10. The child activity's Properties window

393

The child activity will be executed as long as the `WhenCondition` is true. In this case, it will be executed if the task has not yet been completed.

Drag an `OnTaskChanged` activity to this sequence. In the Properties window, select the `CorrelationToken` as `taskToken`, which is the same token used when creating the task. Double-click this activity to generate the event handler. Enter the following code for the implementation of this event handler:

```
private void onTaskChanged_Invoked(object sender, ExternalDataEventArgs e)
{
    SPTaskServiceEventArgs args = (SPTaskServiceEventArgs)e;
    if (args.afterProperties.PercentComplete == 1)
        bTaskComplete = true;
}
```

This code simply checks the `PercentComplete` property and the sets the `bTaskComplete` flag if it's 100 percent complete. Now drag an `IfElseActivity` below the `OnTaskChanged` activity. For the left branch, set the `Condition` property to use the same `completed` condition used for the CAG's `UntilCondition`. The Properties window should look like Figure 14-11.

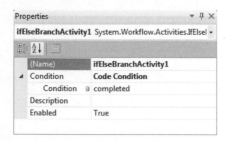

Figure 14-11. The `IfElseActivity` branch properties

Drag a `CompleteTaskActivity` to the left branch of the `IfElseActivity`. In the Properties window, for the `CorrelationToken`, select the same `taskToken` used on the other activities. Double-click this activity to generate the event handler, and enter the following code for its implementation:

```
private void completeTask1_MethodInvoking(object sender, EventArgs e)
{
    CompleteTask task = sender as CompleteTask;
    task.TaskId = taskID;
}
```

This code sets the `TaskId` property using the same value that was set in the `CreateTaskActivity`. The workflow diagram should look like Figure 14-12.

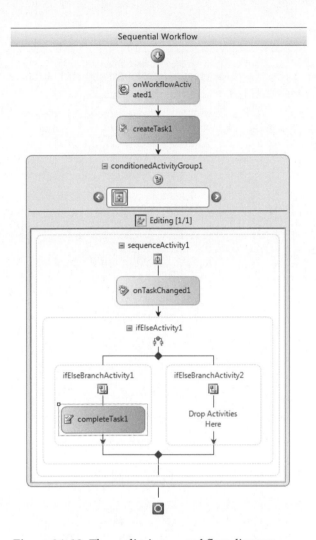

Figure 14-12. The preliminary workflow diagram

This first child activity is complete. It listens for the OnTaskChanged event. If the PercentComplete field is set to 1 (100 percent), the task is completed by using a CompleteTaskActivtity.

■ **Note** The OnTaskChanged event handler is using the PercentComplete property to determine whether the task is done. However, the user could set it to 100 percent complete but leave the status as Not Started or In Progress. From a workflow perspective, the task would still be active. By using the CompleteTaskActivity, you force the task to the Completed status, which will also allow the workflow to complete (once the other activities have also completed).

Designing the Second Child Activity

The second child activity will be used to send a reminder e-mail if the task has not been completed yet. Reminder e-mails will continue to be sent until the task is completed.

Drag another SequenceActivity to the upper part of the CAG. The CAG activity should look like Figure 14-13.

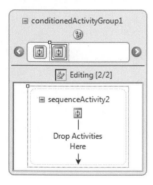

Figure 14-13. A second SequenceActivity in the CAG

Notice that there are two activities in the top section. You can use the arrow buttons on either side of this bar to scroll through the child activities. You can also click one of these to make it the current activity. The current child activity is displayed in the bottom section, which can be either in preview mode or in edit mode.

Click the sequenceActivity2, and in the Properties window, set the WhenCondition using the notCompleted method, just like you did for the first sequence. This child activity, just like the first one, will continue to be executed as long as the task has not been completed.

Drag a DelayActivity to sequenceActivity2. In the Properties window, set the TimeoutDuration property to 00:05:00. This is the notation for a TimeSpan value. The three sections represent the hours, minutes, and seconds of the duration, so 00:05:00 specifies a five-minute wait.

Then drag an IfElseActivity below the DelayActivity. In the left branch, set the Condition property using the notCompleted method. Then drag a SendEmailActivity to the left branch. In the Properties window, for the CorrelationToken, select the workflowToken. Enter appropriate values for the From, To, Subject, and Body properties. The Properties window will look like Figure 14-14.

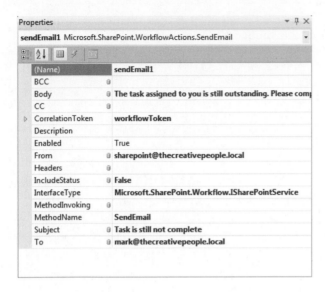

Figure 14-14. The SendEmail Properties window

Your second child activity is now complete. The CAG diagram should look like Figure 14-15.

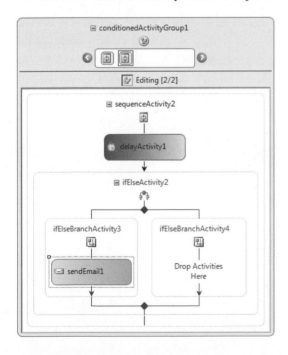

Figure 14-15. The second child activity

The second child activity will wait five minutes and send an e-mail if the task is not yet complete. It will continue to send reminder e-mails every five minutes until the task is complete.

Listing 14-2 shows the complete implementation of the code-behind file.

Listing 14-2. Implementation of the Code-Behind File

```
using System;
using System.ComponentModel;
using System.ComponentModel.Design;
using System.Collections;
using System.Drawing;
using System.Linq;
using System.Workflow.ComponentModel.Compiler;
using System.Workflow.ComponentModel.Serialization;
using System.Workflow.ComponentModel;
using System.Workflow.ComponentModel.Design;
using System.Workflow.Runtime;
using System.Workflow.Activities;
using System.Workflow.Activities.Rules;
using Microsoft.SharePoint;
using Microsoft.SharePoint.Workflow;
using Microsoft.SharePoint.WorkflowActions;

namespace WF_Chapter14.Workflow1
{
    public sealed partial class Workflow1 : SequentialWorkflowActivity
    {
        public Workflow1()
        {
            InitializeComponent();
        }

        public Guid workflowId = default(System.Guid);
        public SPWorkflowActivationProperties workflowProperties
            = new SPWorkflowActivationProperties();

        private Guid taskID = Guid.NewGuid();
        private bool bTaskComplete = false;

        private void createTask1_MethodInvoking(object sender, EventArgs e)
        {
            CreateTask task = sender as CreateTask;
            task.TaskId = taskID;

            SPWorkflowTaskProperties wtp = new SPWorkflowTaskProperties();
            wtp.PercentComplete = (float)0.0;
            wtp.TaskType = 0;
            wtp.DueDate = DateTime.Now.AddDays(1);
            wtp.Title = "Perform some task";

            task.TaskProperties = wtp;
```

```
    }

    private void completed(object sender, ConditionalEventArgs e)
    {
        e.Result = bTaskComplete;
    }

    private void notCompleted(object sender, ConditionalEventArgs e)
    {
        e.Result = !bTaskComplete;
    }

    private void onTaskChanged1_Invoked(object sender, ExternalDataEventArgs e)
    {
        SPTaskServiceEventArgs args = (SPTaskServiceEventArgs)e;
        if (args.afterProperties.PercentComplete == 1)
            bTaskComplete = true;
    }

    private void completeTask1_MethodInvoking(object sender, EventArgs e)
    {
        CompleteTask task = sender as CompleteTask;
        task.TaskId = taskID;
    }
  }
}
```

Using the DelayActivity

The Windows Workflow Foundation (WF) that all SharePoint workflows are based on is designed to support long-running workflows. This means that there can be a long period of time between activities. When a task is created, it could be hours, even days, before the task is completed. When a workflow becomes idle, that is, it is waiting for some external event (such as **OnTaskChanged**), the current state of the workflow is persisted to a database, and the workflow is unloaded from memory. This is very important because if this were not done, there could be thousands of workflow instances taking up system resources. When the user edits the task, the workflow is automatically retrieved from the database and continues processing. This persisting and reloading is going on all the time and is completely transparent to you.

When a **DelayActivity** is used, a timer is created, which sends an event into the workflow after the specified duration. After starting the timer, the **DelayActivity** then waits for an event, just like **OnTaskChanged**. This also causes the workflow to become idle, and it is then persisted and removed from memory. This causes a problem because the workflow cannot handle the timer event since it is no longer running.

To solve this problem, SharePoint uses a windows service called SPTimerV4. It is listed in the control panel as SharePoint 2010 Timer (see Figure 14-16).

Figure 14-16. The SharePoint 2010 timer service

This service periodically checks the persistence store to see whether there are any instances that have expired timers and "wakes" them up. For the most part, this is also transparent to you. However, this service polls the database every five minutes, by default. This means that if you set the duration for five minutes (as you just did), the actual duration can be as long as ten minutes depending when the polling is scheduled.

For most Office workflows, you usually work in units of days, or perhaps hours. An extra five-minute delay is not going to be noticeable. For this project, you set the duration to five minutes, and at 5:01 you'll be wondering where your e-mail is. Allow an extra five minutes because of the polling strategy.

■ **Caution** SharePoint 2007 had lots of issues with this this timer service. In many cases, after the `DelayActivity` was executed, the workflow never resumed. I believe most of these issues have been resolved in SharePoint 2010. However, I have seen some situations where the `DelayActvity` did not work. If you run into this, I have found that restarting the SPTimerV4 service usually rectifies the situation.

Testing Your Workflow

From the Solution Explorer, right-click the WF_Chapter14 project, and choose Deploy, which will install this workflow on the Part4 subsite. Launch the Part4 SharePoint site, and click the Site Workflows link that you'll find on the All Site Content page. You should see the new workflow, as shown in Figure 14-17.

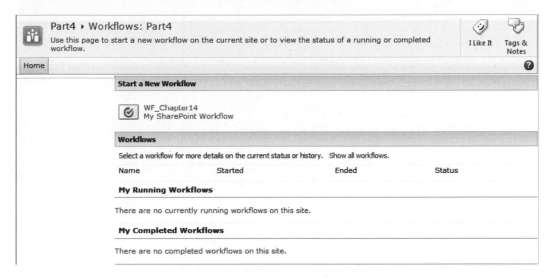

Figure 14-17. Selecting the WF_Chapter14 workflow

Click the *WF_Chapter14* link, which will start the workflow. After the workflow has been started, you should have a task in the Tasks list similar to the one shown in Figure 14-18.

Figure 14-18. Viewing the new task

After waiting a while (up to ten minutes), you should receive an e-mail like the one shown in Figure 14-19.

Figure 14-19. A reminder e-mail

Then edit the task, and set the `PercentComplete` property to 100. The task should then be marked complete, as shown in Figure 14-20.

Figure 14-20. The `Tasks` list showing the completed task

Finally, go back to the Site Workflows page, and the workflow should show that is has been completed (see Figure 14-21).

Figure 14-21. The completed workflow

Summary

In this chapter, you used a `ConditionedActivityGroup` (CAG) to listen for changes to a task and simultaneously send out reminder e-mails. A CAG allows multiple child activities to be executed repeatedly as long as the `WhenCondition` on the child activity is `True` and the `UntilCondition` on the CAG is `False`.

In this project, the first child activity waited for `OnTaskChanged` events until the task was completed. At the same time, the second activity repeatedly sent out reminder e-mails until the task was complete.

CHAPTER 15

■■■

Importing Reusable Workflows

Visual Studio 2010 can import a reusable workflow that was created through some other application such as the SharePoint Designer. This provides the ability to start developing a workflow using a no-code approach and then to import it into Visual Studio where coded features can be added.

■ **Note** Unfortunately, you can't export from Visual Studio. This is primarily because many of the activities in Visual Studio (such as the `CodeActivity`) are not supported in other tools.

In this chapter, you'll create a simple reusable workflow in the SharePoint Designer that generates a task when a new `Calendar` event is created. This workflow will then be imported into Visual Studio where you'll add an extra step that will also send an e-mail. This project will not only demonstrate the import feature but will also give you some insight into how the no-code workflows are implemented.

Creating a Workflow in the SharePoint Designer

To avoid the confusion of having two workflows associated with the same `Calendar` list, you'll implement the first workflow using the Part3 site. The Visual Studio workflow will then use the Part4 site. If you have been working through these projects in order, you should already have a Part3 site. If not, any site created with the Team Site template will work.

Start the SharePoint Designer, and open the Part3 site. In the Navigation pane, click the *Workflows* link. Then click the Reusable Workflow button in the ribbon, as shown in Figure 15-1.

Figure 15-1. Creating a reusable workflow

In the Create Reusable Workflow dialog box that is shown is Figure 15-2, enter the name **Event Review**, and be sure to select the **Event** content type.

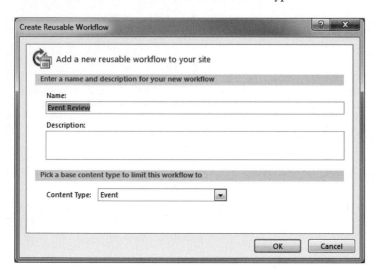

*Figure 15-2. Selecting the **Event** content type*

Designing the Workflow

You can refer to Chapter 7 if you want to review how to implement a workflow using the SharePoint Designer. The initial (blank) design will look like Figure 15-3.

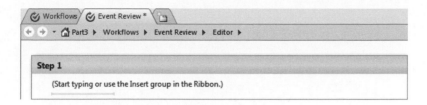

Figure 15-3. A blank workflow design

The orange bar denotes the insertion point where a new action or condition will be added. Type **log**, and press Enter. This will create an action to log a record to the workflow history list. Click the *this message* link, and then click the ellipsis to display the String Builder dialog box. Enter **The workflow has started; the duration is**, and then click the Add or Change Lookup button. In the Lookup for String dialog box, select the `Duration` field from the `Current Item` data source, as shown in Figure 15-4, and click OK.

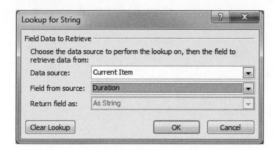

Figure 15-4. Selecting the `Duration` field

Finish the string by adding **seconds**. The completed string should look like Figure 15-5. Click OK to close the dialog box.

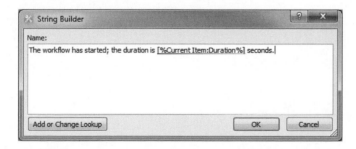

Figure 15-5. The completed string

The insertion point should now be below the item you just added. Type **if c**, and press Enter to add an `If current item field equal value condition`. Click the field link, and select the `Duration` field, as shown in Figure 15-6.

Figure 15-6. Selecting the `Duration` field

Click the *equals* link, and change the operation to `is greater than or equal to`. Click the *value* link, and enter **1800**. This is equivalent to 30 minutes, so this condition will be true if the event is scheduled for 30 minutes or longer. The insertion point should be inside the `If` condition. Type **create l**, and press Enter. This will add the `create list item` action.

Click the *this list* link, which will display the Create New List Item dialog box. For the `List` property, select `Association: Task List`, which should be the first one in the drop-down list. The `Title` field is automatically added to the list of fields because it is required. Select the `Title` field, and click the Modify button, which will display the Value Assignment dialog box. Click the ellipsis next to the value property. In the String Builder dialog box, enter **New Event:**, and then click the Add or Change Lookup button. Select the `Title` field from the `Current Item` data source, as shown in Figure 15-7.

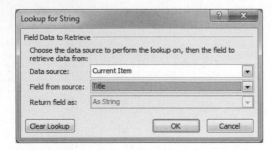

Figure 15-7. Selecting the `Title` field

The completed string should look like Figure 15-8.

Figure 15-8. The completed string

Click the Add button to add another field. In the Value Assignment dialog box, select the field as `Assigned To`. For the value property, click the *fx* button, and select the `Created By` field of the `Current Item` data source, as shown in Figure 15-9.

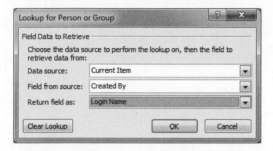

Figure 15-9. Selecting the `Created By` field

This will assign the new task to the user who created the event. The completed Create New List Item dialog box should look like Figure 15-10.

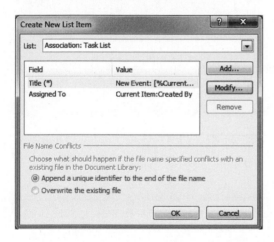

Figure 15-10. The completed Create New List Item dialog box

The completed workflow should look like Figure 15-11.

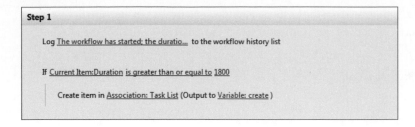

Figure 15-11. The completed workflow design

Testing the Workflow

Click the Publish button in the ribbon, which will validate and save the workflow as well as publish it to the Part3 SharePoint site. Open the Part3 site using a web browser, and select the `Calendar` list. Click the Workflow Settings button that will be on the top-right corner of the Calendar ribbon, as shown in Figure 15-12.

Figure 15-12. The Workflow Settings button

Figure 15-13 shows the Workflow Settings page.

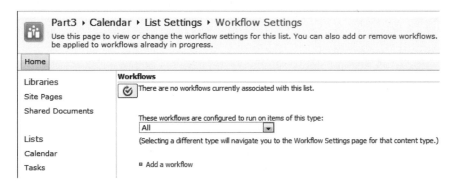

Figure 15-13. The Workflow Settings page

Click the *Add a workflow* link, which will display the Add a Workflow page shown in Figure 15-14.

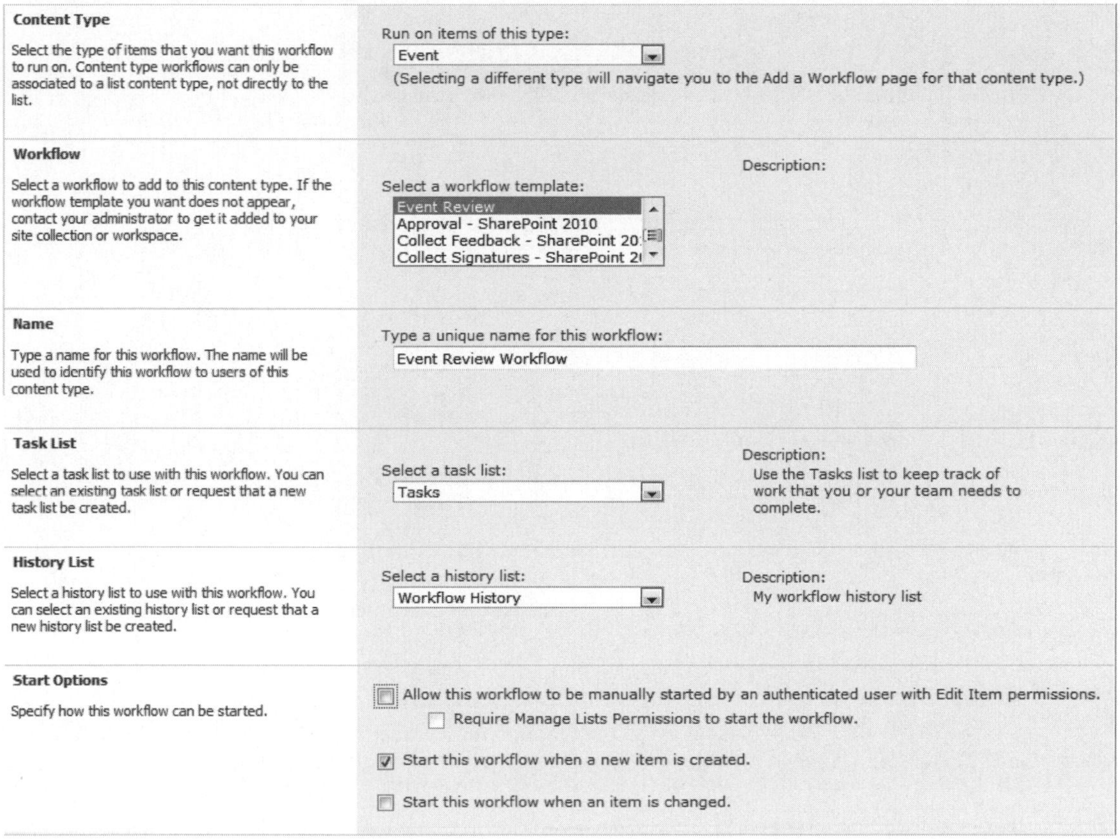

Content Type	Run on items of this type:
Select the type of items that you want this workflow to run on. Content type workflows can only be associated to a list content type, not directly to the list.	Event ▾ (Selecting a different type will navigate you to the Add a Workflow page for that content type.)
Workflow	Description:
Select a workflow to add to this content type. If the workflow template you want does not appear, contact your administrator to get it added to your site collection or workspace.	Select a workflow template: Event Review Approval - SharePoint 2010 Collect Feedback - SharePoint 20 Collect Signatures - SharePoint 2(▾
Name	Type a unique name for this workflow:
Type a name for this workflow. The name will be used to identify this workflow to users of this content type.	Event Review Workflow
Task List	Select a task list: Description:
Select a task list to use with this workflow. You can select an existing task list or request that a new task list be created.	Tasks ▾ Use the Tasks list to keep track of work that you or your team needs to complete.
History List	Select a history list: Description:
Select a history list to use with this workflow. You can select an existing history list or request that a new history list be created.	Workflow History ▾ My workflow history list
Start Options	☐ Allow this workflow to be manually started by an authenticated user with Edit Item permissions. ☐ Require Manage Lists Permissions to start the workflow. ☑ Start this workflow when a new item is created. ☐ Start this workflow when an item is changed.
Specify how this workflow can be started.	

Figure 15-14. Associating a workflow

This workflow was designed to run against items with the `Event` content type. You will need to change the content type to `Event` before the workflow will be available in the drop-down list. Change the content type, and choose the `Event Review` workflow template. Enter the name **Event Review Workflow**, and change the start options so the workflow is started automatically when a new item is created. Click the OK button to complete the association.

Go to the `Calendar` list, and add an event that lasts more than 30 minutes. The workflow should have also generated a task that is similar to the one shown in Figure 15-15.

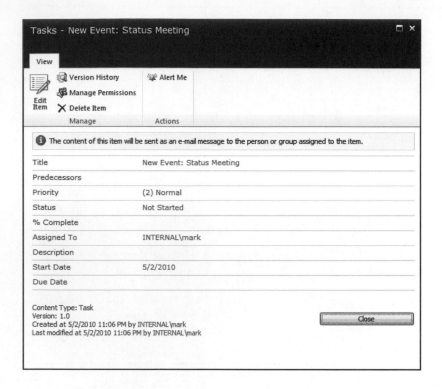

Figure 15-15. The Workflow-generated task

Exporting the Workflow

To import the workflow into Visual Studio, you'll need to first save it as a **.wsp** file. Go to the Workflows page in the SharePoint Designer, and select the Event Review workflow. Then click the Save as Template button that is shown in Figure 15-16.

Figure 15-16. Saving a workflow as a **.wsp** *file*

■ **Caution** You already published the workflow previously so you could test it, so this will not be an issue with this workflow. However, keep in mind that you have to publish the workflow before saving it as a .wsp file. If you don't, the .wsp file will be generated without any errors, but it won't include the workflow.

Site Assets

When you save a workflow template, it is saved to the Site Assets library, as explained by Figure 15-17.

Figure 15-17. Saving the workflow template

The Site Assets document library does not usually have a link to it from the quick links section. Instead, click the *Libraries* link, or choose the *All Site Content* link from the Site Actions menu. Figure 15-18 shows the All Site Content page.

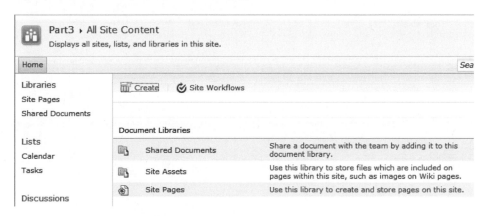

Figure 15-18. Listing all site content links

Click the *Site Assets* link, which will display the Site Assets page showing a single item, as shown in Figure 15-19.

413

	Type	Name	Modified		Modified By
☐	☐	Event Review ⊞ NEW	5/2/2010 11:21 PM		INTERNAL\mark

Figure 15-19. Listing the Event Review file

When you click the *Event Review* link, a download dialog box will appear to choose a suitable place to save this file.

Importing the Workflow

Start Visual Studio 2010, and create a new project using the Import Reusable Workflow template, as shown in Figure 15-20. Enter the project name **WF_Chapter15**.

Figure 15-20. Creating a new project for importing a .wsp file

In the SharePoint Customization Wizard dialog boxes, enter the URL for the Part4 site. In the second dialog box, shown in Figure 15-21, specify the location of the **.wsp** that you downloaded from the Part3 site.

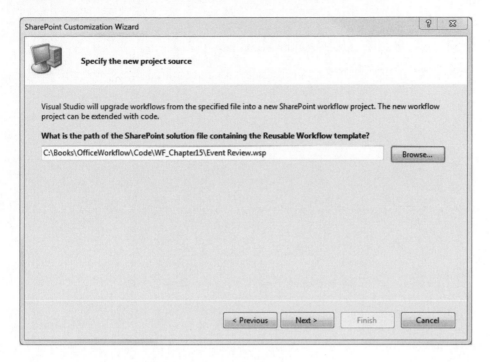

*Figure 15-21. Specifying the location of the **.wsp** file*

The next dialog box, shown in Figure 15-22, lists the workflows that are included in the .wsp file. You can select which ones you want to import. In this case, there is only one, and it should already be selected. Click the Finish button.

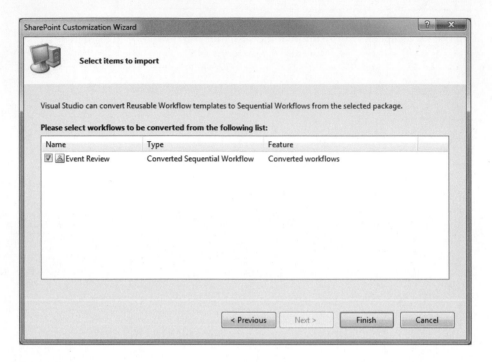

Figure 15-22. Choosing the workflows to import

You should see a message box indicating that the workflow was imported successfully. Figure 15-23 shows the contents of the Solution Explorer. The file names are a little different from other Visual Studio projects.

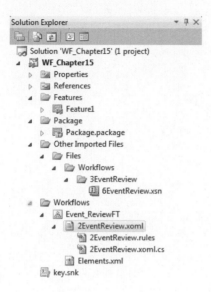

Figure 15-23. The contents of the Solution Explorer

The biggest difference for our purposes is that the workflow is defined in a `.xoml` file.

■ **Note** XOML is based on XML structure and is similar to XAML used by Windows Presentation Foundation (WPF). However, XOML does not rely on the WPF objects. The workflow files you have used so far were expressed in .cs files, which allows for both the workflow design and code to be included in the same class. The XOML format is used when you want code separation, that is, when the workflow file is strictly declarative and any code is placed in a separate class.

Double-click the `2EventReview.xoml` file to see the workflow definition. Figure 15-24 shows a portion of it.

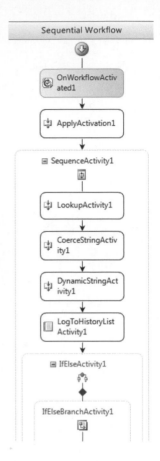

Figure 15-24. The workflow design

At first glance, this may seem like a lot of activities for such a simple workflow. Keep in mind that the SharePoint Designer generates no-code workflows. Operations must be implemented by using primitive activities. For example, the SequenceActivity1 writes an entry to the workflow history log. Its first child activity is a LookupActivity, which retrieves the Duration property for the current item. The CoerceStringActivity is then used to convert this integer value to a string. The DynamicStringActivity is used to concatenate this with some fixed text. Finally, the LogToHistoryListActivity is used to write the data to the history list.

Modifying the Workflow

Scroll to the bottom of the workflow, and drag a SendEmailActivity after the last activity (but still inside the IfElseBranchActivity1). The workflow diagram should look like Figure 15-25.

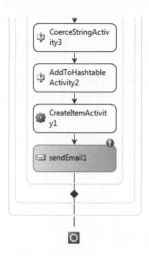

Figure 15-25. Adding the `SendEmailActivity`

In the Properties window, for the `CorrelationToken`, select the existing `refObject`. Enter appropriate values for the `Body`, `From`, `Subject`, and `To` properties. The completed Properties window should look similar to Figure 15-26.

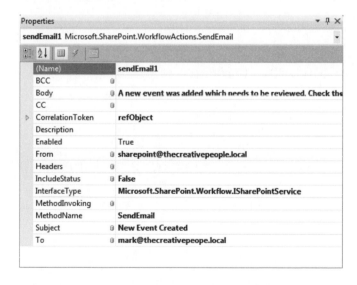

Figure 15-26. The completed Properties window

Associating the Workflow

The easiest way to associate the workflow with the appropriate list is to run the Workflow Customization Wizard. To do that, from the Solution Explorer, click the `Event_ReviewFT` folder. In the Properties window, click the ellipsis next to the `TargetList` property. In the first dialog box, enter the workflow name **WF_Chapter15**, as shown in Figure 15-27. The other options are grayed out because you can't change them once the project has been created.

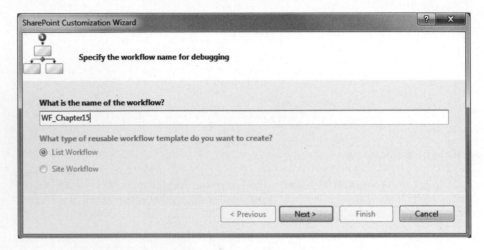

Figure 15-27. *Entering the workflow name*

In the next dialog box, click the check box, and then select the `Calendar` list to associate this workflow with. The form should look like Figure 15-28.

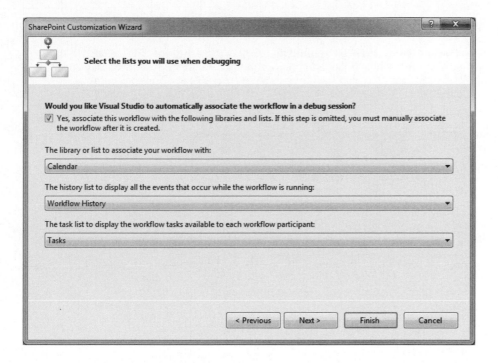

Figure 15-28. Associating with the `Calendar` *list*

In the last dialog box, change the startup options so the workflow is started when an item is created, as shown in Figure 15-29.

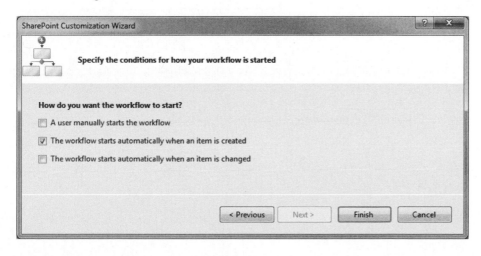

Figure 15-29. Specifying the start options

Testing the Workflow

Now you're ready to test the workflow. Press F5 to build and deploy the solution. This will also launch the Part4 SharePoint site. Go to the Calendar list, and create a new event. Make sure the duration is at least 30 minutes. Then go to the Tasks list. You should have a new task like the one shown in Figure 15-30.

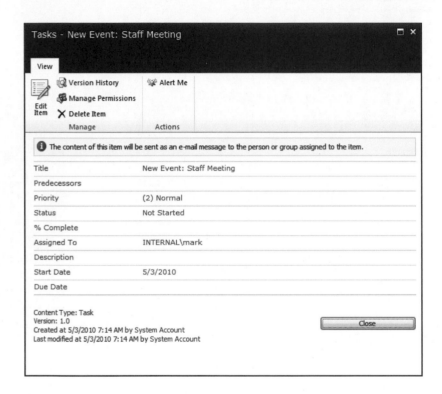

Figure 15-30. *The new task that was created*

You should also receive an e-mail like the one shown in Figure 15-31.

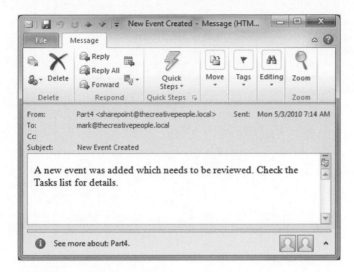

Figure 15-31. The notification e-mail that was added

Summary

You created a simple reusable no-code workflow using the SharePoint Designer and then imported that workflow into Visual Studio. The no-code workflow uses primitive activities to accomplish things that you would normally write in code such as converting data formats or assigning properties. You then modified the workflow in Visual Studio and redeployed it to another site.

This is a useful approach. You can let power users and IT staff build no-code workflows as needed. If these workflows need more advanced features that require a developer, then using this technique, the developer can start with the existing workflow design and simply add the necessary logic.

CHAPTER 16

∎∎∎

Creating Custom Actions

In this chapter you'll create a custom action in Visual Studio 2010 that, once deployed to your SharePoint server, can be used by no-code workflows created with the SharePoint Designer. This demonstrates the flexibility of the tooling options available in Office 2010. You can implement activities with all the power of Visual Studio available to you, including access to the SharePoint object model, which I introduced in Chapter 9. With the technique presented in this chapter, these activities can be packaged into reusable actions that can be employed by power users and other nondevelopment staff.

Setting Up the SharePoint Project

Start Visual Studio 2010, and create an empty SharePoint 2010 project, as shown in Figure 16-1. Enter the project name **WF_Chapter16**.

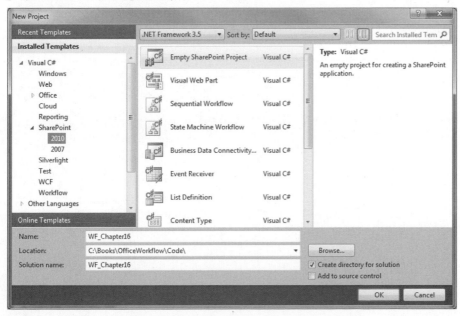

Figure 16-1. Creating an empty SharePoint 2010 project

<section>425</section>

In the SharePoint Customization Wizard that is displayed (see Figure 16-2), enter the URL for the Part4 SharePoint site. Make sure you select the farm solution option.

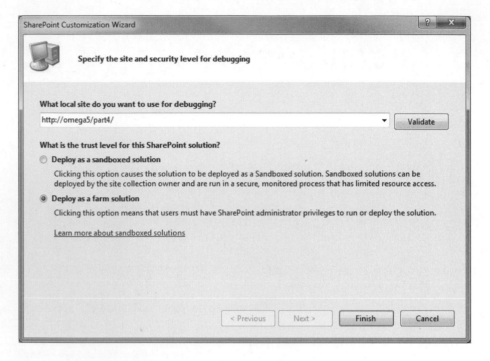

Figure 16-2. Configuring the deployment environment

■ **Note** This project will be used only for packaging and deploying the solution to the SharePoint server. The actual custom activity will be implemented in a different project, which you'll create now.

Designing a Custom Activity

Now you'll use the Workflow Foundation (WF) provided by .NET 3.5 to create the custom activity. From the Solution Explorer, right-click the WF_Chapter16 solution, and choose Add ▶ New Project. Enter **ActivityLibrary** for the project name, as shown in Figure 16-3.

Figure 16-3. Adding an ActivityLibrary project

The template generates an activity named **Activity1.cs**. From the Solution Explorer, right-click this file, and rename it as **CreateEvent.cs**. The pop-up box shown in Figure 16-4 will appear; click Yes to allow Visual Studio to update the references to this file.

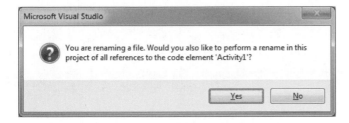

Figure 16-4. Allowing the refactoring of Activity1.cs

Adding the SharePoint References

The template generates this project with all the necessary references for the Workflow Foundation classes; however, you will need to add the SharePoint references. From the Solution Explorer, right-click the ActivityLibrary project, and choose Add Reference. Select the Browse tab, and then navigate to where the SharePoint DLLs are installed. By default, this will be as follows:

```
C:\Program Files\Common Files\Microsoft Shared\Web Server Extensions\14\ISAPI
```

Select the following DLLs, as shown in Figure 16-5:

- `Microsoft.SharePoint.dll`

- `Microsoft.sharepoint.WorkflowActions.dll`

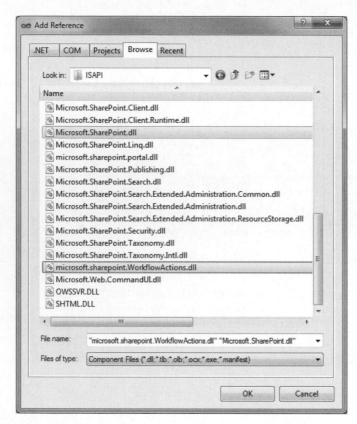

Figure 16-5. Adding references to the SharePoint DLLs

Implementing the Custom Activity

The template generates an activity designer, as shown in Figure 16-6.

Figure 16-6. The workflow activity designer

Right-click this file, and choose View Code. Add the following namespaces, which are provided by the DLLs that you just added references to:

```
using Microsoft.SharePoint;
using Microsoft.SharePoint.Workflow;
using Microsoft.SharePoint.WorkflowActions;
```

Also, the class created by the template, **CreateEvent**, is derived from **SequenceActivity**. Change its parent class to **Activity**. The **CreateEvent.cs** class should look like the code in Listing 16-1. (The new or modified lines are in bold font.)

Listing 16-1. Initial Implementation of CreateEvent.cs

```
using System;
using System.ComponentModel;
using System.ComponentModel.Design;
using System.Collections;
using System.Linq;
using System.Workflow.ComponentModel.Compiler;
using System.Workflow.ComponentModel.Serialization;
using System.Workflow.ComponentModel;
using System.Workflow.ComponentModel.Design;
using System.Workflow.Runtime;
using System.Workflow.Activities;
using System.Workflow.Activities.Rules;

using Microsoft.SharePoint;
using Microsoft.SharePoint.Workflow;
using Microsoft.SharePoint.WorkflowActions;

namespace ActivityLibrary
{
```

```
public partial class CreateEvent : Activity
{
    public CreateEvent()
    {
        InitializeComponent();
    }

    // Add properties here…
}
}
```

Right-click the `CreateEvent.cs` file, and choose View Designer. Notice that the diagram of this activity has changed because the activity is no longer a composite activity (cannot contain other activities).

Dependency Properties

This custom activity will create a new event in the `Calendar` list. To do that, you'll pass in three pieces of information that will be used to configure the event:

- The title of the event

- The date/time the event will start

- The duration of the event (expressed in seconds)

In Workflow Foundation (version 3.5), the technique used to pass arguments into or out of a workflow (or activity) is through *dependency properties*. Dependency properties are used extensively in Windows Presentation Foundation (WPF). Essentially, they allow you to define a wrapper around your class members. You'll need three dependency properties, one for each of the configuration items (`Title`, `StartDate`, and `Duration`).

For each dependency property, you'll define a public property with various attributes applied as well as a `DependencyProperty` definition. Fortunately, Visual Studio makes it easy to enter this. Go back to the code view of the `CreateEvent.cs` file. Put the cursor inside the class definition, just after the constructor. Type **wdp**, and press the Tab key twice. Visual Studio will generate a dependency property named `MyProperty` for you. The text *MyProperty* will be selected. Just type **Title**, and press Tab. The name `MyProperty` will be changed to `Title` every place it is used. The text "string" will now be selected. Since string is the correct data type for this property, you can leave it as is. For other properties, you'll enter the correct data type such as `DateTime` or `int.` When you click off that text, the type will be corrected everywhere.

Using the same approach, add a dependency property named **StartTime** of type **DateTime** and another property named **Duration** of type **int**.

Creating the Event

Add the `Execute()` method shown in Listing 16-2, which creates the event in the `Calendar` list.

Listing 16-2. Implementation of Execute()

```
protected override ActivityExecutionStatus
```

```
Execute(ActivityExecutionContext executionContext)
{
    using (SPWeb web = SPContext.Current.Web)
    {
        SPList calendar = web.Lists["Calendar"];
        SPListItemCollection events = calendar.Items;
        SPListItem item = events.Add();

        item[SPBuiltInFieldId.Title] = Title;
        item[SPBuiltInFieldId.StartDate] = StartTime;
        item[SPBuiltInFieldId.Duration] = Duration;
        item[SPBuiltInFieldId.EndDate] = StartTime + TimeSpan.FromSeconds(Duration);

        item.Update();
    }

    return ActivityExecutionStatus.Closed;
}
```

This code uses the SharePoint object model to add a new event to the Calendar list. The event fields are populated using the values from the dependency properties that you just defined. You can refer to Chapter 9 for more information about using the SharePoint object model.

■ **Tip** Notice the SPWeb class is placed inside a using block. It is a good idea to always use an SPWeb object inside a using block to ensure it is disposed of when you're finished with it.

Listing 16-3 shows the complete implementation of CreateEvent.cs.

Listing 16-3. Final Implementation of CreateEvent.cs

```
using System;
using System.ComponentModel;
using System.ComponentModel.Design;
using System.Collections;
using System.Linq;
using System.Workflow.ComponentModel.Compiler;
using System.Workflow.ComponentModel.Serialization;
using System.Workflow.ComponentModel;
using System.Workflow.ComponentModel.Design;
using System.Workflow.Runtime;
using System.Workflow.Activities;
using System.Workflow.Activities.Rules;

using Microsoft.SharePoint;
using Microsoft.SharePoint.Workflow;
using Microsoft.SharePoint.WorkflowActions;
```

```csharp
namespace ActivityLibrary
{
    public partial class CreateEvent : Activity
    {
        public CreateEvent()
        {
            InitializeComponent();
        }

        // Add properties here...
        public static DependencyProperty TitleProperty =
            DependencyProperty.Register("Title", typeof(string),
                typeof(CreateEvent));

        [Description("Title")]
        [Category("Title Category")]
        [Browsable(true)]
        [DesignerSerializationVisibility(DesignerSerializationVisibility.Visible)]
        public string Title
        {
            get
            {
                return ((string)(base.GetValue(CreateEvent.TitleProperty)));
            }
            set
            {
                base.SetValue(CreateEvent.TitleProperty, value);
            }
        }

        public static DependencyProperty StartTimeProperty =
            DependencyProperty.Register("StartTime", typeof(DateTime),
                typeof(CreateEvent));

        [Description("StartTime")]
        [Category("StartTime Category")]
        [Browsable(true)]
        [DesignerSerializationVisibility(DesignerSerializationVisibility.Visible)]
        public DateTime StartTime
        {
            get
            {
                return ((DateTime)(base.GetValue(CreateEvent.StartTimeProperty)));
            }
            set
            {
                base.SetValue(CreateEvent.StartTimeProperty, value);
            }
        }

        public static DependencyProperty DurationProperty =
```

```
        DependencyProperty.Register("Duration", typeof(int),
            typeof(CreateEvent));

    [Description("Duration")]
    [Category("Duration Category")]
    [Browsable(true)]
    [DesignerSerializationVisibility(DesignerSerializationVisibility.Visible)]
    public int Duration
    {
        get
        {
            return ((int)(base.GetValue(CreateEvent.DurationProperty)));
        }
        set
        {
            base.SetValue(CreateEvent.DurationProperty, value);
        }
    }

    protected override ActivityExecutionStatus
        Execute(ActivityExecutionContext executionContext)
    {
        using (SPWeb web = SPContext.Current.Web)
        {
            SPList calendar = web.Lists["Calendar"];
            SPListItemCollection events = calendar.Items;
            SPListItem item = events.Add();

            item[SPBuiltInFieldId.Title] = Title;
            item[SPBuiltInFieldId.StartDate] = StartTime;
            item[SPBuiltInFieldId.Duration] = Duration;
            item[SPBuiltInFieldId.EndDate] = StartTime + TimeSpan.FromSeconds(Duration);

            item.Update();
        }

        return ActivityExecutionStatus.Closed;
    }
}
}
```

Generating a Strong Name

Assemblies that are deployed to a SharePoint server are placed in the global assembly cache (GAC), which requires your project to have a strong name. When creating a SharePoint project, the template takes care of this for you. Notice there is a **key.snk** file in the WF_Chapter16 project. This is the key file used to generate the strong name. However, the ActivityLibrary project was not set up with a strong name because you used a different template. You'll fix that now so you'll be able to deploy this assembly to SharePoint.

From the Solution Explorer, right-click the ActivityLibrary project, and choose Properties. Go to the Signing tab, and click the *Sign the assembly* check box. You will need to specify a file to hold the assembly key. In the drop-down list, select New, as shown in Figure 16-7.

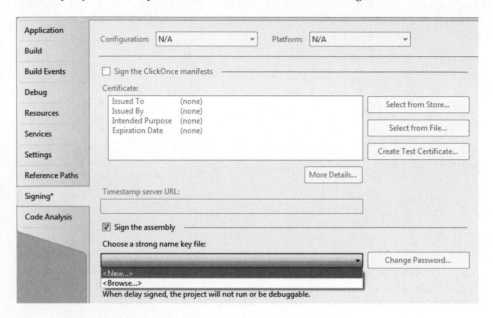

Figure 16-7. Creating a new key file

The pop-up window shown in Figure 16-8 will be displayed. Enter **key.snk**, and deselect the `Protect my key file with a password` check box.

Figure 16-8. Specifying the key file name

Finding the Public Key Token

You will need to know the *public key token*, which is the last 8 bytes of a cryptographic hash of the public key. To get that, first build the solution by pressing F6. Visual Studio provides a Strong Name Utility that, among other things, will extract the public key token from a strongly named assembly.

Run the Visual Studio 2010 command prompt, which you should find in the Start menu under Visual Studio Tools, as shown in Figure 16-9.

Figure 16-9. *Starting the Visual Studio 2010 command prompt*

From the command prompt, navigate to the location of your ActivityLibrary project, and run the following command:

```
sn -T ActivityLibrary.dll
```

The output should look like this:

```
Microsoft (R) .NET Framework Strong Name Utility  Version 4.0.30319.1

Copyright (c) Microsoft Corporation.  All rights reserved.


Public key token is 9d6384a93fc3e8f6
```

Save this token because you will need to specify it in several places.

■ **Caution** Don't use the value of the public key token shown here; make sure you generate one based on your public key.

Defining the Action

The next step is to create an actions file that the SharePoint Designer uses to display and edit this action in the workflow editor. This file must be installed in a special folder on the SharePoint server. Visual Studio provides a feature called *mapped folders*, which allows you to put files in them. These files are then automatically copied to the appropriate folders on the SharePoint server when the solution is deployed.

Adding a Mapped Folder

From the Solution Explorer, right-click the WF_Chapter16 project, and choose Add ▸ SharePoint Mapped Folder, as shown in Figure 16-10.

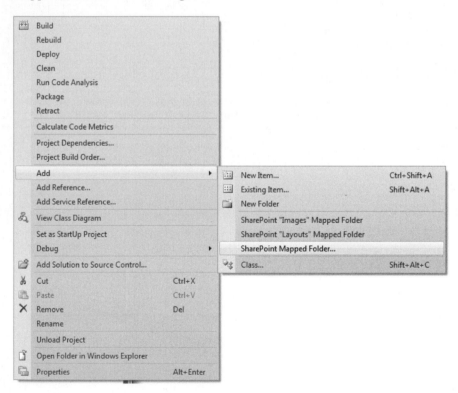

Figure 16-10. Adding a mapped folder

In the Add SharePoint Mapped Folder dialog box, browse to the Workflow folder shown in Figure 16-11.

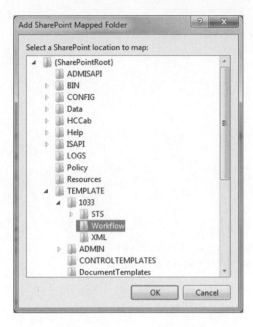

Figure 16-11. Selecting the Workflow folder

Adding an Actions File

To add the actions file here, from the Solution Explorer, right-click the Workflow folder, and choose Add ▸ New Item. In the Add New Item dialog box, select the Data category, and then select the XML File template, as shown in Figure 16-12. Enter the filename **ActivityLibrary.actions**.

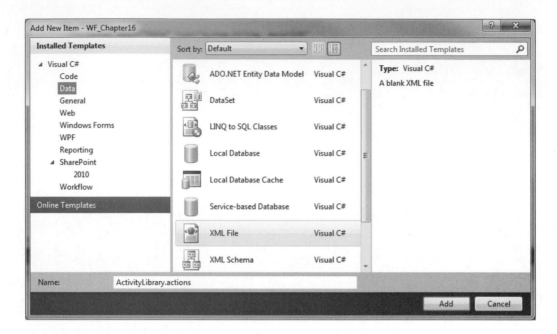

Figure 16-12. *Creating the actions file*

Replace the contents of the `ActivityLibrary.actions` file with the code shown in Listing 16-4.

Listing 16-4. *The Implementation of the Actions File*

```
<WorkflowInfo>
  <Actions Sequential="then" Parallel="and">
    <Action Name="Create Event"
            ClassName="ActivityLibrary.CreateEvent"
            Assembly="ActivityLibrary, Version=1.0.0.0, Culture=neutral,
                      PublicKeyToken=9d6384a93fc3e8f6"
            AppliesTo="all"
            Category="Chapter16">
      <RuleDesigner Sentence="Create Event %1 starting at %2 for %3 seconds.">
        <FieldBind Field="Title" Text="Title" Id="1"
                   DesignerType="Text"/>
        <FieldBind Field="StartTime" Text="Start Time" Id="2"
                   DesignerType="Date"/>
        <FieldBind Field="Duration" Text="Duration (seconds)" Id="3"
                   DesignerType="Integer"/>
      </RuleDesigner>
      <Parameters>
        <Parameter Name="Title" Type="System.String, mscorlib"
                   Direction="In" />
        <Parameter Name="StartTime" Type="System.DateTime, mscorlib"
                   Direction="In" />
```

```
        <Parameter Name="Duration" Type="System.Int32, mscorlib"
                   Direction="In" />
      </Parameters>
    </Action>
  </Actions>
</WorkflowInfo>
```

■ **Caution** Again, make sure you input your own public key token and not the one shown here.

This file will give you an idea of how the workflow editor is built. Notice the second line:

```
<Actions Sequential="then" Parallel="and">
```

Recall from Chapter 7 that subsequent actions in a sequential block are prefixed with the word **then**. The workflow is read as, "Perform action1 and *then* perform action2." However, in a parallel block, the word **and** was used. This actions file defines the actual text used.

■ **Tip** You can open the built-in action files that define the actions and conditions that you have used in the previous projects. They are located in the \Template\1033\Workflow subfolder of the SharePoint installation folder. There are two files, moss.actions and wss.actions. You can open these with a text editor such as notepad. However, make sure you do not change them, or you may break the SharePoint Designer.

Rule Designer

The `RuleDesigner` section starts with the following:

```
Sentence="Create Event %1 starting at %2 for %3 seconds."
```

This specifies the text that is displayed in the workflow editor. It has three placeholders (%1, %2, and %3), which will, initially, be displayed as links. The `FieldBind` items that follow specify how these links should work. In the workflow editor, when you click one of these links, a control is displayed depending on the `DesignerType` that is indicated. If the `DesignerType` is not specified, the default designer will be used, which consists of a text box, an ellipsis control, and a lookup button (fx).

Here is a list of types that are available:

- `Boolean`: Drop-down list box with the choices true and false populated.
- `ChooseDoclibItem`: Document library item selector.
- `ChooseListItem`: Uses the default designer.
- `CreateListItem`: Uses the default designer.

- **Date**: Date/time selector.

- **Dropdown**: Drop-down list box control. Static items can be populated by adding Option elements.

- **Email**: E-mail advanced control. The form displays standard e-mail fields including To, From, CC, Subject, and Body.

- **FieldNames**: Drop-down list box control populated with all field names in the current list or document library.

- **Float**: Text box. Allows entry of floating-point values.

- **Hyperlink**: URL browser. Select local or remote resources using a standard link builder.

- **Integer**: Text box. Accepts non-negative integer values.

- **ListNames**: Drop-down list box control populated with all lists in the current web site.

- **Operator**: Drop-down list box control that includes operators used to evaluate each side of the RuleDesigner sentence. Operators are static and must be added in Options elements.

- **ParameterNames**: Drop-down list box populated with all local variables that have been entered for use by the workflow.

- **Person**: Person or Group selector. You can choose only one person or group from either built-in, local users or groups, or users and groups from a domain.

- **SinglePerson**: Person or Group selector. You choose only one person or group from either built-in, local users or groups, or users and groups from a domain.

- **Stringbuilder**: Inline text box editor. Use to create simple strings.

- **Survey:** Uses the default designer.

- **Text:** Uses the default designer.

- **TextArea:** Uses the default designer.

- **UpdateListItem:** Uses the default designer.

- **writablefieldNames**: Drop-down list box populated either with a list of fields in the current list or with a list of document libraries that are editable. All other fields are hidden.

■ **Note** This list was taken from the MSDN site (http://msdn.microsoft.com/en-us/library/bb897971(v=office.14).aspx). You can find more information there as well as sample code that you may find useful if you plan to take advantage of this functionality in your custom actions.

Some of these controls, such as `Email`, support multiple properties. You've already used the `Email` designer. It presents a separate dialog box where you can specify the From, To, Subject, and Body properties, complete with PeoplePicker controls and a String Builder control.

Deploying the ActivityLibrary

The `ActivityLibrary.dll` file needs to be installed on the SharePoint server when the project is deployed. To do that, you'll need to manually add it to the solution package.

■ **Note** When you started this project, you created an empty SharePoint project (WF_Chapter16). This project is used only as a vehicle for deploying the solution to SharePoint. There is no compiled code in this project; all the code is in the ActivityLibrary assembly. So far, you have one feature in this project, which is the mapped folder that is used to deploy the actions file. Now, you'll add another feature that will deploy the ActivityLibrary assembly.

Adding the Assembly

From the Solution Explorer, double-click the Package folder in the WF_Chapter16 project. Then select the Advanced tab. The package editor should look like Figure 16-13.

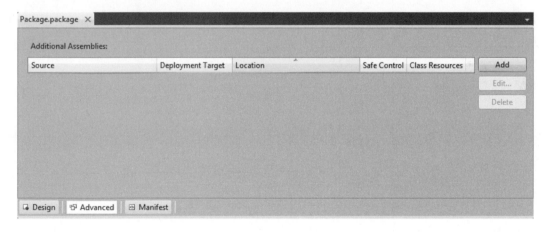

Figure 16-13. The package designer Advanced tab

Click the Add button, and then click the *Add Existing Assembly* link, as shown in Figure 16-14.

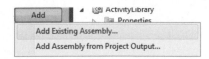

Figure 16-14. Adding an existing assembly

In the Add Existing Assembly dialog box, click the ellipsis next to the **Source Path** field, which will display the Select Assembly dialog box shown in Figure 16-15.

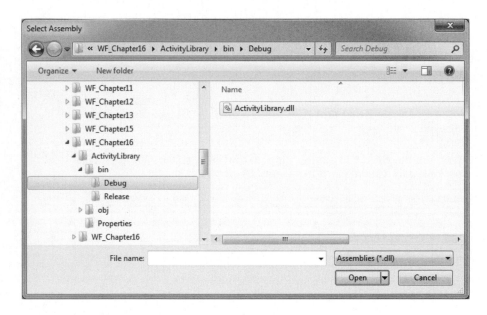

Figure 16-15. Selecting the `ActivityLibrary.dll` *assembly*

Browse to the `ActivityLibrary.dll` assembly, and click the Open button. The file path will be displayed in the Add Existing Assembly dialog box, as shown in Figure 16-16.

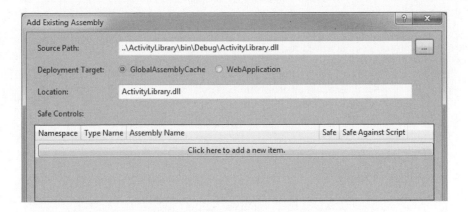

Figure 16-16. The Add Existing Assembly dialog box

Now you'll need to enter the assembly details in the Safe Controls section. Click the *Click here to add a new item* link. Then enter the details as follows:

- `Namespace`: Enter **ActivityLibrary**.

- `Type Name`: Use * (it defaults to this; just leave it as is).

- `Assembly Name`: **ActivityLibrary, Version=1.0.0.0, Culture=neutral, PublicKeyToken=9d6384a93fc3e8f6** (use your own token value here).

- `Safe`: Leave this selected.

- `Safe Against Script`: Leave this unselected.

The completed dialog box should look like Figure 16-17.

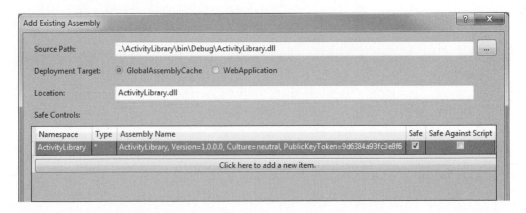

Figure 16-17. Completed Add Existing Assembly dialog box

Click the OK button to add this assembly to the solution package.

Defining a Feature

Next, you'll define a feature for your custom action. From the Solution Explorer, right-click the Features folder (in the WF_Chapter16 project), and choose Add Feature. The feature designer should be displayed. Change the Scope drop-down list to `WebApplication`.

When a feature is deployed, events are raised at appropriate points during the installation process. The feature needs to provide event handlers to respond to the desired events. This is their opportunity to make site-specific configuration changes. To accomplish this, you'll add an event receiver for this feature.

Implementing an Event Receiver

In the Solution Explorer, right-click the `Feature1` feature, and choose Add Event Receiver, as shown in Figure 16-18.

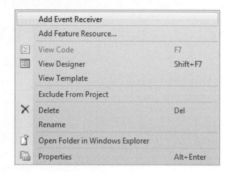

Figure 16-18. *Adding an event receiver*

Visual Studio generates a `Feature1.EventReceiver.cs` class, which is derived from the base `SPFeatureReceiver` class. This class includes an event handler for each of the possible events:

- `FeatureActivated`

- `FeatureDeactivating`

- `FeatureInstalled`

- `FeatureUninstalling`

- `FeatureUpgrading`

However, each of these event handlers is commented out. To support the `FeatureActivated` event, you'll remove the comments and provide an implementation. Add the following namespace to this file:

```
using Microsoft.SharePoint.Administration;
```

Listing 16-5 shows the implementation for the `FeatureActivated` event. Enter this code into the `Feature1.EventReceiver.cs` class.

Listing 16-5. Implementation of the FeatureActivated Event

```
public override void FeatureActivated(SPFeatureReceiverProperties properties)
{
    // Create a configuration object
    SPWebConfigModification config = new SPWebConfigModification();
    config.Type =
        SPWebConfigModification.SPWebConfigModificationType.EnsureChildNode;
    config.Owner = "ActivityLibrary";
    config.Name = "authorizedType[@Assembly='ActivityLibrary']
            [@Namespace='ActivityLibrary'][@TypeName='*'][@Authorized='True']";
    config.Path =
        "configuration/System.Workflow.ComponentModel.WorkflowCompiler/authorizedTypes";
    config.Value = @"<authorizedType Assembly=""ActivityLibrary, Version=1.0.0.0,
        Culture=neutral, PublicKeyToken=9d6384a93fc3e8f6""
        Namespace=""ActivityLibrary"" TypeName=""*"" Authorized=""True"" />";

    // Get the web applications for this feature
    SPWebApplication app = (SPWebApplication)properties.Feature.Parent;

    // Apply the configuration changes
    app.WebConfigModifications.Add(config);
    app.WebService.ApplyWebConfigModifications();
}
```

■ **Caution** The values for the config.Name and config.Value properties are wrapped to fit on the page. However, when you enter this in your code, they must be on a single line. Also, make sure you enter your public key token instead of the value shown here.

This code adds a reference to your assembly into the SharePoint configuration database.

Testing Your Custom Action

Press F6 to build the solution, and fix any errors that may exist. From the Solution Explorer, right-click the WF_Chapter16 project, and choose Deploy. This will install the custom action on the Part4 SharePoint site.

Creating a Site Workflow

Start the SharePoint Designer, and open the Part4 site. Click the *Workflow* link in the Navigation page. Click the Site Workflow button in the ribbon to create a new site workflow. In the Create Site Workflow dialog box, enter the name **WF_Chapter16**, as shown in Figure 16-19.

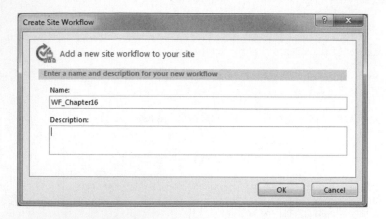

Figure 16-19. Adding a new site workflow

Let's make sure your custom action is available. Click the Action button in the ribbon. You should see the `Create Event` action in the Chapter16 group similar to Figure 16-20.

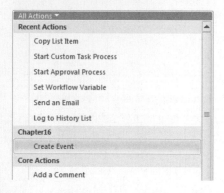

Figure 16-20. The action list

Using the Create Event Action

Now click the insert point. Type **cre**, and press Enter. The workflow editor should have found two matching actions, as shown in Figure 16-21.

Figure 16-21. Listing the matching actions

Notice that the custom actions work just like the built-in actions when searching for an action. Select **Create Event**, and press Enter. The workflow editor should look like Figure 16-22.

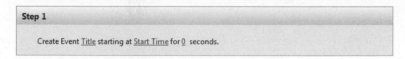

Figure 16-22. The initial Create Event action

This action has three links, corresponding to the three dependency properties that were defined for this activity. Click the *Title* link, and you should have three options for entering this value, as demonstrated in Figure 16-23.

Figure 16-23. The Title entry options

You can enter the Title in the text box, click the ellipsis to set the Title using the String Builder, or click the *ƒx* button to look up a value from an existing list or property. Just enter a title such as **Staff Meeting** in the text box. Next, click the *Start Time* link, and click the ellipsis to display the Date Value dialog shown in Figure 16-24.

Figure 16-24. Entering the Start Time value

Specify a date/time, and click OK to save this value. Finally, click the *0* link, and enter the number of seconds that the meeting should last.

■ **Tip** If only meetings were really measured in seconds! You could change the action so the duration was entered in minutes (instead of seconds). The implementation of the CreateEvent activity would then multiply this by 60 when creating the Event object. I'll leave that for you to work on.

The final implementation of this action should look like Figure 16-25.

Figure 16-25. The final action definition

Testing the Workflow

Click the Publish button in the Workflow ribbon to save and publish this simple workflow. Launch the SharePoint site in a browser window. Open the Part4 site, and then go to the All Site Content page. Click the *Site Workflows* link to display the page shown in Figure 16-26.

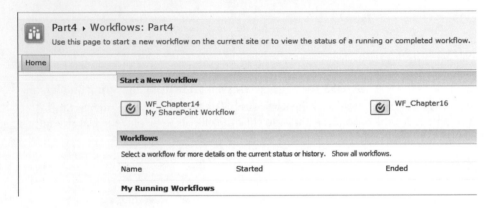

Figure 16-26. Listing the available site workflows

Click the *WF_Chapter16* link to start this workflow. It will display a blank initiation page; just click the Start button to begin the workflow. After a second or two, the page should update and show a completed workflow like the one shown in Figure 16-27.

Workflows

Select a workflow for more details on the current status or history.   Show all workflows.

Name	Started	Ended	Status
My Running Workflows			
There are no currently running workflows on this site.			
My Completed Workflows			
WF_Chapter16	5/7/2010 10:34 PM	5/7/2010 10:35 PM	Completed

Figure 16-27. Showing the completed workflow

Now open the `Calendar` list. It should have a new event, as shown in Figure 16-28.

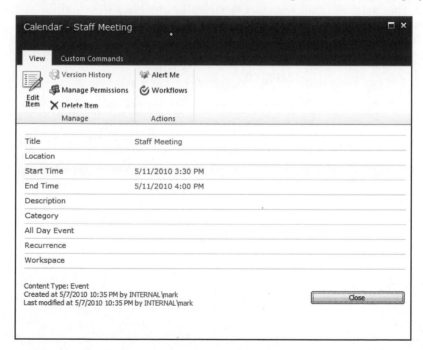

Figure 16-28. The Calendar showing the new event

You should see a new event on the date that you specified when designing the workflow. If you click the *Staff Meeting* link, the event details shown in Figure 16-29 will be displayed.

Calendar - Staff Meeting	□ ×

| View | Custom Commands |

Edit Item · Version History · Manage Permissions · Delete Item | Alert Me · Workflows

Manage | Actions

Title	Staff Meeting
Location	
Start Time	5/11/2010 3:30 PM
End Time	5/11/2010 4:00 PM
Description	
Category	
All Day Event	
Recurrence	
Workspace	

Content Type: Event
Created at 5/7/2010 10:35 PM by INTERNAL\mark
Last modified at 5/7/2010 10:35 PM by INTERNAL\mark

[Close]

Figure 16-29. Displaying the event details

■ **Caution** Microsoft Office stores date/time values in Coordinated Universal Time (UTC) and relies on the client to convert to and from local time. This works really well and is, for the most part, transparent to the end user. You may have noticed in this exercise I entered 10:30 a.m. for the starting time. However, when the event was viewed, the start time was displayed as 3:30 p.m. The time was entered in the SharePoint Designer in local time, and the value was simply stored in the event without any conversion. It should have been converted to UTC before saving it. To fix this, go to the `CreateEvent.cs` class, and use the `ToUniversalTime()` method on the `DateTime` class.

Summary

In this chapter you created a custom action in Visual Studio using the Workflow Foundation (WF) classes. This was then deployed to a SharePoint site and accessed by the SharePoint Designer. Admittedly, the process was a little tedious. Normally, when creating a SharePoint project, the project templates takes care of most of these details. Because you used a workflow template, these SharePoint details had to be implemented manually.

However, once this is done, you can add any number of custom actions to this project. So if you need another custom action, just add it to the same project. The `ActivityLibrary` assembly and the actions file can contain any number of custom actions.

Your custom actions are not limited to just Office-type actions (such as adding an event to the `Calendar` list). You can also write code to update your enterprise business application data. For example, you can create an action that places a product order or enters a customer's comment. I will cover Business Connectivity Services (BCS) in the next section, but I wanted you to see that providing custom actions is another way to integrate Office workflows into your back-end systems.

■ ■ ■

CHAPTER 17

Pluggable Workflow Services

When building workflow solutions, you may need to make a call into an external system to retrieve data or perform some processing. Often, that call can take some time to complete, and it is undesirable to tie up resources on the SharePoint server while waiting for the activity to finish. The Workflow Foundation (WF) provides the ability to make a call and then enter an idle state while waiting for a response. During the idle state, the workflow data is persisted, and the instance is unloaded from memory.

In SharePoint 2007, however, this feature was not available to SharePoint workflows because of limitations in the SharePoint-hosted runtime implementation. The SharePoint 2010 release has fixed this, and in this chapter I'll show you how to use this functionality.

This technique is called *pluggable workflow services*. The external call is implemented as a local service and invoked through the `CallExternalMethodActivity`. When the work has completed, the service then raises an event, which is received by the `HandleExternalEventActivity`.

■ **Note** The term *service* has several connotations. The services that I'm discussing in this chapter are referred to as *local services*. These should not be confused with *web services* (services hosted in IIS) or *Windows services*. A local service resides on the same computer as the client that invokes it. The client accesses the service through an interface that defines the method parameters.

Creating the Workflow Project

Start by creating a new project that will implement the SharePoint workflow. Use the SharePoint 2010 Sequential Workflow template, as shown in Figure 17-1. Enter the project name **WF_Chapter17**.

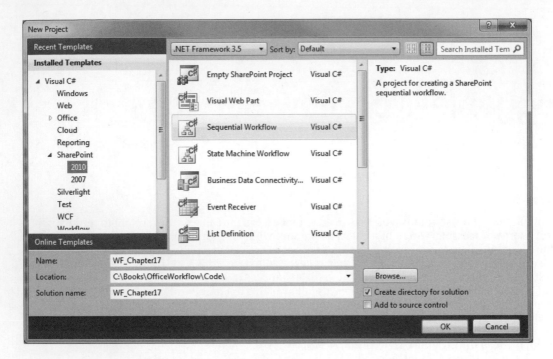

Figure 17-1. Creating a sequential workflow project

In the SharePoint Customization Wizard that is shown in Figure 17-2, enter the URL for the Part4 SharePoint site.

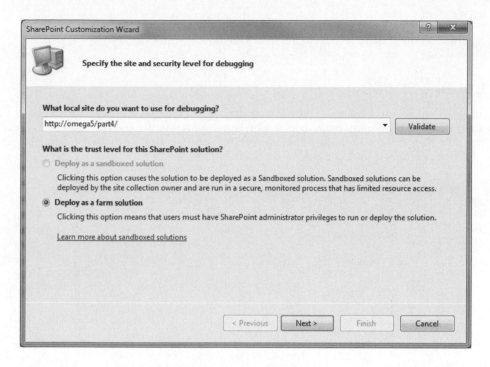

Figure 17-2. Selecting the test site

In the next dialog box, select the site workflow option, and enter the name of the workflow
WF_Chapter17, as shown in Figure 17-3.

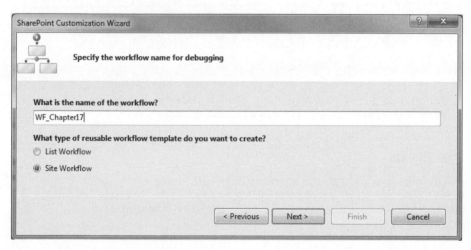

Figure 17-3. Creating a site workflow

For the last two dialog boxes, just use all the default values. This will associate the standard `Workflow History` and `Tasks` lists and set the startup options for manual initiation.

Creating a Local Service

Next you'll create a separate project to implement the local service. This service will simply return a list of files and folders found at a specified path. From the Solution Explorer, right-click the WF_Chapter17 solution, and choose Add ▶ New Project. In the Add New Project dialog box, select the Class Library template, and enter **FileService** for the project name, as shown in Figure 17-4.

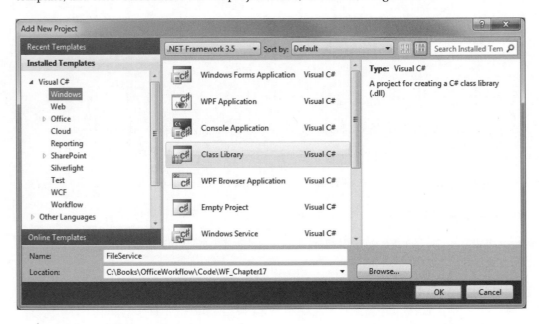

Figure 17-4. Creating a class library project

From the Solution Explorer, right-click the FileService project, and choose Add Reference. From the .NET tab, select `System.Workflow.Activities` and `System.Workflow.Runtime`.

Defining the Interface

The first step in creating the service is to define the interface that it will implement. From the Solution Explorer, right-click the FileService project, and choose Add ▶ New Item. In the Add New Item dialog box, select the Interface template, as shown in Figure 17-5. Enter the name **ICustomService.cs**.

Figure 17-5. Adding the service interface

Enter the code shown in Listing 17-1 for the implementation of this interface.

Listing 17-1. Implementation of ICustomService.cs

```
using System;
using System.Collections.Generic;
using System.Workflow.Activities;

namespace FileService
{
    [Serializable]
    public class CustomEventArgs : ExternalDataEventArgs
    {
        public CustomEventArgs(Guid id)
            : base(id)
        {
        }

        public List<string> contents;
    }

    [ExternalDataExchange]
    public interface ICustomService
    {
        event EventHandler<CustomEventArgs> DataOutput;
```

```
        void GetFolderContent(string path);
    }
}
```

This code first defines a class derived from **ExternalDataEventArgs**. This will be used to provide the data to the client when the service has finished. It contains a single member, **contents**, which is a collection of **string** objects. This represents the contents of the specified folder.

Next, the **ICustomService** interface is defined. It has a single event named **DataOutput** and a method called **GetFolderContent()**. The **GetFolderContent()** method will be called by the client, and the **DataOutput** event will be raised when the work is complete.

Implementing the Service

Now you'll provide the implementation of this service. You'll need to add a reference to the SharePoint DLL. From the Solution Explorer, right-click the FileService project, and choose Add Reference. Select the Browse tab, and then navigate to where the SharePoint DLLs are installed. Normally this will be the following location:

```
C:\Program Files\Common Files\Microsoft Shared\Web Server Extensions\14\ISAPI
```

Select the **Microsoft.SharePoint.dll** file, as shown in Figure 17-6.

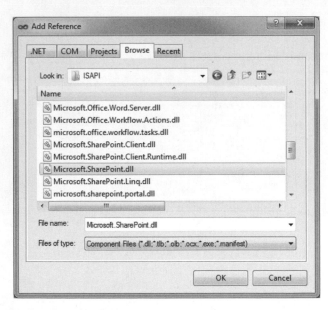

Figure 17-6. Adding references to the SharePoint DLLs

The template generated a class named **Class1.cs**. From the Solution Explorer, rename this file as **CustomService.cs**. Listing 17-2 shows the implementation of this file.

Listing 17-2. Implementation of CustomService.cs

```csharp
using System;
using System.Collections.Generic;
using Microsoft.SharePoint;
using Microsoft.SharePoint.Workflow;
using System.Threading;
using System.IO;
using System.Workflow.Runtime;

namespace FileService
{
    //---------------------------------------------------------
    // This class is used to pass the SharePoint and
    // workflow data between threads
    //---------------------------------------------------------
    internal class ServiceState
    {
        internal SPWeb _web;
        internal Guid _instanceID;
        internal string _path;

        public ServiceState(SPWeb web, Guid instanceID, string path)
        {
            _web = web;
            _instanceID = instanceID;
            _path = path;
        }
    }


    //---------------------------------------------------------
    // This class implements the ICustomService interface
    //---------------------------------------------------------
    public class CustomService : SPWorkflowExternalDataExchangeService,
                                 ICustomService
    {
        //---------------------------------------------------------
        // Implement the ICustomService interface
        //---------------------------------------------------------
        public event EventHandler<CustomEventArgs> DataOutput;

        public void GetFolderContent(string path)
        {
            // Schedule the work on a different thread
            ThreadPool.QueueUserWorkItem
                (GetFolderContent,
                 new ServiceState(CurrentWorkflow.ParentWeb,
                                  WorkflowEnvironment.WorkflowInstanceId,
                                  path));
```

```
    // This method returns as soon as the work is scheduled
}

//---------------------------------------------------
// This method performs the work on a different thread
//---------------------------------------------------
private void GetFolderContent(object state)
{
    ServiceState s = state as ServiceState;

    // Get the folders
    List<string> contents =
        new List<string>((System.IO.Directory.GetDirectories(s._path)));

    // Add the files
    contents.AddRange(System.IO.Directory.GetFiles(s._path));

    // Return the results
    RaiseEvent(s._web,
               s._instanceID,
               typeof(ICustomService),
               "DataOutput",
               new object[] { contents });
}

//---------------------------------------------------
// This method responds to the RaiseEvent call to
// format and send the event
//---------------------------------------------------
public override void CallEventHandler
    (Type eventType,
     string eventName,
     object[] eventData,
     SPWorkflow workflow,
     string identity,
     IPendingWork workHandler,
     object workItem)
{

    switch (eventName)
    {
        case "DataOutput":
            CustomEventArgs e = new CustomEventArgs(workflow.InstanceId);
            e.Identity = identity;
            e.WorkHandler = workHandler;
            e.WorkItem = workItem;
            e.contents = (List<string>)eventData[0];

            // Raise the event
            DataOutput(null, e);
            break;
    }
```

```
        }

        //------------------------------------------------
        // Provide an implementation for the remaining
        // SPWorkflowExternalDataExchangeService methods
        //------------------------------------------------
        public override void CreateSubscription
            (System.Workflow.Activities.MessageEventSubscription subscription)
        {
            throw new NotImplementedException();
        }

        public override void DeleteSubscription(Guid subscriptionId)
        {
            throw new NotImplementedException();
        }
    }
}
```

The ServiceState class is used to store information about the service call, which is needed to pass data between the threads.

The CustomService class, which implements the ICustomService interface, is derived from the abstract SPWorkflowExternalDataExchangeService class. This base class provides helper methods as well as information about the SharePoint site. The GetFolderContent() method simply schedules a work item on the thread pool by calling the static ThreadPool.QueueUserWorkItem() method. This method takes two parameters. The first is the name of the function delegate, and the second is an object, which is an instance of the ServiceState class.

The actual work is done by the second GetFolderContent() method, which takes ServiceState object as a parameter. This method executes on a separate thread and is called as soon as a thread is available. It uses the Directory class to get a list of folders and files. It then calls the RaiseEvent() method, which is provided by the base class.

The RaiseEvent() method relies on you providing an implementation of CallEventHandler(). One of the parameters of CallEventHandler() is the eventName because the service can support multiple events. So, the logic in CallEventHandler() is wrapped in a switch statement so you can provide logic specific for each event. The data provided to the CallEventHandler() method is passed as an array of objects (object[]), which allows for any type of data to be used. It is assumed that each event will know how to interpret the data. In this case, the first object in the array is a List<string> that specifies the folder contents.

The CustomEventArgs class is created, and the various properties are set using data passed to CallEventHandler(). Finally, the DataOutput event is raised, passing the CustomEventArgs class.

The abstract SPWorkflowExternalDataExchangeService class also requires you to provide an implementation for the CreateSubscription() and DeleteSubscription() methods. These are implemented to throw the NotImplementedException if called since we do not expect these to be used.

Generating a Strong Name

This local service is implemented in a separate assembly from the WF_Chapter17 workflow project. Just like in the previous chapter, in order to install this on the SharePoint server, you'll need to generate a strongly named assembly. From the Solution Explorer, right-click the FileService project, and choose

Properties. Go to the Signing tab, and click the `Sign the assembly` check box. You will need to specify a file to hold the assembly key. In the drop-down list, select New, as shown in Figure 17-7.

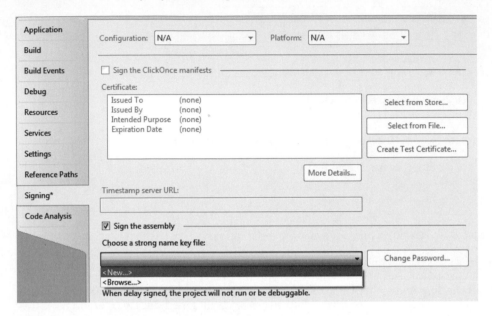

Figure 17-7. Creating a new key file

The pop-up window shown in Figure 17-8 will be displayed. Enter **key.snk**, and deselect the `Protect my key file with a password` check box.

Figure 17-8. Specifying the key file's name

Press F6 to build the assembly. Run the Visual Studio 2010 command prompt, which you should find in the Start menu under Visual Studio Tools. From the command prompt, navigate to the location of your FileService project, and run the following command:

```
sn -T FileService.dll
```

The output should look like this:

```
Microsoft (R) .NET Framework Strong Name Utility  Version 4.0.30319.1

Copyright (c) Microsoft Corporation.  All rights reserved.


Public key token is 75da00303dcde51d
```

Save this token because you will need to specify it in several places. Make sure you use the token generated from your assembly instead of the value shown here.

Deploying the FileService Assembly

Next, you'll manually add the FileService assembly to the WF_Chapter17 solution package just like you did in the previous chapter. From the Solution Explorer, double-click the Package folder in the WF_Chapter17 project. Then select the Advanced tab. The package editor should look like Figure 17-9.

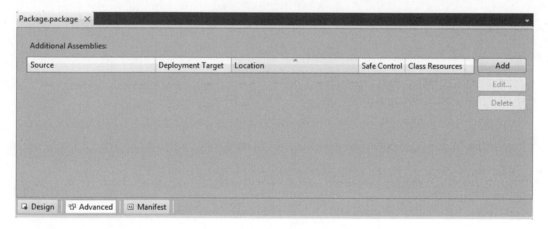

Figure 17-9. The package designer's Advanced tab

Click the Add button, and then click the *Add Existing Assembly* link, as shown in Figure 17-10.

Figure 17-10. Adding an existing assembly

In the Add Existing Assembly dialog box, click the ellipsis next to the `Source Path` field, which will display the Select Assembly dialog box. Browse to the `FileService.dll` assembly, and click the Open button. The file path will be displayed in the Add Existing Assembly dialog box, as shown in Figure 17-11.

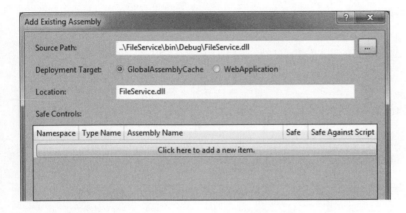

Figure 17-11. The Add Existing Assembly dialog box

Now you'll need to enter the assembly details in the Safe Controls section. Click the *Click here to add a new item* link. Then enter the details as follows:

- `Namespace`: Enter **FileService**.

- `Type Name`: Use * (it defaults to this; just leave it as is).

- `Assembly Name`: Enter **FileService, Version=1.0.0.0, Culture=neutral, PublicKeyToken=75da00303dcde51d** (use your own token value here).

- `Safe`: Leave this selected.

- `Safe Against Script`: Leave this unselected.

The completed dialog box should look like Figure 17-12.

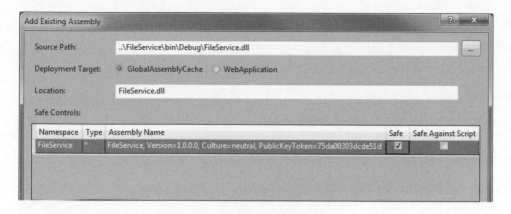

Figure 17-12. Completed Add Existing Assembly dialog box

Click the OK button to add this assembly to the solution package

Implementing an Event Receiver

Next, you'll define a feature for the FileService assembly. From the Solution Explorer, right-click the Features folder (in the WF_Chapter17 project), and choose Add Feature. The feature designer should be displayed. Change the `Scope` drop-down list to `WebApplication`. In the Solution Explorer, right-click the `Feature2` feature, and choose Add Event Receiver, as shown in Figure 17-13.

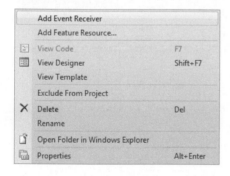

Figure 17-13. Adding an event receiver

■ **Note** Refer to Chapter 16 for more information about event receivers.

The `Feature2.EventReceiver.cs` class should be open. Add the following namespace to this file:

```
using Microsoft.SharePoint.Administration;
```

Listing 17-3 shows the implementation for the FeatureActivated event. Enter this code into the Feature2.EventReceiver.cs class.

Listing 17-3. Implementation of the FeatureActivated Event Handler

```
public override void FeatureActivated(SPFeatureReceiverProperties properties)
{
    // Create a configuration object
    SPWebConfigModification config = new SPWebConfigModification();
    config.Type =
        SPWebConfigModification.SPWebConfigModificationType.EnsureChildNode;
    config.Owner = "WF_Chapter17";
    config.Name = "WorkflowService[Class='FileService.CustomService']";
    config.Path = "configuration/SharePoint/WorkflowServices";
    config.Value = @"<WorkflowService Assembly=""FileService, Version=1.0.0.0, " +
        @"Culture=neutral, PublicKeyToken=75da00303dcde51d"" " +
        @"Class=""FileService.CustomService"" />";

    // Get the web applications for this feature
    SPWebApplication app = (SPWebApplication)properties.Feature.Parent;

    // Apply the configuration changes
    app.WebConfigModifications.Add(config);
    app.WebService.ApplyWebConfigModifications();
    app.Update();
}
```

This event receiver is adding the FileService assembly to the Workflow Service section of the web.config file. This will enable SharePoint to find and execute this service when invoked by a workflow activity.

The local service is implemented and set up to be configured when your project is deployed. It is now ready to be used from within your workflow. Your next step is to modify the workflow design to use this service.

Implementing the Workflow

Open the workflow in the WF_Chapter17 project that was generated by the template. It should have only the OnWorkflowActivated event handler. Right-click the WF_Chapter17 project, and choose Add Reference. From the Projects tab, select the FileService project.

Implementing CallExternalMethodActivity

Drag a CallExternalMethodActivity to the workflow. In the Properties window, select the InterfaceType property, and click the ellipsis next to it. In the dialog box shown in Figure 17-14, select the ICustomService interface.

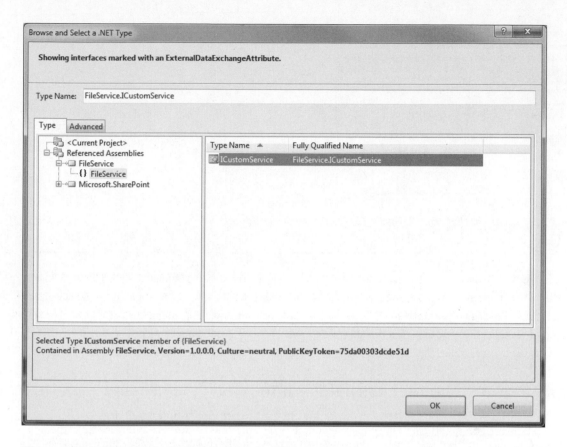

Figure 17-14. Selecting the ICustomService interface

In the Properties window, select the MethodName property, and then select GetFolderContent from the drop-down list. That should be the only method listed since there is only one method defined on this interface. If there were other methods defined for this interface, they would be included in the drop-down list.

Notice that the path property appeared once the MethodName was chosen. Additional properties are automatically added based on the parameters of the method being called. In this case, GetFolderContent() expects a single parameter named path. Click the path property, and enter a valid path. The Properties window should look like Figure 17-15.

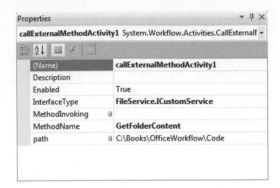

Figure 17-15. The `CallExternalMethodActivity` *Properties window*

■ **Tip** The `MethodInvoking` property is not specified in this project. This is an event handler that is invoked just before the method is called. You could implement this event handler to set some of the properties of the activity. For example, if the value of the `path` property needs to be dynamic, you could implement this event handler to set this property in code. If you double-click this activity, this event handler is generated for you.

Implementing HandleExternalEventActivity

Drag a `HandleExternalEventActivity` to the workflow. In the Properties window, select the `InterfaceType` property, and click the ellipsis next to it. Select the `ICustomService` interface from the dialog box that is displayed just like you did with the `CallExternalMethodActivity`. For the `EventName` property, select the `DataOutput` event from the drop-down list. Again, there is only one event in the list because the interface defined only a single event.

Notice that an **e** parameter appeared. This is the `CustomEventArgs` class that is passed when the event is raised. It contains the data returned by the local service. Select the **e** property, and click the ellipsis. In the dialog that is displayed, select the second tab, and enter **eventArgs** for the member name, as shown in Figure 17-16.

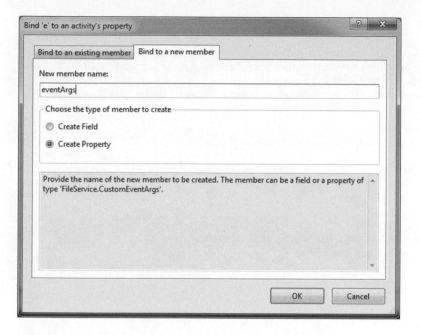

Figure 17-16. *Creating a new member*

This will create a dependency property that is bound to the **e** property. After this activity has executed, the **eventArgs** property will have the **CustomEventArgs** class returned by the **GetFolderContent()** method. The completed Properties window should look like Figure 17-17.

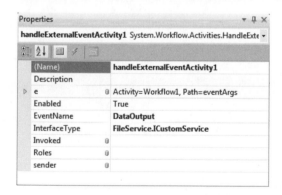

Figure 17-17. The completed HandleExternalEventActivity *properties*

467

Sending an E-mail

The last step of this workflow is to send an e-mail with the results of this method call. Drag a `SendEmail` activity to the workflow. In the Properties window, for the `CorrelationToken`, select `workflowToken`. Enter an appropriate value for the `From`, `Subject`, and `To` properties.

Double-click this activity to generate the `MethodInvoking` event handler. Listing 17-4 shows the implementation for this method.

Listing 17-4. Implementation of the SendEmail1_MethodInvoking() Method

```
private void sendEmail1_MethodInvoking(object sender, EventArgs e)
{
    SendEmail email = sender as SendEmail;
    if (email != null)
    {
        email.Body = "The content of this directory are: <br><br>";
        foreach (string s in eventArgs.contents)
        {
            email.Body += " - " + s + "<br>";
        }
    }
}
```

This code formats the **Body** of the e-mail using the data from the **eventArgs** property. Go back to the design view. The Properties window should look like Figure 17-18.

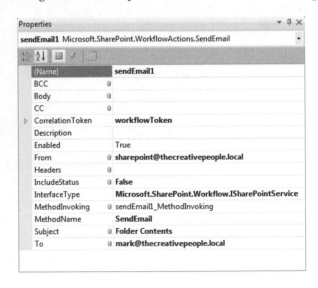

Figure 17-18. The completed SendEmail Properties window

■ **Note** Look at the Properties window for the SendEmail activity. Does anything look familiar? Notice the InterfaceType and MethodName properties. These are the same properties that are on the CallExternalMethodActivity. That's because the SendEmail activity is derived from CallExternalMethodActivity. It is just a specialized implementation of the CallExternalMethodActivity. Also, look at the Properties window for the OnWorkflowActivated event handler. Notice that it has an InterfaceType and EventName properties. That's right; this activity is derived from HandleExternalEventActivity. Most of the built-in SharePoint activities are derived from either CallExternalMethodActivity or HandleExternalEventActivity. These are provided as local services implemented by the SharePoint DLLs. The built-in activities are added to make it easier to call them (and listen for their events).

Figure 17-19 shows the completed workflow diagram.

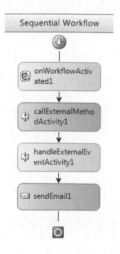

Figure 17-19. The final workflow diagram

Testing the Workflow

Press F6 to build the solution, and fix any errors you may have. From the Solution Explorer, right-click the WF_Chapter17 project, and choose Deploy.

Launch SharePoint from a browser window, and open the Part4 site. Go to the All Site Content page, and then click the *Site Workflow* link. The Workflows page shown in Figure 17-20 should include a *WF_Chapter17* link to start this workflow.

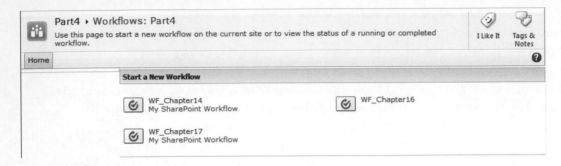

Figure 17-20. The Workflows page showing the WF_Chapter17 workflow

Click the *WF_Chapter17* link. After processing, the home page should be displayed. Navigate back to the Workflows page, and you should see a completed instance of WF_Chapter17, as shown in Figure 17-21.

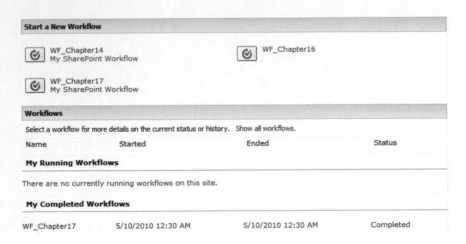

Figure 17-21. The Workflows page showing a completed instance

Now check your e-mails. You should have one that lists the contents of the specified folder similar to Figure 17-22.

Figure 17-22. The e-mail sent from the workflow with the folder contents

Summary

In this chapter, you implemented a workflow that determined the contents of a folder and provided that information in an e-mail. Admittedly, this is a pretty simple application, and you could have easily implemented this in a `CodeActivity`. However, the approach used here demonstrated two key concepts that you will undoubtedly find very useful in more complex workflow solutions:

- You executed a method outside the workflow project. This enables you to invoke external systems in your workflow design.

- You implemented an asynchronous process. After invoking the call, the workflow listened for the response. This allows the workflow to be unloaded while waiting for long-running operations. The workflow could also perform other activities while waiting on this one.

You also got a glimpse into how the built-in workflow activities are implemented. Most of them are based on the `CallExternalMethodActivity` and `HandleExternalEventActivity` design pattern.

PART 5

■ ■ ■

Business Connectivity Services (BCS)

In this part of the book, you'll integrate external data into your SharePoint solution using Business Connectivity Services (BCS). BCS is a significant improvement over the Business Data Catalog (BDC) provided with SharePoint 2007. With BCS, you'll create an external content type (ECT) that represents data from an external data source. Then you can create a list based on this content type, which will function like the native SharePoint lists.

In Chapter 18, you'll create ECTs using the SharePoint Designer, which connects to a SQL Server database. You will also create multiple ECTs that are associated based on a common field and see how the forms provide an instance picker based on this association. In Chapter 19, you will build a .NET Assembly Connector in Visual Studio 2010. This will allow you to create an ECT to any data that you can access from your .NET code. Chapter 20 will demonstrate how these lists can be integrated into Outlook 2010.

The sample projects use the tables that are provided in the AdventureWorks sample SQL Server database. If you do not have an SQL Server with the AdventureWorks database, you can download the latest version at http://msftdbprodsamples.codeplex.com/releases/view/24854. I have the SQL 2008 R2 version installed, but previous versions should work fine as well.

CHAPTER 18

■ ■ ■

Creating External Content Types

In this chapter you'll use the SharePoint Designer to create *external content types*, which will provide external data as if it were a native SharePoint list. You will use the same SharePoint site for all projects in this part of the book. Create a new site named **Part5** using the Blank Site template, as shown in Figure 18-1.

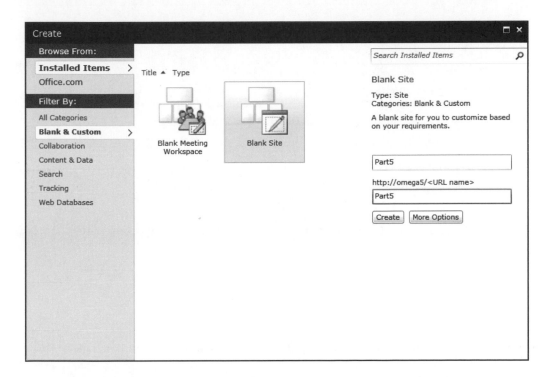

Figure 18-1. Creating a Part5 subsite.

Creating a Read-Only List

Open the Part5 site that you just created. From the Site Actions menu, click *Edit Site in SharePoint Designer*, which will launch the SharePoint Designer and open this site. From the Navigation menu, select External Content Types, as shown in Figure 18-2.

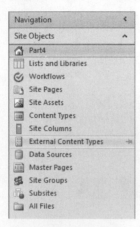

Figure 18-2. Selecting External Content Types

This will display a list of the existing ECTs, which should be empty.

Creating an External Content Type

Click the External Content Type button in the ribbon, as shown in Figure 18-3.

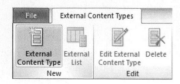

Figure 18-3. Clicking the External Content Type button

This will create a new external content type and display the form shown in Figure 18-4 to define its properties.

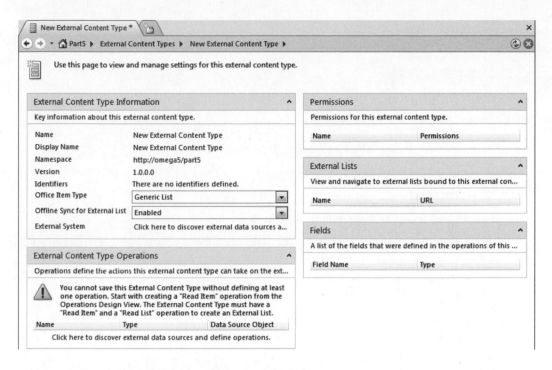

Figure 18-4. The initial External Content Type definition

Change the name to **Employee,** and the display name should change as well. Click the *Click here to discover external data sources and define operations* link. This will display the operation designer.

Creating a Database Connection

You must first create a connection to the `AdventureWorks` database. Click the Add Connection button, as shown in Figure 18-5.

Figure 18-5. Clicking the Add Connection button

There are three types of connections that are supported, as shown in Figure 18-6.

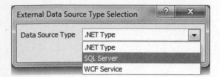

Figure 18-6. The supported data source types

External content types can connect to the following data sources:

- .NET assembly (I'll cover this in the next chapter)

- SQL Server database

- Windows Communication Foundation (WCF) web service

Choose the SQL Server option, which will display the SQL Server Connection dialog box, as shown in Figure 18-7.

Figure 18-7. Specifying the database connection properties

Enter the information that is appropriate for your environment, and click OK. This should add a connection to the Data Source Explorer. From here you can browse the database objects including tables, views, and stored procedures. Expand the view list, and select the **vEmployee** view. The form should look like Figure 18-8.

Figure 18-8. Expanding the vEmployee *view*

■ **Note** External content types work on the principle of implementing the operations known by the *CRUD* acronym, which stands for **C**reate, **R**ead, **U**pdate, and **D**elete. By implementing these basic operations, the external content type provides complete control over the external data. There are actually two read operations. Read Item returns a single record based on an identifier that is supplied. Read List returns a set of records, which may be the entire table or a subset based on filters that are defined. As you create external content types, you will implement one or more of these operations.

Creating a Read Item Operation

Right-click the **vEmployee** view, and select *New Read Item Operation,* as shown in Figure 18-9.

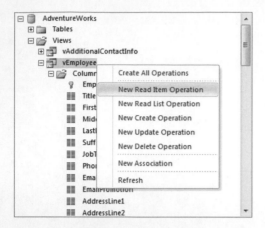

Figure 18-9. *Creating the Read Item operation*

The first page of the Read Item dialog box shown in Figure 18-10 will then display.

Read Item

Operation Properties	**Operation Properties**
Input Parameters	Choose basic settings like display name for this operation.
Return Parameter	

Operation Name: `vEmployeeRead Item`

Operation Display Name: `Read Item Employee`

Operation Type: Read Item

This operation is the default Read Item operation as it is the only Read Item operation on this External Content Type.

Errors and Warnings

To configure Input Parameters, click Next.

`< Back`   `Next >`   `Finish`   `Cancel`

Figure 18-10. *Specifying the operation parameters*

You can leave all the default values and click Next, which will display the second page shown in Figure 18-11.

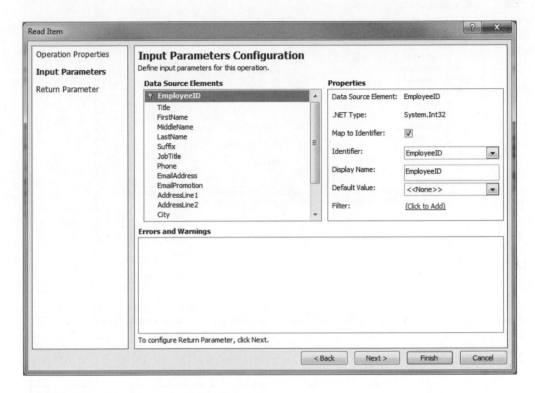

Figure 18-11. Specifying the input parameters

Each of the columns included in the **vEmployee** view are listed in the Data Source Elements list. You can select each one and review the default settings. Since this will be a read-only list, some of these properties such as **Required** and **Default Value** are not important. The SharePoint Designer defaults these settings based on the column's database properties.

You will need one field marked as the identifier, which is used when retrieving a single record from the database. The **EmployeeID** field is selected as the identifier, which is correct. Click Next to display the final page of this dialog box, which is shown in Figure 18-12.

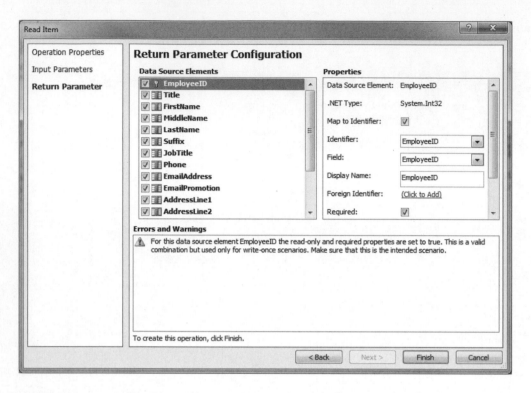

Figure 18-12. Specifying the return parameter

You can leave all the default settings for the return parameter and click Finish. The External Content Type Operations section will list the Read Item operation that you just created, as shown in Figure 18-13.

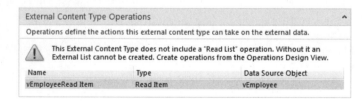

Figure 18-13. The External Content Type operations list

Creating a Read List Operation

Notice the warning that is displayed. An external content type must have both a Read List as well as a Read Item operation. Right-click the **vEmployee** view, and choose *Create Read List Operation*, as shown in Figure 18-14.

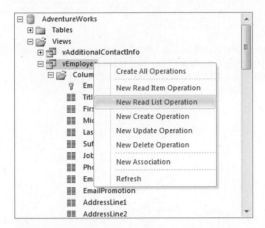

Figure 18-14. Adding the Read List operation

Repeat the same steps to create the Read List operation. The second page of the Read List dialog box shown in Figure 18-15 allows you to define filters to restrict the records that are returned.

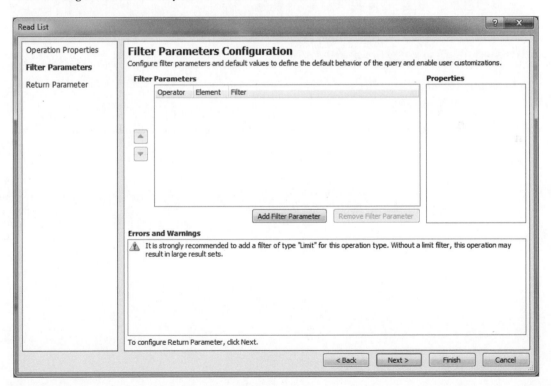

Figure 18-15. Specifying filters for the Read List operation

Adding a Limit Filter

Unless you know that there will not be many items in the list, you should add a limit filter to set the maximum number of items that will be returned. To do that, click the Add Filter Parameter button, which will create a blank filter. In the Properties window, click the *Click to add* link to display the Filter Configuration dialog box shown in Figure 18-16.

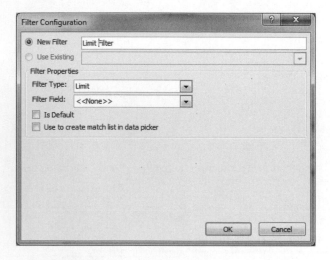

Figure 18-16. Configuring the limit filter

Change the name to **Limit Filter**, and select the `Filter Type` as `Limit`. Click OK. In the Properties window, enter **100** for the `Default Value`. The completed dialog box should look like Figure 18-17.

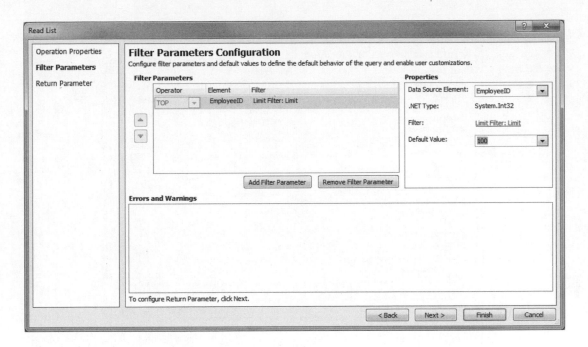

Figure 18-17. The completed filter parameters configuration

Figure 18-18 shows the final dialog box.

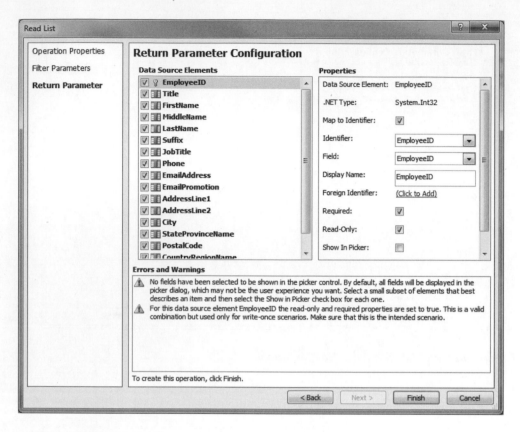

Figure 18-18. Specifying the return parameter configuration

Choosing Fields for the Picker Control

The default settings can be used with one exception. Notice the warning about the picker control. You should select a couple of fields and click their `Show In Picker` check box. If this list will be used to select an employee on a different form, the selected fields will be shown in the picker control. Select the `FirstName` field, and click this check box. Do the same with the `LastName` field. Click the Finish button.

Click the Save button at the top of the SharePoint Designer. The external content type is now complete. Click the Summary View button in the ribbon. The form should look like Figure 18-19.

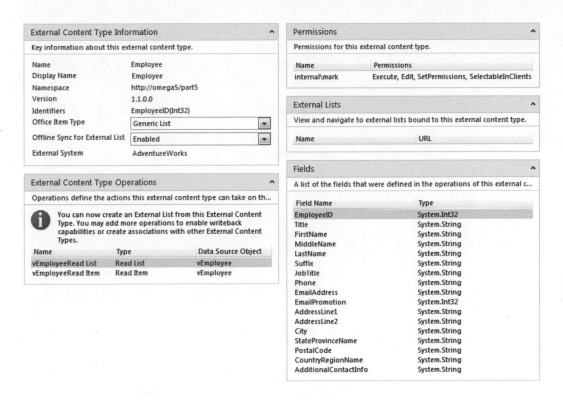

Figure 18-19. The Employee external content type summary information

Setting Permissions

Access to each external content type must be explicitly granted. You can do this from the SharePoint 2010 Central Administration page. You should have a shortcut to this in the Start menu. Figure 18-20 shows the home page.

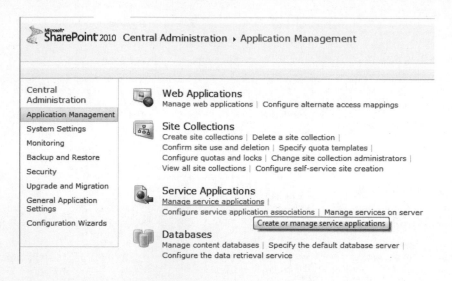

Figure 18-20. SharePoint Central Administration page

Click the *Manage service applications* link in the Service Applications section. This will list all the existing service application, as shown in Figure 18-21.

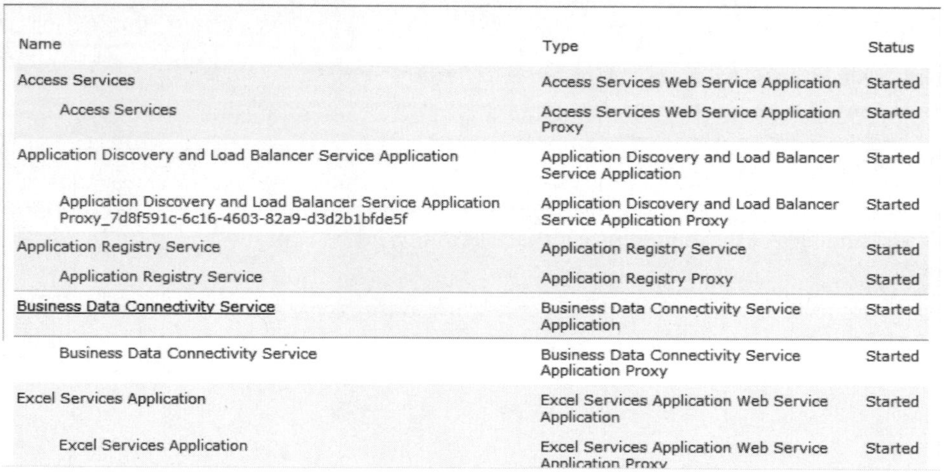

Name	Type	Status
Access Services	Access Services Web Service Application	Started
Access Services	Access Services Web Service Application Proxy	Started
Application Discovery and Load Balancer Service Application	Application Discovery and Load Balancer Service Application	Started
Application Discovery and Load Balancer Service Application Proxy_7d8f591c-6c16-4603-82a9-d3d2b1bfde5f	Application Discovery and Load Balancer Service Application Proxy	Started
Application Registry Service	Application Registry Service	Started
Application Registry Service	Application Registry Proxy	Started
Business Data Connectivity Service	Business Data Connectivity Service Application	Started
Business Data Connectivity Service	Business Data Connectivity Service Application Proxy	Started
Excel Services Application	Excel Services Application Web Service Application	Started
Excel Services Application	Excel Services Application Web Service Application Proxy	Started

Figure 18-21. Business Data Connectivity service application

Click the Business Data Connectivity Service link, which lists details about each external content type. The Employee external content type should be the only one shown (see Figure 18-22).

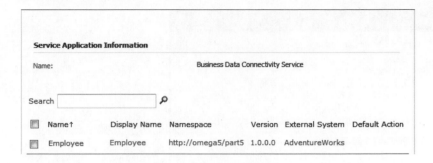

Figure 18-22. Existing external content types

Click the *Employee* link, which will display the details about this external content type. Then click the Set Object Permission button in the ribbon, as shown in Figure 18-23.

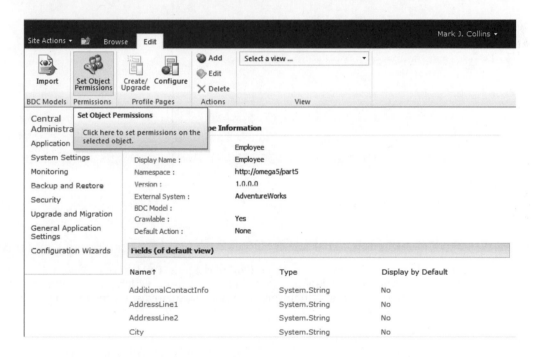

Figure 18-23. Setting the object permissions

In the Set Object Permissions dialog box shown in Figure 18-24, enter a user or group, and click the Add button. Then select all the check boxes to enable all permissions, and click OK.

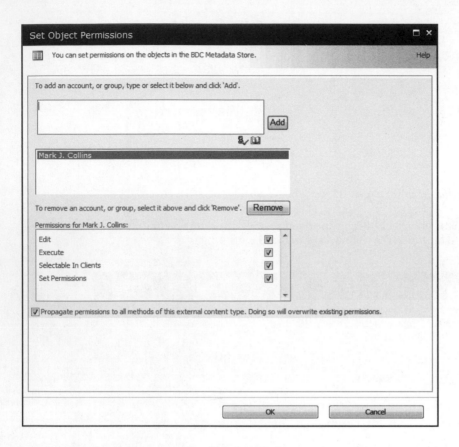

Figure 18-24. Granting access for all permissions

Creating the Employees External List

Close the Central Administration site, and go back to the SharePoint Designer. The External Content Type Operations should now show both the Read Item and Read List operations, which is the minimum required for a read-only list. Now go back one level in the breadcrumb control to display the External Content Types list, as shown in Figure 18-25.

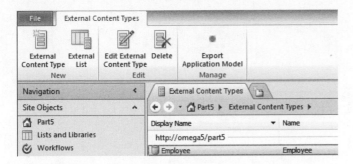

Figure 18-25. Displaying the External Content Types list

Select the **Employee** external content type, and click the External List button in the ribbon. This will create an external list based on this content type. In the Create External List dialog box, enter **Employees** for the name, as shown in Figure 18-26, and click OK.

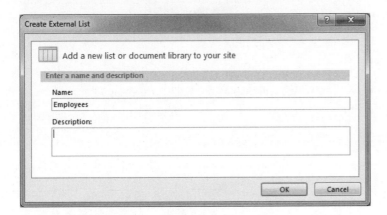

Figure 18-26. Creating a new external list

Open the SharePoint site, and select the **Employees** list, which should look like Figure 18-27.

☐	EmployeeID	Title	FirstName	MiddleName	LastName	Suffix	JobTitle	Phone
	1		Guy	R	Gilbert		Production Technician - WC60	320-555-0195
	2		Kevin	F	Brown		Marketing Assistant	150-555-0189
	3		Roberto		Tamburello		Engineering Manager	212-555-0187
	4		Rob		Walters		Senior Tool Designer	612-555-0100
	5		Thierry	B	D'Hers		Tool Designer	168-555-0183
	6		David	M	Bradley		Marketing Manager	913-555-0172
	7		JoLynn	M	Dobney		Production Supervisor - WC60	903-555-0145
	8		Ruth	Ann	Ellerbrock		Production Technician - WC10	145-555-0130
	9	Ms.	Gail	A	Erickson		Design Engineer	849-555-0139
	10		Barry	K	Johnson		Production Technician - WC10	206-555-0180

Figure 18-27. The Employee list

Click the EmployeeID field on one the records, which will display the View form shown in Figure 18-28.

Figure 18-28. Displaying a single employee

Notice that the edit controls on this form are disabled since you did not provide any of the update methods.

Creating an Updatable List

Now you'll create a second external content type and implement all five operations so it can be updated.

Creating the External Content Type

In the SharePoint Designer, go to the External Content Types list, and select the External Content Type button from the ribbon (just like you did to create the Employee content type). In the External Content

Type form, change the name to **SalesPerson**. Then click the *Click here to discover external data sources and define operations* link.

The **AdventureWorks** data source should already be included in the Data Source Explorer. Expand the list of tables, and select the **SalesPerson** table. Right-click the **SalesPerson** table, and choose *Create All Operations*, as shown in Figure 18-29.

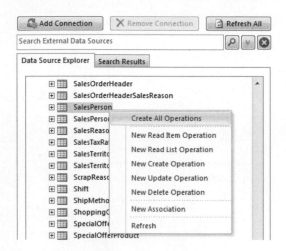

Figure 18-29. Creating all operations

When you use this option, all five operations are created for you, as indicated in the All Operations dialog box, as shown in Figure 18-30.

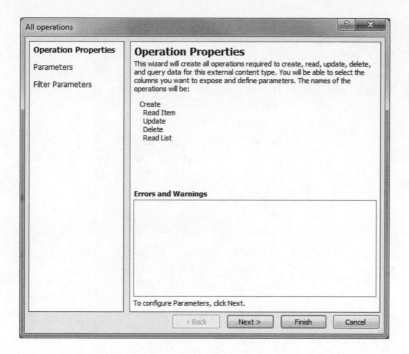

Figure 18-30. The All Operations dialog box

This dialog box will show any errors or warnings that are detected. Click Next to display the next page, as shown in Figure 18-31.

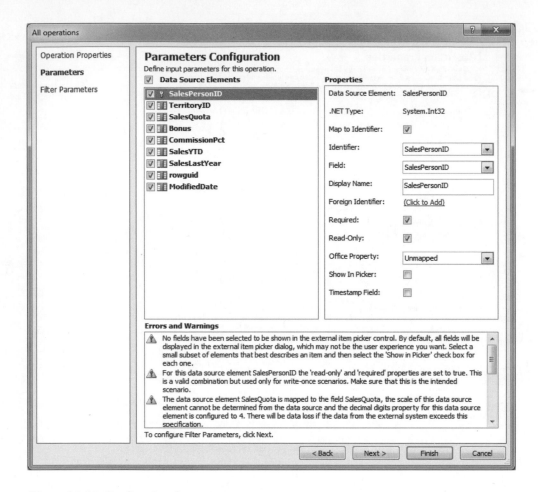

Figure 18-31. Configuring the parameters

Creating all operations at once is most efficient. You only have to go through the fields once, and most of the default settings are correct. There are a few warnings on this page. The first is the same one you saw with the `Employee` external content type regarding the picker control. The `SalesPerson` content type will not be used in a picker control, and there are not any appropriate fields to select, so you can leave it as is without any fields selected.

The second warning has to do with the `SalesPersonID` identifier. It is marked both Read-Only and Required. This means it can be entered when creating a new record but not edited after that. The other warnings are about potential loss of data because of data conversion. You can ignore these.

There is one thing that you should change. For the `ModifiedDate` field, click the `Timestamp Field` check box, as shown in Figure 18-32. This indicates that this field contains the last update timestamp, and SharePoint uses this in its optimizations.

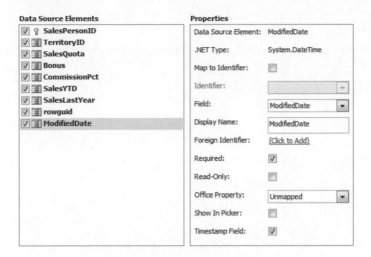

Figure 18-32. Specifying the TimeStamp Field setting

Click Next to display the final page. Set up a limit filter just like you did with the `Employee` external content type. Click Finish, and save the changes. Click the Summary View button; the external content type summary should look like Figure 18-33.

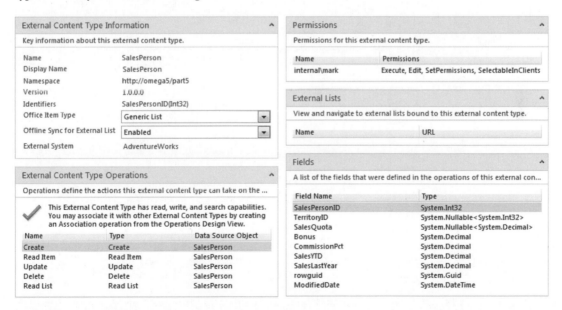

Figure 18-33. The `SalesPerson` external content type summary information

Using the Central Administration application, grant yourself access to the `SalesPerson` external content type just like you did for the `Employee` content type.

Creating the Sales Person List

In the SharePoint Designer, go to the External Content Types list, select **SalesPerson**, and click the External List button, as shown in Figure 18-34.

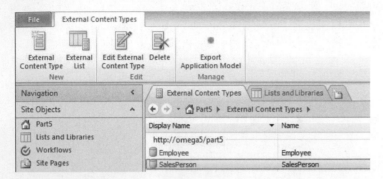

Figure 18-34. Creating an external list

In the dialog box, enter the list name as **Sales Persons**. Start the SharePoint site, and select the **Sales Persons** list, which should look like Figure 18-35.

	SalesPersonID	TerritoryID	SalesQuota	Bonus	CommissionPct	SalesYTD	SalesLastYear
	268			0.0000	0.0000	677558.4653	0.0000
	275	2	300000.0000	4100.0000	0.0120	4557045.0459	1750406.4785
	276	4	250000.0000	2000.0000	0.0150	5200475.2313	1439156.0291
	277	3	250000.0000	2500.0000	0.0150	3857163.6332	1997186.2037
	278	6	250000.0000	500.0000	0.0100	1764938.9859	1620276.8966
	279	5	300000.0000	6700.0000	0.0100	2811012.7151	1849640.9418
	280	1	250000.0000	5000.0000	0.0100	0.0000	1927059.1780
	281	4	250000.0000	3550.0000	0.0100	3018725.4858	2073505.9999
	282	6	250000.0000	5000.0000	0.0150	3189356.2465	2038234.6549
	283	1	250000.0000	3500.0000	0.0120	3587378.4257	1371635.3158
	284			0.0000	0.0000	636440.2510	0.0000
	285	10	250000.0000	5150.0000	0.0200	5015682.3752	1635823.3967
	286	7	250000.0000	985.0000	0.0160	3827950.2380	2396539.7601
	287	1	300000.0000	3900.0000	0.0190	1931620.1835	0.0000
	288			0.0000	0.0000	219088.8836	0.0000
	289	8	250000.0000	75.0000	0.0180	2241204.0424	1307949.7917
	290	9	250000.0000	5650.0000	0.0180	1758385.9260	2278548.9776

✚ Add new item

Figure 18-35. The Sales Persons list

Notice that there is a link to add a new item. This is available because you implemented the Create operation. Select one of the records, and click the Edit Item button, which will display the form shown in Figure 18-36.

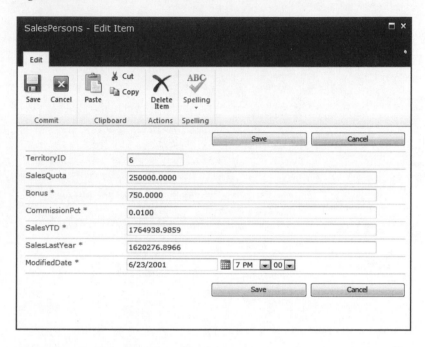

Figure 18-36. Editing a Sales Person record

Update one of the fields, and click the Save button. The list should now reflect the change you just made.

Defining an Association

You may have noticed that the Sales Persons list has a TerritoryID field. Now you'll create an external content type to provide territory information and associate that with the SalesPerson external content type.

Creating the Territory External Content Type

Using the SharePoint Designer, create a Territory external content type just like you did for the vEmployee view except using the SalesTerritory table. Create the Read Item and Read List operations using all the default options. You don't need to provide a limit filter. The completed content type should look like Figure 18-37.

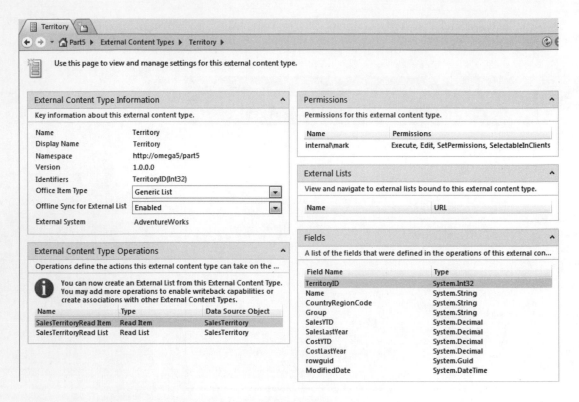

Figure 18-37. The completed `Territory` *external content type*

Adding the Association

Now you'll create an association between the two external content types. Start by selecting `SalesPerson` external content type, and then click the Operations Design View button in the ribbon. Expand the `AdventureWorks` data source, and navigate to the `SalesPerson` table. Right-click the `SalesPerson` table, and select *New Association*, as shown in Figure 18-38.

Figure 18-38. Adding an association

This will display a set of dialog boxes where you will define the association. On the first page, shown in Figure 18-39, you will select the other external content type that this one should be associated with.

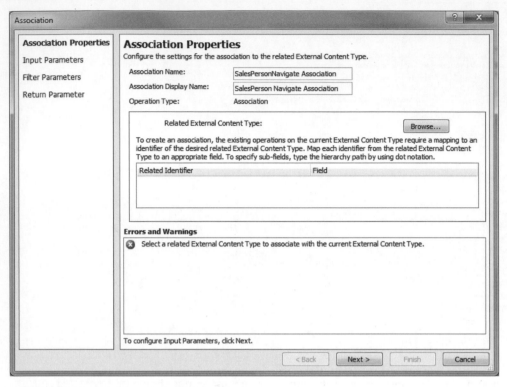

Figure 18-39. *The initial Association dialog box*

Click the Browse button to select the content type. Select the `Territory` external content type, as shown in Figure 18-40, and click OK.

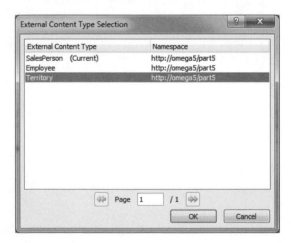

Figure 18-40. *Selecting the `Employee` content type*

Notice that the `SalesPerson` external content type is also listed but is marked as the current content type (the one you're adding the association to).

Configuring the Association

Once you've selected the related external content type, the dialog box is updated, as shown in Figure 18-41.

Figure 18-41. Selecting the identifier

■ **Tip** The `Association Display Name` property is the label that will be displayed on the forms for the `Sales Person` list items. The default value of "SalesPerson Navigate Association" is a little cryptic. The form is indeed navigating an association on the `SalesPerson` external content type. However, it is the `Territory` record that is being retrieved. Change this value to **Territory**.

The identifier of the `Territory` external content type, `TerritoryID`, is automatically selected as the related identifier. Now you must choose the field from the `SalesPerson` external content type that specifies the `TerritoryID`. The `TerritoryID` field should already be selected in the drop-down list. Click the Next button to display the next dialog box.

■ **Note** An Association operation works like a ReadItem operation. You'll supply an identifier as an input parameter, and the operation will return an object containing the field values of the related list. In this case, the parameter is the TerritoryID from the SalesPerson external content type, and a Territory external content type is returned.

In the next dialog box (Input Parameters), select the TerritoryID field, and click the Map to Identifier check box. This will map the TerritoryID field from SalesPerson to an identifier of Territory. The Territory external content type has only a single identifier, TerritoryID, so it is automatically selected. The completed dialog should look like Figure 18-42.

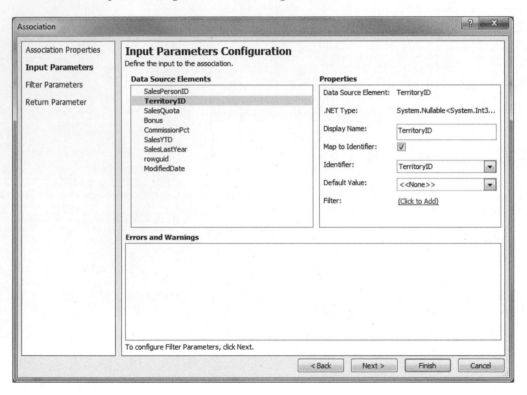

Figure 18-42. Selecting the input parameters

The next dialog box is used to define filters, but none is needed since the association will return only a single object. Click Next to display the final dialog box. For the Return Parameter Configuration, the SalesPersonID needs to be mapped to the SalesPersonID identifier, as shown in Figure 18-43. It should be set up this way by default.

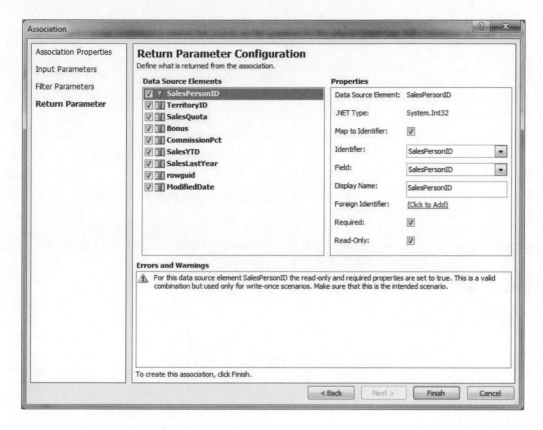

Figure 18-43. Configuring the return parameter

Click the Finish button to complete the association. The list of operations should now include the new association, as shown in Figure 18-44.

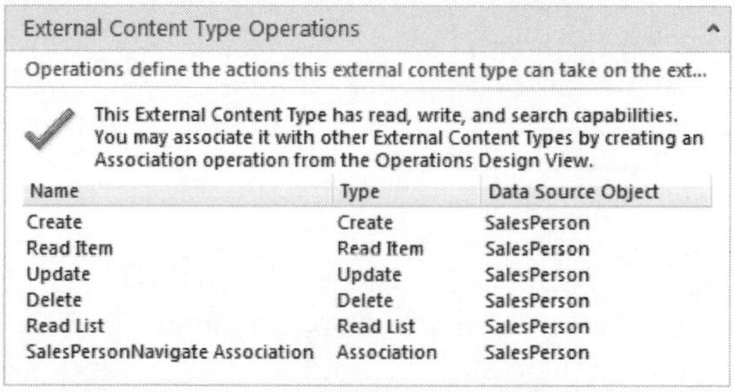

Figure 18-44. The updated list of operations

Save the changes. Again, grant yourself access to the `Territory` external content type using the Central Administration page.

■ **Caution** Delete the `Sales Persons` list, and re-create it from the `SalesPerson` external content type. This will cause the new list to pick up the changes you made to the external content type.

Testing the Changes

Open the SharePoint site, and select the `Sales Persons` list. Edit one of the `Sales Persons` items, which should show an edit form like the one shown in Figure 18-45.

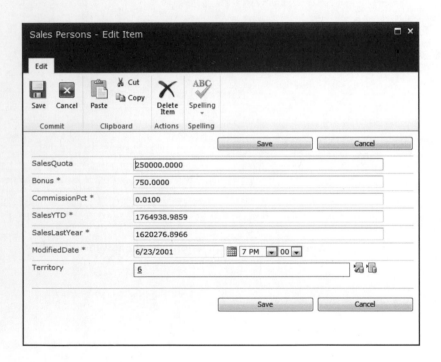

Figure 18-45. The `Sales Persons` edit form

Notice that the `Territory` field now has a picker control. If you click it, the dialog box shown in Figure 18-46 will be displayed.

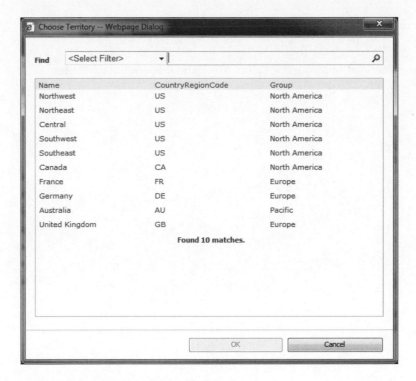

Figure 18-46. The Territory picker list

You can select a territory from this list by double-clicking it. That will close this dialog box, and the corresponding TerritoryID will be shown in the edit form. Click the Save button on the edit form, which will update the external data with the selected territory.

Summary

In this chapter, you created several external content types to access data from an external database. You also created two lists, Employee and Sales Persons. Employee is a read-only list that allows you to view information about existing employees. Sales Persons is an updatable list where you can also create, update, and delete items in the list. The Sales Persons list also uses an associated external content type, which gives you a picker control to select a territory.

To create an external content type, you implemented the CRUD operations, which define how data is accessed in the external source. Specifically, the following operations can be provided:

- Read Item returns a single record specified by an identifier.

- Read List returns all items or a subset defined by one or more filters.

- Create creates a new item.

- Update updates an existing item.

- Delete deletes a single record specified by an identifier.

In addition, you can also create associations, which work like a Read Item operation except the identifier is supplied by one external content type, and the object that is returned is defined by another.

■ ■ ■

CHAPTER 19

Implementing a .NET Assembly Connector

In this chapter you'll create external content types using Visual Studio 2010 by implementing a .NET *Assembly Connector*. This connector will implement the same five CRUD operations that you created in Chapter 18 through the SharePoint Designer. However, because the connector is implemented in .NET code, you can provide an external content type for any data that you can access through .NET. This gives you virtually limitless possibilities.

Creating the Business Data Connectivity Project

Start Visual Studio, and create an empty SharePoint project, as shown in Figure 19-1. Enter the name **WF_Chapter19**.

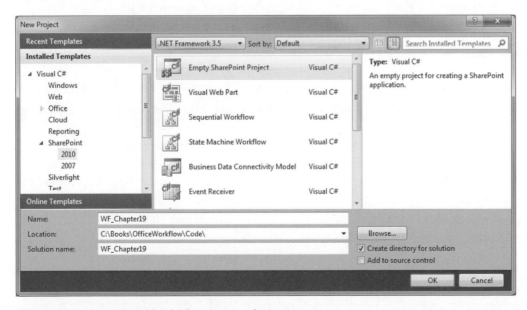

Figure 19-1. Creating a blank SharePoint solution

The SharePoint Customization Wizard shown in Figure 19-2 will be displayed. Enter the URL for the Part5 subsite that you created in the previous chapter. Make sure you also select the radio button to deploy this as a farm solution.

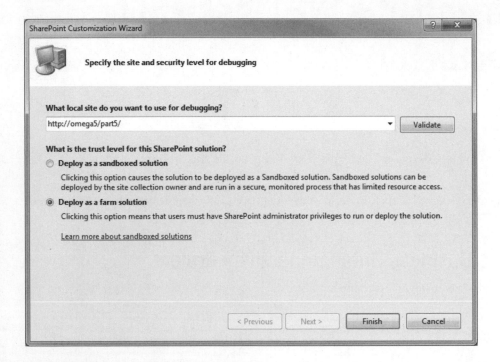

Figure 19-2. Specifying the debugging site

Now you'll need to add an item to this project that will implement the .NET Assembly Connector.

■ **Note** SharePoint 2007 provided a feature called Business Data Catalog (BDC), which is replaced in the 2010 version by Business Connectivity Services (BCS). Visual Studio 2010 provides a template called Business Data Connectivity Model, which creates the .NET Assembly Connector that you'll use in this chapter. It also provides a Business Data Connectivity (BDC) Explorer that you will use to design this connector. The term *BDC* used in Visual Studio should not be confused with Business Data Catalog (BDC) used in SharePoint 2007. In Visual Studio 2010, the acronym BDC stands for Business Data Connectivity.

In the Solution Explorer, right-click the WF_Chapter19 project, and choose Add ▶ New Item. In the Add New Item dialog box, select the Business Data Connectivity Model template, and enter the name **ProductDetail**, as shown in Figure 19-3.

Figure 19-3. Adding a BDCM project

The Solution Explorer should look like Figure 19-4.

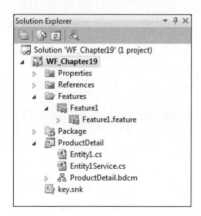

Figure 19-4. The Solution Explorer

The template created a **ProductDetail** folder that contains three files:

- **Entity1.cs**: Contains the data definition
- **Entity1Service.cs**: Implements the CRUD operations
- **ProductDetail.bdcm**: Provides the external content type definition

---

■ **Tip** Instead of creating a blank project and then adding the BDCM item, you could have selected the BDCM template when creating the project so it would be done all in one step. However, that would have generated a file named BdcModel1.bdcm and put your objects in a BdcModel1 namespace. These can be renamed to a more descriptive name (like ProductDetail), but it would require several manual steps. Creating the project in a second step will save you time in the long run.

In the Solution Explorer, right-click the **Entity1.cs** file, and choose Rename. Enter the filename **ProductDetail.cs**. The dialog box shown in Figure 19-5 will appear, asking whether you want to update all references to **Entity1**. Click the Yes button.

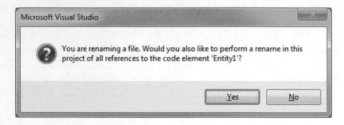

Figure 19-5. Updating references

Also, rename the **Entity1Service.cs** to **ProductDetailService.cs**.

Using the BDC Explorer

The ProductDetail.bdcm file should be open; if not, double-click this file in the Solution Explorer to open it. The top portion of the page provides a graphical representation of the entities defined in your model. The template created a single entity named Entity1, which is shown in Figure 19-6.

Figure 19-6. The BDC entity diagram

The initial entity contains a single identifier, named Identifier1, and the ReadList and ReadItem methods. This is the minimum requirement for a read-only external content type. Click this entity, and change its name to **ProductDetail**, as shown in Figure 19-7.

Figure 19-7. Changing the entity name

In the same way, change the identifier to **ProductID**. In the Properties window, change the type name to System.Int32. In the bottom portion of the page, shown in Figure 19-8, the method details are displayed.

Figure 19-8. The BDC method details

The details of the two methods, ReadList and ReadItem, are shown. This form has three columns. The first indicates the Name of the parameter. The second specifies the Direction, which is generally either In or Return. (Out and InOut are also available but not normally used.) The third column contains the Type Descriptor, which defines the type of data being passed through this parameter. You can edit the Direction column on the form by selecting the appropriate value from the drop-down list. The Name and Type Descriptor settings are modified in the Properties window that is automatically displayed when the property is selected.

Visual Studio does a good job creating the default elements, although the names are somewhat generic, which you'll fix now. The ReadList has a single parameter, which is a return parameter that is a list of entities. The ReadItem method has two parameters: an input parameter, which is the identifier, and a return parameter, which is the entity that is selected. The Instances collection allows you to specify the actual method name in the ProductDetailService class.

Updating the Method Details

Select the Identifier1 Type Descriptor setting for the id parameter. In the Properties window, change the name to ProductID, and set the Type Name property to System.Int32. The Identifier property should already be set to ProductID. The completed Properties window should look like Figure 19-9.

Figure 19-9. Modifying the Identifier parameter

Click the **id** parameter, and change its name in the Properties window to **productID**. Click the **returnParameter** parameter, and change its name to **product**. Click **Entity1 Type Descriptor**, and change its name to **ProductDetail**. Notice that its **Type Name** property is defined as follows:

```
WF_Chapter19.ProductDetail.ProductDetail, ProductDetail
```

This is the fully qualified name of the **ProductDetail** data class. For the **ReadList** method, rename the **returnParameter** to **productList**, and rename the **Type Descriptor** property to **ProductDetailList**. Notice that its **Type Name** property is defined as follows:

```
System.Collections.Generic.IEnumerable`1
    [[WF_Chapter19.ProductDetail.ProductDetail, ProductDetail]]
```

This is an **IEnumerable** collection of **ProductDetail** data classes. Select the **ReadList** instance, and change its **Default Display Name** property to **ProductDetail List**. The Properties window should look like Figure 19-10.

Figure 19-10. ReadList instance Properties window

Notice that the **Type** is defined as **Finder**. The **ReadList** operation is often referred to as a *Finder* operation because it *finds* objects from that data source. The **ReadItem** operation is called a **SpecificFinder**, because it *finds* the specified record. Click the **ReadItem** instance, and change its **Default Display Name** to **Read ProductDetail**. The completed Method Details form should look like Figure 19-11.

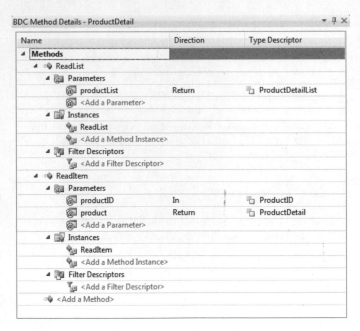

Figure 19-11. The completed Method Details form

Using the BDC Explorer

The BDC Explorer is normally at the top-right corner of the Visual Studio IDE. It provides another view of the BDC model. Figure 19-12 shows its contents when fully expanded.

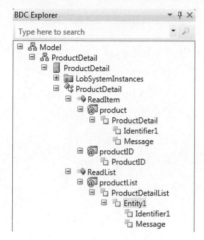

Figure 19-12. The BDC Explorer

When you click one of the nodes, the Properties window displays the details just like the Method Details window did. So, you can navigate and update the model from either of these views using the Properties window.

The BDC Explorer provides an additional detail that is not available from the Method Detail window. It shows the field definitions of the object. Notice the `ProductDetail` node under the `ReadItem` method has two subnodes called `Identifier1` and `Message`. These are the default fields generated by the template. You'll now use the BDC Explorer to define the fields contained in the `ProductDetail` object.

Click the `Identifier1` node under the `ReadItem` method. In the Properties window, change the name to **ProductID**, and set the `Type Descriptor` property to `System.Int32`, as shown in Figure 19-13.

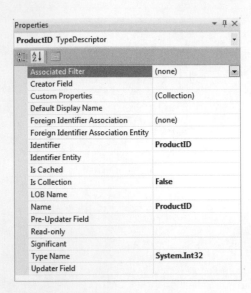

Figure 19-13. The `ProductID` *properties*

Similarly, select the `Message` node, and change the `Name` property to **Name**. You can leave the `Type Name` property as `System.String`. To add more fields, right-click the `ProductDetail` node, and choose Add Type Descriptor, as shown in Figure 19-14.

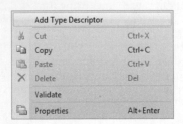

Figure 19-14. Adding more fields

Table 19-1 lists all the fields that should be included in the `ProductDetail` entity and the appropriate `Type Name` property for each. Add the remaining nodes by right-clicking the `ProductDetail` node, adding a `Type Descriptor` object, and changing its `Name` property (and `Type Name` if necessary).

Table 19-1. Fields to Be Included in the ProductDetail Entity

Name	TypeName
ProductID	System.Int32
Name	System.String
ProductNumber	System.String
MakeFlag	System.Boolean
FinishedGoodsFlag	System.Boolean
Color	System.String
StandardCost	System.Decimal
ListPrice	System.Decimal
Size	System.String
Weight	System.Decimal
ProductLine	System.String
Class	System.String
Style	System.String
Category	System.String
Subcategory	System.String
ProductModel	System.String
SizeUOM	System.String
WeightUOM	System.String

The BDC Explorer should look like Figure 19-15.

Figure 19-15. The updated BDC Explorer

Now you'll need to add all the same fields to the **ReadList** method that you added to the **ReadItem** method. Fortunately, there's an easy way to copy them. First, the **ReadList** method has a node called **Entity1**. Right-click the **Entity1** node, and choose Delete. Then right-click the **ProductDetail** node (in the **ReadItem** method), and choose Copy. Finally, right-click the **ProductDetailList** node (in the **ReadList** method), and choose Paste.

The BDC Model File

The BDC model is now complete. The next step is to provide the implementation for the CRUD operations. But first, let's look at the **ProductDetail.bdcm** file that provides the definition of the external content type. It is an XML-formatted text file, and Listing 19-1 shows its contents.

*Listing 19-1. Contents of the **ProductDetail.bdcm** File*

```
<?xml version="1.0" encoding="utf-8"?>
<Model xmlns:xsi="http://www.w3.org/2001/XMLSchema-instance"
       xmlns:xsd="http://www.w3.org/2001/XMLSchema"
       xmlns="http://schemas.microsoft.com/windows/2007/BusinessDataCatalog"
       Name="ProductDetail">
  <LobSystems>
    <LobSystem Name="ProductDetail" Type="DotNetAssembly">
```

```xml
<LobSystemInstances>
  <LobSystemInstance Name="ProductDetail" />
</LobSystemInstances>
<Entities>
  <Entity Name="ProductDetail"
          Namespace="WF_Chapter19.ProductDetail"
          EstimatedInstanceCount="1000"
          Version="1.0.0.62">
    <Properties>
      <Property Name="Class"
                Type="System.String">
        WF_Chapter19.ProductDetail.ProductDetailService, ProductDetail
      </Property>
    </Properties>
    <Identifiers>
      <Identifier Name="ProductID"
                  TypeName="System.String" />
    </Identifiers>
    <Methods>
      <Method Name="ReadList">
        <Parameters>
          <Parameter Direction="Return" Name="productList">
            <TypeDescriptor TypeName=
"System.Collections.Generic.IEnumerable`1
[[WF_Chapter19.ProductDetail.ProductDetail, ProductDetail]]"
                            IsCollection="true"
                            Name="ProductDetailList">
              <TypeDescriptors>
                <TypeDescriptor Name="ProductDetail"
                                TypeName=
"WF_Chapter19.ProductDetail.ProductDetail, ProductDetail">
                  <TypeDescriptors>
                    <TypeDescriptor Name="ProductID"
                                    TypeName="System.Int32"
                                    IdentifierName="ProductID"
                                    IsCollection="false" />
                    <TypeDescriptor Name="Name"
                                    TypeName="System.String" />
                    <TypeDescriptor Name="ProductNumber"
                                    TypeName="System.String" />
                    <TypeDescriptor Name="MakeFlag"
                                    TypeName="System.Boolean"
                                    IsCollection="false" />
                    <TypeDescriptor Name="FinishedGoodsFlag"
                                    TypeName="System.Boolean"
                                    IsCollection="false" />
                    <TypeDescriptor Name="Color"
                                    TypeName="System.String" />
                    <TypeDescriptor Name="StandardCost"
                                    TypeName="System.Decimal"
                                    IsCollection="false" />
                    <TypeDescriptor Name="ListPrice"
```

```
                                        TypeName="System.Decimal"
                                        IsCollection="false" />
                        <TypeDescriptor Name="Size"
                                        TypeName="System.String" />
                        <TypeDescriptor Name="Weight"
                                        TypeName="System.Decimal"
                                        IsCollection="false" />
                        <TypeDescriptor Name="ProductLine"
                                        TypeName="System.String" />
                        <TypeDescriptor Name="Class"
                                        TypeName="System.String" />
                        <TypeDescriptor Name="Style"
                                        TypeName="System.String" />
                        <TypeDescriptor Name="Category"
                                        TypeName="System.String" />
                        <TypeDescriptor Name="Subcategory"
                                        TypeName="System.String" />
                        <TypeDescriptor Name="ProductModel"
                                        TypeName="System.String" />
                        <TypeDescriptor Name="SizeUOM"
                                        TypeName="System.String" />
                        <TypeDescriptor Name="WeightUOM"
                                        TypeName="System.String" />
                      </TypeDescriptors>
                    </TypeDescriptor>
                  </TypeDescriptors>
                </TypeDescriptor>
              </Parameter>
            </Parameters>
            <MethodInstances>
              <MethodInstance Type="Finder"
                              ReturnParameterName="productList"
                              Default="true"
                              Name="ReadList"
                              DefaultDisplayName="ProductDetail List" />
            </MethodInstances>
          </Method>

          <Method Name="ReadItem">
            <Parameters>
              <Parameter Direction="In" Name="productID">
                <TypeDescriptor TypeName="System.Int32"
                                IdentifierName="ProductID"
                                Name="ProductID"
                                IsCollection="false" />
              </Parameter>
              <Parameter Direction="Return" Name="product">
                <TypeDescriptor TypeName=
"WF_Chapter19.ProductDetail.ProductDetail, ProductDetail"
                                Name="ProductDetail">
                  <TypeDescriptors>
                    <TypeDescriptor TypeName="System.Int32"
```

```xml
                              IdentifierName="ProductID"
                              Name="ProductID"
                              IsCollection="false" />
        <TypeDescriptor TypeName="System.String"
                              Name="Name" />
        <TypeDescriptor Name="ProductNumber"
                              TypeName="System.String" />
        <TypeDescriptor Name="MakeFlag"
                              TypeName="System.Boolean"
                              IsCollection="false" />
        <TypeDescriptor Name="FinishedGoodsFlag"
                              TypeName="System.Boolean"
                              IsCollection="false" />
        <TypeDescriptor Name="Color"
                              TypeName="System.String" />
        <TypeDescriptor Name="StandardCost"
                              TypeName="System.Decimal"
                              IsCollection="false" />
        <TypeDescriptor Name="ListPrice"
                              TypeName="System.Decimal"
                              IsCollection="false" />
        <TypeDescriptor Name="Size"
                              TypeName="System.String" />
        <TypeDescriptor Name="Weight"
                              TypeName="System.Decimal"
                              IsCollection="false" />
        <TypeDescriptor Name="ProductLine"
                              TypeName="System.String" />
        <TypeDescriptor Name="Class"
                              TypeName="System.String" />
        <TypeDescriptor Name="Style"
                              TypeName="System.String" />
        <TypeDescriptor Name="Category"
                              TypeName="System.String" />
        <TypeDescriptor Name="Subcategory"
                              TypeName="System.String" />
        <TypeDescriptor Name="ProductModel"
                              TypeName="System.String" />
        <TypeDescriptor Name="SizeUOM"
                              TypeName="System.String" />
        <TypeDescriptor Name="WeightUOM"
                              TypeName="System.String" />
      </TypeDescriptors>
    </TypeDescriptor>
  </Parameter>
</Parameters>
<MethodInstances>
  <MethodInstance Type="SpecificFinder"
                  ReturnParameterName="product"
                  Default="true" Name="ReadItem"
                  DefaultDisplayName="Read ProductDetail" />
</MethodInstances>
```

```
            </Method>
          </Methods>
        </Entity>
      </Entities>
    </LobSystem>
  </LobSystems>
</Model>
```

This file, although somewhat verbose, is fairly easy to follow. The content is laid out in essentially the same order that it is displayed in the Method Details window. If you're comfortable working with XML files, you can edit this file directly instead of using the BDC tools in Visual Studio. To open the raw XML file, right-click the `ProductDetail.bdcm` file, and choose Open With. Then select the XML (Text) Editor.

Implementing the CRUD Operations

Now you're ready to implement the `ReadItem()` and `ReadList()` methods.

Defining the Data Class

Open the `ProductDetail.cs` class. This class specifies a class member for each field that will be provided by the external content type. The template generated an initial version that contains the `Identifier1` and `Message` class members. Replace this with the code shown in Listing 19-2.

Listing 19-2. Implementation of ProductDetail.cs

```
using System;

namespace WF_Chapter19.ProductDetail
{
    public partial class ProductDetail
    {
        public int ProductID { get; set; }
        public string Name { get; set; }
        public string ProductNumber { get; set; }
        public bool MakeFlag { get; set; }
        public bool FinishedGoodsFlag { get; set; }
        public string Color { get; set; }
        public decimal StandardCost { get; set; }
        public decimal ListPrice { get; set; }
        public string Size { get; set; }
        public decimal Weight { get; set; }
        public string ProductLine { get; set; }
        public string Class { get; set; }
        public string Style { get; set; }
        public string Category { get; set; }
        public string Subcategory { get; set; }
        public string ProductModel { get; set; }
```

```
        public string SizeUOM { get; set; }
        public string WeightUOM { get; set; }
    }
}
```

Open the `ProductDetailService.cs` file. Notice that the `ReadItem()` and `ReadList()` methods are already generated with the correct signatures. As you modified the BDC model, this class was updated as well to reflect the design changes.

■ **Note** This class is probably showing some compiler errors. The method implementation that was generated by the template was based on the initial method signatures. Your design changes were reflected in the method signatures, but the implementation was not updated. You will be replacing the implementation anyway.

Using LINQ to SQL

To access the data from the AdventureWorks database, you'll use LINQ to SQL. In the Solution Explorer, right-click the WF_Chapter19 project, and choose Add ▶ New Item. In the Add New Item dialog box, select the LINQ to SQL template, and enter the name **AdventureWorks.dbml**, as shown in Figure 19-16.

Figure 19-16. Adding the LINQ to SQL classes

In the Server Explorer, create a connection to the AdventureWorks database. Expand the list of tables from this connection, and drag the following tables to the `AdventureWorkds.dbml` design surface:

- Product
- ProductCategory
- ProductModel
- ProductSubcategory
- ProductReview
- UnitMeasure

The diagram should be similar to Figure 19-17.

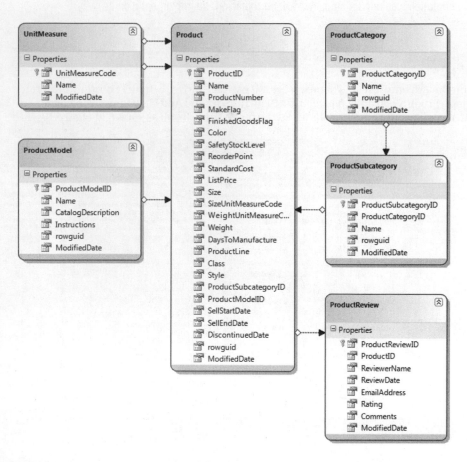

Figure 19-17. `AdventureWorks.dbml` *tables*

Configuring the Database Connection

Now you'll put the database connection string in a settings file so it can be configured. In the Solution Explorer, right-click the WF_Chapter19 project, and choose Add ▶ New Item. In the Add New Item dialog box, select the Settings template from the General group. Enter the name **Settings.settings**, as shown in Figure 19-18.

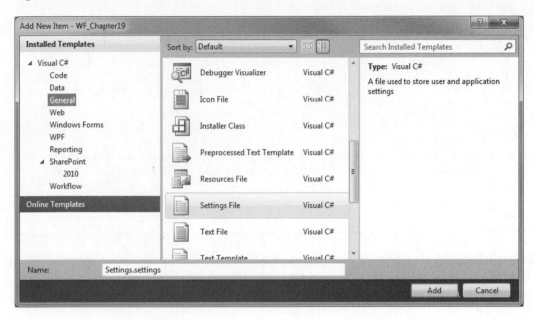

Figure 19-18. Adding a settings file

In the `Settings.settings` file, add a new setting named **AdventureWorksConnectionString**, and change the scope to **Application**. Enter an appropriate connection string for the value field. Your settings file should look like Figure 19-19.

Name	Type	Scope	Value
AdventureWorksConnectionString	string	Application	Data Source=SVR01\SQL8R2;Initial Catalog=AdventureWorks;Integrated Security=True
*			

Figure 19-19. The `AdventureWorksConnectionString` setting

The LINQ to SQL template generated a class named `AdventureWorksDataContext` that provides the data context for the SQL queries. Now you'll implement a partial class to add a default constructor that uses the new settings file. In the Solution Explorer, right-click the WF_Chapter19 project, choose Add ▶ Class, and enter the class name **AdventureWorksDataContext.cs**. Listing 19-3 shows the implementation for this class.

Listing 19-3. Implementation of AdventureWorksDataContext.cs Class

```
using System;

namespace WF_Chapter19
{
    public partial class AdventureWorksDataContext
    {
        public AdventureWorksDataContext() :
            base(global::WF_Chapter19.Settings.Default.AdventureWorksConnectionString,
                mappingSource)
        {
            OnCreated();
        }
    }
}
```

This constructor gets the connection string from the settings file and passes it into the standard constructor. This will allow you to use this class in your operations without needing to deal with the connection string.

■ **Tip** To add the additional constructor, you could have simply edited the class that was generated by the LINQ to SQL template, which is in the `AdventureWorkds.designer.cs` file. However, you should not do that because the file can be regenerated if you make any table changes, and your constructor would be deleted. This is exactly the purpose of partial classes. They allow you to add a method to an existing class while keeping your extensions in a separate file.

Implementing the Operations

Now you're ready to implement the `ReadItem()` and `ReadList()` methods. Open the `ProductDetailService.cs` file, and enter the implementation shown in Listing 19-4.

Listing 19-4. Implementation of ProductDetailService.cs

```
using System;
using System.Collections.Generic;
using System.Linq;

namespace WF_Chapter19.ProductDetail
{
    public class ProductDetailService
    {
        public static ProductDetail ReadItem(int productID)
        {
            AdventureWorksDataContext dc = new AdventureWorksDataContext();
```

```
        Product p = dc.Products.SingleOrDefault(x => x.ProductID == productID);

        if (p != null)
            return ExtractProduct(p);
        else
            return null;
    }

    public static IEnumerable<ProductDetail> ReadList()
    {
        AdventureWorksDataContext dc = new AdventureWorksDataContext();

        List<ProductDetail> list = new List<ProductDetail>();

        IEnumerable<Product> q = dc.Products;
        foreach (Product p in q)
        {
            list.Add(ExtractProduct(p));
        }

        return list.AsEnumerable<ProductDetail>();
    }

    internal static ProductDetail ExtractProduct(Product product)
    {
        ProductDetail d = new ProductDetail();

        d.Class = product.Class;
        d.Color = product.Color;
        d.FinishedGoodsFlag = product.FinishedGoodsFlag;
        d.ListPrice = product.ListPrice;
        d.MakeFlag = product.MakeFlag;
        d.Name = product.Name;
        d.ProductID = product.ProductID;
        d.ProductLine = product.ProductLine;
        d.ProductNumber = product.ProductNumber;
        d.Size = product.Size;
        d.StandardCost = product.StandardCost;
        d.Style = product.Style;

        if (product.ProductModel != null)
            d.ProductModel = product.ProductModel.Name;

        if (product.ProductSubcategory != null)
        {
            d.Subcategory = product.ProductSubcategory.Name;
            if (product.ProductSubcategory.ProductCategory != null)
                d.Category = product.ProductSubcategory.ProductCategory.Name;
        }

        if (product.Weight.HasValue)
```

```
                d.Weight = product.Weight.Value;

            if (product.UnitMeasure != null)
                d.SizeUOM = product.UnitMeasure.Name;
            if (product.UnitMeasure1 != null)
                d.WeightUOM = product.UnitMeasure1.Name;

            return d;
        }
    }
}
```

The implementation provides an `ExtractProduct()` helper method that extracts the properties from the `Product` class that is returned from the LINQ query and copies the data to the `ProductDetail` class that represents the external content type. This method also copies properties from associated tables, providing a slightly flattened view of the product tables.

The implementation of the `ReadItem()` and `ReadList()` method is then a simple matter of executing the query and returning the data using the helper method.

Testing the ProductDetail External Content Type

Press F6 to build the solution, and fix any compile errors. In the Solution Explorer, right-click the WF_Chapter19 project, and choose Deploy. This will install this external content type on the SharePoint server. Launch the SharePoint Central Administration application, and grant yourself access to the `ProductDetail` external content type. The steps for doing this are explained in the previous chapter.

Start a web browser, and go to the Part5 SharePoint site. From the Site Actions menu, choose More Options. Select the External List template, as shown in Figure 19-20, and click the Create button.

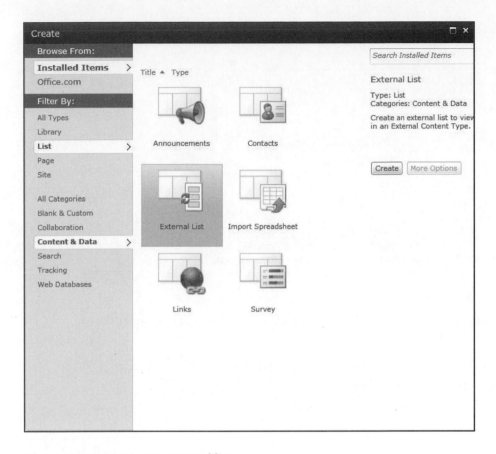

Figure 19-20. Creating an external list

Enter the name of the new list as **Products**. Next to the External Content Type field there is a picker control. Click it to display a list of available external content types. The dialog box shown in Figure 19-21 will be displayed.

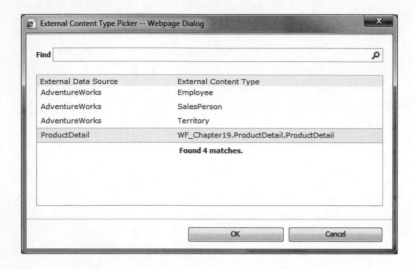

Figure 19-21. Selecting the external content type

Select the `WF_Chapter19.ProductDetail.ProductDetail` external content type, and click OK. Figure 19-22 shows the completed dialog box.

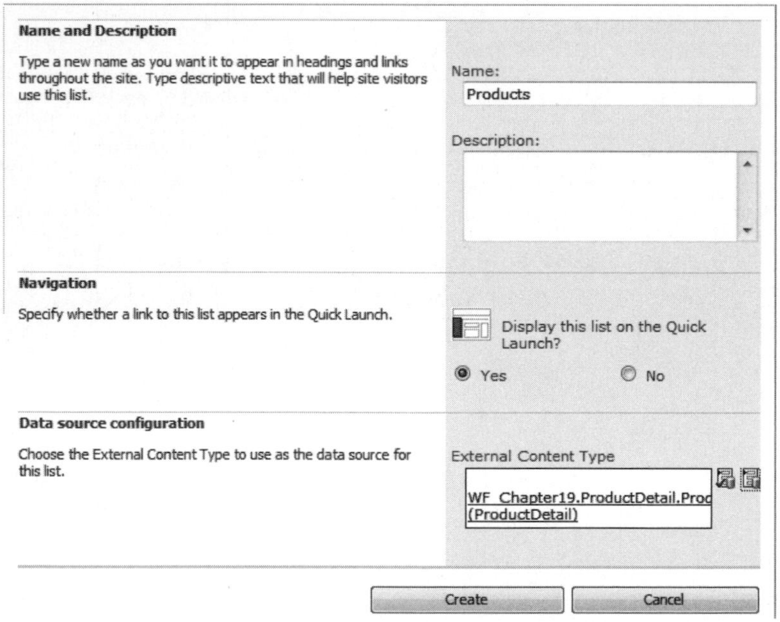

Figure 19-22. The completed External List dialog box

Click the Create button to create the new **Products** list. The **Products** list should look like Figure 19-23.

	ProductID	Name	ProductNumber	MakeFlag	FinishedGoodsFlag	Color	StandardCost	ListPrice
☐	1	Adjustable Race	AR-5381	No	No		0.0000	0.0000
	2	Bearing Ball	BA-8327	No	No		0.0000	0.0000
	3	BB Ball Bearing	BE-2349	Yes	No		0.0000	0.0000
	4	Headset Ball Bearings	BE-2908	No	No		0.0000	0.0000
	316	Blade	BL-2036	Yes	No		0.0000	0.0000
	317	LL Crankarm	CA-5965	No	No	Black	0.0000	0.0000
	318	ML Crankarm	CA-6738	No	No	Black	0.0000	0.0000
	319	HL Crankarm	CA-7457	No	No	Black	0.0000	0.0000
	320	Chainring Bolts	CB-2903	No	No	Silver	0.0000	0.0000
	321	Chainring Nut	CN-6137	No	No	Silver	0.0000	0.0000
	322	Chainring	CR-7833	No	No	Black	0.0000	0.0000
	323	Crown Race	CR-9981	No	No		0.0000	0.0000
	324	Chain Stays	CS-2812	Yes	No		0.0000	0.0000
	325	Decal 1	DC-8732	No	No		0.0000	0.0000
	326	Decal 2	DC-9824	No	No		0.0000	0.0000

*Figure 19-23. A sample view of the **Products** list*

Click the **ProductID** of one of the products to display the view form. It should look similar to Figure 19-24.

Figure 19-24. A sample product item view form

Notice that the edit controls are disabled because you only implemented the read operations.

Creating a Updatable External Content Type

Now you'll implement another external content type that provides access to the product reviews. You will provide all the CRUD operations so items can be added, updated, and deleted from the SharePoint site. Open the `ProductDetail.bdcm` file. Open the Toolbox if it's not already open. Notice that there is an `Entity` control in the Toolbox, as shown in Figure 19-25.

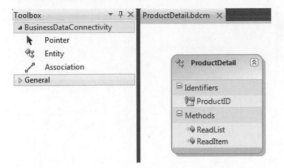

Figure 19-25. The Business Data Connectivity Toolbox

Adding a New Entity

You can easily add additional entities to the BDC model by dragging the `Entity` control to the diagram. Create a new entity, and the diagram should look like Figure 19-26.

Figure 19-26. Adding a new entity to the model

The new entity is called `Entity` and has no identifiers or methods. If you select this entity, the Method Details window will also be empty. The first entity generated by the template had the basic properties to support a read-only external content type. Additional entities, however, are blank.

Click the `Entity`, and change its name to **Review**. Right-click the Identifier section, and choose Add new Identifier. Change the name to **ProductReviewID**. In the Properties window, change the `Type Name` property to `System.Int32`.

Defining the Data Class

Visual Studio automatically created the `ReviewService.cs` class that will implement the operations. However, it did not create a class to define the fields. In the Solution Explorer, right-click the `ProductDetail` folder, choose Add ▶ Class, and enter the class name **Review.cs**. Listing 19-5 shows the implementation for this file.

Listing 19-5. The Implementation of Review.cs

```
using System;

namespace WF_Chapter19.ProductDetail
{
    public partial class Review
    {
        public int ProductReviewID { get; set; }
        public int ProductID { get; set; }
        public string ReviewerName { get; set; }
        public string EmailAddress { get; set; }
        public int Rating { get; set; }
        public string Comments { get; set; }
        public DateTime ReviewDate { get; set; }
        public DateTime ModifiedDate { get; set; }
    }
}
```

Defining the ReadItem Method

Right-click the Methods sections, and choose Add new Method. Change the name to **ReadItem**. In the Method Details window, click the *<Add a Parameter>* control, expand the drop-down list, and click *Create Parameter*, as shown in Figure 19-27.

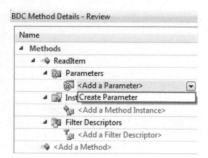

Figure 19-27. Adding a new parameter

In the Properties window, change the `Name` property to **productReviewID**. In the Method Details window, select the corresponding `Type Descriptor`, and in the Properties window change the `Name` property to **ProductReviewID** and the `Type Name` property to `System.Int32`. Also, make sure you update the `Identifier` property by selecting `ProductReviewID` from the drop-down list.

Repeat this step to create the return parameter. Enter the parameter name as **review** and the `Type Descriptor Name` property as **Review**. Change the `Direction` property to `Return`. For the `Type Descriptor` property, in the Properties window, click the second tab named Current Project, shown in Figure 19-28.

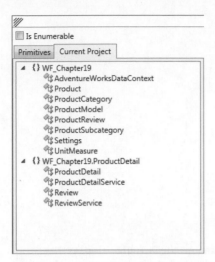

Figure 19-28. Selecting a type from the current project

Select the `Review` class in the `ProductDetail` namespace. The Properties window should look like Figure 19-29.

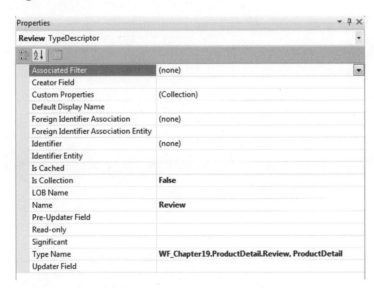

Figure 19-29. The completed Properties window

Next, add a method instance by clicking the *<Add a Method Instance>* control, expanding the drop-down list, and clicking *Create Finder Instance*, as shown in Figure 19-30.

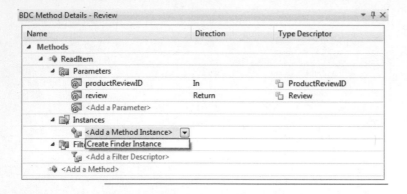

Figure 19-30. Adding a method instance

In the Properties window, change the Name property to **ReadItem** and the Default Display Name property to **Read Review**. Select the Type as **SpecificFinder**, and select the Return Parameter Name as **review**. You'll also need to update the Return Type Descriptor by selecting **Review** from the drop-down list. The completed Properties window should look like Figure 19-31.

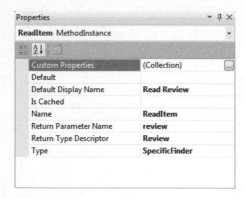

Figure 19-31. The Properties window for the ReadItem method instance

Defining the Review Fields

The last step is to define the fields that are included in the **Review** object. Go to the BDC Explorer, and expand the **Review** entity, as shown in Figure 19-32.

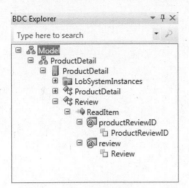

Figure 19-32. Expanding the Review entity

Right-click the last **Review** node, and choose Add Type Descriptor. In the Properties window, change the **Name** property to **ProductReviewID** and the **Type Name** property to **System.Int32**. Also, for the **Identifier** property, select the **ProductReviewID** identifier from the drop-down list. The completed Properties window should look like Figure 19-33.

Figure 19-33. The completed Properties window for ProductReviewID

Table 19-2 lists all the fields that should be included in the **Review** entity and the appropriate **Type Name** property. Add the remaining nodes by right-clicking the **Review** node, adding a **Type Descriptor** property, and changing its **Name** and **Type Name** properties.

Table 19-2. Fields to Be Included in the Review Entity

Name	TypeName
ProductReviewID	System.Int32
ProductID	System.Int32
ReviewerName	System.String
ProductNumber	System.String
EmailAddress	System.String
StandardCost	System.Decimal
Rating	System.Int32
Comments	System.String
ReviewDate	System.DateTime
ModifiedDate	System.DateTime

The BDC Explorer should look like Figure 19-34.

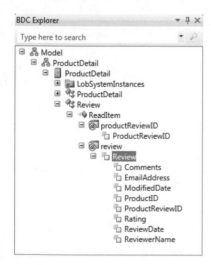

Figure 19-34. The ReadItem nodes

Creating the Remaining Operations

Now you'll implement the remaining methods, which will go a lot faster because Visual Studio will generate most of the details for you using the information you entered for the `ReadItem` method. In the Method Details window, click the *<Add a Method>* control, and then click *Create Finder Method*, as shown in Figure 19-35.

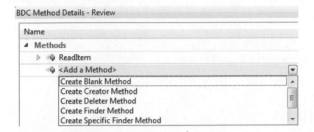

Figure 19-35. Adding a finder method

This will generate a `ReadList` method, and the parameter and method instance are set up just like the `ReadItem` was. For the `ReadItem` method, the first character of the parameter name was lowercase, and the first character of the parameter type was uppercase. This same naming convention is carried forward to the `ReadList` method. Even the fields in the BDC Explorer are copied from the `ReadItem` method.

Repeat this step to generate `Creator`, `Deleter`, and `Updater` methods.

Removing Fields

When creating a new `Review`, we don't want all the fields provided by the client. The identifier, `ProductReviewID`, for example, will be generated by the database when the insert is performed. Also, the `ReviewDate` and `ModifiedDate` fields should not be set by the user; instead, they are set by the system using the current date/time. We could just ignore these fields when implementing the create method. However, these fields would still be on the form, and the user would need to provide something just to have it ignored.

We can have a different set of fields on each method. The best approach is to simply remove these fields from the method definition. Go to the BDC Explorer, and expand the `Create` node. Notice that there are two sets of fields. The `newReview` object represents the data being passed in, and the `returnReview` is the data being passed back. At first, this might seem redundant since they should be the same. But this is exactly what we need to handle this situation. The `newReview` object will have a subset of the fields, while the `returnReview` object will have the complete object. Remove the following nodes from the `newReview` object:

- `ProductReviewID`
- `ReviewDate`
- `ModifiedDate`

When updating a record, you may not want certain fields to change, or you'll want to control the value of those fields. The `ProductID` is a good example. Once a review is created for a product, we don't usually want to assign that review to a different product. The ProductID should not change once the record is created. The same is true with the ReviewDate. Also, the ModifiedDate should be set by the system, not the user. Remove the following fields from the Update method:

- ProductID

- ReviewDate

- ModifiedDate

You will also mark these same fields as read-only on the ReadItem method. This will specify that these fields should not be included on the edit form. Expand the ReadItem node, and select the ProductID node. In the Properties window, set the Read-only property to True. Do the same thing to the ReviewDate and ModifiedDate fields.

Implementing the CRUD Operations

Now you're ready to implement the methods defined in the BDC model. Open the ReviewService.cs class. Notice that all five methods have been generated with no implementation (actually, the implementation simply throws an exception). Listing 19-6 shows the initial implementation.

Listing 19-6. The Initial Implementation of ReviewService.cs

```
using System;
using System.Collections.Generic;
using System.Linq;
using System.Text;
namespace WF_Chapter19.ProductDetail
{
    public partial class ReviewService
    {
        public static Review ReadItem(int productReviewID)
        {
            throw new System.NotImplementedException();
        }

        public static IEnumerable<Review> ReadList()
        {
            throw new System.NotImplementedException();
        }

        public static Review Create(Review newReview)
        {
            throw new System.NotImplementedException();
        }

        public static void Delete(int productReviewID)
        {
            throw new System.NotImplementedException();
        }
```

```
        public static void Update(Review review)
        {
            throw new System.NotImplementedException();
        }
    }
}
```

To implement these methods, you'll use the same LINQ classes that you generated previously. Listing 19-7 shows the complete implementation of this class.

Listing 19-7. The Final Implementation of ReviewService.cs

```
using System;
using System.Collections.Generic;
using System.Linq;

namespace WF_Chapter19.ProductDetail
{
    public partial class ReviewService
    {
        public static Review ReadItem(int productReviewID)
        {
            AdventureWorksDataContext dc = new AdventureWorksDataContext();

            ProductReview pr = dc.ProductReviews
                .SingleOrDefault(x => x.ProductReviewID == productReviewID);

            if (pr != null)
                return ExtractReview(pr);
            else
                return null;
        }

        public static IEnumerable<Review> ReadList()
        {
            AdventureWorksDataContext dc = new AdventureWorksDataContext();

            List<Review> list = new List<Review>();

            IEnumerable<ProductReview> q = dc.ProductReviews;
            foreach (ProductReview pr in q)
            {
                list.Add(ExtractReview(pr));
            }

            return list.AsEnumerable<Review>();
        }

        public static Review Create(Review newReview)
        {
            AdventureWorksDataContext dc = new AdventureWorksDataContext();
```

```
    // Create and initialize a ProductReview
    ProductReview pr = new ProductReview();

    pr.Comments = newReview.Comments;
    pr.EmailAddress = newReview.EmailAddress;
    pr.ProductID = newReview.ProductID;
    pr.Rating = newReview.Rating;
    pr.ReviewerName = newReview.ReviewerName;

    pr.ReviewDate = DateTime.UtcNow;
    pr.ModifiedDate = DateTime.UtcNow;

    // Insert the record
    dc.ProductReviews.InsertOnSubmit(pr);
    dc.SubmitChanges();

    // Now read it back
    ProductReview pr1 = dc.ProductReviews
        .SingleOrDefault(x => x.ProductReviewID == pr.ProductReviewID);

    if (pr1 != null)
        return ExtractReview(pr1);
    else
        return null;
}

public static void Delete(int productReviewID)
{
    AdventureWorksDataContext dc = new AdventureWorksDataContext();

    ProductReview pr = dc.ProductReviews
        .SingleOrDefault(x => x.ProductReviewID == productReviewID);

    if (pr != null)
    {
        dc.ProductReviews.DeleteOnSubmit(pr);
        dc.SubmitChanges();
    }
}

public static void Update(Review review)
{
    AdventureWorksDataContext dc = new AdventureWorksDataContext();

    ProductReview pr = dc.ProductReviews
        .SingleOrDefault(x => x.ProductReviewID == review.ProductReviewID);

    pr.Comments = review.Comments;
    pr.EmailAddress = review.EmailAddress;
    pr.Rating = review.Rating;
    pr.ReviewerName = review.ReviewerName;
```

```
        pr.ModifiedDate = DateTime.UtcNow;

        // Update the record
        dc.SubmitChanges();
    }

    internal static Review ExtractReview(ProductReview review)
    {
        Review r = new Review();

        r.Comments = review.Comments;
        r.EmailAddress = review.EmailAddress;
        r.ProductID = review.ProductID;
        r.ProductReviewID = review.ProductReviewID;
        r.Rating = review.Rating;
        r.ReviewDate = review.ReviewDate;
        r.ReviewerName = review.ReviewerName;
        r.ModifiedDate = review.ModifiedDate;

        return r;
    }
  }
}
```

This code uses standard LINQ methods to read and write the data from and to the database. It uses a helper method called `ExtractReview()` to copy the fields from the `ProductReview` LINQ class.

■ **Tip** Since the members of the Review class are identical to the LINQ class (ProductReview), you could have just used the ProductReview class. With that approach, you don't need this mapping method. However, often the members are different, and you'll need this mapping code. Using it here doesn't add much overhead, and it keeps your design cleaner to have a separation between the external content type definition and the table definition.

Testing the Review External Content Type

Now you're ready to test. Press F5 to build the solution, and fix any compiler errors. From the Solution Explorer, right-click the WF_Chapter19 project, and choose Deploy. Using the SharePoint Central Administration application, grant yourself access to the `Review` external content type as explained previously. Start a web browser, and go to the Part5 SharePoint site. You'll create a new external list the same way you created the `Products` list earlier. From the Site Actions menu, choose More Options. Select the External List template, and click the Create button. Enter the list name as **Product Reviews**. Click the picker control, and select the `Review` external content type.

Open the SharePoint site, and select the `Product Reviews` list. Select one of the records to display the view form, which is shown in Figure 19-36.

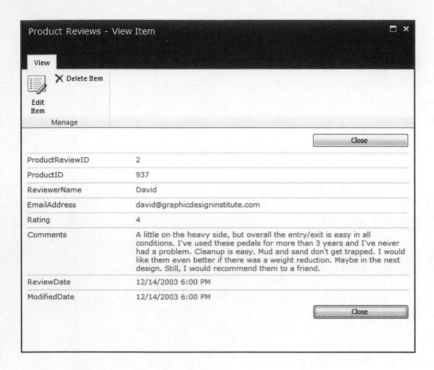

Figure 19-36. Displaying a product review

Notice that the edit and delete controls on the form are enabled. Also, the list should have a link to create a new item. Click it to display the new item form, as shown in Figure 19-37.

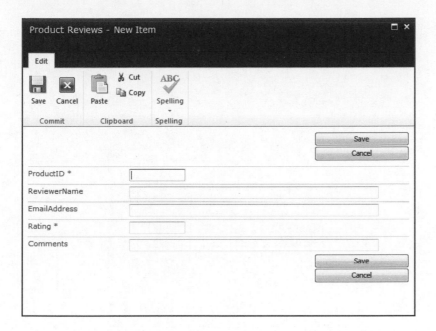

Figure 19-37. Creating a new product review

Notice that some of the fields are missing because these are being set by the system.

Creating an Association

Now you'll create an association between these two external content types. Open the
ProductDetail.bdcm file. Notice in the Toolbox that there is an Association control. Click it, click the
ProductDetail entity, and then click the Review entity.

Defining Associations

The Association Editor shown in Figure 19-38 will be displayed.

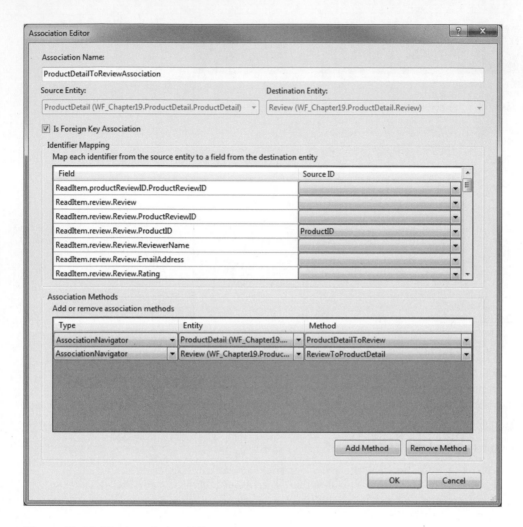

Figure 19-38. The Association Editor

Most associations are based on a common field. A field in one entity, called a *foreign key*, is used as a primary key in another entity. In our case, the `ProductID` in the `Review` entity serves as a foreign key to the `ProductDetail` entity. When creating an association based on a foreign key, the top portion of this form allows you to indicate the foreign key fields and which field represents the primary key in the related entity.

■ **Tip** If you deselect the *Is Foreign Key Association* check box, the Identifier Mapping section will be grayed out so you cannot define any mapping.

Every place that `ProductID` appears in the `Field` column, select `ProductID` from the associated drop-down list in the `SourceID` column. Make sure you update all instances of `ProductID`; there are four of them. For each one, select `ProductID` as the `SourceID`.

The bottom portion of the form defines the methods that are used to implement the association. These are generated for you automatically. There is a method for each entity that returns the related objects. For example, the `ProductDetail` entity will have a method that returns all the `Review` entities for that product.

Click OK to close the form. Notice in the BDC model shown in Figure 19-39 that there is a line between the two entities representing the association you just defined.

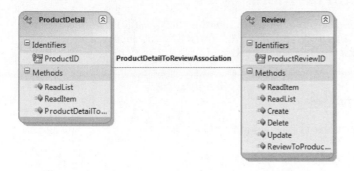

Figure 19-39. The BDC model showing an association

There is also an additional method in each entity. This method is included in the Method Details window shown in Figure 19-40.

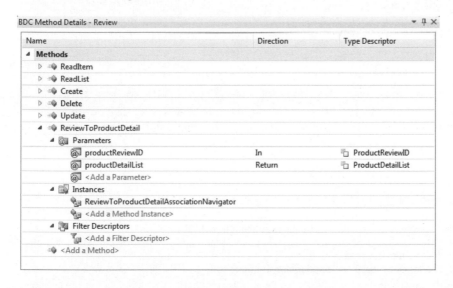

Figure 19-40. The Method Details window with the association method

549

The new method is called **ReviewToProductDetail**, and the method instance is named **ReviewToProductDetailAssociationManager**. By default, this rather long name will be used for the label in the SharePoint forms. Click this method instance, and in the Properties window, set the **Default Display Name** property to **Reviews**. If this property is specified, it will be used on the forms instead of the **Name** property.

Likewise, click the **ProductDetail** entity, and select the method instance for that association method. Change its **Default DisplayName** to **Product**.

Implementing the Association Methods

Open the **ProductDetailService.cs** class, and scroll to the bottom of the file. You should notice that a new method called **ProductDetailToReview** has been generated for you. It takes a **ProductID** as a parameter and returns a collection of **Review** entities. You'll need to supply the implementation using the code shown in Listing 19-8.

Listing 19-8. Implementation of ProductDetailToReview

```
public static IEnumerable<Review> ProductDetailToReview(int productID)
{
    AdventureWorksDataContext dc = new AdventureWorksDataContext();

    IEnumerable<ProductReview> q = dc.ProductReviews
        .Where(x => x.ProductID == productID);


    List<Review> list = new List<Review>();
    foreach (ProductReview pr in q)
    {
        list.Add(ReviewService.ExtractReview(pr));
    }

    return list.AsEnumerable<Review>();
}
```

This code simply looks up the **ProductReview** records with the specified **ProductID**. Now open the **ReviewService.cs** file, and enter the implementation for its association method using the code shown in Listing 19-9.

Listing 19-9. Implementation of ReviewToProductDetail

```
public static IEnumerable<ProductDetail> ReviewToProductDetail(int productReviewID)
{
    AdventureWorksDataContext dc = new AdventureWorksDataContext();

    ProductReview pr = dc.ProductReviews
        .Single(x => x.ProductReviewID == productReviewID);

    List<ProductDetail> list = new List<ProductDetail>();
```

```
IEnumerable<Product> q = dc.Products.Where(x => x.ProductID == pr.ProductID);
foreach (Product p in q)
{
    list.Add(ProductDetailService.ExtractProduct(p));
}

return list.AsEnumerable<ProductDetail>();
}
```

Even though the method returns a collection of `ProductDetail` entities, the collection will have, at most, one object in it.

Testing the Changes

Before testing these changes, you'll need to go to the SharePoint site and delete the existing `Products` and `Product Reviews` lists. You will re-create these after you have updated the external content types. You won't lose any data by deleting the lists since the lists don't actually store any data. The data, including any changes you've made, are stored in the external data store, the AdventureWorks database, in this case.

Press F6 to rebuild the solution, and fix any compiler errors. Then from the Solution Explorer, right-click the WF_Chapter19 project, and choose Deploy, which will deploy the updated content types to your SharePoint site. Re-create both the `Products` and `Product Reviews` lists just like you did earlier.

Go to the SharePoint site, and display the `Product Reviews` list. Scroll to the bottom of the list, and click the link to create a new item. The new item form shown in Figure 19-41 will be displayed.

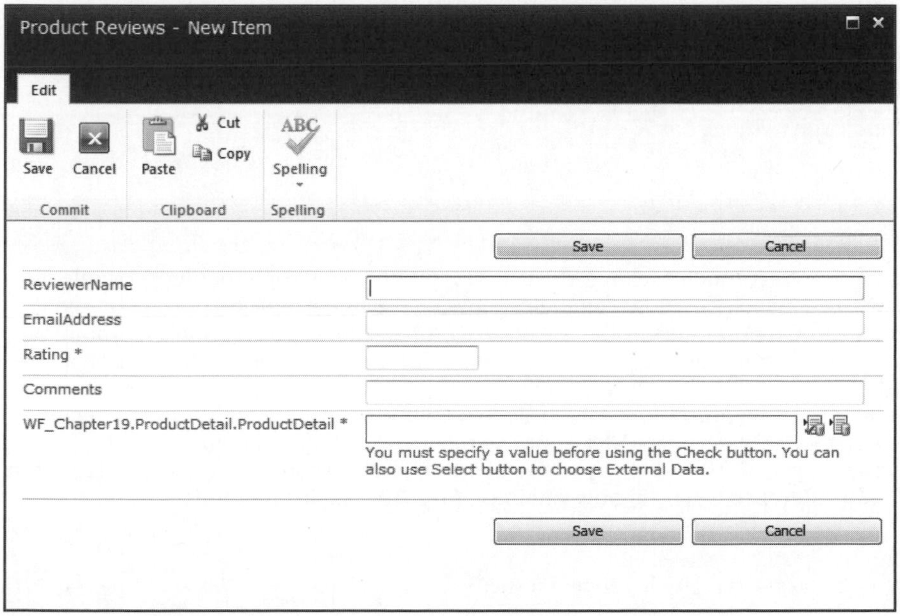

Figure 19-41. The Product Review new item form

551

Notice there is a picker control next to the `Product` field. This allows you to verify or search for a `ProductID`. Click the picker control, and the search dialog box shown in Figure 19-42 will be displayed.

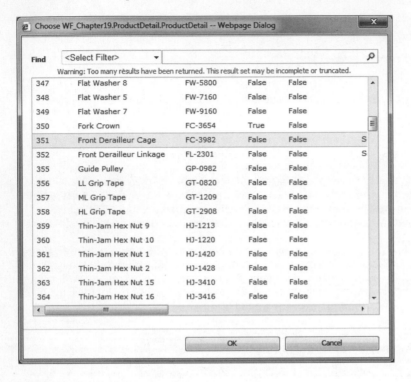

Figure 19-42. The product search dialog box

Summary

The project in this chapter was very much like the project in Chapter 18. You implemented a couple of external content types with an association between them, allowing the use of a picker control on the forms. The basic concepts are the same such as the use of CRUD operations and creating a method to implement an association. The technique used, however, is very different. In Chapter 18 you used a no-code approach, while this one requires writing code in Visual Studio 2010.

This project used the same AdventureWorks database to simplify the implementation. But I want you to see that any data that you can get from .NET code can be provided to SharePoint using this technique. You can access proprietary data formats, interrogate external systems, or aggregate data from multiple sources. The only difference will be in how you implement the service methods.

■ ■ ■

Using External Lists in Outlook

In this chapter I'll show you how you can integrate external lists into Outlook 2010. You'll use the Employee list that you created in Chapter 18 and link it as a contact list in Outlook 2010. The employee data in the AdventureWorks database can then be viewed in Outlook with the same rich-client experience.

■ **Note** This chapter requires the solution described in Chapter 18. If you have not implemented that yet, you'll need to first create the Employee and Territory external content types and then create the Employees external list.

Linking the External Content Type

Launch the SharePoint Designer, and navigate to the Part5 site. Click the *External Content Types* link in the Navigation pane. If you've been working the projects for each chapter, you should have five external content types listed, as shown in Figure 20-1.

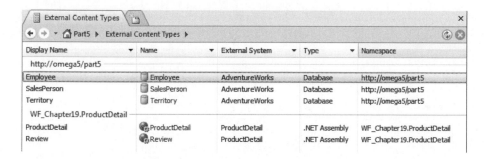

Figure 20-1. Listing the existing external content types

Mapping to Office

Select the `Employee` external content type. The External Content Type Information section should look like Figure 20-2.

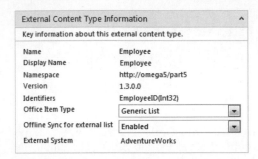

Figure 20-2. The Employee External Content Type Information section

There are two properties here that I did not explain when this content type was created. The `Office Item Type` property is set by default to `Generic List`, and the `Offline Sync for external list` property is `Enabled`. To be able to link this list in Outlook, you'll need to specify the appropriate Outlook item type to map this to. Expand the drop-down list, and you'll see the available choices. Select `Contact`, as shown in Figure 20-3.

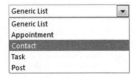

Figure 20-3. Selecting the `Contact` item type

Now notice the warning in the External Content Type Operations section shown in Figure 20-4.

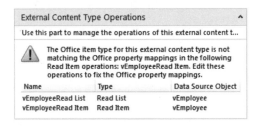

Figure 20-4. The External Content Type Operations section showing a warning

To finish this process, you'll also need to map the columns in the external content type to the appropriate properties of the `Contact` object. The `Contact` requires that at least the `LastName` property must have a value, and this warning appears because no column is yet mapped to this property. This warning also lets you know that it is the `ReadItem` operation that is used to define the mapping to Outlook. You don't have to map the other operations.

Double-click the `ReadItem` operation, and click the Next button twice to display the Return Parameter Configuration dialog box. Select the `LastName` column. Notice that the `Office Property` is currently set to `Custom Property`. This is the default value that all the columns are mapped to. In the `Office Property` drop-down list, select `Last Name`, as shown in Figure 20-5.

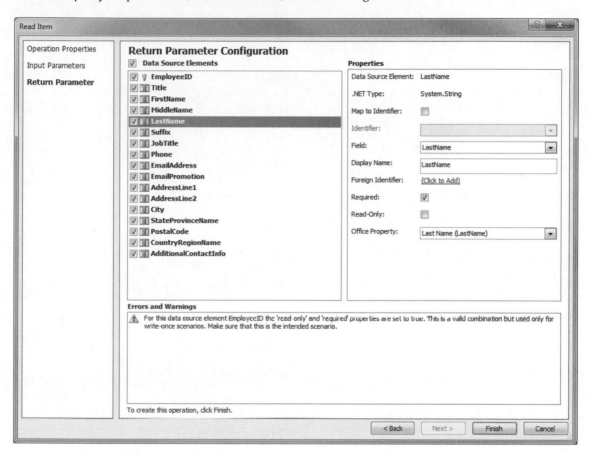

Figure 20-5. Specifying the Office Property setting

That takes care of the minimum requirement. However, you should also map as many of the other columns as you can. There are a lot of `Contact` properties to choose from. Table 20-1 shows how I mapped mine, but you can choose to use other properties if you prefer.

Table 20-1. Column Mapping

ECT Column	Office Property
EmployeeID	Custom Property
Title	Title
FirstName	First Name
MiddleName	Middle Name
LastName	Last Name
Suffix	Suffix
JobTitle	Job Title
Phone	Business Telephone Number
EmailAddress	Email 1 Address
EmailPromotion	Custom Property
AddressLine1	Business Address Street
AddressLine2	Business Address
City	Business Address City
StateProvinceName	Business Address State
PostalCode	Business Address Postal Code
CountryRegionName	Custom Property
AdditionalContactInfo	Custom Property

When you're done mapping the columns, click the Finish button. Click the Save button in the SharePoint Designer. This will update the metadata store.

Connecting to Outlook

At this point, the `Employee` external content type has been configured, so it knows how to map to Outlook. Go to the Part5 SharePoint site, and select the `Employees` list. In the List ribbon, click the Connect to Outlook button, as shown in Figure 20-6.

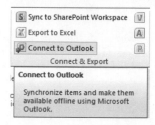

Figure 20-6. Connecting to Outlook

The SharePoint Designer generated an installation package. This needs to be installed on the local Office client for every user who wants to link to the `Employee` list. SharePoint makes this easy through what is referred to as a *ClickOnce installation*. The Connect to Outlook button will start this installation. You should see the prompt shown in Figure 20-7. Click the Install button to confirm the installation.

Figure 20-7. Installing the Office customization

■ **Tip** This dialog box appears because the package autogenerated by SharePoint is not signed with a trusted certificate. To prevent this dialog box, you'll need to provide a certificate to SharePoint that is trusted by your client. For more information, see the article at `http://msdn.microsoft.com/en-us/library/ff394644(v=office.14).aspx`.

When the installation has finished, you should see the notification shown in Figure 20-8.

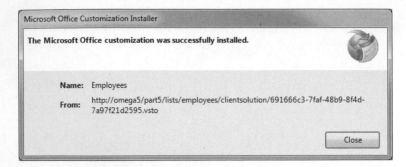

Figure 20-8. *Installation confirmation*

After a few seconds, Outlook 2010 should start and display the employees in a contact list similar to Figure 20-9.

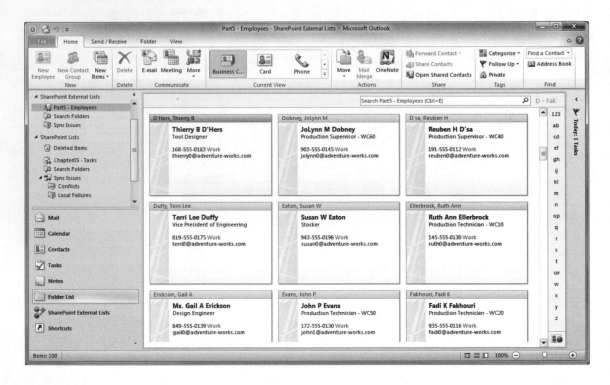

Figure 20-9. *Outlook displaying the Employee list*

With the data now in Outlook, you can use Outlook's organization tools to format the data to suit your needs. There are several predefined views that you can select from the ribbon. You can create your own custom views as well.

Double-click one of these employees. You should see a details window similar to Figure 20-10.

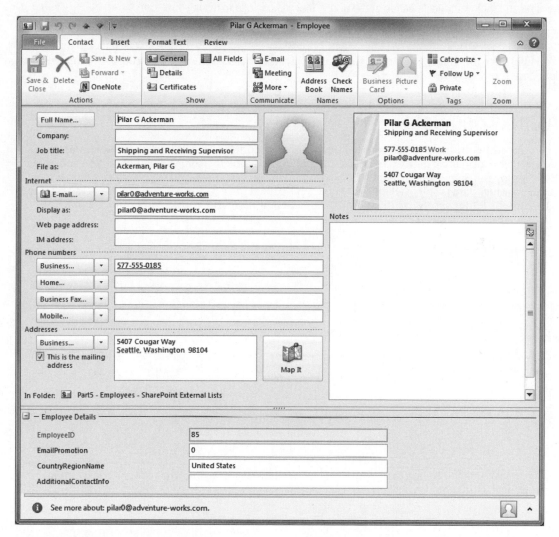

Figure 20-10. Employee details window

Notice the Employee Details pane at the bottom of the window. All the columns that were mapped as `Custom Property` are displayed here. This allows you to include custom data items not supported by the standard `Contact` object.

■ **Note** If there are five or less custom columns, they are displayed at the bottom of the window, as shown in Figure 20-10. However, if there are more than five columns, they will be displayed in a separate form. In this case, there will be an Employee Details button in the ribbon that you can use to display this form.

You also have the ability to create a custom view where you can control which custom properties are displayed and how they are organized.

Synchronizing Data

Outlook created a copy of the data provided by the external content type. When you view contacts, Outlook is accessing a local data cache and is not pulling this directly from the database. You can prove this by stopping the SQL Server instance. Close the Outlook application, and then restart it. You'll see that all the contact data is still available.

The Outlook folder list shown in Figure 20-11 has a new item under the SharePoint External Lists section called `Part5 - Employees`.

Figure 20-11. The Outlook folder list

You can force the local data to be synchronized with the server by right-clicking this folder and choosing Sync now, as shown in Figure 20-12.

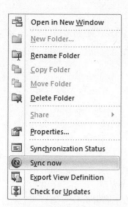

Figure 20-12. Selecting the Sync now command

You can also use the Synchronization Status option to see the details of the most recent synchronization. This will display the Synchronization Status window shown in Figure 20-13.

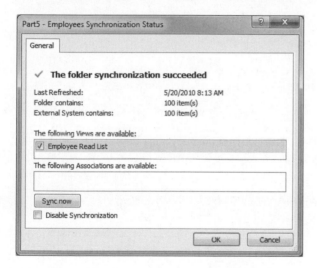

Figure 20-13. The Synchronization Status window

Changing the Limit Filter

You may have noticed that exactly 100 employees were synchronized. This is because when the external content type was created, the default limit filter was set to 100. Now you'll modify this limit value so all the employees will be brought into Outlook.

Open the Part5 SharePoint site, and select the `Employees` list. In the ribbon, click the List Settings button, as shown in Figure 20-14.

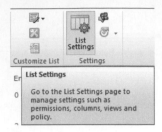

Figure 20-14. Clicking the List Settings button

The existing views are listed at the bottom of the List Settings page, as shown in Figure 20-15.

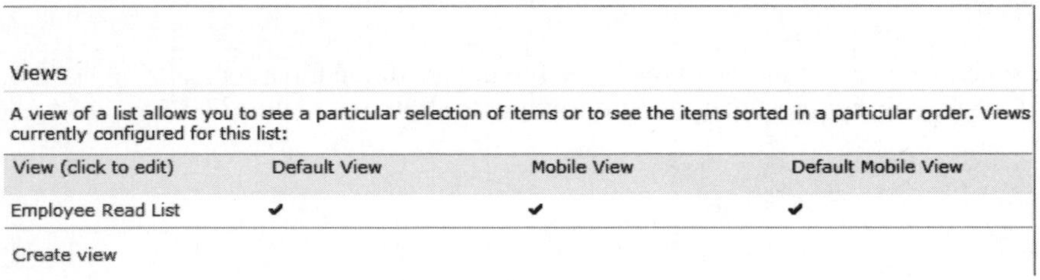

Views

A view of a list allows you to see a particular selection of items or to see the items sorted in a particular order. Views currently configured for this list:

View (click to edit)	Default View	Mobile View	Default Mobile View
Employee Read List	✔	✔	✔

Create view

Figure 20-15. Displaying the existing views

The `Employee Read List` view is used to synchronize the list in Outlook. You can determine this because this is specified in the Synchronization Status dialog box shown in Figure 20-13. Click the *Employee Read List* link to view and edit the view definition. The page shown in Figure 20-16 will be displayed.

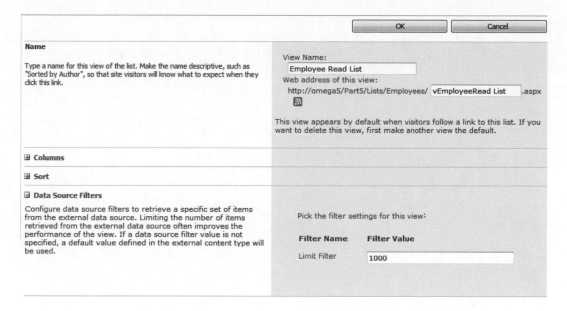

Figure 20-16. The Edit View page

In the Data Source Filters section, change the `Limit Filter` setting to **1000**, and click the OK button.

■ **Tip** You could create a new view instead and in the Synchronization Status dialog box select the new view. Then the web page will display only 100 employees, but all employees will be included when synchronizing with Outlook. Also, you can provide additional filtering if you want only a subset of the employees to be included in Outlook. You could even create multiple views with different filtering options, and each user could choose which view to use. This will allow each user to have a different contact list all from the same common repository.

Applying the Changes

For Outlook to pick up this change, you will need to reinstall the Office customization package. To do this, right-click the Part5 - Employees folder, and choose Check for Updates, as shown in Figure 20-17.

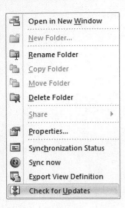

Figure 20-17. Checking for package updates

Follow the instructions, which will probably include closing Outlook. After it has finished installing, Outlook will be resynchronized. If you display the Synchronization Status dialog box, you should see a different number of employees that were synchronized, as shown in Figure 20-18. (Your count can be different from what is shown here.)

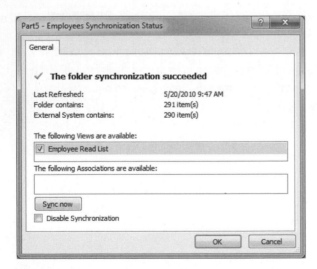

Figure 20-18. The Synchronization Status dialog box

Linking the Territories List

The Employee external content type is read-only. It is based on a read-only database view, and only the ReadItem and ReadList operations were implemented. So, you will not be able to modify any of the employee data from Outlook. To demonstrate the two-way synchronization, you'll now link an external content type that allows both read and write operations.

Modifying the Territory External Content Type

The Territory external content type that you created in Chapter 18 has only the ReadItem and ReadList operations. You'll now add the Create and Update operations. Launch the SharePoint Designer, and then open the Part5 site. Select External Content Types from the Navigation pane, and then select the Territory external content type. Click the Operations Design View button in the ribbon. In the Data Source Explorer, right-click the SalesTerritory table, and choose New Create Operation, as shown in Figure 20-19.

Figure 20-19. Adding the Create operation

Click the Next button twice, and then click the Finish button to accept all the default settings. Right-click the SalesTerritory table again, and choose New Update Operation. Accept all the default settings. Click the Save button to update the metadata store. Click the Summary View button in the ribbon. The summary view should look like Figure 20-20.

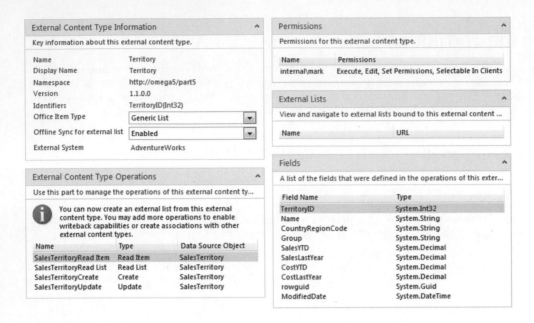

Figure 20-20. The summary view of the `Territory` *external content type*

Mapping to Office

Now you'll need to map the `Territory` external content type to an Office item. There really isn't one that fits well. In that case, you should use the `Post` item because it is the most generic item type. In the External Content Type Information section, select `Post` in the `Office Item Type` drop-down list.

You'll get the same warning as you did with `Employee` because no column is mapped to the mandatory property, which is the `Subject` property. Double-click the `ReadItem` operation. Click the Next button twice to display the Return Parameter Configuration dialog box. Click the `Name` column, and then select `Subject` for the `Office Property`, as shown in Figure 20-21.

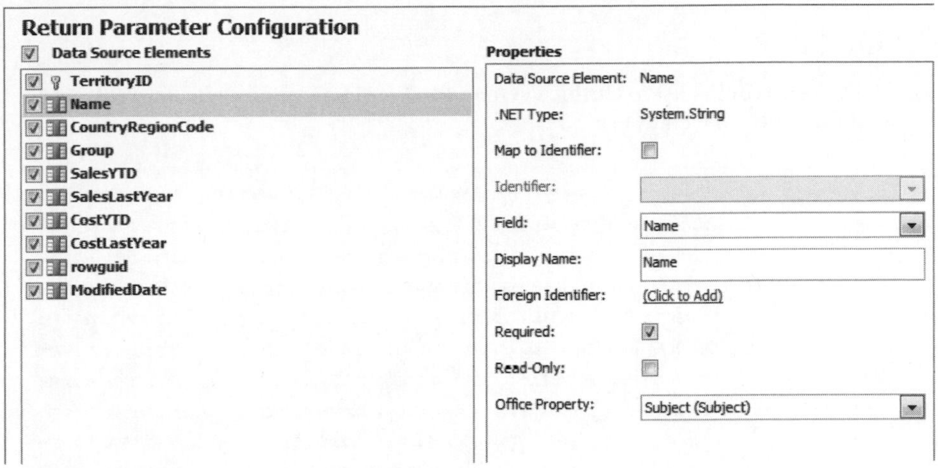

Return Parameter Configuration

☑ **Data Source Elements**

☑ ⦵ **TerritoryID**
☑ ▤ **Name**
☑ ▤ **CountryRegionCode**
☑ ▤ **Group**
☑ ▤ **SalesYTD**
☑ ▤ **SalesLastYear**
☑ ▤ **CostYTD**
☑ ▤ **CostLastYear**
☑ ▤ **rowguid**
☑ ▤ **ModifiedDate**

Properties

Data Source Element:	Name
.NET Type:	System.String
Map to Identifier:	☐
Identifier:	▾
Field:	Name ▾
Display Name:	Name
Foreign Identifier:	(Click to Add)
Required:	☑
Read-Only:	☐
Office Property:	Subject (Subject) ▾

Figure 20-21. Mapping the `Subject` *property*

Click the Finish button, and then click the Save icon to save these changes. Navigate back to the page that lists the external content types. Select the `Territory` external content type, but don't click the link that will open it. Click the External List button in the ribbon. In the Create External List dialog box, enter the `Name` property as **Territories**, as shown in Figure 20-22, and click the OK button.

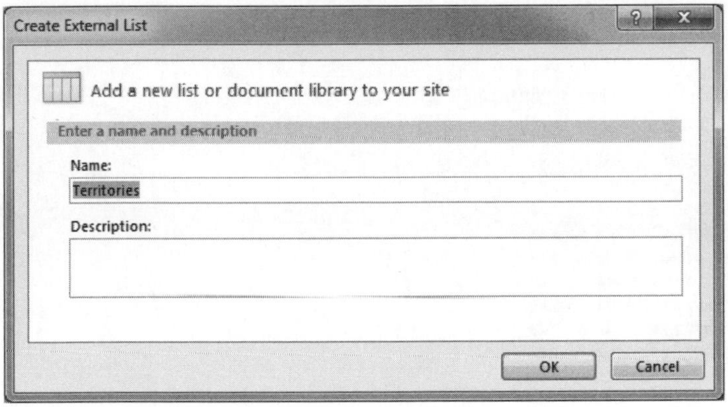

Create External List

▦ Add a new list or document library to your site

Enter a name and description

Name:

Territories

Description:

[OK] [Cancel]

Figure 20-22. Creating a new external list

Connecting to Outlook

Now you're ready to link the **Territories** list to Outlook. Open the Part5 SharePoint site, and select the **Territories** list. The list should look like Figure 20-23.

	TerritoryID	Name	CountryRegionCode	Group	SalesYTD	SalesLastYear	CostYTD	CostLastYear	ModifiedDate
☐	1	Northwest	US	North America	5767341.9752	3298694.4938	0.0000	0.0000	5/31/1998 7:00 PM
	2	Northeast	US	North America	3857163.6331	3607148.9371	0.0000	0.0000	5/31/1998 7:00 PM
	3	Central	US	North America	4677108.2690	3205014.0767	0.0000	0.0000	5/31/1998 7:00 PM
	4	Southwest	US	North America	8351296.7411	5366575.7098	0.0000	0.0000	5/31/1998 7:00 PM
	5	Southeast	US	North America	2851419.0435	3925071.4318	0.0000	0.0000	5/31/1998 7:00 PM
	6	Canada	CA	North America	6917270.8842	5693988.8600	0.0000	0.0000	5/31/1998 7:00 PM
	7	France	FR	Europe	3899045.6940	2396539.7601	0.0000	0.0000	5/31/1998 7:00 PM
	8	Germany	DE	Europe	2481039.1786	1307949.7917	0.0000	0.0000	5/31/1998 7:00 PM
	9	Australia	AU	Pacific	1977474.8096	2278548.9776	0.0000	0.0000	5/31/1998 7:00 PM
	10	United Kingdom	GB	Europe	3514865.9051	1635823.3967	0.0000	0.0000	5/31/1998 7:00 PM

Figure 20-23. The Territories *list*

In the List ribbon, click the Connect to Outlook button. Follow the instructions to install this package just like you did for the **Employees** list. After it has been installed and synchronized, the list in Outlook should look like Figure 20-24.

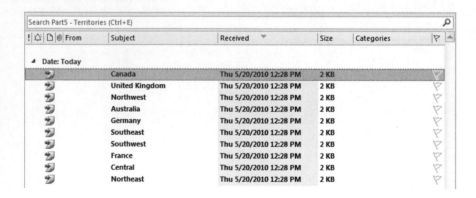

Figure 20-24. The Territories *list in Outlook*

Double-click one of these territories, and then click the Territory Details button in the ribbon. The form should look like Figure 20-25.

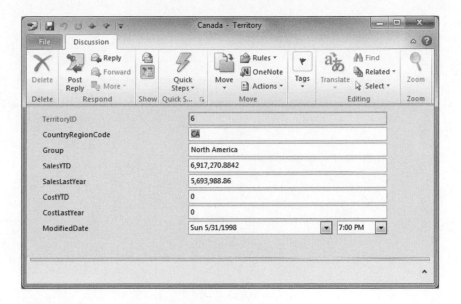

Figure 20-25. Displaying the `Territory` *details*

Enter a value for the `CostYTD` field, save this record, and close the form. In the folder list, right-click the `Part5 - Territories` list, and choose Sync now. You can check the Synchronization Status information to verify the synchronization was successful. Go back to the `Territories` list in the SharePoint site, and refresh the page. You should see that this field has been updated, as shown in Figure 20-26.

TerritoryID	Name	CountryRegionCode	Group	SalesYTD	SalesLastYear	CostYTD	CostLastY
1	Northwest	US	North America	5767341.9752	3298694.4938	0.0000	0.0000
2	Northeast	US	North America	3857163.6331	3607148.9371	0.0000	0.0000
3	Central	US	North America	4677108.2690	3205014.0767	0.0000	0.0000
4	Southwest	US	North America	8351296.7411	5366575.7098	0.0000	0.0000
5	Southeast	US	North America	2851419.0435	3925071.4318	0.0000	0.0000
6	Canada	CA	North America	6917270.8842	5693988.8600	1000000.0000	0.0000
7	France	FR	Europe	3899045.6940	2396539.7601	0.0000	0.0000
8	Germany	DE	Europe	2481039.1786	1307949.7917	0.0000	0.0000
9	Australia	AU	Pacific	1977474.8096	2278548.9776	0.0000	0.0000
10	United Kingdom	GB	Europe	3514865.9051	1635823.3967	0.0000	0.0000

Figure 20-26. The updated `Territories` *list*

If you're really skeptical, you can query the SQL database and verify the update has been made there as well.

Adding a Territory

Go back to Outlook, and click the New Territory button. Enter the territory name in the **Subject** field. In the ribbon, click the Territory Details button, and enter the other fields. The form should be similar to Figure 20-27.

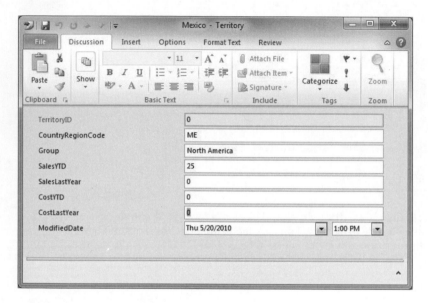

Figure 20-27. Adding a new territory

Inserts are synchronized in real time, if possible. Go back to the **Territories** list on the SharePoint site, and refresh the page. You should see the new territory listed, as shown in Figure 20-28.

TerritoryID	Name	CountryRegionCode	Group	SalesYTD	SalesLastYear	CostYTD	CostLastYear	ModifiedDate
1	Northwest	US	North America	5767341.9752	3298694.4938	0.0000	0.0000	5/31/1998 7:00 PM
2	Northeast	US	North America	3857163.6331	3607148.9371	0.0000	0.0000	5/31/1998 7:00 PM
3	Central	US	North America	4677108.2690	3205014.0767	0.0000	0.0000	5/31/1998 7:00 PM
4	Southwest	US	North America	8351296.7411	5366575.7098	0.0000	0.0000	5/31/1998 7:00 PM
5	Southeast	US	North America	2851419.0435	3925071.4318	0.0000	0.0000	5/31/1998 7:00 PM
6	Canada	CA	North America	6917270.8842	5693988.8600	1000000.0000	0.0000	5/31/1998 7:00 PM
7	France	FR	Europe	3899045.6940	2396539.7601	0.0000	0.0000	5/31/1998 7:00 PM
8	Germany	DE	Europe	2481039.1786	1307949.7917	0.0000	0.0000	5/31/1998 7:00 PM
9	Australia	AU	Pacific	1977474.8096	2278548.9776	0.0000	0.0000	5/31/1998 7:00 PM
10	United Kingdom	GB	Europe	3514865.9051	1635823.3967	0.0000	0.0000	5/31/1998 7:00 PM
11	Mexico		North America	25.0000	0.0000	0.0000	0.0000	5/20/2010 1:00 PM

Figure 20-28. The `Territories` *list with a new territory*

Summary

In this chapter, you took two external lists (based on external content types) and pushed them to Outlook 2010. Now the same data can be viewed (and edited) from the following locations:

- Your LOB applications accessing the SQL database
- The SharePoint site
- Outlook clients

Using Outlook to view and edit the data provides an out-of-the-box rich-client interface. Users can use the familiar Outlook application to manage their LOB data.

Using Outlook also adds another enormous benefit in that it uses a synchronized data cache. This means that Outlook can be used on a laptop or mobile device and the data is still available even when disconnected from the internal network. Changes made while offline are automatically synchronized when Outlook is reconnected.

Index

You Need the Companion eBook

Your purchase of this book entitles you to buy the companion PDF-version eBook for only $10. Take the weightless companion with you anywhere.

We believe this Apress title will prove so indispensable that you'll want to carry it with you everywhere, which is why we are offering the companion eBook (in PDF format) for $10 to customers who purchase this book now. Convenient and fully searchable, the PDF version of any content-rich, page-heavy Apress book makes a valuable addition to your programming library. You can easily find and copy code—or perform examples by quickly toggling between instructions and the application. Even simultaneously tackling a donut, diet soda, and complex code becomes simplified with hands-free eBooks!

Once you purchase your book, getting the $10 companion eBook is simple:

❶ Visit **www.apress.com/promo/tendollars/**.

❷ Complete a basic registration form to receive a randomly generated question about this title.

❸ Answer the question correctly in 60 seconds, and you will receive a promotional code to redeem for the $10.00 eBook.

THE EXPERT'S VOICE™

233 Spring Street, New York, NY 10013

Offer valid through 11/10.